CHURCH DOGMATICS

D1546057

For further resources, including the forewords to the original 14-volume edition of the *Church Dogmatics*, log on to our website and sign up for the resources webpage: http://www.continuumbooks.com/dogmatics/

KARL BARTH
CHURCH DOGMATICS

VOLUME II

THE DOCTRINE
OF GOD

§ 32–33

THE ELECTION OF GOD I

EDITED BY
G. W. BROMILEY
T. F. TORRANCE

t & t clark

Published by T&T Clark

A Continuum Imprint

The Tower Building, 11 York Road, London, SE1 7NX
80 Maiden Lane, Suite 704, New York, NY 10038

www.continuumbooks.com

Translated by G. W. Bromiley, J. C. Campbell, Iain Wilson, J. Strathearn McNab, T. H. L. Parker, W. B. Johnston, Harold Knight, J. L. M. Haire, R. A. Stewart

Copyright © T&T Clark, 2010

Authorised translation of Karl Barth, *Die Kirchliche Dogmatik II*
Copyright © Theologischer Verlag Zürich, 1940–1942
All revisions to the original English translation and all translation of Greek, Latin and French
© Princeton Theological Seminary, 2009

British Library Cataloguing-in-Publication Data
A catalogue record for this book is available from the British Library

ISBN13: 978-0-567-43701-3

Typeset by Interactive Sciences Ltd, Gloucester, and Newgen Imaging Systems Pvt Ltd, Chennai
Printed and bound in Great Britain by CPI Antony Rowe, Chippenham, Wiltshire

PUBLISHER'S PREFACE TO THE STUDY EDITION

Since the publication of the first English translation of *Church Dogmatics I.1* by Professor Thomson in 1936, T&T Clark has been closely linked with Karl Barth. An authorised translation of the whole of the *Kirchliche Dogmatik* was begun in the 1950s under the editorship of G. W. Bromiley and T. F. Torrance, a work which eventually replaced Professor Thomson's initial translation of *CD I.1*.

T&T Clark is now happy to present to the academic community this new *Study Edition* of the *Church Dogmatics*. Its aim is mainly to make this major work available to a generation of students and scholars with less familiarity with Latin, Greek, and French. For the first time this edition therefore presents the classic text of the translation edited by G. W. Bromiley and T. F. Torrance incorporating translations of the foreign language passages in Editorial Notes on each page.

The main body of the text remains unchanged. Only minor corrections with regard to grammar or spelling have been introduced. The text is presented in a new reader friendly format. We hope that the breakdown of the *Church Dogmatics* into 31 shorter fascicles will make this edition easier to use than its predecessors.

Completely new indexes of names, subjects and scriptural indexes have been created for the individual volumes of the *Study Edition*.

The publishers would like to thank the Center for Barth Studies at Princeton Theological Seminary for supplying a digital edition of the text of the *Church Dogmatics* and translations of the Greek and Latin quotations in the original T&T Clark edition made by Simon Gathercole and Ian McFarland.

London, April 2010

HOW TO USE THIS
STUDY EDITION

The *Study Edition* follows Barth's original volume structure. Individual paragraphs and sections should be easy to locate. A synopsis of the old and new edition can be found on the back cover of each fascicle.

All secondary literature on the *Church Dogmatics* currently refers to the classic 14-volume set (e.g. II.2 p. 520). In order to avoid confusion, we recommend that this practice should be kept for references to this *Study Edition*. The page numbers of the old edition can be found in the margins of this edition.

CONTENTS

§ 32–33

THE PROBLEM OF A CORRECT DOCTRINE OF THE ELECTION OF GRACE

The doctrine of election is the sum of the Gospel because of all words that can be said or heard it is the best: that God elects man; that God is for man too the One who loves in freedom. It is grounded in the knowledge of Jesus Christ because He is both the electing God and elected man in One. It is part of the doctrine of God because originally God's election of man is a predestination not merely of man but of Himself. Its function is to bear basic testimony to eternal, free and unchanging grace as the beginning of all the ways and works of God.

1. THE ORIENTATION OF THE DOCTRINE

The time has now come to leave the doctrine of the knowledge of God and the reality of God. We have tried to learn the lofty but simple lesson that it is by God that God is known, and that He is the living God as the One who loves in freedom; living both in the unity and also in the wealth of His perfections. Our starting-point in that first part of the doctrine of God was neither an axiom of reason nor a datum of experience. In the measure that a doctrine of God draws on these sources, it betrays the fact that its subject is not really God but a hypostatised reflection of man. At more than one stage in our consideration of the earlier history of the doctrine we have had to guard steadfastly against the temptation of this type of doctrine. We took as our starting-point what God Himself said and still says concerning God, and concerning the knowledge and reality of God, by way of the self-testimony which is accessible and comprehensible because it has been given human form in Holy Scripture, the document which is the very essence and basis of the Church. As strictly as possible we have confined ourselves to the appropriation and repetition of that self-testimony as such. As strictly as possible we have let our questions be dictated by the answers which are already present in the revelation of God attested in Holy Scripture. In so doing we have listened gratefully to the voices of the [004] Church as well, both old and new. But we have continually measured those voices by the only voice which can reign in the Church. Whether we could follow them or not, we allowed ourselves to use them only in order that we might learn the better to hear and understand that voice which reigns in the Church as the source and norm of all truth. It was in that way that we came to perceive the lofty but simple truth concerning the knowledge and reality of God. It was in that way that we rendered our account of what is pure and correct doctrine in this matter.

But the voice which reigns, the voice by which we were taught by God Himself concerning God, was the voice of Jesus Christ. Along all the path now behind us we could not take a single step without stumbling again and again across that name. And "across that name" does not mean across an empty title. It does not mean across a form or figure in which God could declare Himself to us or exist for us and yet be quite different in and by Himself. It does not mean across a name which is only a means or medium, and which God could ultimately discard, because ultimately it is not the real name of God, but only of a divine arrangement which in the last analysis is quite different from God Himself. The truth is that we continuously stumbled across that name in matter and substance. We stumbled across it necessarily. For as we proceeded along that path, we found that that name was the very subject, the very matter, with which we had to deal. In avoiding the different sources of error, we saw that they had one feature in common: the negligence or arbitrariness with which even in the Church the attempt was made to go past or to go beyond Jesus Christ in the consideration and conception and definition of God, and in speech about God. But when theology allows itself on any pretext to be jostled away from that name, God is inevitably crowded out by a hypostatised image of man. Theology must begin with Jesus Christ, and not with general principles, however better, or, at any rate, more relevant and illuminating, they may appear to be: as though He were a continuation of the knowledge and Word of God, and not its root and origin, not indeed the very Word of God itself. Theology must also end with Him, and not with supposedly self-evident general conclusions from what is particularly enclosed and disclosed in Him: as though the fruits could be shaken from this tree; as though in the things of God there were anything general which we could know and designate in addition to and even independently of this particular. The obscurities and ambiguities of our way were illuminated in the measure that we held fast to that name and in the measure that we let Him be the first and the last, according to the testimony of Holy Scripture. Against all the imaginations and errors in which we seem to be so hopelessly entangled when we try to speak of God, God [005] will indeed maintain Himself if we will only allow the name of Jesus Christ to be maintained in our thinking as the beginning and the end of all our thoughts. We recall how in our consideration of the divine perfections everything became clear and orderly when He, Jesus Christ, emerged as the perfect One, the fulness of the love and freedom of God Himself, the love and freedom of God in which all the divine perfections are neither more nor less than God Himself. So long as we remained true to the witness of Holy Scripture there was no alternative but to follow this line and to hold fast by it. For witnessing to God, the Old and New Testament Scriptures also witness to this name, and to the fulness of God which it encloses and represents, which cannot be separated from it, which cannot precede or follow it, but in it begins and continues and ends.

This is the decisive result of all our previous discussion. This is the sum and substance of the whole doctrine of the knowledge and reality of God. But that means that the Christian doctrine of God cannot end with the matter which we have treated so far. In a Christian doctrine of God our concern is to define and expound the Subject of all that the Christian Church receives and proclaims. If it is true, then, that this Subject is disclosed only in the name of Jesus Christ, that it is wholly and entirely enclosed in Him, then we cannot stop at this point, defining and expounding the Subject only in and for itself. We tried to do that on the earlier part of our way. But we should be overlooking and suppressing something essential, and a serious gap would be left in our reflection on the Word of God as the norm of Christian proclamation, if we now tried to proceed without treating of what the Church must receive and proclaim as the work of this Subject, the activity of God as Creator, Reconciler and Redeemer. We should still not have learned to say "God" correctly (i.e., as understood in the Christian Church on the basis of Holy Scripture) if we thought it enough simply to say "God." However well-grounded or critical our utterance, if it has a logical exclusiveness, if it is only "God," it will not suffice. For if it is true that in Jesus Christ there dwells the fulness of the Godhead bodily (Col. 2^9), then in all the perfection with which it is differentiated from everything that is not God, and thus exists for itself, the Subject God still cannot, as it were, be envisaged, established and described only in and for itself. We must not be so exact, so clever, so literal, that our doctrine of God remains only a doctrine of God. We must demonstrate its Christian character by avoiding such abstraction. In virtue of the truth of its specific content it must burst through the frame which apparently—but only apparently—surrounds it. Otherwise the highest reality can, and inevitably will, be reduced to the flattest unreality. All that we have previously said concerning this Subject will be enveloped again in darkness. From the very outset a new obscurity will, in fact, extend over all that we have still to say concerning the work of this Subject. To be truly Christian, the doctrine of God must carry forward and complete the definition and exposition [006] of the Subject God. It must do this in such a way that quite apart from what must be said about the knowledge and the reality of God as such, it makes the Subject known as One which in virtue of its innermost being, willing and nature does not stand outside all relationships, but stands in a definite relationship *ad extra* to another. It is not as though the object of this relationship, the other, constitutes a part of the reality of God outside of God. It is not as though it is in any other way comparable with God. It is not as though God is forced into this relationship. It is not as though He is in any way constrained or compelled by this other. As we have often enough seen and asserted, there can be no question of any such compulsion coming upon God from without. God is love. But He is also perfect freedom. Even if there were no such relationship, even if there were no other outside of Him, He would still be love. But positively, in the free decision of His love, God is God in the very fact, and in such a way, that He does stand in this relation, in a definite relationship with the other. We cannot go back on this decision if we would know God and speak accurately of God. If we did, we should be betrayed into a false abstraction which sought to speak only of God, not recognising that, when we speak of God, then in consideration of His freedom, and of His free decision, we must speak also of this relationship. This relationship belongs to the Subject God, and to the doctrine of God in the narrower sense, to the extent that it rests upon a definite attitude of God which, when we speak of God, we must always and in all respects take into consideration. And that we have never so far failed to do. For how could we have said anything about the knowledge and reality of God had we not considered this positive attitude, learning from it how God gives Himself to be known, and what He is both in Himself and in all His works? But this fact, that God is God only in this way and not in any other, must now be made explicit. We move on to solid ground when we seek to learn from this positive attitude that which can be learned concerning the knowledge and reality of God, considering Him and conceiving of Him in the constant light of His revelation and all His works. For the divine attitude is not a matter of chance. It is not revocable or transitory. God lays upon us the obligation of this attitude because first of all He lays it upon Himself. In dealing with this attitude, we have to do with His free but definitive decision. We cannot abstract from it without falling into arbitrary speculation. But we cannot ignore it. Once made, it belongs definitively to God Himself, not in His being in and for Himself, but in His being within this relationship. It belongs to the reality of God which is a reality not apart from but in this decision. It is so adjoined to this reality that we must not allow any objectivity of logic to prevent us from introducing the adjunct as an element in our knowledge of God. We cannot [007] speak correctly of God in His being in and for Himself without considering Him always in this attitude, without allowing both our questions and answers to be dictated by it. We cannot speak accurately or confidently of the work of God unless first we see clearly that the attitude which God has taken up, and by which His work is determined, belongs to God Himself, and cannot in any way be isolated from Him. For that reason, the question of this attitude must be raised specifically and independently within the framework of the doctrine of God. In a Christian doctrine of God, if God is to be exhaustively described and represented as the Subject who governs and determines everything else, there must be an advance beyond the immediate logical sense of the concept to the actual relationship in which God has placed Himself; a relationship outside of which God no longer wills to be and no longer is God, and within which alone He can be truly honoured and worshipped as God. If it is true that it pleased the fulness of God to dwell in Jesus Christ (Col. 1^{19}), then in a Christian doctrine of God this further step is unavoidable. And it is immediately apparent in which direction the step must be taken.

Jesus Christ is indeed God in His movement towards man, or, more exactly, in His movement towards the people represented in the one man Jesus of Nazareth, in His covenant with this people, in His being and activity amongst and towards this people. Jesus Christ is the decision of God in favour of this attitude or relation. He is Himself the relation. It is a relation *ad extra*, undoubtedly; for both the man and the people represented in Him are creatures and not God. But it is a relation which is irrevocable, so that once God has willed to enter into it, and has in fact entered into it, He could not be God without it. It is a relation in which God is self-determined, so that the determination belongs no less to Him than all that He is in and for Himself. Without the Son sitting at the right hand of the Father, God would not be God. But the Son is not only very God. He is also called Jesus of Nazareth. He is also very man, and as such He is the Representative of the people which in Him and through Him is united as He is with God, being with Him the object of the divine movement. That we know God and have God only in Jesus Christ means that we can know Him and have Him only with the man Jesus of Nazareth and with the people which He represents. Apart from this man and apart from this people God would be a different, an alien God. According to the Christian perception He would not be God at all. According to the Christian perception the true God is what He is only in this movement, in the movement towards this man, and in Him and through Him towards other men in their unity as His people.

That other to which God stands in relationship, in an actuality which can neither be suspended nor dissolved, is not simply and directly the created world as such. There is, too, a relationship of God to the world. There is a work of God towards it and with it. There is a history between God and the world. [008] But this history has no independent signification. It takes place in the interests of the primal history which is played out between God and this one man and His people. It is the sphere in which this primal history is played out. It attains its goal as this primal history attains its goal. And the same is true both of man as such and also of the human race as a whole. The partner of God which cannot now be thought away is neither "man" as an idea, nor "humanity," nor indeed a large or small total of individual men. It is the one man Jesus and the people represented in Him. Only secondarily, and for His sake, is it "man," and "humanity" and the whole remaining cosmos. Even human nature and human history in general have no independent signification. They point to the primal history played out within them between God and the one man, and all other men as His people. The general (the world or man) exists for the sake of the particular. In the particular the general has its meaning and fulfilment. The particular is that other over against God which cannot be thought away, which is outside of God, which is the object of the divine movement, which is so adjoined now to the reality of God that we cannot and should not say the word "God" without at once thinking of it. We must think at once, then, of Jesus of Nazareth and of His people. The attitude or relation for which God has once

5

and for all decided, to which He has committed us and wills to be committed by us, is the relation or attitude to Jesus Christ. In the person of His eternal Son He has united Himself with the man Jesus of Nazareth, and in Him and through Him with this people. He is the Father of Jesus Christ. He is not only the Father of the eternal Son, but as such He is the eternal Father of this temporal man. He is, then, the eternal Father, the Possessor, the Lord and the Saviour of the people which this man represents as King and Head. In this determination, as carried through by His own decision, God is, therefore, the Subject of everything that is to be received and proclaimed in the Christian Church. All His work takes place according to this plan and under this sign. As such it has, of course, a wider reach. The other towards which God moves in this wider sphere is, of course, the created world as a whole. It is, of course, "man" and "humanity." But everything which comes from God takes place according to this plan and under this sign. Everything is from this beginning and to this end. Everything is in this order and has this meaning. Everything happens according to this basic and determinative pattern, model and system. Everything which comes from God takes place "in Jesus Christ," i.e., in the establishment of the covenant which, in the union of His Son with Jesus of Nazareth, God has instituted and maintains and directs between Himself and His people, the people consisting of those who belong to Him, who have become His in this One. The primal history which underlies and is the goal of the whole history of His relationship *ad extra*, with the creation and man in general, is the history of this covenant. The primal history, and with it the covenant, are, then, the attitude and relation in which by virtue of the decision of His free love God wills to be and is God. And this relation cannot be separated from the Christian conception of God as such. The two must go together if this conception is to be truly Christian. For that reason, this relation must form the subject of a second part of our doctrine of God.

[009]

But as we approach this particular subject, two aspects of the one truth must be considered and two spheres of investigation are disclosed.

It is at once apparent that in the decision by which He institutes, maintains and directs this covenant, in His decision "in Jesus Christ," God on His side does accomplish something quite definite. He executes this decision in His movement towards man, towards the man Jesus Christ and the people which He represents. And this movement is an act of divine sovereignty. To characterise it as such we must select from the fulness of His essential attributes. We must say: This act demonstrates His mercy and righteousness, His constancy and omnipotence. It is as the Lord who lives in the fulness of these perfections that God acts when He institutes and directs this covenant. He constitutes Himself the Lord of the covenant. He is, therefore, its free author. He gives it its content and determines its order. He maintains it. He directs it to its goal. He governs it in every respect. It is His decision that there is a covenant-partner. It is also His decision who this partner is, and what must befall him. It is only as He wills it that the covenant arises at all. The covenant-member is the one whom He ordains. It is what He wills that takes place within the covenant. All that we have to say concerning this aspect of the divine movement may be summed up in the concept which is the title of this chapter: that of the election in the sense of the election of divine grace, the choice which God makes in His grace, thus making this movement, and instituting, maintaining and directing this covenant. In accordance with the theological tradition of the Reformed Churches (and especially the German-speaking), what we have in mind is the election of grace (in translation of ἐκλογὴ χάριτος, Rom. 11⁵); and it may be noted how the term reflects the being of God as we have hitherto sought to understand and explain it. It is a question of grace, and that means the love of God. It is a question of election, and that means the freedom of God.

Here, again, we must deal first with grace. The fact that God makes this movement, the institution of the covenant, the primal decision "in Jesus Christ," which is the basis and goal of all His works—that is grace. Speaking generally, it is the demonstration, the overflowing of the love which is the being of God, that He who is entirely self-sufficient, who even within Himself cannot know isolation, willed even in all His divine glory to share His life with another, and to have that other as the witness of His glory. This love of God is [010]
His grace. It is love in the form of the deepest condescension. It occurs even where there is no question of claim or merit on the part of the other. It is love which is overflowing, free, unconstrained, unconditioned. And we must add at once: It is love which is merciful, making this movement, this act of condescension, in such a way that, in taking to itself this other, it identifies itself with its need, and meets its plight by making it its own concern. And we must add at once: It is love which is patient, not consuming this other, but giving it place, willing its existence for its own sake and for the sake of the goal appointed for it. For the moment, however, it is important to stop at the first concept, the concept of grace. God's decision in Jesus Christ is a gracious decision. In making it, God stoops down from above. In it He does something which He has no need to do, which He is not constrained to do. He does something which He alone can constrain Himself, and has in fact constrained Himself, to do. In entering into this covenant, He freely makes Himself both benefactor and benefit. It will be seen that the whole sovereignty of this act is contained already in the concept of grace. Because grace is here the Alpha and Omega, it cannot be otherwise than that, in the total manner already indicated, God should be the Lord "in Jesus Christ." But with this concept the other aspect forces itself to the forefront, and must there remain—that "in Jesus Christ" we have to do with a divine benefit or favour. It is a matter of God's love. If in His majesty He establishes fellowship with the other which does not partake of His majesty, but in its otherness stands in the very depths over against Him, that means favour. In showing His grace, God proves Himself both Saviour and Helper. He does so freely as the Lord. But this exercise of lordship is kind as well as good, communicating and sharing its goods. The doctrine of the divine

7

election of grace is the sum of the Gospel. It is the content of the good news which is Jesus Christ.

The other part of the concept cannot and should not alter this fact in the least. Election should serve at once to emphasise and explain what we have already said in the word grace. God in His love elects another to fellowship with Himself. First and foremost this means that God makes a self-election in favour of this other. He ordains that He should not be entirely self-sufficient as He might be. He determines for Himself that overflowing, that movement, that condescension. He constitutes Himself as benefit or favour. And in so doing He elects another as the object of His love. He draws it upwards to Himself, so as never again to be without it, but to be who He is in covenant with it. In this concept of election there is reflected more clearly, of course, the other element in the being of God: the freedom in which He is the One who eternally loves. The concept election means that grace is truly grace. It means that [011] God owes His grace to no one, and that no one can deserve it. It means that grace cannot be the subject of a claim or a right on the part of the one upon whom it is directed. It means that it is the determination and decision of the will of God. Again, God elects that He shall be the covenant-God. He does so in order not to be alone in His divine glory, but to let heaven and earth, and between them man, be the witnesses of His glory. He elects the way in which His love shall be shown and the witness to His glory established. He elects creation, man, the human race, as the sphere in which He wills to be gracious. But the existence of creation and of the human race does not constrain Him in the future exercise of grace. He elects even within this sphere. He elects the man of Nazareth, that He should be essentially one with Himself in His Son. Through Him and in Him He elects His people, thus electing the whole basis and meaning of all His works. He elects, i.e., He is free, and He remains free, both in what He does and in what He permits. He does what He does, but without any claim arising that He must do it, or that He must do it in this or that way. Over against Him no claim can ever arise. Nothing can precede His grace, whether in eternity or time, whether from the beginning or in the process of development. In all its manifestations, in all its activity, His grace is free grace. It is the Lord who is the Saviour and Helper. His taking to Himself of that other is an act of unconditioned sovereignty. This is what the word "election " tells us as the second component of the concept "election of grace." It cannot possibly mean any restriction of the evangelical character of the concept. It reminds us emphatically, however, that the good news summarised in this concept is good news only because it proclaims to us the salvation which is the will of the real Lord both of our life and of all life. The truth to which the whole concept points is the specific subject to which we must address ourselves in this seventh chapter.

The doctrine of God's covenant-relation with the people represented in the man Jesus is the fulfilment of the doctrine of God in the narrower sense of the term. But it is not exhausted by the doctrine of the election of grace. God acts in His free grace, but He also wills and expects and demands something from His covenant-partner. To the majesty of that activity which no claim can condition, there corresponds the unconditional nature of the very definite claim which He Himself must advance. Encountering man in His free love, God becomes the companion of man. That is what He determined to do "in Jesus Christ." That is the foundation-plan and sign of all His works. But in virtue of His absolute ascendancy, in virtue of the fact that in this relationship He must have both the first and the last word concerning His partner, He is of necessity the Judge. We use the expression here in its most comprehensive sense. God is for His covenant-partner both the One by whom he will be judged and also the [012] One according to whom he must judge himself. God is for him the criterion, the standard, the question of the good or the evil, the rightness or the wrongness, of his being and activity. God ordained and created him as partner in this covenant; God elected and called him to that position; and in that position He makes him responsible. How could God draw him to Himself, as He does, without making him responsible? God constitutes this "being responsible" the whole meaning of his existence. He shows him His own way as the only one which he can tread. He calls him to order and keeps him in order, revealing to him His own order and seeing that he keeps to it. Even this He does in genuine fulfilment of His love and grace. Here too, then, we have to do with the Gospel. But we have to do with the Gospel in so far as it has always the form of the Law. The practical significance of the freedom of grace, of the sovereignty in which God elects, is this: that in his very election the one elected finds a Master and Lord. Grace does not will only to be received and known. As it is truly received and known, as it works itself out as the favour which it is, it wills also to rule. But it rules by offering God to His covenant-partner as Lord of the covenant. That is the second basic point which we must make concerning the life of God "in Jesus Christ," in and with His people. We must be constantly aware of this point as we consider all the divine work grounded upon the grace of God and the divine election of grace. There is no grace without the lordship and claim of grace. There is no dogmatics which is not also and necessarily ethics. The basic points in the inter-relationship between divine grace and the divine claim will occupy us in the next chapter (which will also serve as a foundation for "theological ethics") under the title *"The Command of God."* The theme which first confronts us (and it is most intimately connected with the second) is the divine election of grace.

As we take up this theme, we enter the field of theology which is known in the history of dogma as the doctrine of predestination. Before we do anything more, it is essential that we should make emphatically the first affirmation inscribed in the synopsis at the head of this section. The truth which must now occupy us, the truth of the doctrine of predestination, is first and last and in all circumstances the sum of the Gospel, no matter how it may be understood in detail, no matter what apparently contradictory aspects or moments it may present to us. It is itself evangel: glad tidings; news which uplifts and comforts and sustains. Once and for all, then, it is not a truth which is neutral in face of the antithesis of fear and terror, of need and danger, which the term itself suggests. It is not a mere theorem whose content does not amount to anything more than instruction in, or the elucidation of, something which is quite unaffected by the distinction between right and wrong or good and evil. Its content is instruction and elucidation, but instruction and elucidation which [013] are to us a proclamation of joy. It is not a mixed message of joy and terror, salvation and damnation. Originally and finally it is not dialectical but non-dialectical. It does not proclaim in the same breath both good and evil, both help and destruction, both life and death. It does, of course, throw a shadow. We cannot overlook or ignore this aspect of the matter. In itself, however, it is light and not darkness. We cannot, therefore, speak of the latter aspect in the same breath. In any case, even under this aspect, the final word is never that of warning, of judgment, of punishment, of a barrier erected, of a grave opened. We cannot speak of it without mentioning all these things. The Yes cannot be heard unless the No is also heard. But the No is said for the sake of the Yes and not for its own sake. In substance, therefore, the first and last word is Yes and not No.

We must establish this at the outset because, as the "doctrine of predestination," the doctrine of the divine election of grace has fallen under something of a shadow during the course of its history. The shadow has become so pronounced that when one mentions the terms "election of grace" or "predestination " one must expect to awaken in one's hearers or readers associations which necessarily confuse and thus make impossible the necessary recognition of the great truth with which we have to do at this point. The association may be resentment against the "pathetic inhumanity" of the doctrine (as in Max Weber, *Ges. Aufs. z. Rel. Soz.* I, 1922, 93), or perhaps against the danger of dialectical ambiguity, or worse than both these, against what we mentioned earlier: the idea that in this matter we are dealing only with an abstract and neutral theorem. If we glance at the history of the doctrine, even as presented by its greatest and profoundest exponents, we cannot simply dismiss these associations as completely without foundation. Everywhere this shadow is in the ascendancy. A good deal has, in fact, been said in such a way as to give rise to confusion, to savage hostility, to well-meant but fatal misrepresentations of what ought to be received, indeed to a whole mass of misunderstanding and indifference with regard to the doctrine. "I may go to hell, but such a God (as that of the Calvinistic teaching) will never command my respect"—that was the cry of John Milton (according to M. Weber, *op. cit.*, p. 91), and openly or secretly how many others have made some similar utterance. For that reason it cannot be our present task simply to take one of the classical forms of the traditional doctrine and to present it as integrally as possible—as, in the case of the Calvinistic form, Loraine Boettner has recently attempted to do in his book, *The Reformed Doctrine of Predestination*, 1932. The task which confronts us is rather a critical one, even in face of the very best tradition. The task is imposed by the nature of the matter, as was the case, although rather differently, in the first part of our doctrine of God. If the doctrine is to shed forth its light, then the shadow must be dispersed. The dispersing of this shadow will be our definite objective in the polemical discussions throughout this whole chapter. We cannot be too soon, or too radical, in the opposition which we must offer to the classical tradition, or rather in the attempt to do justice to the particular and justifiable and necessary intention which underlies that tradition. And we introduce the first and most radical point with our thesis that the doctrine of election must

1. The Orientation of the Doctrine

be understood quite definitely and unequivocally as Gospel; that it is not something neutral on the yonder side of Yes and No; that it is not No but Yes; that it is not Yes and No, but in its substance, in the origin and scope of its utterance, it is altogether Yes.

The election of grace is the sum of the Gospel—we must put it as pointedly as that. But more, the election of grace is the whole of the Gospel, the Gospel [014] *in nuce*[EN1]. It is the very essence of all good news. It is as such that it must be understood and evaluated in the Christian Church. God is God in His being as the One who loves in freedom. This is revealed as a benefit conferred upon us in the fact which corresponds to the truth of God's being, the fact that God elects in His grace, that He moves towards man, in his dealings within this covenant with the one man Jesus, and the people represented by Him. All the joy and the benefit of His whole work as Creator, Reconciler and Redeemer, all the blessings which are divine and therefore real blessings, all the promise of the Gospel which has been declared: all these are grounded and determined in the fact that God is the God of the eternal election of His grace. In the light of this election the whole of the Gospel is light. Yes is said here, and all the promises of God are Yea and Amen (2 Cor. 1^{20}). Confirmation and comfort and help are promised us at this point, and they are promised us at every point. Whatever problems or contradictions we may encounter elsewhere, they all cease to be such, they become the very opposite, when we see them in their connexion with the real truth which we must receive and proclaim here. On the other hand, if it is the shadow which really predominates, if we must still fear, or if we can only half rejoice and half fear, if we have no truth at all to receive or proclaim but only the neutral elucidation of a neutral subject, then it is quite certain that we can never again receive or proclaim as such the Gospel previously declared. In this sphere, too, the shadow will necessarily predominate.

Many of the great exponents of the doctrine of predestination in the history of the Church have clearly expressed the basic character of the doctrine of the divine election of grace even from the positive standpoint, at any rate in some leading passages. We may note the definition of Augustine: *Haec est praedestinatio sanctorum, nihil aliud: praescientia sc. et praeparatio beneficiorum Dei, quibus certissime liberantur quicumque liberantur*[EN2] (*De dono persev.* 14, 35). Predestination, according to Luther, is *voluntas Dei ordinantis suo consilio, quos et quales praedicatae et oblatae misericordiae capaces et participes esse velit*[EN3] (*De servo arb.* W.A. 18, 684, 35). Even Calvin assures us that here it is not a question of an *arguta vel spinosa speculatio, quae absque fructa ingenia fatiget*[EN4], but of a *disputatio solida et ad pietatis usum maxime accommoda; nempe, quae et fidem probe aedificet et nos ad humilitatem erudiat et in admirationem extollat immensae erga nos Dei bonitatis et ad hanc celebrandam excitet. Nulla aedificandae fidei aptior est ratio, quam dum audimus electionem illam, quam spiritus Dei cordibus*

[EN1] in a nutshell

[EN2] This is the predestination of the saints, and nothing else: the foreknowledge, that is to say, the preparation of the benefits of God, by which whoever is freed is most certainly freed

[EN3] the will of God who ordains in his counsel whom and in what manner he wills to be the right participants in the proclaimed mercy he has offered

[EN4] disputed or thorny speculation, which wearies minds without benefit

11

nostris obsignat, in aeterno et inflexibili Dei beneplacito consistere, ut nullis mundi procellis, nullis satanae insultibus, nulli carnis vacillationi sit obnoxia. Tunc enim demum nobis certa est nostra salus, quum in Dei pectore causam reperimus. Sic enim vitam in Christo manifestatam fide apprehendimus, ut eadem fide duce procul intueri liceat, ex quo fonte vita prodierit[EN5] (*De aet. Dei praed.*, 1552, *C.R.* 8, 260). even if they do also make specific mention of a *decretum horribile*[EN6] (*Instit.* III. 23, 7): *In ipsa quae terret caligine non modo utilitas huius doctrinae, sed suavissimus quoque fructus se profert. Nunquam liquido ut decet persuasi erimus salutem nostram ex fonte gratuitae misericordiae Dei fluere, donec innotuerit nobis aeterna eius electio*[EN7] (*Instit.* III, 21, 1). Intentionally, I have quoted only

[015] what these passages say positively about the doctrine of election as such. In the same context all of them do speak of the non-election or rejection which accompanies election. But in face and in spite of this second and accompanying aspect, they ascribe to the doctrine as such and in its entirety this redemptive and evangelical character. "The godlike consideration of Predestination, and our Election in Christ, is full of sweet, pleasant and unspeakable comfort to godly persons" (The *Irish Articles* of 1615, cf. E. F. Karl Müller, 528). Always and in all circumstances the doctrine must be understood according to this character, even in the detailed exposition of the second aspect. The Lutheran *Formula of Concord* is undoubtedly right when it finds in such understanding a criterion of correctness of doctrine in this matter: *Haec nequaquam erit vera et sana sententia aut legitimus usus doctrinae de aeterna praedestinatione Dei quibus vel impoenitentia vel desperatio in hominum mentibus excitatur aut confirmatur. Neque vero nobis scriptura hanc doctrinam aliter quam hoc modo proponit, ut nos ad verbum Dei revelatum fide amplectendum ableget, ad poenitentiam agendam hortetur, ad pie vivendum invitet*[EN8] (*Sol. decl.* XI, 12). *Doctrina illa amplissimam consolationis verae materiam nobis suppeditabit*[EN9] (43). If the preaching of the Gospel brings with it instead of consolation either despair or a false assurance, then it is certain *quod articulus de electione non ad normam et iuxta voluntatem Dei sed secundum humanae rationis caecae indicium et ex impulsu atque instinctu diaboli male et perverse doceatur* (91). *Quodsi nobis per scripturam consolatio illa vel enervatur vel eripitur, certo certius est scripturam contra sententiam et mentem Spiritus Sancti explicari et intelligi*[EN10] (92). This could not be said against Calvin and the Calvinists except through misunderstanding, or with reference to certain inferences which seriously embarrass their

---

[EN 5] solid consideration, extremely fitting and useful for piety, indeed which rightly builds up faith and teaches us humility. It lifts us to admiration of the immeasurable goodness of God to us and awakens us to celebrate it. No means is more appropriate for building up faith than as we hear of that election which the Spirit of God seals in our hearts, that it consists in the eternal and inflexible decree of God, such that it is not subject to any storms of the world, to any of the accusations of Satan, nor to any doubting of the flesh. For then at last our salvation is certain to us, since we have found its origin in the heart of God. For thus we apprehend by faith our life manifested in Christ, so that with that same faith as our guide we are permitted to regard him from afar – him, the fount from which our life has proceeded

[EN 6] terrible decree

[EN 7] In frightening gloom, not only the usefulness of this doctrine, but also very sweet enjoyment is offered. For we will never be persuaded as we should that our salvation flows from the fount of the free mercy of God, until our eternal election has come to our attention

[EN 8] It would by no means be a true and sound opinion or a legitimate use of the doctrine of the eternal predestination of God if either impenitence or desperation in the minds of men were aroused or confirmed. Indeed, Scripture does not advance this doctrine to us except to send us to the revealed word of God, to be embraced by faith. It exhorts us to repent, and invites us to godly living

[EN 9] That doctrine furnishes us with a most abundant basis for true consolation

[EN10] the article of election is being wickedly and perversely taught according to the judgment of blind human reason and by the impulse and instinct of the devil (91). But if that consolation is either weakened or disrupted by Scripture, then it is quite certain that Scripture is being explained and understood against the opinion and mind of the Holy Spirit

teaching. The Calvinists themselves might well have spoken, and did in fact speak, in the very same way. One can only wish that they had done so more emphatically in order that misunderstanding might have been avoided.

In this matter the real source and goal of all thought and utterance must be the Gospel itself, and that in a comprehensive, and to a certain extent compendious, sense. This will at once be apparent when we cast a first and general glance at the part played by the concept of election in the testimony of Holy Scripture. In the Old Testament it is the basic category used to describe the relationship between *Yahweh* and His people Israel. From its election, and as a result of the elections which constitute its history, there follow all the blessings visited upon this people by its God. In some degree the election is the fundamental blessing with which it has been and in detail continues to be visited. It is true that the rejection of Israel was determined when it stubbornly resisted the Gospel. Yet in face and in spite of that rejection, the fundamental blessing, the election, is still confirmed. Its confirmation is both the starting-point and the goal even of the crooked path of the chief New Testament passage in this matter: Rom. 9–11. In these chapters there are many apparent hesitations and contradictions which we shall have to consider and reckon with; and yet we cannot overlook the fact that their final word is one of testimony to the divine Yes to Israel (to the Israel which had crucified Christ). Only when they are understood in the light of this final word can they be understood aright. So, too, the content and purpose of the other New Testament passages which touch on the election is always testimony to divine favour; or, more exactly, to the one ultimate and decisive presupposition of all divine favour. The fact that they are elected should make clear to Christians the fact that they are the new and the true Israel, the people of God partaking of all the promises (1 Pet. 2⁹). It should make clear to them the fact that they are called unto salvation in sanctification (2 Thess. 2¹³); that they are called of God, justified and already glorified (Rom. 8³⁰); that unto them is given the mystery of the kingdom of God (Mk. 4¹¹); that they are blessed by God, the Father of Jesus Christ (Eph. 1³ᶠ·). It is grace itself which visits them, and it does so because they have been appointed thereto by the divine election of grace—by grace to grace. In the New Testament election is the divine ordination to discipleship, to the apostolate, to the community: to the apostolate in so far as this constitutes the community and to the community in so far as this is constituted by the apostolate; but either one way or the other, the divine ordination to participation in the salvation of the Messianic future. The "book" spoken of by God in Ex. 32³² has always, and quite rightly, been connected with the election of grace. In Ps. 69²⁹ it is called unequivocally the "book of the living" (Prayer Book Version),* and it is described as the "book of life" in the New Testament (Phil. 4³; Rev. 3⁵, 17⁸, 20¹², ¹⁵). One's name may not be in this book. It can be blotted out from it. And yet there are not two columns, but only one. Similarly, the concept of the divine πρόθεσις^{EN11} used in Rom. 8²⁸ and 9¹¹ and Eph. 1¹¹ etc. relates to the divine election to salvation, but only to that election as such, and not to the accompanying non-election, or rejection. The problem began to be obscured when the "book of life" came to be spoken of as though it had in it a death-column; when the divine election and the divine rejection came to be spoken of as inter-connected divine acts similar in character and determination; when they came to be regarded and understood as though they could both be grouped under the one over-ruling concept.

When we look at the matter, it is here that there is a movement away from the biblical testimony even in Augustine. Augustine wanted to know why some believe and are saved, and others do not believe and are damned. He found the answer (supposedly in relation to

[016]

---

* In the A.V. and R.V. "the book of life," Ps. 69²⁸ (R.V. margin "the living"). Trans.
^{EN11} fore-ordination

certain texts in Rom. 9) in the fact of a double divine decision from all eternity, i.e., a decision with two parallel sides: *Multi audiunt verbum veritatis; sed alii credunt, alii contradicunt. Volunt ergo isti credere, nolunt autem illi. Quis hoc ignoret? Quis hoc neget? Sed cum aliis praeparetur, aliis non praeparetur voluntas a Domino; discernendum est utique, quid veniat de misericordia eius, quid de iudicio* (*De praed. sanct.* 6, 11). *Cur ergo non omnes docet, ut veniant ad Christum, nisi quia omnes quos docet, misericordia docet, quos autem non docet, iudicio non docet?* (*ib.*, 8, 14). *Scimus iis quibus datur misericordia Dei gratuita dari. Scimus iis, quibus non datur, iusto iudicio non dari*EN12 (*Ep.* 217, 5, 16). It is certainly true that God's mercy and righteousness are both active in God's dealings with believers and unbelievers. But in view of the unity of the divine essence, we must at once ask whether it is possible to allocate the two attributes to different dealings of God, as though only His mercy were at work in the one case and only His righteousness in the other. Above all, we must ask what biblical or inherent authority Augustine has for relating God's dealings in this way, as though we had only to look at God's work here and His work there and to understand them as a unity in order to find the premiss for this interrelationship. At any rate, in Holy Scripture there is no parallelism of this kind in the treatment and proclamation of the divine election and rejection.

Augustine himself did receive here a salutary check, as is shown by the fact that on the whole he avoided reducing God's twofold dealings to one common denominator, even in concept. By *praedestinatio*EN13 he always (or almost always) understood *praedestinatio ad gratiam*EN14 (a definition taken over by Peter Lombard, *Sent.* I, *dist.* 40 A) and therefore *praedestinatio ad vitam*EN15. Predestination consists positively in *electio*EN16, and does not include *reprobatio*EN17. Thomas Aquinas held a similar concept. For him predestination was *ratio transmissionis vitae aeternae praeexistens in Deo*EN18 (*S. th.* I, *qu.* 23, *art.* 1 *c*), or, according to a later definition: *quaedam praeordinatio ab aeterno de his quae per gratiam Dei sunt fienda in tempore*EN19 (*S. th.* III, *qu.* 24, *art.* 1 *c*). Thomas, like Augustine, does set the two alongside: *voluit Deus in hominibus quantum ad aliquos, quos praedestinavit, suam bonitatem repraesentare per modum misericordiae, parcendo—et quantum ad aliquos, quos reprobat, per modum iustitiae, puniendo*EN20 (*qu.* 23, *art.* 5 *ad.* 3). But more clearly than Augustine he regards *reprobatio*EN21 as in fact a separate genus, quite apart from and standing to some extent only in the shadow of *praedestinatio*EN22. A similar view was held in the 14th century even by such strong "predestinarians" as Gregory of Rimini and John Wyclif.

[017]

EN12 Many hear the word of truth; but some believe, and some deny it. So, the former will to believe, the latter will not to believe. Who can escape this? Who can deny it? For some, the will is prepared by God, for others the will is not prepared. It must particularly be noted how it he treats some with mercy, and others with judgment (6,11). Why then does he not teach all to come to Christ, except because all whom he teaches he teaches with mercy, but those whom he does not teach, in judgment he does not teach (8,14). We know that for those to whom it is given, the mercy of God is given freely. And we know that for those to whom it is not given, it is in righteous judgment that it is not given

EN13 predestination

EN14 predestination to grace

EN15 predestination to life

EN16 election

EN17 reprobation

EN18 means, pre-existing in God, of the transmission of eternal life

EN19 a predestination from eternity for those things which are to exist, by the grace of God, in time

EN20 God willed among men a number whom he predestined, to be given his goodness according to the manner of his mercy by which they are spared; and a number whom he reprobated, by the manner of his justice, by which they are punished

EN21 reprobation

EN22 predestination

1. The Orientation of the Doctrine

Already, however, Isidore of Seville in the 7th and Gottschalk in the 9th century had taught a doctrine which differed formally from that of Augustine: *Gemina est praedestinatio, sive electorum ad requiem, sive reproborum ad mortem*[EN23] (Isidore, *sent.* 2, 6, 1). *Sicut electos omnes (Deus) praedestinavit ad vitam per gratuitum solius gratiae suae beneficium ... sic omnino et reprobos quosque ad aeternae mortis praedestinavit supplicium per iustissimum videlicet iustitiae suae iudicium*[EN24] (Gottschalk, according to Hinkmar, *De praed.* 5). In this case predestination is an over-ruling concept, including both election and rejection. This was the usage adopted by the Reformers. In Luther's *De servo arbitrio*, in Zwingli's *De providentia* and in the writings of Calvin, predestination means quite unequivocally double predestination: double in the sense that election and rejection are now two species within the one genus designated by the term predestination. It is true that not only in Luther but in Calvin too there are passages in which the matter is expounded with the same disproportion, the same overemphasis upon the positively evangelical element, as had obviously appeared necessary to Thomas. Yet of Calvin it must be said that at any rate in his stricter teaching he did not think it possible to dispense with this fatal parallelism of the concepts election and rejection: *Fateri necesse est, Deum aeterno suo beneplacito, cuius aliunde causa non pendet, quos illi visum est, destinasse ad salutem, aliis relictis et quos gratuita adoptione dignatus est, spiritu suo illuminare, ut vitam in Christo oblatam recipiant, alios ita sponte esse incredulos, ut fidei luce destituti in tenebris maneant*[EN25] (*De aet. Dei praed.* C.R. 8, 261 f.). So, too, in the famous definition in the *Institutio* (III, 21, 5): *Praedestinationem vocamus aeternum Dei decretum, quo apud se constitutum habuit, quid de unoquoque homine fieri veuet. Non enim pari conditione creantur omnes: sed aliis vita aeterna, aliis damnatio aeterna praeordinatur. Itaque prout in alterutrum finem quisque conditus est, ita vel ad vitam vel ad mortem praedestinatum dicimus*[EN26]. It was quite in the spirit of Calvin, and yet quite fatal, when many of the older Reformed dogmaticians thought that they ought to balance against the concept of the election of grace that of an election of wrath. Although they attempted to amend the doctrine, it is noteworthy that even the Arminians could not escape the concept of a "double" predestination in this sense: *Est praedestinatio Dei decretum divinum, quo pro voluntatis suae beneplacito constituit ante tempora saecularia fideles in Jesum Christum Filium suum eligere, in filios adoptare, iustificare, et, si in fide perseverent, aeternum glorificare—infideles vero ac contumaces reprobare, excoecare, indurare, et, si in contumacia sua perseverent, in aeternum damnare*[EN27] (P. a Limborch, *Theol. chr.*, 1686, IV, 1, 5).

As against that, it is one of the merits of the *Canones* of the Synod of Dort (1619) that a definition of predestination was there given (I, 7) which, although it did not, of course, exclude the divine reprobation, did not include or append it as an autonomous truth, being

---

[EN23] Predestination is twofold: either of the elect for rest, or of the reprobate for death

[EN24] Just as God has predestined all the elect to life by the free gift of his grace alone ... so he has also predestined every reprobate to the punishment of eternal death, by what is most evidently the most just judgment of his righteousness

[EN25] It is necessary to say that God, by his eternal decree, of which the cause depends on nothing else, has destined for salvation those whom he pleased, and whom – leaving others out – he graced with his free adoption to enlighten them by his own Spirit, that they might receive the life offered to them in Christ. But he decreed also that others should be freely unbelieving, so that destitute of the light of faith, they should remain in the darkness

[EN26] We call the eternal predestination of God that decree in which he has it established in himself what he wills to become of each man. For all were not created in a like state. Rather, eternal life is foreordained for some, and eternal damnation for others. Therefore, just as each person is made for one or other of these ends, so we can say that they are predestined either for life or for death

[EN27] The predestination of God is that divine decree by which he established in the decree of his will before all temporal ages to choose those who believe in his Son Jesus Christ, to adopt them as his sons, to justify them, and if they persevere in the faith, to glorify them eternally.

content rather to state positively what *electio*[EN28] is: the *immutabile Dei proposition, quo ante iacta mundi fundamenta e universo genere humano, ex primaeva integritate in peccatum et exitium sua culpa prolapso, secundum liberrimum voluntatis suae beneplacitum, ex mera gratia, certam quorundam hominum multitudinem, aliis nec meliorum, nec digniorum, sed in communi miseria cum aliis iacentium, ad salutem elegit in Christo, quem etiam ab aeterno mediatorem et omnium electorum caput, salutisque fundamentum constituit, atque ita eos ipsi salvandos dare, et ad eius communionem per verbum et spiritum suum efficaciter vocare ac trahere seu vera in ipsum fide donare, iustificare, sanctificare et potenter in Filii sui communione custoditos tandem glorificare decrevit, ac demonstrationem suae misericordiae et laudem divitiarum gloriosae suae gratiae*[EN29]. Whatever else
[018] one may think of the formula, in this form the doctrine of predestination certainly did take on again the character of evangelical proclamation which it had lost in the definitions in which it referred simultaneously and equally to grace and non-grace, salvation and reprobation.

While they could not evade the importance of the content of his doctrine, some of Calvin's more timid contemporaries were much exercised about the danger of misunderstanding. They expressed the view that the doctrine of predestination ought to be reserved as a kind of secret wisdom for theologians of sobriety and discretion, and not published abroad amongst the people. Calvin made the forceful answer that true discretion cannot consist in burying away a truth to which all true servants of God testify, but only in the sober and reverent yet quite open confession of what is learned in the school of the heavenly Teacher (*De aet. Dei praed. C.R.* 8, 347). It would not be a true Christian simplicity, *eorum, quae Deus ostendit scientiam noxiam refugere*[EN30] (*ib.*, 264). What is revealed to us in Scripture is as such necessary and useful and worthy to be known by all. On no account, then, must the doctrine of predestination be withheld from believers (*Instit.* III, 21, 3). *Sicut enim praedicanda est pietas ut rite colatur Deus, ita et praedestinatio, ut, qui habet aures audiendi, de gratia Dei, in Deo, non in se glorietur*[EN31] (*De aet, Dei praed. ib.*, 327). Calvin was right. But although his point was right, he could have made it more emphatically and impressively if his understanding of predestination had been less speculative and more in accordance with the biblical testimony; if it had been a strictly evangelical understanding. And with its *parallelismus membrorum*[EN32], with that balanced assertion of the twofold dealings of God, as a doctrine of double predestination, this is precisely what it is not. The balance gives to the doctrine a neutrality which is almost scientific. It does not differentiate between the divine Yes and the divine No. It does not come down on the side of the divine Yes. On the very same level as the

---

But he chooses to reprobate/reject, to blind and to harden those hard-hearted unbelievers, and if they persist in their hard-heartedness, to condemn them in eternity
[EN28] election
[EN29] the immutable decree of God in which, before the foundations of the world were laid, according to the most free decree of his will, out of his undiluted grace, he elected in Christ unto salvation a definite multitude of certain men (out of the whole human race which had fallen from its original wholeness into sin and death by its own fault) neither better nor more worthy than others, but laid up in the same wretched state as those others. He established Christ as the mediator from eternity, the head of all the elect, the basis of salvation, and decreed to give to him those who are to be saved, and effectually to call and bring them to communion with him through his own Word and Spirit, to give them true faith in him, to justify, to sanctify, and in the end to glorify those he had powerfully kept in communion with his Son, as a demonstration of his mercy and for the praise of the glorious riches of his grace
[EN30] to flee from the 'harmful knowledge' of the things which God has revealed
[EN31] For just as holiness is to be preached so that God might be correctly worshipped, so also should predestination, so that those who have ears to hear may, by the grace of God, glory in God and not in themselves
[EN32] parallel lines

Yes it registers an equally definitive divine No concerning man. In such a form it is inevitable that the No should become much the stronger and ultimately the exclusive note. It is inevitable that the doctrine should in the last resort be understood as δυσαγγέλιον EN33, and that as such it should be repudiated with horror (and not without inward cause). It is not surprising, then, that the same miserable counsel once defeated by Calvin could 150 years later be reintroduced by Samuel Werenfels as the latest wisdom—just as though nothing had happened—and that since that time it has achieved something of the dignity of an *opinio communis*EN34 amongst the half-hearted.

The basic demand by which any presentation of the doctrine must be measured, and to which we ourselves must also conform, is this: that (negatively) the doctrine must not speak of the divine election and rejection as though God's electing and rejecting were not quite different, as though these divine dealings did not stand in a definite hierarchical relationship the one with the other; and that (positively) the supremacy of the one and subordination of the other must be brought out so radically that the Gospel enclosed and proclaimed even in this doctrine is introduced and revealed as the tenor of the whole, so that in some way or other the Word of the free grace of God stands out even at this point as the dominating theme and the specific meaning of the whole utterance. It is along these lines that it will be proved whether or not the doctrine is understood in conformity with the Bible and therefore with divine revelation. Only if understood in this way can it lay claim to the full publicity within the Church rightly defended by Calvin. If not understood in this way, then even as a secret wisdom for theologians it can have no real significance, or rather it can have only a very dangerous significance.

The specific proof of this thesis can be introduced connectedly only in and with the doctrine of predestination grounded upon it. Our preliminary concern is to show how right and necessary it is to set up this thesis at the very outset as a kind of working hypothesis.

We may establish first a point which all serious conceptions of the doctrine [019] have in common. They all find the nerve of the doctrine, the peculiar concern which forces them to present and assert it, in the fact that it characterises the grace of God as absolutely free and thereby divine. In electing, God decides according to His good-pleasure, which as such is holy and righteous. And because He who elects is constant and omnipotent and eternal, the good-pleasure by which He decides, and the decision itself, are independent of all other decisions, of all creaturely decisions. His decision precedes every creaturely decision. Over against all creaturely self-determination it is pre-determination—*prae-destinatio*. Grace is the divine movement and condescension on the basis of which men belong to God and God to men. Whether offered or received, whether self-revealing and reconciling or apprehended and active in faith, it is God's dealing, God's will and God's work, God's lordship, God Himself in all His sovereignty. Grace cannot be called forth or constrained by any claim or merit, by any existing or future condition, on the part of the creature. Nor can it be held up or rendered nugatory and ineffective by any contradiction or opposition on the part of the creature.

EN33 bad news
EN34 consensus view

Both in its being and in its operation its necessity is within itself. In face of it there is no place for the self-glorying or the self-praise of the creature. It comes upon the creature as absolute miracle, and with absolute power and certainty. It can be received by the creature only where there is a recognition of utter weakness and unworthiness, an utter confidence in its might and dignity, and an utter renunciation of wilful self-despair. What the creature cannot claim or appropriate for itself, it cannot of itself renounce when it does partake of it, nor can it even will to deprive itself of it. The decision by which it receives and affirms grace takes place in fulfilment of the prior divine decision. It cannot, then, be asserted over against God as a purely creaturely achievement, nor can it be revoked. As the fulfilment of that prior divine decision, it redounds *per se*[EN35] to the praise of the freedom of grace: of its independence both of the majesty and of the misery of our human volition and achievement; of the sovereignty in which it precedes and thus fully over-rules our human volition and achievement. All serious conceptions of the doctrine (more or less exactly and successfully, and with more or less consistency in detail) do at least aim at this recognition; at the freedom of the grace of God. We can put it more simply: They aim at an understanding of grace as grace. For what kind of grace is it that is conditioned and constrained, and not free grace and freely electing grace? What kind of a God is it who in any sense of the term has to be gracious, whose grace is not His own most personal and free good-pleasure.

[020] *Quidquid est in homine ordinans ipsum in salutem, totum comprehenditur sub effectu praedestinationis, etiam ipsa praeparatio ad gratiam: neque enim hoc fit nisi per auxilium divinum*[EN36] (Thomas Aqu. *S. th.* I, *qu.* 23, *art.* 5 *c*). It is certain *que Dieu nous a esleus, voire non seulement devant que nous le cogneussions, mais devant que nous fussions nais, et avant que le monde fut creé; et qu'il nous a esleus par sa bonté gratuite, et qu'il n'a point cerché la cause ailleurs; qu'il a deliberé ce propos en soy-mesme, et qu'il faut que nous cognoissions cela, afin qu'il soit glorifié de nous comme il appartient. Or la gloire telle qu'elle luy est deue, ne luy peut estre rendue sans cela …* [EN37] (Calvin, *Congrég. sur l'Election ét.*, 1562, *C.R.* 8, 103). We must *Deo reddere, quod suum est*[EN38] (*De aet. Dei praed.*, 1552, *C.R.* 8, 261). *Proprio cordis motu*[EN39] we are just as little ordained (*ordinati*) for fellowship with God as the world is self-created (*ib.*, 299). *Ut Deus cultores suos diligat, necesse est, ut, dum adhuc omni bono vacui sunt, gratuito amore praeveniat indignos et illis donet, quod postea amore prosequatur. Hanc vero primam gratiam dat quibus vult*[EN40] (*ib.*, 306).

[EN35] in itself

[EN36] Whatever is in respect of a person ordaining him to salvation, it must all be understood as the working of predestination. That is the preparation for grace. For this does not happen except by divine assistance

[EN37] that God has elected us, is evident not only because we know Him, but because we have been known, even before the world was created; and that we have been elected by His goodness, and that He did not look for any reason for it; that He deliberated this decree in Himself, and that it was necessary that we might know it, so that He might be glorified by us as he ought. So, the glory such as is due to Him cannot be rendered to him without that

[EN38] return to God that which is his own

[EN39] According to the motives of our hearts

[EN40] In order that God might love his worshippers, it is necessary that while they were still empty of all goodness, he went ahead to those who were unworthy with his free love, and gave to them what he afterwards continued to give in love. So he gives this first grace to those he wills

1. The Orientation of the Doctrine

Quand il dit que Dieu a deliberé en soy-mesme ce propos, c'est à dire, qu'il n'est point sorty hors de soy, qu'il n'a point ietté les yeux çà ne là, pour dire: Je serai esmeu à ce faire[EN41] (*Congrég.*, 1562, *ib.*, 95). *Clarissime Dominus pronuntiat, nullam hominibus benefaciendi rationem in ipsis se habere, sed a sola sua misericordia sumere; ideoque suum esse opus suorum salutem. Quum tuam in se uno salutem Deus statuat, cur ad teipsum descendes? Quum unam tibi suam misericordiam assignet, cur ad propria merita decurres? Quum tuam cogitationem in sua miseratione contineat, cur ad operum tuorum intuitum partem reflectes?*[EN42] (*Instit.* III, 22, 6). This note is still sounded in the older Reformed dogmatics: *Deus est liberrimae potestatis et solus vere* ἀνυπεύθνος. *Deuss igitur de suo fecit, quod sibi placuit, ac proinde creaturas suas praedestinavit quo voluit …. Nihil est in ulla creatura rationali, quod ei gratiam apud Deum conciliet; sed Deus ipse sibi gratos et acceptos in Filio suo fecit quos voluit. Nec Deus est cuiquam obligatus, ut ei teneatur quicquam dare*[EN43] (Polanus, *Synt. Theol. chr.*, 1609, *col.* 1561 f.). But the teaching of the *Formula of Concord* has the same emphasis: It is an error *quod non sola Dei misericordia et sanctissimum Christi meritum, sed etiam in nobis ipsis aliqua causa sit electionis divinae, cuius causae ratione Deus nos ad vitam aeternam elegerit*[EN44] (Ep. XI, 20, cf. *Sol. decl.* XI, 88). *Electio nostra ad vitam aeternam non virtutibus aut iustitia nostra sed solo Christi merito et benigna coelestis patris voluntate nitatur, qui seipsum negare non potest*[EN45] (*Sol. decl.* XI, 75). For Quenstedt, too, the *causa agens*[EN46] of election is *Dei unitrini voluntas libere decernens*[EN47] (*Theol. did. pol.*, 1685, III, *c.* 2, sect. 1, *th.* 9); its *causa movens interna: gratia Dei mere gratuita, excludens omne omnino operum humanorum meritum sive omne id, quod nomine operis vel actionis, sive per gratiam Dei, sive ex viribus naturae factae venit. Elegit enim nos Deus non secundum opera, sed ex mera sua gratia. Etiam fides ipsa huc non pertinet, si spectatur tanquam conditio, magis vel minus digna, sive per se, sive ex aestimio per voluntatem Dei, fidei superaddito, quod nihil horum decretum electionis ingrediatur tanquam causa movens aut impellens Deum ad tale decretum faciendum, sed id purae putae gratiae Dei est adscribendum*[EN48] (*ib.*, th. 10).

[EN41] When it is said that God has deliberated his decree in Himself, that does not mean that He has gone forth from Himself or that he Has cast His eye here and there in order to say, 'I will be moved to do this'

[EN42] The Lord pronounces most clearly that he has no reason to be gracious to men on their own account, but draws solely upon his own mercy, and therefore that their salvation is his own work. Since God establishes your salvation in his one self, why do you stoop to (attributing it to) yourself? Since he assigns to you one mercy, why do you run back to your own merits? Since he holds your thought in his compassion, why do you regard and contemplate the role of your works?

[EN43] God is possessed of utterly free power and is alone truly unaccountable. Therefore God, of his own (volition), does what he pleases, and he predestines his creatures as he wills. There is nothing in any rational creature which would attract favour to it from God; but God himself makes whom he wills pleasing to himself, and accepted in his Son. God is not obliged to anything, such that he is bound to give anything to it

[EN44] not only the mercy of God and the most holy merit of Christ, but also that there might be in ourselves some cause of divine election, by reason of which cause God elects us to eternal life

[EN45] Our election to eternal life rests not on our virtues or righteousness, but only on the merit of Christ and on the good will of our heavenly Father, who cannot deny himself

[EN46] acting cause

[EN47] the free decreeing will of the triune God

[EN48] internal motive cause: the grace of God, purely free, which excludes altogether every merit of human work; everything – whether it comes in the name of 'work' or 'action'; whether through the grace of God, or through the power of created nature. For God does not choose us according to works, but out of his undiluted grace. Even faith itself is not relevant here, whether considered (as a more, or less important condition) either in itself, or in some estimation of the divine will in conjunction with it. Because none of these encroaches upon the decree of election as a motive cause which could force God to create such a decree. Rather, that is to be attributed to the pure, to the perfectly pure, grace of God

19

§ 32. *The Problem of a Correct Doctrine of the Election of Grace*

All serious conceptions of the doctrine also agree that in this free decision of God we have to do with the mystery of God, i.e., with the divine resolve and decree whose basis is hidden and inscrutable. We were not admitted to the counsel of God as He made His election, nor can we subsequently call Him to give account or to make answer in respect of it. The will of God knows no Wherefore? It is an absolute Therefore, the ultimate Therefore of all. And it is as such that it wills to be known and honoured and obeyed. We resist the very being of this election as an election of grace, as a decision in accordance with the good-pleasure of the holy and righteous, the constant and omnipotent and eternal God; we resist the very being and existence of God Himself, if we raise even a question concerning the purpose and validity of this election, if we do not recognise that any such question is already answered by the fact that it is God who here decides and elects.

[021]

Sic inquirenda est ratio praedestinationis, sicut inquirilur ratio divinae voluntatis[EN49] (Thomas Aqu., *S. th.* I, *qu.* 23, *art.* 5 *c*). It was in recognition of this fact that Luther gave full vent to his wrath against Erasmus: *Quid quaeritur? Voluntati eius quis resistet? Hoc est illud, quod ratio neque capere, neque ferre potest, hoc offendit tot viros excellentes ingenio tot saeculis receptos. Hic expostulant ut Deus agat iure humano et faciat quod ipsis rectum videtur, aut Deus esse desinat. Nihil illi profuerint secreta maiestatis, rationem reddat, quare sit Deus, aut quare vellit aut faciat, quod nullam speciem iustitiae habeat, ac si sutorem aut zonarium roges iudicio se sistere. Non dignatur Deum caro gloria tanta, ut credat iustum esse et bonum, dum supra et ultra dicit el facit, quam definivit Codex Justiniani vel quintus liber Ethicorum Aristotelis. Cedat maiestas creatrix omnium feci uni creaturae suae et Coricius ille specus metuat versa vice spectatores suos. Igitur absurdum est, ut damnet eum, qui vitare non potest meritum damnationis. Et propter hanc absurditatem falsum esse oportet, quod Deus, cuius vult, miseretur, quem vult indurat, sed redigendus est in ordinem et praescribendae illi leges, ut non damnet quenquam nisi qui nostro iudicio id meruerit*[EN50] (*De servo arb.* W.A. 18, 729, 13). Calvin likewise drew attention to the mystery of the election of grace: *Il est donc ici question d'adorer les secrets de Dieu qui nous sont incompréhensibles. Et sans cela iamais nous ne gouterons les principes de la foy. Car nous sçavons que nostre sagesse doit commencer touisours par humilité; et ceste humilité-là emporte que nous ne veniens point avec nostre balance pour peser les iugemens de Dieu, que nous n'en vueillions point estre iuges ni arbitres: mais que nous soyons sobres, voyant la petitesse de nostre Esprit, voyant que nous sommes grossiers et lours, que nous magnifions Dieu, et que nous disions (comme nous*

[EN49] Thus is the basis of predestination to be investigated, just as the means of the divine will is investigated

[EN50] "Why does he find fault? Who can resist his will?" (Rom 9.19). This is something which reason can neither grasp nor bear. This has been a stumbling-block to so many brilliant men, who have come down to us, from so many centuries. Here they demand that God act according to human law, and does what seem right to them, or else cease to be God. To such a person, the secrets of his majesty are of no help to his case: let him give a reason why he be God, or why he wills or does that which has no appearance of justice, as you might summon a cobbler or a girdlemaker to stand in court. The flesh does not dignify God with such glory that it believes him to be righteous and good when he speaks and acts above and beyond what the Justinian Code or the fifth book of Aristotle's Ethics define. Here, the majesty which created all things, must yield to one of the dregs of his creation, and the cave of Corycos (the entrance to the underworld) must, conversely, be afraid of its those who see it. Therefore it is absurd that he damn someone who cannot avoid deserving damnation. And on account of this absurdity, it must be false that God has mercy on whom he wills, and hardens whom he wills. He must be brought to order and laws must be prescribed for him, such that he does not condemn any-one, except one who in our judgment deserves it

sommes enseignez par l'Escriture saincte), *Seigneur, c'est un abysme trop profond que ton conseil, nul ne le peut raconter*[EN51] (*Serm. on Eph.* 1³ᶠ· *C.R.* 51, 260 f.). *Non alia nos cognitio iuvet, quam quae admiratione claudatur. Rideant nos qui volent: modo stupori nostro Deus e coelo annuat et angeli applaudant*[EN52] (*De aet. Dei praed. C.R.* 8, 292). We might also bring in as an instructive indirect confirmation some words of Kant on this subject: "That there should be at work in man a heavenly grace which not by any merit of works but by an unconditioned decree grants its aid to one and refuses it to another, predestinating one part of our race to salvation and the other to eternal perdition, does not give us any concept of divine righteousness, but must necessarily be referred to a wisdom whose canon is to us an absolute mystery. Concerning such mysteries, in so far as they touch on the moral history of every individual—how it comes about, for instance, that there is good and evil in the world at all, or (if the latter is in all and at all times) how the former can arise out of it and be restored in any man, or why, if this does take place in some, others are excluded therefrom—God has not revealed anything to us, nor indeed can He, for we would not understand it even if He did" (*Rel. innerh. d. Grenzen d. blossen Vernunft*, 1793, ed. K. Vorländer, 166). And elsewhere rather less morosely: "If we represented this faith itself as having such mystical (or magical) power that, although so far as we know it ought to be regarded as merely historical, it could yet radically improve a man (make of him a new man) if accepted with all its attendant emotions, then we should have to regard the faith itself as mediated and given directly from heaven (with and under historical faith), in which case everything that has to do with the moral activity of man would come back ultimately to an unconditioned decree of God: He hath mercy on whom He will, and whom He will He hardeneth; a sentence which, taken literally, is the *salto mortale*[EN53] of human reason" (*op. cit.*, p. 139).

And now we can mention a third point which unites all serious conceptions of the doctrine. To the confession of the mystery of God's freedom in the election of grace they all quite definitely relate, in some sense as a basis, the confession that in the mystery of His freedom God always does that which is worthy of Himself, i.e., the confession of His righteousness. As we regard the work of God in the election of grace we must always remember Rom. 9²⁰: "Nay but, O man, who art thou that repliest against God?" We must recognise the sovereignty of God and the inscrutability of His election, respecting the Therefore of it which no Wherefore can circumvent. Yet in so doing—if we really have God before us as the Subject of this work—we honour the source and citadel of all equity and judgment: not merely the wisdom which *must* silence the objections of our thinking and feeling, as though we were confronted by a *brutum factum*[EN54]—as though all discussion were terminated at this point by [022]

[EN51] Here, then, it is a question of adoring the secrets of God which are incomprehensible to us. And without that we will never taste the principles of faith. For we know that our wisdom must always begin with humility; and that humility removes the possibility that we come with our balance for weighing the judgments of God, of whom we should not wish in any way to be the judges or arbiters. Rather, we should be sober, seeing the smallness of our spirits, seeing that we are rude and dull, that we should magnify God, that we should say (as we are taught by Holy Scripture), 'Lord, it is too profound a mystery that no one is able to tell forth your counsel'

[EN52] No other thought aids us except that which is stopped by wonder. Let them mock us who will; God approves of our amazement from heaven, and the angels applaud it

[EN53] death-defying leap

[EN54] brute fact

force—by a "higher" force, but still by force; but the wisdom before which we *can* only be silent. We are not bowing before the caprice of a tyrant. Our submission cannot be such that it is accompanied by a still-remaining and ever-increasing inward complaint and resistance. Rather, of ourselves, of our own better knowledge, we will to be silent. It is not that our mouth is stopped—for then our silence would not be a voluntary act of obedience, but an act of disobedience which has been prevented and suppressed. It is rather because our ears have heard the Therefore which is the truly satisfying and convincing answer to every Wherefore. We are persuaded, and have no more questions to put. God Himself, and in Him wisdom itself and righteousness itself, has communicated Himself to us and given us Himself as the answer. What God does in freedom is in order. And in that it is done in freedom, we can and must perceive and recognise that it is in order without first measuring it by our own conceptions of order and only then recognising it to be such. It belongs to God that He should teach us what order is. It belongs to us to measure our conceptions of order by His decision, and to learn from Him what order is. In so doing we do not make any *sacrificium intellectus*[EN55], but we become and are truly wise: so assuredly is the fear of the Lord the beginning of wisdom. "O man, who art thou that repliest against God?" And the answer is: "Thou art a fool. It is high time to learn wisdom and to leave off thy disputing. In the mystery of God's freedom in His election thou mayest contemplate and adore the only and true righteousness, and in such contemplation and adoration thou mayest be truly wise."

In the history of the doctrine the justifiable concern to bring out this aspect of the matter has inspired innumerable efforts which have done further violence to the only possible form of such an acknowledgment as we have here tried to sketch it. It was not thought sufficient simply to assert that in the freedom of His decision God Himself is as such righteousness and the Teacher of righteousness, and that the sum of all wisdom consists in listening to Him as such a Teacher. There was a desire to be wise in respect of God before learning wisdom from God Himself. Thus there sprang up within the sphere of this doctrine all those attempts which resulted in violence being done to the freedom of God by the indication of certain external conditions of God's work in the light of which the validity and order of His election could again be measured by our conceptions of order, and thus acknowledged as righteous and worthy of God without that silence, without that listening to God Himself. It is self-evident that in greater or lesser degree all such attempts must call in question the divine mystery which Kant found so strange and repugnant but the denial of which could provoke a Luther to such great indignation. Attempts of this kind have been made again and again since the Gottschalk controversy of the 9th century. We do not take part in them, but we can and must appreciate that their appearance points to an underlying concern which must be vindicated in some form or other. It is all the more interesting to hear Calvin on this point, for he did not wish the slightest diminution of the freedom of the divine election, but the preservation in all circumstances of the divine mystery. And yet he showed the righteousness of this election, and the need for us to do justice to it as an act, as *the* act, of the only and true wisdom, with an impressiveness hardly surpassed by any other writer. It is true that when any

[023]

[EN55] sacrifice of the intellect

question was raised concerning the basis or ground of the divine decision Calvin loved—and rightly—to quash it at once simply along the line of Rom. 9^{20}: *Il y en a qui trouvent estrange quand on ne leur donne point de resolution qui soit facile. Et je voudroye qu'on me dit les choses plus clairement, que j'aperceusse pourquoy telle chose se fait. Mon amy, il te faut aller cercher une autre escole, puis que tu es si presomptueux, que tu ne veux point donner gloire à Dieu, sinon que tu voyes les enseignes. Or va cercher une autre escole que celle du sainct Esprit*[EN56] (*Congrég. C.R.* 8, 108). *Nous savons quelle est l'audace des hommes; et il n'y a celuy qui n'en ait l'experience en soy, qu'il est bien difficile de dompter nos esprits, tellement que nous recevions en paix et humilité tout ce qu'on nous declare. Il faut qu'un homme soit bien matté de Dieu devant qu'il se reigle là .... Ces objections qui se font, doivent estre repoussés par ce mot seulement de l'autorité de Dieu: assavoir quelle maistrise et préeminence est-ce qu'il doit avoir par dessus nous*[EN57] (*op. cit.*, p. 104). *Iniquum est calculo nostro subiici profunda illa iudicia, quae sensus omnes nostros absorbent*[EN58] (*Instit.* III, 23, 1). *In sola eius voluntate quiescendum est: ut quod illic placere intelligimus, cuius nos causa fugit instar mille rationum sufficiat*[EN59] (*De aet. Dei praed. C.R.* 8, 312). *Adeo enim summa est iustitiae regula Dei voluntas, ut quicquid vult, iustum habendum sit. Ubi ergo quaeritur, cur ita fecerit Dominus, respondendum est: Quia voluit .... Quod si ultra pergas rogando cur valuerit, maius aliquid quaeris et sublimius Dei voluntate, quod inveniri non potest*[EN60] (*Instit.* III, 23, 2). But Calvin did not rest content with that. He followed the line of Rom. 9^{20} to its conclusion : *Quod tibi sonat Dei nomen?*[EN61] he demanded of those to whom it appeared *molestum ac odiosum*[EN62] that God should have been able to do and should have done more than their reason could comprehend (*De aet. Dei praed. C.R.* 8, 262). The very name of God is our guarantee that it is sensible to be silent at this point: *Quavis enim sapientia praestantior est sobrietas, quae Dei timore subacta intra praescriptum ab eo intelligendi modum se continet*[EN63] (*ib.*, 8, 263). But we must say too, and just as definitely, that in God we are not dealing with a tyrant, or a God of caprice: *Non fingimus Deum exlegem, qui sibi ipsi lex est .... Dei voluntas non modo ab omni vitio pura, sed summa perfectionis regula, etiam legum omnium lex est*[EN64] (*Instit.* III, 23, 2). *Nous disons, que ceste volonté*

[EN56] There are some who find it strange when they are not given an easy answer. I myself would like to be told things more clearly, and would like to discern why such-and-such a thing takes place. My friend, you must go and find another school, since you are so presumptuous that you are not willing to give glory to God unless you see the reasons. Go, then, and find a school other than that of the Holy Spirit

[EN57] We know how great the audacity of men is. And there is no one who has not had the experience himself of how difficult it is to tame our spirits, such that we receive peacefully with humility everything which is declared to us. It is necessary that a man be well conquered by God before he directs himself to that ... These objections which are made must be pushed away on the authority of God alone by this word: Know what Lordship and pre-eminence we must have over us

[EN58] It is wicked to subject to our reckoning those profound judgments which absorb all our senses

[EN59] There is rest to be found in his will alone. As we understand what pleases him – of which the reason escapes us – this value is worth a thousand reasons

[EN60] For the will of God is so much the highest rule of justice, that whatever he wills must be considered just. So when it is asked why God acts in such-and-such a way, it must be replied, 'Because he wills'. But if you go further, and ask why he has willed it, you ask for something greater and more sublime than the will of God, which cannot be found

[EN61] What does God's name mean to you

[EN62] troublesome and despicable

[EN63] For the moderation, which is constrained by the fear of God and keeps itself within the means of understanding prescribed by him, is more excellent than any wisdom

[EN64] We are not describing a lawless God, who is a law unto himself ... The will of God is not only pure of all wickedness, but is the purest rule of perfection, even the law of all laws

de Dieu est ordonnée et tellement ordonnée que c'est la source de tout équité et iustice[EN65] (*Congrég. C.R.* 8, 115). *Si velle se ac iubere pronuntiet mortalis homo ut pro ratione sit sua voluntas, tyrannicam esse vocem fateor: sed id ad Deum transferre sacrilegi est furoris, Neque enim quidquam Deo immoderatum affingere licet, ut in eo sicut in hominibus exsultet libido: sed merito hoc honoris defertur eius voluntati, ut pro ratione valeat; quando omnis iustitiae fons est ac regula*[EN66]. To distinguish between a *voluntas Dei ordinata*[EN67] and *absoluta*[EN68] is a blasphemy from which we can only recoil in horror. *Ego autem ex adverso contendo, adeo nihil esse in Deo inordinatum, ut inde potius fluat, quidquid est in coelo et in terra ordinis. Quum ergo in summum gradum evehimus Dei voluntatem, ut sit omni ratione superior, absit ut eum quidquam nisi summa ratione velle imaginemur; sed simpliciter sentimus, eum iure suo tantum habere potestatis, ut solo eius nutu contento esse nos oporteat .... An mihi portentum hoc unquam venit in mentem, nullam Deo consilii sui rationem constare? Dum ego Deum praesidem totius mundi statuo, qui incomprehensibili et mirifico consilio gubernet modereturque omnia: an illum fortuito huc illuc raptari, vel caeca temeritate eum facere quod facit, quisquam ex verbis meis colliget? ... Gloriae suae rationem in actis suis omnibus habet Dominus. Nempe hic universalis est finis ...* [EN69]. (*De aet. Dei praed. C.R.* 8, 310 f.). And finally therefore: *Praedestinatio nihil aliud est quam iustitiae occultae quidem sed inculpatae dispensatio*[EN70] (*Instit.* III, 23, 8).

[024]

We have emphasised three points (we shall have to treat them more fully in detail) common to all conceptions of the doctrine: the freedom of God, the mystery of God, and the righteousness of God in His election of grace. We have done this because as we consider these three points we cannot refrain from asking a question of the exponents of the dogma (no matter how they may interpret it in detail). This question will occupy us in different forms as we proceed. We now put it for the first time in this way: Are we at liberty to accuse or blame these exponents because as Christian theologians they did speak in this way of the freedom, the mystery and the righteousness of God in His election of grace; because they did speak of the freedom, the mystery and the righteousness of the triune God, the Father revealed in the Son by the Holy Ghost, as testified in Holy Scripture; because they did not wander off and

---

[EN65] We say that this will of God is ordered, and so ordered that it is the source of all equity and justice

[EN66] If a mortal man pronounced that he willed or commanded that his will was to be reason, I would say his statement was tyrannical. But to extend that to God is a terrible sacrilege. For it is not permissible to attach anything improper to God, such as that desire springs up in him as it does in men. But by this merit of honour, it is attributed to his will that it be worthy of being reason, since it is the fount and rule of all justice

[EN67] an ordered will of God

[EN68] an absolute will of God

[EN69] But I contend, on the contrary, that there is nothing in God which is not ordered, and from that follows whatever is orderly in heaven and earth. So when we lift the will of God up to the highest degree, so that it is superior to all reason, then we will be far from imagining that he wills anything except by the highest reason. We should simply think that he has so much power in his law, that it is right for us to be content merely with a mere nod from him. Or does this portent ever come into my mind, that there is no reason in the counsel of God? I acknowledge that God presides over all the world, and governs with his incomprehensible and marvellous counsel and moderates all things. Or could anyone gather from my words that he rushes around randomly from here to there, or that he made everything which he made in blind rashness? The Lord has reason in all of his acts – the reason of his glory. Indeed, he is the goal of all things

[EN70] Predestination is nothing other than the dispensation of justice, secret – yes – but also blameless

speak of a "supreme being" posited by human invention and, as the absolutised image of man, endowed with certain pre-eminent qualities; because they did not speak of the ostensible freedom, the ostensible mystery and the ostensible righteousness of this being? There can be no doubt that when we consider the serious exponents of the doctrine we have reason on the whole to return a favourable answer to the question, unconditionally so when we take into account their intention. The theologians we have in mind did wish to be Christian theologians, and in the particular form in which it was presented their doctrine of predestination was meant to be the exposition of Scripture, and therefore a testimony to the revelation of the triune God. There was, then, no question of arbitrary speculation concerning an arbitrarily conceived absolute, but rather an obedient reckoning with the One whom Jesus Christ called His Father, and who called Jesus Christ His Son. In so far as we hold fast by their intention, we think we shall still be in agreement with them when we add at once that the freedom, mystery and righteousness of God in the election of grace must be understood in terms of Christian theology. Only as understood in this way are they the truth which must be received and proclaimed in the Church. But if this is the case, it is settled once and for all that in the doctrine of election we have to do with the sum of the Gospel. This is the theme which we must now finally develop.

We did not form at random the concept of the election of grace. In it we [025] described the choice of God which, preceding all His other choices, is fulfilled in His eternal willing of the existence of the man Jesus and of the people represented in Him. If we are to understand and explain the nature of this primal and basic act of God, we cannot stop, then, at the formal characteristic that it is a choice. We must resist the temptation to absolutise in some degree the concept choosing or electing. We must not interpret the freedom, the mystery and the righteousness of the election of grace merely as the definitions and attributes of a supreme form of electing posited as absolute. We must not find in this supreme form as such the reality of God. Otherwise we shall be doing what we ought not to do. We shall be forging and constructing (out of this very characteristic) a supreme being. And it is difficult to imagine how the description of the activity of this being can ever become a Gospel. If the distinctive and ultimate feature in God is absolute freedom of choice, or an absolutely free choice, then it will be hard to distinguish His freedom from caprice or His mystery from the blindness of such caprice. It will be no less hard to maintain His righteousness in any form except that of mere assertion. It will then be difficult to make it clear that God is not merely a tyrant living by His whims, that He is not merely blind fate, that He is something other than the essential inscrutability of all being. It cannot well be denied that there has taken place such an absolutising of the concept of electing, or of its freedom, with the accompanying influence of a non-Christian conception of God, in the history of the doctrine. Nor can it be denied that as a result the utterances on the subject have to a greater or lesser extent been obscured, and in any case

25

fairly generally distorted. As against that, we must take as our starting-point the fact that this divine choice or election is the decision of the divine will which was fulfilled in Jesus Christ, and which had as its goal the sending of the Son of God. As such, it has always in God Himself, as a spontaneous *opus internum ad extra*EN71 of the trinitarian God, and to that extent originally and properly, the character of grace. Its freedom is indeed divine and therefore absolute. It is not, however, an abstract freedom as such, but the freedom of the One who loves in freedom. It is He Himself, and not an essence of the freedom of choice, or of free choice, who is the divine Subject of the electing which takes place at this point. We must not seek the ground of this election anywhere but in the love of God, in His free love—otherwise it would not be His—but still in His love. If we seek it elsewhere, then we are no longer talking about this election. We are no longer talking about the decision of the divine will which was fulfilled in Jesus Christ. We are looking beyond these to a supposedly greater depth in God (and that undoubtedly means nothingness, or rather the depth of Satan). What takes place in this election is always that God is for us; for us,

[026] and therefore for the world which was created by Him, which is distinct from Him, but which is yet maintained by Him. The election is made with a view to the sending of His Son. And this means always that in Him and through Him God moves towards the world. It means not merely that He creates and sustains the world, but that He works on it and in it by (miracle of all miracles) giving Himself to it. It means that the will for fellowship, which is His very being and to which the world owes its existence, is actively demonstrated to the world in a way which surpasses anything that could be expected or claimed. If we describe this movement as election, then it is only because we would thereby emphasise that it is the active demonstration of His love. Would it be love—the love of the personal God, and as such real love—if it were not an electing? As electing love it can never be hatred or indifference, but always love. And the active demonstration of that love is this: "God so loved the world, that he gave his only begotten Son, that whosoever believeth in him should not perish, but have everlasting life" (Jn. 3¹⁶). Whatever may be the inner link in God's election between that giving of His only-begotten Son and the faith in Him by which the intended salvation is effected, this much is certain, that in this election (in giving Himself to this work, and in electing as the object of this work the man Jesus from among the world of men, and in Him the whole race) God loved the world. It is certain that this election is a work in which God meets the world neither in indifference nor in enmity, but in which at the very highest and lowest levels (in the giving of His only-begotten Son) He is for this man Jesus, and in Him for the whole race, and therefore for the world. That God wills neither to be without the world nor against it can never be stated more clearly or forcibly than when we speak of His election. At bottom, then, to speak of the election means necessarily to speak of the Gospel. In our teach-

---

EN71 internal work outside of himself

ing concerning the election we must always bring in the fact, definitely and basically and as the meaning and substance of all our assertions, that of and from Himself God has decided for this loftiest and most radical movement towards His creation, ordaining and constituting Himself its Friend and Benefactor. It is in this way, in the form of this election, that God has made His decision. And the tidings of the divine decision in this form are glad tidings. It is as such and in such a sense that they must be delivered: without any concealment of the fact that God does elect (for what need is there of concealment?); without any transmutation of God's way of loving the world into some other way, a general "loving" which involves no election and which is not really love; without any suppression or obfuscation of the fact that in this way and in the form of this election God has truly loved the world. In this form and this form alone the tidings of the divine decision made in Jesus Christ are glad tidings directed to all men, directed indeed to the whole world. It is also true that in the world there is opposition to the love of God, indeed that this opposition [027] constitutes the being of the world as such. The text itself points indirectly but quite definitely to this fact when it says: "Whosoever believeth in him should not perish." But the will and the power of God smash this opposition. Where the opposition does not break down in faith in the Son given, even the love of God must itself be destructive. To an opposing world the election must of the same force and necessity become non-election, or rejection. And it is for this reason, and to this extent, that there does exist a definite sphere of damnation ordained and determined by God as the negation of the divine affirmation, the work of the almighty non-willing which accompanies God's willing. But the divine affirmation, the divine willing as such, is salvation and not damnation. The divine election as such does not negate creation but affirms it. The message of God's election means always the message of the Yes determined and pronounced by God. Another message can, of course, be given apart from that of God's election, e.g., the message of the blind election of fate, or of the supposedly most enlightened election of our own judgment. Here we shall be told something quite different from the divine affirmation. But we cannot hear of God's election without also hearing God's Yes. If we truly hear, then in face of this election and its meaning it is not possible for us not to be able to hear or obey that Yes, not to will to be amongst those who are affirmed by God. This is not a possibility but an impossibility. It is a turning of the sense of that election into nonsense. It is a descent into the abyss of the divine non-willing and the divine non-electing. Even in such a descent the creature cannot escape God. Even in this abyss it is still in the hands of God, the object of His decision. Yet that does not mean that it has been flung, or even allowed to fall, into the abyss by God Himself. God is and God remains the One who has decided for the creature and not against it. It is by love itself that the creature is confounded. Even there, in the midst of hell, when it thinks of God and His election it can think only of the love and grace of God. The resolve and power of our opposition cannot put any limit to the power and resolve of God. Even in our opposition there comes upon us that which God has foreordained for us. But that means that what comes upon us cannot alter in the slightest the nature and character of the foreordination which is God's decree. In that decree as such we find only the decree of His love. In the proclaiming and teaching of His election we can hear only the proclaiming of the Gospel.

With this in mind we may now take up again the three points on which we found agreement amongst the different exponents of the doctrine.

[028]

In the light of an evangelical understanding of the election of grace, what is the meaning of the freedom of God in this His work? In His grace God is the One who unconditionally precedes the creature. Man with his decision can only follow. He cannot forestall God with any claim, or condition, or ground of action. But this fact carries within itself the final and severest humiliation of the creature. If it is really the case, then over against God the creature cannot produce or proclaim any inherent dignity, anything that is good within itself. It is obviously the creature's destiny to owe all that is good in its nature and existence as a creature to God alone. On account of that good it has no claim to be elected by God. But it seems evident, too, that before God even the good of its creatureliness as such is null and void. Before God the creature has lost and forfeited that good. It stands accused because it has misused that good, because it has not been thankful in respect of it. Even out of its gratitude there cannot arise, then, any expectation of divine election. The freedom of the divine election means that over against God the creature finds itself within the cordon not merely of its creatureliness but of its sin. It is not only little before God but blameworthy. Against the love of God it is in a state of opposition in which that love turns to its destruction and in which fellowship with God can result only in judgment and perdition. That is what the freedom of grace means for the creature towards whom it is directed. That is the self-knowledge which is demanded of the creature side by side with the knowledge of God's freedom. In the depth of its plight there is reflected the foreordination under which it stands when God is gracious to it on the basis of His free election. With the radicalness therein implied it must renounce everything which might be regarded as earning or even partially meriting its election. But that is not all that God's freedom in this work means for the creature, for this freedom is His freedom in respect of this particular work, the freedom of His grace. Grace is the Nevertheless of the divine love to the creature. The election consists in this Nevertheless. It is indeed election. It is indeed grace, and for that reason it is free. How could the divine love to the creature be really love, how could it be divine, unless it were free? But it is grace, loving-kindness, favour. In it God says Yes to the creature and not No. He says it of Himself. He says it without the creature having any right or claim to it. He says it, then, in freedom. But what He says, He says as the One who loves in freedom. He does not say No but Yes. Against our No He places His own Nevertheless. He is free in the very fact that the creature's opposition to His love cannot be any obstacle to Him. He is free, too, in the fact that He cannot be satisfied merely with smashing this opposition, and thus allowing the creature to be confounded by His love. He could have been satisfied with that. But He need not. And in His free grace He will not and is not. He is not free, then, merely in the fulfilling of His will for fellowship with the creature by allowing it to perish beneath the hand which it has rejected but still cannot escape. He is free rather, and His hand is almighty, in the fact that He can rescue the creature from the destruction into which it has plunged itself by its opposition. He is free in the fact that He can turn it in [029] spite of itself to the salvation and life which are the positive and distinctive meaning and goal of His love. And it is that which God elects. It is that which He does in the election of His grace. He chooses the Yes and not the No, inevitable as the latter seems in face of the attitude of the creature. He elects grace as grace and not as judgment, which the attitude of the creature seems inevitably to have made it. He elects the fulfilment and not the non-fulfilment of the purpose and meaning of love, even though the creature seems as though it must inevitably be confounded by that love, even though His will seemingly can only take its course in the non-fulfilment, in the damnation of the creature, in its destruction and perdition. There is nothing inevitable against which the love of God must for its part be shattered. God elects, then, not the punishment but the undeserved rewarding of the creature, not its death but the life which it had forfeited, not its non-being but its impossible being. He elects. Neither to the creature nor to Himself is He under an obligation to elect in this way. But He does elect in this way. This means the freedom of God for His creature. And if it means the final and severest humiliation of the creature, it does not mean that it is driven to despair. It means that despair of self, which appears to be its only remaining portion, is forbidden as mere wilfulness. It means that such despair loses its point because it is unnecessary. It means that it is made quite impossible because it is deprived of its object. Where God does not despair, the creature cannot despair. And grace, the freedom of the election of grace, means that God does not despair of the creature. Not only does He not despair of it, but in all the riches of His own glory He moves towards it and interests Himself in it. The sovereignty of God is not only confirmed by the fact that the creature cannot escape Him, that it must fulfil the divine will even in its condemnation. It is also confirmed by the fact that God's last word to it and the positive goal of His will is always one of blessedness. It is confirmed in the Nevertheless with which He rescues the creature from condemnation and ordains it to blessedness, notwithstanding the decision of the creature, in opposition to it, in reversal of that mistaken decision, in the reconstitution of it by His own prior decision. The sovereignty of God is thus confirmed by the freedom of the election of grace, and that means for the creature not simply humiliation, but the humiliation which is really and in the same moment exaltation. If a man has not been allowed to fall by God, then He cannot fall at all, and least of all can he cause himself to fall. God Himself in His freedom has decided that he shall stand, that he shall be saved and not lost, that he shall live and not die. He cannot take these things, but they are given to him in the freedom of God. He himself has no freedom for God. He cannot assert any such freedom over against God. He has no freedom in which [030] he may will to help himself. But God in His freedom stands substitute for him. And in that very fact he has his own real freedom for God and for the purpose of the will of God; the freedom to obey Him and to live by Him. That he is elected by the grace of God means also, then, that he too becomes free: free from the threat of the accusation laid against him, free from the curse of his own proven guilt, free from the bondage in which the curse works itself out, free from death, in which its end is finally attained; free for the thankfulness which he can never again deny to God now that his ingratitude has been passed over, free for the service of which he is now made worthy without any merit of his own, free for a joy which only now can live again and which is unfathomable in its depths. And all this means the freedom of the grace of God for the humiliated who has no help apart from God, who even now can only cling to the grace of God as such. This is the incomparable and inexhaustible blessing visited upon him in the election of God. This is the blessing held out to every man who hears; the blessing which must always be proclaimed as the final word whenever we make mention of the doctrine of the divine election of grace.

We ask further: In the light of an evangelical understanding of the election of grace, what is the meaning of the mystery of the freedom of this divine work? The will of God in His grace knows no Wherefore. God's decision is grounded in His good-pleasure, and for that reason it is inexplicable to us. If we tried to call God to account for His decision we should be questioning and indeed denying God Himself. But if this is the case, then it means that the creature must bow before the gracious God and submit itself to Him. Confronted with the mystery of God, the creature must be silent: not merely for the sake of being silent, but for the sake of hearing. Only to the extent that it attains to silence, can it attain to hearing. But, again, it must be silent not merely for the sake of hearing, but for that of obeying. For obedience is the purpose and goal of hearing. Our return to obedience is indeed the aim of free grace. It is for this that it makes us free. It is for this that it confronts us as a mystery, as a supreme court, as a verdict against which there can be no appeal, as a decision the lightness of which cannot be tested by the standards of other decisions because, on account of the One who made it, it is inherently right. In its very character as unsearchable the election of God demands as such our obedience. It is not proclaimed to us, nor does it reach us, but as an election of the creature it is the mere imagination of the creature, if in and with that election there is no summons to obedience—quite irrespective of the accusation laid against us, the curse resting upon us, the death shadowing our whole life. From these very things the election of grace has, in fact, released us. And in so doing it has undermined the pretence and subterfuge that we had no power to obey, that the demand laid upon us by God was too great. In the

demand He makes God does not ask us concerning ourselves: He asks us   [031]
rather concerning our acknowledgment of that which He in His grace has
determined and adjudged concerning us. We are not summoned to an active
demonstration of our own powers. We are summoned to live in the power of
His grace. But to that we are summoned, being confronted by the omnipotent
and unsearchable Therefore of God, which in its unsearchability both cuts off
our retreat and drives us forward. Drives us forward: for no longer can we
sustain ourselves with anything but the positive meaning and purpose of the
will of God, in the power of which we are saved and ought to live, to whose pre-
determination our own self-determination is subject. Everything else is the old
past of which we can never again lay hold. The mystery of grace is the middle-
point in our lives, divisive and disturbing. And by this fact it is decided that
God's will is our salvation. This is what the mystery means for the creature. But
there is more to it than that. It was necessary to point out that the mystery of
the election of God summons to obedience. It does so because it is the mystery
of the living and life-giving God, and not of an enthroned but lifeless idol
beside which we could only sit in an equally lifeless fear or confidence. But
now we must maintain, and, if possible, emphasise even more strongly, the
other side of the matter: that when the mystery of God in election comes into
the life of the creature, demanding, compelling and disturbing, it is really
grace and loving-kindness and favour which visits the creature. When this happens, God is in fact saying Yes to it. And it is God who says Yes. It is, therefore, a
Yes which is unconditional in its certainty, preceding all self-determination
and outlasting any change in self-determination on the part of the creature. It
is the foreordination under which the creature must always live. It disturbs us
but does not disquiet us. The sphere of disquiet is the sphere outside the divine election of grace, the sphere of the creature resisting the love of God. The
creature is restless, and necessarily so, having brought about its own fall by this
resistance. Once it has left its only possible and real resting-place, it seeks
another in vain. It has no rest because that resistance has made it completely
untrustworthy and yet it would trust in itself. By the divine election of grace,
however, it is removed from this sphere of unrest. And the mystery of this
election means for the creature that it is set at rest. The rest of decision and
obedience: for it is the mystery of the living and the life-giving God. But truly
at rest: for it is the mystery of the constant God, who gives to the creature
whose interests He espouses a part in His own constancy. When God says Yes to
the creature, He does say Yes; without any if or but, without any afterthought
or reservation, not temporarily but definitively, with a fidelity which is not par-
tial and temporal, but total and eternal. Once the election has taken place,
there is no further question as to the validity or non-validity of this Yes. There is
no further anxiety as to how such a Yes can be fashioned or maintained. There
is no further despair in face of the ever-present and total impossibility of living   [032]
by one's own strength in the light of this Yes. All this lies behind the creature—
as the old past. As truly as God has said Yes, as truly as God is God, the creature

is affirmed, and it has no other life than life in the light of this Yes. The obedience demanded of it by the divine election of grace, what else is it but the self-evident authorisation of the creature elected and therefore affirmed by God? And so the decision which in this election is made concerning the creature cannot mean that it is placed under the alien law of an all-powerful destiny, which it must restlessly fulfil, tormented by the consciousness of its own insufficiency in the face of its greatness and demand. What indeed is there to fulfil when by the divine Yes the law of its life has not merely been established but fulfilled? All that is left for it to do is simply to live the life ordained for it, and to live therefore at peace. All that is left to it is wonder, reverent astonishment, at the fact of the mystery that it can live this life affirmed by God: not an idle wonder, but not one which could lead to new unrest; wonder at the God who in advance has answered all our questions, removed all our anxiety and taken away the object of all our self-despair, by Himself, i.e., by His intervention for us, in which account is already taken of our insufficiency, and by which He has created a perfect sufficiency for us. Inasmuch as He does not allow Himself to be called to account for His election, God permits and commands the creature to surrender to Him the responsibility for its existence. Inasmuch as in the election He disposes of us without allowing any questions as to the grounds of His action, we can and must reckon with the fact that the dispositions concerning our conduct have already been made, and need not be made again by us, but need only be recognised as already made. Inasmuch as in the election He has made Himself the object of our worship, all the demand now made of us consists in the one thing—that we should really offer Him this worship. This is the rest which is signified by God's election of grace even for the creature which is rigorously and inexorably claimed for service. Thus claimed, it has no longer any need to justify itself, to defend itself, or to save itself. It may be silent and still before this mystery. Even as it runs, it may wait for the joyous revelation of this mystery. In God's election of grace it is visited by an incomparable and inexhaustible blessing even from this second standpoint; even in the very fact that it is always God's mystery, that in it God disposes of us, not allowing us to approve of the disposition made, but only to acknowledge it as something already accomplished. And that is the blessing held out to every man who hears; the blessing which must always be proclaimed as the final word whenever we make mention of the doctrine of the divine election of grace.

[033] And now, thirdly, we ask: In the light of an evangelical understanding of the election of grace, what is the meaning of the divine righteousness of this event? Undoubtedly the first meaning is this, that in this work God exercises judgment on the creature—He who has and alone has the right and the discernment for such a task. It means that in this work God creates order—He who is the source and norm of all order, who is Himself the order by whose standard all other order is still, or yet again, disorder. It means that God maintains His own worth over against the creature—He who in His wisdom knows, and alone knows, what is worthy of Himself. And so again the knowledge of the

righteousness of the divine election means that we are made aware of our own limitations. Who is there can come before the judgment-seat of God with the consciousness that he has a good case and nothing therefore to fear? Who is there can discuss or argue with God as to what constitutes order? Who can anticipate God's wisdom with his own judgment, or even wish to find it confirmed thereby? Before the mystery of His freedom we not only must, but can only be silent. And when we know this, and will to be really silent, then this willing becomes the confession of those who acknowledge themselves to be in the wrong before Him, who find in themselves no grounds either of justification or even excuse, no grounds, therefore, for a divine pardon, no grounds which could move God to elect them. It is inevitable that the righteousness of the divine election, when recognisable by us as such, should remind us that of ourselves we must stand outside in the realm of non-election, and therefore perdition. It is inevitable that the known righteousness of God in His election should constantly lead the creature to the fact that it is in opposition to the love of God directed towards it in that election, thus making itself unworthy of it. The known righteousness of the divine election of grace has for the creature the significance of a glimpse into the abyss into which it has caused itself to fall and from which it has no power to save itself. But, again, that is not all. The righteousness of God utterly crushes us. In it God asserts and vindicates His own worth over against the creature. Yet in the election of the creature even this righteousness reveals itself as the grace and loving-kindness and favour of God directed towards it. It is not out of negligence or procrastination, not out of any kind of weakness, but in the relentless vindication and exercise of His righteousness that God, in electing, is merciful towards the creature, espousing its cause, giving to it in its poverty, need and suffering His own substance, creating its righteousness, guaranteeing its future. For, according to the judgment of His wisdom, it is His substance and righteousness which comes upon it. It is arrested in that self-caused fall, it is kept and delivered from the abyss, it is allowed to live by the ordination and power of God, quite irrespective and even in spite of its deserts, and with a clear indication of its limitations. And it is this which God regards as worthy of Himself, which is therefore truly worthy of Himself. It is in this way that He wills to maintain and vindicate Himself over against the creature. This is the righteous order which He creates and establishes. He opposes to the creature the fact of His loving-kindness. He avenges sin not by regarding but by forgiving it. He attacks and overcomes the unreason of our opposition by His peace, which is higher than all reason of ours, and which is therefore revealed as the true, divine wisdom. The righteousness of God in His election means, then, that as a righteous Judge God perceives and estimates as such the lost case of the creature, and that in spite of its opposition He gives sentence in its favour, fashioning for it His own righteousness. It means that God does not acquiesce in the creature's self-destruction as its own enemy. He sees to it that His own prior claim on the creature, and its own true claim to life, is not rendered null and void. He cares for the creature as for His

[034]

own possession. And in seeking its highest good, He magnifies His own glory. We cannot distinguish God's kingly righteousness from His mercy. We need not deny it for the sake of His mercy. It is in that righteousness that He says Yes to the creature in the mystery of His freedom. And that is what makes the Yes so stirring as a challenge and so firm as a basis of the sure confidence in which the creature can live. It lifts the accusation from us and yet it does not expose God Himself to accusation. It is rather the revelation of the reasonableness of His work, in which we may recognise that work as well-founded, and accept it, and allow it to come upon us as a blessing—the great blessing with which He has visited us. Once again, it is a question of the incomparable and inexhaustible blessing which is for all those who may hear. And from this third standpoint, too, this blessing must always be proclaimed as the final word if we are to speak rightly and evangelically of the doctrine of the divine election of grace.

Such, then, are the stipulations of an understanding of the three basic concepts of the doctrine of predestination—stipulations which we had to bring out at once with a view to the further investigation and exposition of the doctrine. The doctrine of election is the sum of the Gospel.

2. THE FOUNDATION OF THE DOCTRINE

What is the source of the doctrine of predestination? This is the second preliminary question to which we must now turn. What we mean by it is this: What are the truths and realities thereby presented to us? What is the specific knowledge which compels us to think and speak about this matter, and to think and speak about it in this particular way? What impression is it that will and must find in this doctrine its expression? What is the particular concern [035] which has the power, a power at once stimulating, dynamic and formative, an authorising and commanding and directive power, to make this doctrine both possible and necessary, and to give to it this or that specific form?

There is reason to ask ourselves this question with particular care and candour at this specific juncture. Consciously or unconsciously, all conceptions of the doctrine must, of course, glance in this direction. But we may glance at many different aspects of the matter. And ever after our doctrine of predestination will assume a different form, and with it our whole dogmatic system, and the Church proclamation informed by that system. In the first part of our discussion it has become clear that we have reached a point in Christian doctrine which is vital for the whole, and yet also very vulnerable. And the most common failure has been an insufficient notice or investigation of the question which is the real starting-point for what we have to think and say in this connexion. On the basis of presupposedly self-evident answers to the question, courses have been adopted—and very definite courses in spite of the untested nature of the answers—which can lead to the most momentous decisions and statements. And such decisions and statements have then established themselves by their own natural weight, and have thus been able to characterise and even dominate the whole of Christian doctrine. It is only natural that in spite of all the accompanying good intentions and moments of truth, such statements and decisions are endangered by their doubtful and possibly erroneous starting-point. It is only natural that they can themselves become a danger, perhaps inevitably so. We must at this point recall the basic rule of all Church dogmatics: that no single item of Christian doctrine is legitimately grounded, or rightly developed or expounded, unless it can of itself be understood and explained as a part of the responsibility laid upon the hearing and teaching Church towards the self-revelation of God attested in Holy Scripture. Thus the doctrine of election cannot legitimately be understood or represented except in the form of an exposition of what God Himself has said and still says concerning Himself. It cannot and must not look to anything but the Word of God, nor set before it anything but the truth and reality of that Word. It can seek its basis and necessity only in the knowledge of the God self-manifested there. It can seek to give expression only to the impression of that Word. It can seek to meet only the one concern, receiving its stimulus and dynamic and form only from the fact that this Word must always be heard and validated in the Christian Church because this Word has constituted itself its basis and the nourishment by which it must live. Before we seek to discuss generally the implications of this basic principle, it is necessary, as matters stand, to execute certain specific defensive movements.

1. To begin with something apparently self-evident, yet not generally recognised to-day, it is not simply a matter of proceeding to develop the doctrine along lines which allow the tradition of the Church to prescribe and lay down [036] in advance the theme and programme of its exposition. In the matter of election the best ecclesiastical tradition can indeed serve both as an occasion and an ancillary. But it cannot be the subject and norm of dogmatic effort. On the contrary, in this matter we must ask even of the best ecclesiastical tradition what is its true origin, and to what extent it may or may not be properly adapted in this respect to serve as an ancillary.

It is remarkable enough that in the question of the election this warning must today be addressed to a certain movement in Reformed theology. It is a well-known historical fact that more than any other doctrine the doctrine of predestination stamped itself upon the face of the Reformed Church, or rather of 16th and 17th century Reformed theology, thus distinguishing it from others. This fact can and ought to stimulate Reformed theology to concern itself especially seriously with this doctrine. But it cannot serve as a basis for the doctrine. We cannot regard any doctrine of election as Reformed, or prove it Reformed (let alone Christian), merely in virtue of the fact that it maintains as such the historical characteristics of the Reformed confession and theology, seeking, if possible, to resurrect the doctrine in its historical form, or in the form of the most accurate possible repetition of the Reformed teaching. The book of Loraine Boettner already mentioned begins with the words: "The purpose of this book is ... to give a re-statement to that great system, which is known as the Reformed faith or Calvinism, and to show that this is beyond all doubt the teaching of the Bible and of reason." And directly afterwards the author thinks it necessary to commend himself by saying that he is a "Calvinist without reserve." But this is simply to say that he has set himself a task which is scholastic in the wrong sense of the word, and completely at variance with the basic principle even of Reformed dogmatics. The reproduction of the Calvinistic system is a necessary, rewarding and instructive exercise within the sphere of ecclesiastical or dogmatic history. But we cannot substitute it for, or confuse it with, the task of presenting Christian, and even Reformed Christian doctrine. Nor can such doctrine be presented in the form of a reproduction of "Calvinism." Consultation of the Bible must mean something more than simply giving a supplementary proof—side by side with the consultation of reason—that the doctrine of the Bible is identical with that of Calvin. Calvinism may be a good and praiseworthy thing from the human standpoint, even if we give to the concept more than its historical sense. But from the standpoint of a strict Christian theology there is no such thing as "Calvinism," just as there ought never to have been any such thing as "Lutheranism." Calvinism does not exist as a subject and norm of Christian doctrine. Calvin and the older Reformed Church did present in all seriousness the doctrine of predestination. They did so in a specific form. We may accept their work, and always keep it in mind, as a penetrating approach to the question, as a contribution to its treatment which we must respect and value. But we shall be doing Calvin the most fitting honour if we go the way that he went and start where he started. And according to his own most earnest protestations, he did not start with himself, nor with his system, but with Holy Scripture as interpreted in his system. It is to Scripture that we must again address ourselves, not refusing to learn from that system, but never as "Calvinists without reserve." And it is to Scripture alone that we must ultimately be responsible. Modern Neo-Calvinism involves at once, on its formal side, a mistaken re-introduction of the Catholic principle of tradition repudiated by all the Reformers, and most sharply of all by Calvin. Out of loyalty to Calvin himself we must never begin by treating the doctrine of predestination as a kind of *palladium*[EN72] of the older Reformed Church. Our point of departure must never be the particular form of the doctrine as there presented.

[037]   2. If we are to understand the doctrine of election rightly, we may not substitute for its foundation what we think must in any case be acknowledged as its didactic value, or its pedagogic usefulness in the cure of souls. We may not set before us this value and usefulness, only, and inevitably, to construct and expound the doctrine in accordance with the usefulness and value which we think ought to be ascribed to it. The order of procedure must be the very opposite. We must enquire into the foundation of the doctrine in the divine revelation quite independently of its value and usefulness, and the doctrine must then be constructed and expounded in accordance with that foundation. Only as that is done will the fact and the extent of its didactic and pedagogic value and usefulness really emerge.

At the very beginning of his exposition in the *Institutio* (III, 21, 1) Calvin maintained the *utilitas*[EN73], indeed the *suavissimus fructus huius doctrinae*[EN74], along three lines: first, that it teaches us to put our trust wholly in the mercy of God; second, that it demonstrates to us the glory of God in its full grandeur; and third, that it inclines us to a true humility (*humilitas*). There is no doubt that factually we can only agree with him on these points. Heinz Otten (*Calvins theol. Anschauung von der Praedestination*, 1938, 34) writes in this regard: "When we

---

[EN72] talisman
[EN73] usefulness
[EN74] sweetest fruit of this doctrine

treat of these impulses towards edification, we introduce the particular concern or interest of Calvin in the matter of predestination." But it is precisely in this kind of "particular concern or interest" that there lurk the main sources of dogmatic error. For such "particular interests" have it within themselves to shift quite remarkably both in purpose and emphasis as the years pass. It needed only the gradual disappearance of respect for the Word of God as such which characterised the age which followed; it needed only the increased prevalence of arbitrariness in systematisation, to transform the *utilitates*^{EN75} of Calvin into formally didactic and pedagogic axioms which as such claimed a permanent importance and the value of basic principles. Once that was done, it was these axioms which inevitably gave to the doctrine its shape and form. Already with Beza and Gomarus the glory of God had given rise to the concept of His comprehensive and exclusive action and efficacy. In the *Westminster Confession* the sure confidence in God's mercy had become the absolute assurance of the elect. Throughout the Reformed world *humilitas*^{EN76} had become the highly practical and in time all too practical sense of the Christian world-citizen, whom Max Weber and others have described as the specific outcome and result of the Reformed doctrine of election; a world-citizen lowly indeed before God but for that reason all the more self-assured in his conduct upon earth. If from the very first the doctrine was worked out with a view to such results it was inevitable that it should develop in this direction. But it can also happen that many Christians and theologians have a natural sympathy with particularly hard and mysterious and high-soaring teachings which stand in the sharpest possible antithesis to ordinary human thought, and for that reason they are inclined to have a positive interest in this very doctrine. It cannot be denied that the doctrine may also commend itself from what is to some extent an aesthetic standpoint. But what if this aspect, and the formal pleasure which it awakens, become the dominating motif in its development? Again, L. Boettner seems quite prepared to accept it as a recommendation—presumably in an apologetic interest—"that among non-Christian religions Mohammedanism has so many millions who believe in some kind(!) of predestination, that the doctrine of Fatalism has been held in some form or other in several heathen countries, and that the mechanistic and deterministic philosophies have exerted such great influence in England, Germany and America" (p. 2). However that may be, it is always a serious matter when, on his own confession, a theologian approaches this matter with so wishful a picture in his mind. What is certain about all bases of this type is that they always leave us at a point where the Yes only too easily becomes a No and the confirmation a denial. Very different judgments can be passed on the value and usefulness of the doctrine, as history has in fact demonstrated. Where Calvin and his followers saw nothing but *suavissimum fructum*^{EN77}, the Lutherans of the 16th and 17th centuries, and many others too, saw only an endangering of assurance of salvation, the sense of responsibility, etc., or even an open relapse into Stoicism, Manicheism, Quietism and Libertinism. Boettner appears to rejoice at the supposed kinship between the doctrine of predestination, as understood Calvinistically, and the teaching of Islam. But this supposed kinship was the very reason why the older Lutherans sought to discredit the Calvinists by describing them as secret adherents of the Eastern Antichrist. While the one can never cease to find aesthetic edification in the paradox of the doctrine, the other will find in that paradox the reason for an angry repudiation of it. It is impossible to build upon the foundation of such value-judgments or predilections, and it is as well to maintain a radical and consistent reserve in such matters, grounding the doctrine first in the Word of God, and then letting its value and usefulness speak for themselves.

[038]

---

^{EN75} usefulness
^{EN76} humility
^{EN77} sweetest fruit

3. There is a third possibility, more serious than the first two and the more decidedly to be rejected. This is the possibility of basing the doctrine of election upon a datum of experience, presumed or actual. On this view our concern is with what we observe to be the evident contrast between those who through the Church hear the Gospel and those who never have the opportunity to hear it at all; or, again, between those who hear it obediently and with profit, and so to salvation, and those who hear with open hostility, or without any result at all, and so finally to condemnation. How—it is asked—are these facts to be explained? And how especially is it to be explained that there seem to be those who either outwardly or inwardly cannot hear the Gospel? And if this is a fact, what is its bearing on our understanding of the other observation, that there are some who do seem actually to hear the Gospel? To answer this question the Bible is consulted (although only in a secondary capacity), and it is shown that some are elected by God and some rejected. But this raises the further question: Is it right to go to the Bible with a question dictated to us by experience, i.e., with a presupposition which has only an empirical basis, in order then to understand the statements of the Bible as an answer to this question, which means chiefly as a confirmation of the presupposition which underlies the question? Ought our observation and judgment in regard to the external and internal relationship of men to the Gospel really to force us to the position where we may recognise in this distinction between men the divine decision of the election of grace to which the Bible testifies? Can this observation impress itself upon us as all that significant? Can the standards by which we judge be as accurate and serviceable as that? After all, the resultant judgment is ours and not God's. And we have no right to proceed at once to understand the divine judgment of the election to which Scripture testifies simply from this external judgment, and to some extent as the divine ratification of it. If it is to be a question of the divine judgment, as it must be in dealing with the doctrine of election, then Scripture must not be brought in simply as an interpretation of the facts of the case as given by our own judgment. The very facts which we consider must be sought not in the realm of our experience but in Scripture, or rather in the self-revelation of God attested in Scripture.

[039]

We have already seen how Augustine began quite expressly with the question of a would-be experience. And after him Calvin in particular demands careful watching. I could not say that he made the experience in question the basis of his doctrine of predestination. But he did buttress his doctrine so emphatically by the appeal to it that we can hardly fail to recognise that much of the pathos and emotional power with which he defended it, and to an even greater extent the form in which he did so, were determined by this experience, the effects of which were inevitably serious from the point of view of the purity of the doctrine. This is particularly the case in the work *De aet. Dei praed.*, 1552, in which there is a constant appeal (e.g., *C.R.* 8, 261, 275, 292, 298, 317) to the *convincere*[EN78] or *docere*[EN79] or *demonstrare*[EN80] of

---

[EN78] convincing
[EN79] teaching
[EN80] demonstrating

experientia[EN81], to *palam apparet*[EN82] or *palam constat*[EN83], whenever the question arises of the basis of the assertion that from the very first men stand in a different relationship to the Gospel; a difference which can be explained only by a difference in the divine decree made concerning them. But in the *Institutio*, too, we read: *Apud centum eadem fere habetur concio, viginti prompta fidei oboedientia suscipiunt; alii vel nullius pensi habent, vel rident, vel explodunt, vel abominantur*[EN84] (III, 24, 12). *Experientia docet, ita (Deum) velle resipiscere quos ad se invitat, ut non tangat omnium corda*[EN85] (III, 24, 15). Indeed, the whole exposition begins with the methodologically only too revealing words: *Quod non apud omnes peraeque homines foedus vitae praedicatur et apud eos, quibus praedicatur, non eundem locum vel aequaliter vel perpetuo reperit: in ea diversitate mirabilis divini iudicii altitudo se profert. Nec enim dubium quin aeternae Dei electionis arbitrio haec quoque varietas serviat. Quod si palam est Dei nutu fieri ut aliis ultro offeratur salus, alii ab eius aditu arceantur: hic magnae et arduae protinus emergunt quaestiones, quae aliter explicari nequeunt, quam si de electione ac praedestinatione constitutum habeant piae mentes quod tenere convenit*[EN86] (III, 21, 1). The answer to these questions is then strikingly given in the famous definition: *Non pari conditione creantur omnes, sed aliis vita aeterna, aliis damnatio aeterna praeordinatur*[EN87] (III, 21, 5). According to the tenor of all these statements the fact which above all others inspired Calvin, and was thus decisive for the formation of his doctrine, was not at all the contrast between the Church on the one hand, and on the other the heathen world entirely unreached by the Gospel. It could not be said that Calvin particularly concerned himself with this aspect of the problem within the context of the doctrine of predestination. Again, it was not the positive observation that at all times the Gospel has both reached so many externally and also seemed to prevail over them internally. Of course, this aspect of the matter does enter in strongly—the thankfulness of the Church which hears and receives God's Word. And obviously Calvin might very well have put this aspect in the foreground, and begun his thinking at this point. But because in this connexion he already thought of this positive aspect as a fact of experience, it was inevitable that he should regard it as limited by that other fact of experience which excites both pain and anger, the fact of the opposition, the indifference, the hypocrisy and the self-deception with which the Word of God is received by so many of those who hear it (80 per cent according to the estimate there given). And it is this limiting experience, the negative in conjunction with the positive, which is obviously the decisive factor as Calvin thought he must see it. It was out of this [040] presupposition, laid down with axiomatic certainty, that there arose for him the *magnae et*

[EN81] experience

[EN82] 'it is plainly apparent'

[EN83] 'it is plainly the case'

[EN84] Almost every meeting of a hundred people will be the same: about twenty undertake the prompt obedience of faith, the others will either have no thought of it, or laugh, or hiss, or abominate it

[EN85] Experience teaches that God wills that those whom he calls to himself come to their senses, just as he does not touch the hearts of all

[EN86] The covenant of life is not preached equally among all men, and among those to whom it is preached it does not find the same place in equal measure or with equal permanence. In that diversity the wonderful depth of the divine judgment offers itself. For there is no doubt that even this variety serves the will of God's eternal election. If it is plain that it happens by God's approval that salvation is offered to some on the one hand, but others are kept from approaching him. Here, great difficult questions arise, which cannot be explained, except that pious minds must hold to what there is to hold concerning election and predestination as established

[EN87] All are not created in the same condition, but eternal life is ordained for some, and eternal damnation for others

arduae quaestiones[EN88] for which he saw an answer in what he found to be the teaching of Scripture concerning the election; questions which he thought he himself ought to answer in his doctrine of election supposedly gathered from Scripture. Within the sphere of the Church he saw men in whose being, words and actions when confronted by the Gospel proclaimed to them he thought he could recognise only that which Scripture describes as the divine rejection, and therefore the hardening accompanying the divine election. It is true that he saw in these men and their like only a foil to what, on the other hand, he thought he could gratefully recognise as the positive result of the divine election in the living faith of the Church and also, of course, in his own personal faith. He knew, too, with a perfect clarity that it was not of his own or of any other believer's merit that he did not belong equally well to the number of those rejected and hardened by God: *Si quis respondeat, diversitatem ex eorum provenire malitia et perversitate, nondum satisfactum fuerit: quia et illorum* (of believers) *ingenium eadem malitia occuparetur, nisi Deus sua bonitate corrigeret. Ideoque semper implicabimur, nisi succurrat illud Pauli: Quis te discernit? (1 Cor. 4⁷). Quo significat non propria virtute, sed sola Dei gratia alios aliis praecellere*[EN89] (III, 24, 12). And he also knew that there are no absolutely unequivocal marks of the divine rejection of certain men, and that there can be no absolutely unequivocal perception of the reprobate state of this or that individual. He knew, too, that the election of a man cannot be gathered with absolute certainty from a fact of experience. He recognised with Augustine (*De corr. et gratia* 14, 45): *Nescimus quis ad praedestinatorum numerum pertineat vel non pertineat*[EN90] (III, 23, 14). He knew and constantly acknowledged that the Lord knoweth them that are His. And yet it is only too evident that Calvin thought himself competent to recognise very well, if not the reprobate, at least the stupid and deceived and wicked who in that age formed so distressingly large a majority of men. He thought himself competent to distinguish all kinds of fools, scoundrels and wretches, both the crass and the subtle. He thought that he could recognise the *canaille*[EN91] in all its forms. He thought that he could know those who must at any rate be suspected of the divine rejection and hardening, especially in the case of theological opponents, in whom such a characteristic might be noted with a sureness which bordered on absolute certainty. Both in word and deed he obviously dealt with such people in accordance with that knowledge. It would be petty to seek to dispute with Calvin on this issue. Unless we can see what he saw, and for similar reasons, we have no right whatever to do so. One of the characteristic traits of this Reformer was a torturing exposedness and sensitiveness to all that mass of most radical wrongdoing which just at that period, and in direct opposition to the whole preaching of the Gospel, extended itself quite shamelessly over every section of human life (acutely so in the ecclesiastical, and most acutely of all in the theological world). And even if it were partly conditioned by his spleen, who is there would not really maintain that this was one of his great characteristics? It should be remembered, too, that the age of Calvin was that of the Counter-Reformation: a time which saw the harassing resurgence of temporal and spiritual powers against the but newly attempted renovation of the Church; a time which exposed the painful weaknesses, negligences and perversities of the supposedly renovated Church itself; a time which knew all the self-willed and ill-conceived and dangerous parallel movements within that renovation; a time, then, which might very well cause a clever and determined

---

[EN88] great difficult questions
[EN89] If anyone responds that the difference between them consists in malice and perversity, that would not yet be sufficient, because the minds of believers are occupied with the same malice, unless God in his goodness corrects them. Therefore we will always be involved, unless the statement of Paul helps us: 'Who can discern you?' By this it is meant that they excel others not by their own virtue, but by the grace of God
[EN90] We do not know who belongs to the number of the predestined, and who does not
[EN91] scoundrel

man to keep and turn away himself with grief and horror from the majority of his contemporaries. The fact which Calvin believed he experienced so definitely was that of the contrast and the appalling numerical discrepancy between the multitude of those who were useless in one way or another, the 80 per cent, whom one could meet only with a 100 per cent. aversion, and the tiny company of those who were "right." And when and where did that fact [041] not obtrude itself, even in the sphere of the Church? Calvin was, indeed, comparatively tolerant when he believed that he could estimate the strength of the latter group as 20 per cent, of the whole. Yet even when we grant him that, even when we agree that the experience which claimed his attention was and is solidly founded, and does in some way obtrude itself, it must still be held against him that such experience can never claim more than human value and relevance. No matter what practical or theoretical results it may have, according to Calvin's own presuppositions it could not and cannot ever claim the character of a revelation. It could not and cannot be adapted as an axiom in accordance with which Scripture itself must be interrogated and expounded. We may already ask, and we cannot simply presuppose that it is decided in advance, whether a doctrine of election which is obedient to Scripture is required without further ado to answer the questions—no matter how pressing—forced upon us by the contrast either between the Church and the world or between the true Church and the false. We may ask whether in Scripture the divine electing and rejecting are related to one another in the same way as are Christendom and heathendom according to the construct of our experience, or as the small company of the righteous and the great multitude of *canaille* within the Church itself according to the construct which Calvin found so particularly impressive. If the undoubted statistics of this construct are taken as the point of departure for reflection on the divine election of grace, strengthened by the influence of so clever and determined a perception as that of Calvin, then quite obviously Scripture is no longer able to say freely what it wills to say. It can only answer the questions put to it by man. What it wills to do first is to give us with its answers the right questions. "At the very outset, before he consulted the Bible," Calvin had "reached a decision which—quite independently of the answer of Scripture—determined the character of his outlook on predestination in accordance with the question put by experience" (H. Otten, *op. cit.*, p. 29). But that is the very thing which should not happen. If it does, then there is a pressing danger—which Calvin himself did not escape—that the divine election which it is our task to explore and expound will take on far too great a similarity with the perhaps very well-grounded and very praiseworthy but still human electing of the outstanding theological thinker, and that the electing God there revealed will come to resemble far too closely the electing, and more particularly the rejecting theologian. Whether and how far the work and being of God in this matter have anything to do with the positive and negative constructs of our experience can only be discovered, like the generally admitted usefulness of the doctrine, when without any reference to such constructs, indeed with a setting aside so far as possible of all existing constructs, the doctrine has been grounded upon God's own Word and has already taken shape. Not before!

We must go on at once to give to this delimitation greater precision and content.

If the doctrine of election is grounded upon supposed or real facts of experience, materially that obviously means that it is grounded with reference to man in general. In one way or another the election is thought of as the description of a differing and differentiating attitude of God towards the totality of individual men as such; an attitude in which God (according to some, more or less completely in accordance with His own mysterious good-pleasure;

according to others, with more or less regard to the attitude of men towards Himself) divides this totality of individuals into two sections or groups, electing here and not electing or rejecting there, with the aim and result of salvation and blessedness in the case of the former, perdition and damnation in the case of the latter. The divine electing and human election (and the negative counterpart of both) are thus understood in some sense as the ordaining of a private relationship between God and each individual man as such. Thus it is possible and necessary on the one side to consider God in His private relationship with each individual, and on the other side to consider each individual in his private relationship with God. The action of God in the plenitude of these private relationships cannot as such, of course, become the subject of our experience. Yet the individuals in their election or non-election can enter in as such a subject of experience. The differences between them in relation to the Gospel, the difference between heathen and Christians, or between good Christians and bad, may be taken as a cause for enquiry concerning their private relationship with God, or at least for the assertion of the existence of such a relationship (which by its very nature cannot perhaps be defined in detail with any certainty). Upon the basis of that assertion it is then possible to speak of the divine electing and human election (and the negative counterpart of both). Even where great caution is exercised in the foundation of the doctrine in accordance with experience, it is naturally presupposed that there is at all events a connexion between the doctrine of election and these private relationships between God and each individual as such; between the doctrine of election and the positive or negative character of the decision made between God and every individual man. In such circumstances the first and final purpose of the doctrine is to denote and describe what the relationship with God determines, as grace or as non-grace, for the totality of these individuals, each of whom exists and must be considered equally in and for himself. In some measure it is the first and final word of a doctrine of man as the creature of God subjected to the divine decision, of his exodus and entry to salvation or perdition, to life or death, as determined by his relationship with God. It is the first and final word of a rightly conceived anthropology, i.e., an anthropology which takes into account the relationship with God.

It cannot be denied that such private relationships between God and each individual do exist, and that in these relationships there is in fact a first and final divine decision. How can God be God, how can He be in every respect the Lord of the creature, unless He is sovereign as the Lord and God of each individual as such, unless for the individual as such the first and final decision is in fact made in his relationship with God? It also cannot be denied that the divine election stands in a radically necessary connexion with the ordination of the plenitude of these relationships between God and the individual, and with the decisions made in these relationships. How can it be otherwise? As we concluded in our first sub-section, the election is always God's decision over

against man as His creature, a decision which was fulfilled in Jesus Christ, and   [043]
in virtue of which God wills to be, not without this creature, but with it, as the
One who in His free love has bound Himself to it. But this creature, man, exists
concretely in the plenitude of individual men. Thus the divine election does
indeed determine and ordain the plenitude of the private relationships
between God and every individual. What they may or may not be is decided in
God's election. That is not to say, however, that God's election as such is identical with the determination of these private relationships as already made. This
is a presupposition which has been taken too much for granted. What we
ought rather to ask in this connexion is whether the electing God as such, as
self-revealed, and attested in Holy Scripture, is in fact simply this counterpart
of the individual as such, fixed and rigid in His decision one way or the other.
Is it practicable, therefore, to consider Him merely with reference to individuals, asking whether He has perhaps elected these or not elected those? And,
on the other hand, is it practicable to consider individuals as such in relation
to Him, enquiring whether they are elected or rejected? Is there any justification for such a conception when we have regard to the electing God as self-
revealed and attested in Holy Scripture? It cannot be questioned that the
election of God does concern all men, and that in it the will of God is determined concerning all men. The question is, however, whether the divine election is for this reason to be understood as an already made and existent
determination of all men; whether it is meaningful or possible to understand
each man as such as already either "elected" or "rejected," i.e., in the light of
this determination. *For* this determination—yes. To be determined by God's
election is the final—but really the final mystery of every human life. But this
does not mean that the mystery as such derives from the "determining" in the
sense that every human life has already received the determination corresponding to it. The election is decisively important for each individual, but it
does not follow that it is for the individual a character already imparted to him,
immanent in him from the very first. It does not follow that it is bound up with
his very existence. It is still the activity of the free love of God. As such, it is
intended for every man, and it concerns and determines every man. But it
does so without necessitating that he should be elected or rejected immediately and in advance. According to Scripture, the divine election of grace is an
activity of God which has a definite goal and limit. Its direct and proper object
is not individuals generally, but one individual—and only in Him the people
called and united by Him, and only in that people individuals in general in
their private relationships with God. It is only in that one man that a human
determination corresponds to the divine determining. In the strict sense only
He can be understood and described as "elected" (and "rejected"). All others
are so in Him, and not as individuals. It is not right, therefore, to take it as self-
evident, as has so frequently been the case, that the doctrine of predestination   [044]
may be understood and presented as the first and final word of a general
anthropology. On the contrary, it is right and necessary to get back from

things supposedly self-evident to the true sources, the self-revelation of God and the testimony of Holy Scripture, and to discover the definite form in which the electing God encounters and confronts humanity as a whole, and in which humanity also confronts and encounters the electing God. Without a reference to the specific form of this encounter, it would be premature to attempt an investigation of man as such and in general, and of the private relationships between God and the individual. In such an investigation we should remain completely blind to what election is and what it really means both for all men and also for each of those private relationships.

This question takes us deep into the main problem of the doctrine. We had to raise it here because the dubious basing of the doctrine on certain experiences has its root in the supposedly self-evident presupposition that the divine election is a direct determination of human existence as such. Once we are freed from this presupposition, there is no further point in attempting in some way or other to derive the divine election of grace from the existence of heathen and Christians, or of good Christians and bad. There is no further point in attempting to understand and fashion the doctrine of election as an answer to questions raised by the facts of experience.

4. Another foundation which must be taken seriously, but all the more carefully avoided, is that which begins with the concept of God as omnipotent Will, governing and irresistibly directing each and every creature according to His own law, and thus disposing also of the salvation and perdition of men. The concept *praedestinatio* (foreordination or pre-decision) is not unequivocal, nor are the biblical concepts πρόθεσις, πρόγνωσις EN92 and προορισμός EN93 if once divorced from their contexts. Who and what is it that in authority, time and logic is "prior" to everything else—"prior," then, to human decision, whether to the right hand or to the left? It cannot be denied that it is God who even in this sense is "prior" to everything else, that He is the absolute *prius* EN94. He is so even in His election. Otherwise He would not be God. He is the Almighty, and in His almightiness He is free. There can be no question of any diminution of this fact. But here error can also arise: the error of supposing that God is irresistibly efficacious power *in abstracto* EN95, naked freedom and sovereignty as it were; and in respect of the election, the error of supposing that this is a manifestation of this free sovereignty, and that the doctrine of election is only a matter of deducing and asserting, in relation to the positive or negative destiny of men, the logical consequences of the notion of a being who is sovereign over the whole world and whose operations are therefore necessary, as though the eternal salvation or perdition of men, like anything and everything else that takes place in the created order, could be traced back to the righteous decision of the will of this most necessary being. On such a

[045]

EN92 foreordination, foreknowledge
EN93 pre-decision
EN94 prior
EN95 in the abstract

view predestination is only one moment within the world-order established and executed by the principle of freedom and necessity proclaimed under the name of God. The doctrine of predestination is only one moment in a deterministic scheme. When we oppose this view we must beware of coming down on the side of indeterminacy. But we must also assert that we do not exhaustively define or describe God when we identify Him with irresistible omnipotence. Indeed, if we make this identification *in abstracto*^{EN96}, we do not define or describe God at all. Irresistible omnipotence cannot be made the beginning and end of the being of God. And even if we do not make or intend this abstraction, we must still ask whether we understand the election aright if we understand it from the very first within the framework of the presumably superior reality of the divine government of the world, as one specific act of this general divine activity. That it is logically convenient to do this is quite evident. But what we must enquire is whether it is in fact correct to do it; whether we ought not rather to understand the divine government of the world in the light of the divine election of grace. May it not be that we can believe and understand, not merely the election itself, but the fact that God and not a blindly determining and deciding something rules the world, and that the world is really ruled by Him, only when we recognise and proclaim in God the electing God, and as such the Lord, the Subject of that all-comprehensive activity? May it not be that it is as the electing God that He is the Almighty, and not *vice versa*?

A classical statement of the position which we must oppose is that of Thomas Aquinas. It is so because in content it is certainly not deterministic. For that reason, its critical character for the methodological question which here concerns us is all the more evident. According to Thomas, the doctrine of predestination belongs directly to that of the divine providence. Providence is God's ordering and directing of all things to their appointed end in virtue of His knowledge and will. To the knowledge and will of God, and therefore to His providence, all things are subordinate: *non (tantum) in universali, sed etiam in particulari*^{EN97} (*S. theol.* I, *qu.* 22, *art.* 2 *c*). And this includes man with his free will and his own human *providentia*^{EN98} in matters of good and evil (*ib.*, *ad* 4). Predestination is *quaedam pars providentiae*^{EN99}. Its specific concern is with the ordering and directing of man to eternal life, which he cannot as such attain by his own powers. He must be dispatched (*transmittitur*) towards this mark like the archer's arrow. And as for every event, so for this event in particular, there is a pre-existent *ratio*^{EN100} in God Himself. This *ratio transmissionis creaturae rationalis in finem vitae aeternae*^{EN101}, this particular instance of general providence, is predestination (*qu.* 23, *art.* 1 *c*). From this standpoint—it is a matter of the execution of one specific purpose of the Creator in respect of one of His creatures, but a purpose which basically and formally is in line with all His purposes—Thomas then attempted to treat and to solve all the problems of predestination in detail. He carried this so far that sometimes he could say quite expressly

---

EN 96 in the abstract
EN 97 not only in the universal, but also in the particular
EN 98 providence
EN 99 a certain part of providence
EN100 reason
EN101 means of bringing the rational creature to the goal of eternal life

that the concept grace does not in itself belong to the definition of predestination. It does so only in so far as it is here the specific effect and purpose of the divine work (*qu.* 23, *art.* 3, *ad.* 4). Bonaventura, too (*Breviloq.* I, 9), spoke of predestination entirely from the standpoint of the divine omnipotence and free will: *Est enim voluntas Dei prima et summa causa omnium specierum et motionum. Nihil enim fit visibile aut intelligibile in ista totius creaturae amplissima quadam universaque republica, quod non de illa imperiali aula summi imperatoris aut iubeatur aut permittatur*[EN102]. That is the major: the general divine world-government. And: *Quia* (*voluntas Dei*) *efficassima est, nullo modo potest aliquis aliquid efficere nisi ipsa cooperante et coefficiente; nullus deficere vel peccare potest, nisi ipsa iuste deserente.*[EN103]. That is the minor: predestination, as Bonaventura sees it. Zwingli's teaching was exactly the same: *Ex providentiae loco praedestinationis, liberi arbitrii meritique universum negotium pendet*[EN104] (*Comm. de vera et falsa relig.*, 1525, *ed.* Schuler u. Schulth., Vol. 3, 163). *Est autem providentia praedestinationis veluti parens* (*ib.*, p. 282). *Nascitur praedestinatio* (*quae nihil aliud est, quum si tu dicas praeordinatio*) *ex providentia, imo est ipsa providentia*[EN105] (*ib.*, p. 283).

We must count it highly in Calvin's favour that methodologically at least he broke with this tradition, treating the doctrine of providence (*Instit.* I, 16–18) in conjunction with that of creation, and the doctrine of predestination (III, 21–24) as the climax of that of the communication of the grace of God manifested and active in Jesus Christ. Of course, when we come to his arguments and statements at this latter point, we must constantly ask whether in matters of detail he does justice to the movement which this separation rightly indicates. Is it not the case that some of the decisive insights which dominate his doctrine of predestination derive from the generally acquired conception of the governance of God's omnipotence and will in the world at large? At the former point, too, we must ask whether it is not the case that predestination is already asserted in a different way—but still predestination according to the peculiar understanding of the term? That predestination should not only be subordinate to providence but superior to it was apparently not what Calvin intended, although in the second draft of the *Institutio* (1539 f., *cap.* 14, 1) it is noteworthy that it is at least given the precedence over it (cf. Heinz Otten, *op. cit.*, p. 99 f.).

It is not surprising, then, that amongst the very orthodox, amongst those who thought that they were following Calvin most faithfully, there took place the converse of a quite distinct subordination of the doctrine of predestination to that of providence. It is true that many of these placed the doctrine of predestination in some sense at the very head of the dogmatic system, immediately after the doctrine of God. But a closer inspection reveals at once (as with Polanus, *Synt. Theol. chr.*, 1609, *col.* 1559, and Wolleb, *Chr. Theol. Comp.*, 1626, I, *cap.* 4) that, although general providence is only named and developed as such later, it is already presupposed in fact under the title *decretum generale*[EN106], forming the pattern for an understanding of predestination. Even as early as Polanus (*col.* 1560) there is a distinct reappearance of the Thomistic statement: *praedestinatio pars est providentiae*[EN107]. On the

---

[EN102] For the will of God is the first and highest cause of all that is seen and every movement. For nothing becomes visible or intelligible in the most wide and universal state of all creation which is not either commanded or permitted by that imperial power of its most high ruler

[EN103] Because it (the will of God) is most efficacious, nothing can in any way cause anything, except as the will of God is cooperative and co-efficient. Nothing can lack anything, or even sin, unless the will of God justly abandons it to do so

[EN104] From the locus of the providence of predestination, the whole business of the free will and of merit hangs

[EN105] But the providence is as the parent of predestination: predestination (which is nothing other than what one would call foreordination) is born from providence, or rather is providence itself

[EN106] general decree

[EN107] predestination is part of providence

other hand, with him too we see the tendency towards that broadening of the concept of predestination as such which made possible the understanding of the doctrine of predestination as the comprehensive doctrine of the divine world-governance, which includes as a specific application God's dealings with those elected or rejected by Him. That is how the Supralapsarian F. Gomarus put it: There is a *praedestinatio universalis, quae res omnes spectat totumque Dei decretum est*[EN108] and a *praedestinatio particularis, quae ad quasdam earum tantum pertinet et pars aeterni atque universalis illius decreti existit*[EN109] (*Disp. de div. hom. praed., th.* 15, *op.* III, 1644). By *praedestinare*[EN110] (and indeed by the $\pi\rho o o\rho i\zeta\epsilon\iota\nu$[EN111] of Rom. 8²⁹ and Eph. 1⁵) Gomarus did not mean to understand the divine *eligere*[EN112] in particular, but generally and abstractly the divine *decernere*[EN113] as such (*ib., coroll.* 1). Into the doctrine of predestination there was now brought as a ruling concept that of the general, absolutely free divine disposing. Fundamentally, the thought was the same even where the doctrine was treated at a later stage, ostensibly as a basis for the atoning work of Jesus Christ, as in the Infralapsarian *Synopsis purior. Theol.* of Leiden (1624). Here, too, we read: *Sumitur haec praedestinationis vox vel generalius de actionibus divinae providentiae tam in bono quam in malo ... vel de ordinatione personarum ad certum et supernaturalem finem*[EN114] (*Disp.* 24, 4). And it is one of the peculiar features of the latest defence of the older Reformed doctrine by L. Boettner that he begins, as though there were no alternative, with the assertion that the doctrine of predestination is the representation of the absolute and unconditional purpose of the divine will, which is independent of all creation and grounded solely in God's eternal counsel. Everything outside of God is enclosed by this decree. All creatures owe their creation and preservation to the divine will and power (*The Ref. Doctr. of Pred.*, 1932, 13). Everything which exists does so only as a medium through which God in some way manifests His glory. The doctrine of predestination is no more than the application of this perception to the doctrine of the salvation of man (p. 14). When He created the world, God had a plan, like any "rational and intelligent man," like Napoleon before his Russian campaign (!). It is this plan which He executes. To confess that is to confess predestination, and the true and Calvinistic confession of predestination is the confession that God does everything, whether great or small, in accordance with this plan. To put it more exactly, predestination is the choice of this plan, now to be executed unquestioningly and unalterably. The whole history of the world is nothing other than the execution of it (p. 20 f.). "What can give the Christian more satisfaction and joy than to know that the whole course of the world is ordered with reference to the establishment of the kingdom of heaven and the manifestation of the divine glory; and that he is one of the objects upon which infinite love and mercy is to be lavished?" (p. 25). When with all thinking men we confess that our lives are over-ruled—we were not asked whether we wished to enter the world or not, or when, or where, or in what capacity we should be born, whether in the 20th century or before the Flood, whether as white men or black, whether in America or China—we confess as Christians that it is God who rules and determines all these things, as He does everything else in the world; and if we hold fast by the perception of this truth, then we are already adopting the Calvinistic position (p. 30). It

[047]

[EN108] universal predestination which pertains to all things, where all is the decree of God

[EN109] particular predestination, which pertains only to some of those things and exists as part of his eternal and universal decree

[EN110] predestination

[EN111] predestination

[EN112] election

[EN113] decree

[EN114] This word predestination is taken either more generally, as the actions of divine providence whether in good or evil circumstances ... or as the ordination of people to their definite and supernatural destiny befits the sovereignty of God to be able to do everything consonant with His nature. He can dispose of the creature as of His property. He can over-rule man in every aspect of his being, and He does so according to His own good-pleasure: whether in what he is or is not, in what he has or has not, in what he ought to become or ought not to become (p. 36). Like everything else, these things all happen as they are definitely ordained by God for the attainment of the end which God has set for Himself and for all things: "Every raindrop and every snowflake which falls from the clouds, every insect which moves, every plant which grows, every grain of dust which floats in the air, has had certain definite causes and will have certain definite effects. Each is a link in the chain of events, and many of the great events of history have turned on these apparently insignificant things" (p. 37). In this connexion God deals with each creature according to its own nature, and therefore according to His own most proper will (p. 38). And if we remember that all that God foreordained and infallibly executes He equally infallibly foresaw, that is only to say that everything which happens does so exactly as God has prescribed (p. 42 f.). This is the basis upon which Boettner undertakes to present the doctrine of predestination. He can hardly have imagined that he stood in the succession of Calvin in so doing, for the context at least of Calvin's doctrine points only too clearly in a different direction. What we can say, however, is that with a painful fidelity Boettner has reproduced the older Reformed method as used by Gomarus. In so doing he has brought new credit to the method of Thomas. Now naturally there can be no question of casting doubt upon all these statements about the freedom and omnipotence of God and

[048] the sovereignty of his ruling and disposing. Boettner has said something which has to be said concerning the divine government of the world and its definitiveness as a sovereign act of power. His statements are rather trite, but they are correct in content, and finely put. What is missing is the answer to two questions: (1) On what basis and with reference to what subject should these statements be made? How are they to be distinguished from what a Jew or Mohammedan or Stoic might say in this respect? What is the role of divine grace in the designation and description of the divine government of the world? Can it and should it play a purely supplementary and subordinate role, as one mode of divine action side by side with others? And if it can, do these utterances really bring us within the sphere of the Christian confession, and if so, to what extent? And (2) if we accept all this, what has it to do with predestination? There may be a formal interconnexion, consisting in the fact that in the one as in the other we are concerned with the sovereign will of God, in the one case with that will in general, in the other with a particular application of it. But is that interconnexion really sufficient to justify the deducing of the doctrine of predestination from that of providence, like a species from a genus?—the more so when the Christian character of that doctrine of providence has not yet been shown, and the doctrine is in all likelihood incomplete. Is it not the case that when God elects (in the sense in which He proclaims Himself the electing One and is attested as such in Holy Scripture) something more takes place than simply one manifestation among others of His willing and working? Do we not here find ourselves at the beginning of all God's ways and works, which as such must be considered in and for itself, and in the light of which the divine world-government is alone real or recognisable? Once again we must say that use has been made here of a presupposition which is not so self-evident as it makes itself out to be. Recourse has been had here to an apparent movement in formal logic from the general to the particular, without any demonstration whether or not such a procedure corresponds to the specific logic of this subject. As an obtrusive experience was followed in respect of the object of election, an obtrusive logical necessity is here followed in respect of its Subject. The one was and is just as arbitrary as the other, and just as little adapted to the theme. In this respect, too, we shall have to open up afresh certain matters which have been all too self-evidently closed.

At this point the necessary delimitation must take on a definite character in respect of its content. We have already seen that if the doctrine of election is grounded upon the facts of experience this means that it is abstractly grounded as far as concerns elected man. If it is grounded upon the logical necessity of the free and omnipotent divine will active both in general matters and in particular, both in the world as a whole and also in relation to the salvation or damnation of man, this means that it is just as abstractly grounded so far as concerns the electing God. On the one hand, regard is had to man in general and to the differences between individuals, and the phenomenon is then explained by the fact that individuals are what they are because they are elected or rejected by God. On the other hand, there is the thought of God in general, the concept of one Individual absolutely controlling everything else, of a *summus imperator*[EN115], and from that concept it is most logically deduced that amongst all the other things it belongs to the free power of God either to elect man and to bring him to salvation or to reject him and allow him to be lost.

Latet periculum in generalibus[EN116]: we were forced to say this of the first error, and we must now repeat it with reference to the second. In the first case we were forced to challenge the general character of the presupposed view of humanity. In the second, we must challenge the general character of the presupposed concept of God. When we deal with what is called God's electing in God's self-revelation and the testimony of Holy Scripture, what authority have we to seek its meaning simply and solely in the alleged definitiveness of the private relationship between God and the individual as such? And now farther: What authority have we to interpret this electing as the act of a God alleged to be divine merely in His naked sovereignty? When we do such things, do we not misunderstand at the very outset, in the one case the view of elected man, and in the other the concept of the electing God, as these should be normative for a Christian doctrine of election and therefore for the doctrine of election in Church dogmatics? And supposing there develops a friendly rivalry between the two misapprehensions, as was very largely the case in the traditional teaching? Supposing it becomes impossible to correct the mistaken view by the correct concept, and the mistaken concept by the correct view—a thing not impossible in itself? Supposing the one misapprehension almost necessarily gives rise to the other? Supposing the same fundamental error is at work in both? In such circumstances, will it be at all surprising if the doctrine of election becomes, as Calvin himself once described it (*Comm. on Rom.* 9^14, *C.R.* 49, 180), a "labyrinth," in which only the very humblest may at a pinch detect any great part of the way, and from which even many of the cleverest and greatest—let alone the great majority whether in the world or the Church—will prefer to remain in perplexed aloofness? Will it be at all surprising if the doctrine cannot at any rate shed that light which properly it could and should shed if grounded upon a true view of man and a true concept of God? There is, indeed, every reason to proceed critically at this point.

[049]

If we allow God's self-revelation and the testimony of Scripture to prescribe our concept, then the Subject of election, the electing God, is not at all the

---

[EN115] most high ruler
[EN116] Danger lies in the generalities

absolute World-ruler as such and in general. We cannot, therefore, understand the election as one of the many functions of world-government exercised by Him, nor can we deduce it from, or establish it as a consequence and application of, that one basic principle. The Subject of the election, of this election, the Subject with which the Christian doctrine of election must reckon, is not in the least a "God in general," as he may be conceived and systematically constructed from the standpoint of sovereignty, of omnipotence, of a first cause, of absolute necessity. It is always unconditioned thinking which undertakes to construct such a "God in general," and (notwithstanding all the theoretical protestation against *potentia absoluta*[EN117]) the result of such unconditioned thinking must always be an unconditioned God, a God who is free *in abstracto*[EN118]. Even if the concept freedom is filled out by that of love, it makes no essential difference, unless by both concepts we understand the one decisive thing: that the true God is the One whose freedom and love have nothing to do with abstract absoluteness or naked sovereignty, but who in His love and freedom has determined and limited Himself to be God in particular and not in general, and only as such to be omnipotent and sovereign and the possessor of all other perfections. The true God (true according to His self-revelation and the biblical testimony), the God who is the object of thinking

[050]   which is conditioned in a way conformable with His self-revelation, is, of course, the sovereign Lord and Ruler of all things and all events, from the greatest to the smallest. Naturally, then, there is nothing outside of Him. There is nothing which is efficacious or significant or even existent except only by His will. There is nothing which in respect both of its being and its nature is not predetermined by Him. But from that it does not at all follow that to conceive of God Himself we need only conceive of a being which rules absolutely. On the contrary, such a concept in itself might well and indeed must be the concept of a false god, an idol, the exact opposite of the true God. If we are to lay hold of the concept of the true God, we shall do so only as we conceive of Him in His *dominium*[EN119], in His actuality as Lord and Ruler. We shall do so only as we conceive of Him in the determination and limitation which are peculiar to Him, which He has not taken upon Himself as something additional, in His relationship with the world or as an accommodation to it, but which are the characteristics of His presence and activity in the world because they are the determination and limitation proper to His own eternal being, so assuredly has He decided for them by the decree of His eternal will. God does rule. Yet it is not the fact that He rules that makes Him the divine Ruler, for false gods and idols also rule. The mere fact of ruling with infinite power in an infinite sphere does not make God the divine Ruler, for that is the very thing

---

EN117 absolute power
EN118 in the abstract
EN119 dominion

which He does not do. Infinite power in an infinite sphere is rather the characteristic of the government of ungodly and anti-godly courts. God Himself rules in a definite sphere and with a definite power. What makes Him the divine Ruler is the very fact that His rule is determined and limited: self-determined and self-limited, but determined and limited none the less; and not in the sense that His caprice as such constitutes His divine being and therefore the principle of His world-government, but in such a way that He has concretely determined and limited Himself after the manner of a true king (and not of a tyrant); in such a way, then, that we can never expect any decisions from God except those which rest upon this concrete determination and limitation of His being, upon this primal decision made in His eternal being; decisions, then, which are always in direct line with this primal decision, and not somewhere to right or left of it in an infinite sphere. If we begin quite simply with the divine world-government which holds sway in and over all things, if we think that the election should be subordinated to this world-government as one specific instance of it, then it is difficult to escape a twofold danger: first, that of losing sight of the primal decision which is identical with the basis of the election, and therefore of the eternal divine being in the determination and limitation in which it is the divine being; and second, and in consequence, that of missing the line or succession of the later divine decisions which derive from this primal decision. If we do that, then ultimately and in effect we can describe the divine world-government, and with it the over-ruling of divine [051] providence, only as the sequence and inter-relation of the actions of absolute caprice. And we can present the divine predestination only as one of such capricious actions. It is necessary then, as we consider predestination and form our concept of it, to consider and to form a concept of the deity of God which is true deity because it is self-determined and self-limited. In so doing we shall perceive both the fact and the extent that the true God is as such the true Ruler of the world, the omnipotent sovereign over all things both great and small, and to that extent "God in general." He is that, and He wills to be acknowledged and worshipped as such. And it is for that reason, and to attain that end, that our thinking on the subject of the election cannot begin arbitrarily with the concept of a World-ruler as such. We must know first who this Ruler is and what He wills and does in that rule. But this concrete aspect of His rule results from our consideration and concept of the election. It is there that God is (and is self-revealed as) who and what He is, in contrast with all false gods and idols. It is there, in the election itself so to speak, and not in an underlying higher principle from which it must be deduced, that its true basis must be sought. It is there, in the singularity of this activity itself, and not in what it has in common with all God's other activities. It is there; so that only from that point can we perceive and understand the divine providence and world-government, and not only that, but creation too, and not only creation, but the totality of all God's other activities.

It is easy to see the link between the correction necessary here and that which we made earlier. In the doctrine of predestination we have to do with the understanding both of God and of man in particular; in the particular relationship in which God is the true God and man true man. In itself, and as such, the particular leads us to the general, which it includes within itself. For finally, of course, the election has to do with the whole of humanity and therefore with each individual, although materially it has to do first and exclusively only with the one man, and then with specific members of the people which belongs to Him, which is called by Him and which is gathered around Him; a people which as such is not identical either with the whole of humanity or with an aggregate of individuals. Finally, then, the election has to do with the sovereign rule of God and His omnipotent world-government, although materially it has to do with the specific being and activity of God in His relationship with this particular man and the people represented in Him. It is a matter of the specific attitude of God in which He fulfils the primal decision which as such is the basic law of His lordship and sovereign rule as a whole. The doctrine of election is rightly grounded when in respect of elected man as well as the electing God it does not deal with a generality or abstraction in God or man, but with the particularity and concretion of the true God and true man. It is rightly grounded when only from that starting-point it goes on to perceive and to understand whatever there is of consequence about God or man in general; from that starting-point alone, and not *vice versa*.

[052] We can now make an attempt to give a positive answer to the question of the origin of the doctrine of election. The two answers just mentioned and rejected have been and have to be taken seriously because they do contain decisive moments of truth. It is undoubtedly the case (and considerations advanced in the first sub-section have prepared us for this conclusion) that the election does in some sense denote the basis of all the relationships between God and man, between God in His very earliest movement towards man and man in his very earliest determination by this divine movement. It is in the decision in favour of this movement, in God's self-determination and the resultant determination of man, in the basic relationship which is enclosed and fulfilled within Himself, that God is who He is. The primal relationship belongs, therefore, to the doctrine of God. The doctrine of God would be incomplete without the extension necessitated by this relationship, without the inclusion of the decision which precedes and characterises and gives rise to all God's work *ad extra*[EN120]; the decision in which God gives Himself to another, to man, and on the basis of which He is the One who has willed and done this, who has indeed given Himself to man. If their incorrect form is ignored, and they are taken together, the two answers just mentioned and rejected do have the merit of indicating the real problem of the doctrine: God as the Subject of the election and man as its object. In so doing, they point to the fact that they, too, in their own way derive from the perception which is basic and normative in this matter; that they, too, in their own way, have been presented within the sphere of the Christian Church. Because of their incorrect form we must reject them as answers to the question of the basis of the doctrine, but we must keep their substance in so far as it indicates the two

---

[EN120] outside of himself

poles of the problem, God on the one side and man on the other. They fail because prematurely, and with serious consequences for the purity of the doctrine from the Christian standpoint, they think that the two poles are to be found, not in their particularity, but in a general view of man and a general concept of God. It is with this point that we must begin as we seek to be taught by the self-revelation of God attested by Holy Scripture.

When Holy Scripture speaks of God, it does not permit us to let our attention or thoughts wander at random until at this or that level they set up a being which is furnished with utter sovereignty and all other perfections, and which as such is the Lord, the Law-giver, the Judge and the Saviour of man and men. When Holy Scripture speaks of God it concentrates our attention and thoughts upon one single point and what is to be known at that point. And what is to be known there is quite simple. It is the God who in the first person singular addressed the patriarchs and Moses, the prophets and later the apostles. It is the God who in this "I" is and has and reveals sovereignty and all other perfections. It is the God who wills to be known and worshipped and reverenced as such. It is the God who created His people Israel by His Word, and separated them from all other peoples, and later separated the Church from Israel. It is the God who exercises His rule in what He wills and does with this people, the people first called Israel and later the Church. It is He, this God, who as the Lord and Shepherd of that people is also, of course, the World-ruler, the Creator of all things, the Controller of all events, both great and small. But in every way His government of the world is only the extension, the application and the development of His government in this one particular sphere. He does the general for the sake of the particular. Or to put it in another way, He does the general through the particular, and in and with it. That is God according to His self-revelation. [053]

We may look closer and ask: Who and what is the God who is to be known at the point upon which Holy Scripture concentrates our attention and thoughts? Who and what is the God who rules and feeds His people, creating and maintaining the whole world for its benefit, and guiding it according to His own good-pleasure—according to the good-pleasure of His will as it is directed towards this people? If in this way we ask further concerning the one point upon which, according to Scripture, our attention and thoughts should and must be concentrated, then from first to last the Bible directs us to the name of Jesus Christ. It is in this name that we discern the divine decision in favour of the movement towards this people, the self-determination of God as Lord and Shepherd of this people, and the determination of this people as "his people, and the sheep of his pasture" (Ps. 100³). And in this name we may now discern the divine decision as an event in human history and therefore as the substance of all the preceding history of Israel and the hope of all the succeeding history of the Church. What happened was this, that under this name God Himself became man, that He became this particular man, and as such the Representative of the whole people that hastens towards this man and derives from Him. What happened was this, that under this name God Himself realised in time, and therefore as an object of human perception, the self-giving of Himself as the Covenant-partner of the people determined by Him from and to all eternity. What happened was this, that it became a true fact that under this name God Himself possesses this people: possesses it no less than He does Himself; swears towards it the same fidelity as He exercises with Himself; directs upon it a love no less than that with which in the person of the Son He loves Himself; fulfilling His will upon earth as in the eternal decree which precedes everything temporal it is already fulfilled in heaven. What happened was this, that under this name God Himself established and equipped the people which bears the name to be "a light of the Gentiles," the hope, the promise, the invitation and the summoning of all peoples, and at the same time, of course, the question, the demand and the judgment set over the whole of humanity and every individual man. As all these things happened

[054] under this name, the will of God was done. And according to God's self-revelation attested in Scripture, it is wholly and utterly in these happenings that we are to know what really is the good-pleasure of His will, what is, therefore, His being, and the purpose and orientation of His work, as Creator of the world and Controller of history. There is no greater depth in God's being and work than that revealed in these happenings and under this name. For in these happenings and under this name He has revealed Himself. According to Scripture the One who bears this name is the One who in His own "I" introduces the concept of sovereignty and every perfection. When the bearer of this name becomes the object of our attention and thoughts, when they are directed to Jesus Christ, then we see God, and our thoughts are fixed on Him.

As we have to do with Jesus Christ, we have to do with the electing God. For election is obviously the first and basic and decisive thing which we have always to say concerning this revelation, this activity, this presence of God in the world, and therefore concerning the eternal decree and the eternal self-determination of God which bursts through and is manifested at this point. Already this self-determination, as a confirmation of the free love of God, is itself the election or choice of God. It is God's choice that He wills to be God in this determination and not otherwise. It is God's choice that He moves towards man, that He wills to be and is the Covenant-partner of man. It is God's choice that under the name of Jesus Christ He wills to give life to the substance of His people's history and to that people itself, constituting Himself its Lord and Shepherd. It is God's choice that in this specific form, in one age, in the very midst of that people's history, He acts on behalf of all ages, thus giving to all created time, becoming indeed, its meaning and content. It is God's choice that for the sake of the Head whose name it bears He has created and established this particular body, this people, to be the sign of blessing and judgment, the instrument of His love and the sacrament of His movement towards men and each individual man. It is God's choice that at every stage in its history He deals with this people with that purpose in view. It is in the utter particularity of His activity, and therefore of His volition, and to that extent of His self-determined being, that He is the electing God. He is so at that one point upon which Scripture concentrates our attention and thoughts. He is so in that He is the Lord and Shepherd of His people. He is so in Jesus Christ, in His only-begotten Son, and therefore from all eternity in Himself. To put it the other way round: If we would know who God is, and what is the meaning and purpose of His election, and in what respect He is the electing God, then we must look away from all others, and excluding all side-glances or secondary thoughts, we must look only upon and to the name of Jesus Christ, and the existence and history of the people of God enclosed within Him. We must look only upon the divine mystery of this name and this history, of this Head and this body.

It is exactly of a piece with this that when Scripture speaks of man it does not   [055] allow our attention or thoughts to lose themselves in any self-selected generalities. In the Bible we are not concerned with the abstract concept of man, or with the human race as a whole, or with the being and destiny of the individual man as such.

It is true that in the beginning Scripture does tell us about Adam, the progenitor and representative of the whole race. But the further course of the record makes it clear that the object of the story is not universal history and its problems. After Adam there are a few almost incidental side-glances at the further propagation and extension of the race, and then we pass directly to Noah, and from Noah to Abraham, and from Abraham to Jacob-Israel. We are led most firmly and definitely from the general to the particular. Here and always it is in the sphere of the particular that the events are played out which it is the purpose of the Bible to record concerning man. It is for the sake of the particular that the Bible is interested and seeks to interest its readers in man. In this series the individual man is not important because he is a particular specimen in the propagation and extension of the race, or because in some way this propagation and extension is set forward by him. On the contrary, he is interesting because within this succession of events, as one of the many sons or grandsons of the one father, he is always a special case, and because there will always be similar special cases amongst his own sons and grandsons. The whole history from Adam onwards aims ultimately at the emergence of the particular man Jacob-Israel, the ancestor of the twelve tribes of the chosen people. It is in this most narrowed future that the meaning and necessity of the history is to be found, so that looking backward even Adam is ultimately or primarily important (and is thought of) as *the* man in the Old and New Testaments, not because he is the father of the human race, but because he is the first of these special cases, the first in this succession of particular men—and more expecially because this succession was to make possible the existence of Jacob-Israel. See above.

And the narrowing down does not cease with the man Jacob-Israel and his descendants. It is not the case that from his time onwards there existed in the form of the people named after him a kind of lesser humanity within the whole; a race which as such, in all its members, constitutes the particular envisaged in the whole. What is attained, or rather manifested, from Jacob-Israel (better, from the succession Abraham-Isaac-Jacob) onwards is simply the existence of a specific people as such. It is revealed that each of the special cases had its meaning only in the existence of a whole. In the narrowing down which took place from the very first it was not and is not simply a question of the individual as an individual, but of the many in the individual. It is a question, indeed, of a definite aggregate, of the necessary and intimate connexion, the obvious coherence and unity of the many, as it has all been realised in this one people. But only in this way. For "the people Israel" as such, as a community of blood and speech and history, is still only a sign of this definite aggregate within humanity as a whole. Israel is self-deceived when it thinks that in itself, as the people Jacob, as the community of blood and race and history, it can recognise this particular humanity within humanity in general. It had, in fact, hardly existed as a people in this sense before there began a further narrowing down within itself, the cutting off of whole generations and whole sections of the people (already foreshadowed in the cutting away of Ishmael and Esau, and impressively declared by the covenant sign of circumcision). And this process constantly gained ground, constantly diminishing what was left of the particularity imparted to this people in its forefather; a process which was apparently a vast retrogression to the narrowing

[056]   down which was involved in and commenced with the existence of the one man Adam. The people still lived, but it lived only as a sign of the people obviously envisaged. The specific purpose of its history approximated more and more to that of the preceding history of the propagation and extension of the race from the time of Adam to that of the patriarchs. It lived on as a people, but, like the race in that earlier period, it did so only as it prepared and made possible the existence of a special case. Its life was directed towards one individual figure. Whose is that figure? If we take the Old Testament, the record of its history, only in and for itself, then without doubt we must return at once the answer: the figure of King David. In the powerful and righteous kindom of David the promise given to the descendants of Jacob, that they should possess the land of Canaan, found fulfilment in a way which apparently cannot be, and (in the direct sense) never has been, surpassed. When this man was brought forth and attained to the kingship. Israel reached the end of all its ways. It was towards this king, and to become his people, subject to him as such, that all its life had been directed during the whole of this second Old Testament period. Even in the establishment of the people, which was the specific aim of the first period, this king had been intended; for the people established was the people which should have David as its powerful and righteous sovereign.

But now, surprisingly, a new period began. It lasted from David to the Exile. Its peculiar feature was this. The dissolution of the historical existence of the people as such, a dissolution already proclaimed clearly at such turning-points as the journey through the wilderness and the conquest of Canaan, and in the very personal climax of the rejection of Saul, now became the true and proper subject of the history and its record. The promise to Israel had been conclusively fulfilled in the figure of David, but it now became clear that that fulfilment was only a repetition of the promise. Even the reign of David as such was only a sign. Indeed, it was upon the Son of David that David himself fixed all his hopes, as though he himself were not the end of all Israel's ways thus far. And Solomon did, in fact, mount the throne of David. He reigned on that throne with a wisdom and glory which overshadowed all that David was and did. He could do what even David was not permitted to do—build the temple. To that extent it did seem as though the promise had at last found its true fulfilment. By its rapid appearance, however, this supposedly true fulfilment, the *regnum gloriae*[EN121] which only followed the Davidic *regnum gratiae*[EN122], served merely to emphasise the fact that David himself was the purpose of the previous existence of Israel: not, of course, as an end, but for his son's sake; as the beginning of a new way. And by its equally rapid disappearance it served merely to emphasise the fact that while Solomon did, of course, represent and declare the wisdom and glory of the Son of David, he could not himself be the Son promised and awaited, but could only act as another of His representatives. And then there began

---

[EN121] reign of glory
[EN122] reign of grace

irresistibly the dissolution which the prophets did not arrest but step by step announced and proclaimed to be inevitable. Its result was the manifestation of yet another son of David; the Jehoiachin or Jeconiah who reigned only three months as next to the last king in Jerusalem and was then overthrown by Nebuchadnezzar and led away captive to Babylon. This son was in everything the direct opposite of David—we need only read what is written about him in Jer. 22$^{24-30}$—and in him the goal of Israel seemed to have become its end, the gracious separation a wrathful rejection. And yet, even in his function as a powerless, dethroned and exiled king, he belonged no less to the Davidic monarchy than his forefather David himself. In his own way he represented the promised Son of David no less than Solomon. According to the likeliest interpretation, the Suffering Servant of Is. 49 ff. is not merely Israel as such, not merely Jeremiah seen as a monumental figure, not merely an unknown prophet of the Exile, not merely the quintessence of all the prophets, but (together with all these) it is in the first instance this pitiful ex-king and shadow-ruler Jeconiah, of whom, significantly enough, the record of 2 K. 25$^{27f.}$ tells us that not only was he graciously favoured and kindly spoken to by Evil-Merodach in Babylon, but that his throne was set above the thrones of all the kings that were there with him. [057]

But this figure is found only at the very beginning of the Exile. He is the Son of David who represents the people punished and cast off for their sin. Obviously he is not the One who is to come, the expected Son. But then a fourth Old Testament period began. Punished and cast off, Israel was not allowed to fall from God. In the second part of the Book of Isaiah the promise was made yet again and still more comprehensively. Israel was to return. And another Davidic line was raised up, with Zerubbabel, the grandson of Jehoiachin, at its head. He was not king, of course, for Israel would never again be a kingdom. Those signs had been given and would not recur. There is always a similarity in this history, but there is never simple recurrence. The commission given this new David by the prophet Haggai was rather that he should build again the ruined temple, "not by might, nor by power, but by my spirit" (Zech. 4^6). For the rest, he was only a deputy-ruler, standing side by side with the high-priest Joshua as one of the two olive-trees beside the seven-branched candlestick. It seemed that Israel had now become a people without a king. Was it a people at all? Was not this the end of all that had been promised? But the question we ought really to put is quite different: Was not this son of David, Zerubbabel, the clearest of all the signs, just because he was only a deputy-ruler who stood side by side with the high-priest, not having any proper office but only the non-political task of directing the restoration of the temple? Did he not bear the highest political testimony to something which David and Solomon had also to attest, but as holders of direct political power could not do so as clearly, something which the political rulers of the succeeding house of David had denied, namely, that God Himself is (both in word and deed) the King of this people and that his human representative is summoned only to make good the destruction of His earthly sanctuary? Is it not perhaps the case that in this way and at this time, by becoming no more than Jewry inhabiting the land of Palestine, Israel achieved visible unity under this King as the true people of God? That it should become such a people was the promise and the offer with which this fourth period began— and ended. It ended with the birth of the promised Son of David Himself, the one who in His own person was David and Solomon, Jeconiah and Zerubbabel, and more than they all. After all that had gone before, none but God Himself could take the throne as David's Son, fulfilling all the promises at one blow. The Word—that Word which created Israel, and accompanied and directed it as prophetic judge and comforter—the Word itself became flesh. The Word Himself became the Son of David. Now at last there had come the special case for which there had had to be all those others from Adam to Zerubbabel, and for which Israel had had to be separated out from the whole race, and Judah from Israel. This coming was to the detriment of Israel. Face to face with its Messiah, the Son of David who was also the Son of God, Israel knew no better than to give Him up to the Gentiles to be put to death on the cross. In so doing, they confirmed the rightness of God's dealings with them from the very first, when He cut them off and destroyed them. And yet because the righteousness of God stands fast like the mountains against the unrighteousness of man, this coming was also to the benefit of Israel, and of the Gentiles, and of the world. In the crucifixion of Jesus Christ the world was shown to be a co-partner in guilt with Israel, but only in order that it might be shown a co-partner in the promise with Israel. The promise could not be destroyed or overthrown. Only now was it completely fulfilled. And its fulfilment was made manifest in the resurrection of Jesus Christ. Jews and Gentiles were in the same guilt of disobedience. But now they could hear the same words: You, my people; I, God, in the person of David's [058] Son, your King. Those who are called by this King, and hear this King, whether they are Jews or Gentiles, constitute the people whose existence was envisaged throughout the whole of that long history. In the person of this King there enters the man as whose type Adam had already been *the* man. In Adam's case, it was man the creature of God, and forthwith the sinful creature. In this case it is man the Son of God, more powerful and righteous than David, more wise and glorious than Solomon. It is also, of course, the man who has to suffer shame and insult, although quite differently from Jeconiah. It is also the man who rebuilds the temple, although quite differently from Zerubbabel. This man is the Holy One who in His suffering and triumph gathers the sinner under His wings and by Himself covers and saves him. This is the man who is the fulfilment of the promise and hope of His people, and the meaning and purpose of its existence and history. As such He is very man.

This man, who as God's Son is the King of His people, is elected man. In Him and through Him those who are His subjects and the members of His people are elected. Even under this aspect it is obviously a question of God's choice. None of the figures mentioned appointed itself a special case, a link in that chain, and in its particular function a sign of the special case to which they must all point and for which they must all prepare. From the standpoint of the general it must always be demanded: Why this one and that one? Why not this other, or that other? And always there is only one answer to such a demand, and that is the event as a fact, the existence of the cases as such. But that means a choice which was not made by the men themselves, but which came upon them, and which cannot, therefore, be explained by anything in the men themselves. Obviously, then, it is wholly because of a choice of which man himself is not the subject that within the sphere of humanity, and not some other sphere, there should take place this sequence of events, these special cases. Obviously the people whose establishment was at once the goal and the new starting-point in this sequence did not choose for itself this position and function. If it had regarded it as a matter of its own choosing, and fulfilled it accordingly, it would already have forfeited it. The extent, the completeness, with which God is the electing One in all these happenings is revealed by the continual cutting and falling away of countless numbers—something which does not make the promise null and void as given to the whole, but which indirectly confirms it, because the whole must be always the whole which is elected by God and the bearer and recipient of His promise. The extent to which God is the electing One in these happenings is revealed in the remarkable way in which the promise is constantly fulfilled only to be renewed, until at last the fulfilment is before us in all its singularity, itself the true promise unequivocally revealed. Even the fulfilment, even the purpose and meaning of these happenings, has still to be God's choice. And it is only really God's choice when this sequence of special cases, the sign of the coming One, their goal, is shown not to be infinite, but to be bounded by the one special case in which their goal is revealed, by the one case which is also a sign—it is so as the true fulfilment, as the promise unequivocally revealed—but which as a sign is also and at the same time the thing signified.

If we listen to what Scripture says concerning man, then at the point where our attention and thoughts are allowed to rest there is revealed an elect man, *the* elect man, and united in Him and represented by Him an elect people. But just as truly there is revealed at that same point the electing God. The elect One is true man according to God's self-revelation, and that revelation, being God's, has the decisive word concerning man too. And once again we must put it the other way: If we would know what election is, what it is to be elected by God, then we must look away from all others, and excluding all side-glances or [059] secondary thoughts we must look only upon the name of Jesus Christ and upon the actual existence and history of the people whose beginning and end are enclosed in the mystery of His name.

We perceive that the statements of Scripture concerning God and those concerning man converge at this point. And it is as statements concerning what takes place at this point that the statements concerning God's election of man must be formulated and understood. For it is at this point that election takes place. If this perception is right, and if we feel bound always to base the doctrine of election upon the self-revelation of God according to the witness of Scripture, then we have answered positively the question of the basis of the doctrine and the standpoint which we ought to take up in relation to it. If our perception has been fundamentally correct in this preparatory survey, then the necessity of the doctrine has been decided once and for all. We are not free either to give ourselves to this matter or not to give ourselves to it, either to take seriously the knowledge of divine predestination or not to take it seriously. Election is that which takes place at the very centre of the divine self-revelation. In the light of this fact we can understand the emphasis with which the doctrine of predestination has been presented by all the great doctors of the Church. And in particular, we need feel no shame at the witness of the Reformed Church, in which from the outset this doctrine has played so outstanding a role. We must admit rather (not out of mere conservatism or the impulse to imitate, but out of inner necessity) that our forefathers were right. And we shall regard ourselves as bound to follow in their footsteps. But if in this survey our perception has been a right one, then it is also the case that the form in which we must take up and present the doctrine has been radically decided. In face of the whole history, even the Reformed history, of the doctrine, a corrective has been inserted and a standard brought to light. It is the name of Jesus Christ which, according to the divine self-revelation, forms the focus at which the two decisive beams of the truth forced upon us converge and unite: on the one hand the electing God and on the other elected man. It is to this name, then, that all Christian teaching of this truth must look, from this name that it must derive, and to this name that it must strive. Like all Christian teaching, it must always testify to this name. On the way now before

59

us we must never allow this name to fade or to be blurred in favour of abstract presuppositions concerning God or man, or of the abstract consequences of such abstract presuppositions. We can advance on this way only if in conformity with our attempted survey we confirm and develop the presuppositions which in respect of the divine election of man are contained in the name of Jesus Christ. In the measure that we hold fast to this principle, we shall find ourselves on solid ground as we advance into this as into every other sphere of

[060] dogmatic enquiry and presentation. It will not be the ground of arbitrary speculation. It will be that of the responsibility and stewardship laid upon the Church (and upon theology in particular) with regard to the theme of its proclamation, the theme which is also the basis of its existence and the standard of its truth.

It is not as though we are really making an innovation when we describe the name of Jesus Christ as the basis of the doctrine of election. There has been much regrettable deviation at this point in the way of the abstractions mentioned, but even so the Church and theology have always kept before their eyes certain utterances in the New Testament witness which reminded them clearly enough, and not altogether ineffectively, that knowledge of the election is only a distinctive form of the knowledge of Jesus Christ. Chief amongst such utterances is Eph. 1$^{4f.}$, where we read that God "has chosen us (the Church) in him ($\dot{\epsilon}\nu$ $\alpha\dot{\nu}\tau\hat{\omega}$) that we should be holy and without blame before him," that "before the foundation of the world" ($\pi\rho\grave{o}$ $\kappa\alpha\tau\alpha\betao\lambda\hat{\eta}s$ $\kappa\acute{o}\sigma\muou$), "according to the good pleasure of his will" ($\kappa\alpha\tau\grave{\alpha}$ $\tau\grave{\eta}\nu$ $\epsilon\dot{\nu}\deltao\kappa\acute{\iota}\alpha\nu$ $\tauo\hat{\nu}$ $\theta\epsilon\lambda\acute{\eta}\mu\alpha\tauos$ $\alpha\dot{\nu}\tauo\hat{\nu}$), "that in him we might be predestinated unto the adoption of children by Jesus Christ to himself" ($\deltai\grave{\alpha}$ $\mathit{Ἰ}\eta\sigmao\hat{\nu}$ $X\rho\iota\sigmato\hat{\nu}$ $\epsilon\dot{\iota}s$ $\alpha\dot{\nu}\tau\acute{o}\nu$). And again: "In him ($\dot{\epsilon}\nu$ $\alpha\dot{\nu}\tau\hat{\omega}$, $\dot{\epsilon}\nu$ $\hat{\omega}$) we have obtained an inheritance, being predestinated according to the purpose of him who worketh all things after the counsel ($\betaou\lambda\acute{\eta}$) of his will, that we should be to the praise of his glory, who had before first trusted in him" ($\tauo\grave{\nu}s$ $\pi\rhoo\eta\lambda\pi\iota\kappa\acute{o}\tau\alpha s$ $\dot{\epsilon}\nu$ $X\rho\iota\sigma\tau\hat{\omega}$, Eph. 1^{11}). And again: "To the intent that now unto the principalities and powers in the heavenly places might be known by the existence of the church ($\dot{\epsilon}\kappa\kappa\lambda\eta\sigma\acute{\iota}\alpha$) the manifold wisdom of God, according to the eternal purpose ($\kappa\alpha\tau\grave{\alpha}$ $\pi\rho\acute{o}\theta\epsilon\sigma\iota\nu$ $\tau\hat{\omega}\nu$ $\alpha\dot{\iota}\acute{\omega}\nu\omega\nu$) which He purposed ($\mathring{\eta}\nu$ $\dot{\epsilon}\pioi\eta\sigma\epsilon\nu$) in Christ Jesus our Lord, in whom we have (therefore) boldness and access with confidence by the faith of him" (Eph. 3^{10}). Another passage is Rom. 8$^{29f.}$, where we read: "For whom he did foreknow (i.e., the called according to his purpose), he also did predestinate "—$\pi\rhoo\acute{\epsilon}\gamma\nu\omega$ ^{EN123} and $\pi\rho\omega\acute{\rho}\iota\sigma\epsilon\nu$ ^{EN124} are not two different and consecutive acts, but, according to Paul's consistent usage of the connecting $\kappa\alpha\acute{\iota}$^{EN125}, they are one and the same divine act described with additional distinctness—"to be conformed to the image of his Son" (i.e., according to Col. 1^{15}, to that image which His own Son is), that "he might be the first-born among many brethren." And "whom he did predestinate, them he also called, them he also justified, them he also glorified." Now all these statements show us quite plainly that when we have to do with the reality indicated by the concept of election or predestination we are not outside the sphere of the name of Jesus Christ but within it and within the sphere of the unity of very God and very man indicated by this name. Indeed, the great exponents of the doctrine have not hesitated to point most emphatically to Jesus Christ when speaking of the knowledge of election. The only exception is Thomas Aquinas. He did

---

^{EN123} foreknow
^{EN124} predestinate
^{EN125} and

quote Eph. 1^4 (*S. th.* I, *qu.* 23), but in his interpretation he succeeded in not paying any attention to the *in ipso*^{EN126}. Only in a much later context did he treat *De praedestinatione Christi*^{EN127} (*S. th.* III, *qu.* 24).

Quite different was Augustine before him, and to Augustine we owe a christological explanation of predestination to which we must return more penetratingly at the appropriate place. Quite different, above all, was the older Luther, who declared with the greatest possible emphasis that there is only one way which our thinking can take with the text: "Many are called, few are chosen": "We must leave the predestinating God undisturbed in His majesty. For He is incomprehensible. And it is not possible for man not to be offended at such thoughts, whether by falling into despair, or by sinking into utter godlessness and recklessness. To know God and the way of God rightly, we must follow the right way, and then we shall be edified and not offended. But the right way is the Lord Christ, as He Himself says, [061] 'No man cometh unto the Father but by me.' To know the Father rightly and to come to Him, you must come first to Christ and learn to know Him, thus: Christ is the Son of God, and the almighty eternal God. What does the Son of God do? He becomes man for our sakes; He becomes obedient to the law to redeem us from the law. He lets Himself be crucified and dies on the cross to pay the price for our sins, and He rises again from the dead to open up for us by His resurrection a way to eternal life, and to help us against eternal death, and He sits now at the right hand of God to represent us, and to send us the Holy Ghost, and by the Holy Ghost to rule and guide believers and to guard them against all the assaults of the devil and temptation. To know that is to know Christ rightly. When that knowledge is well and truly in your heart, then set forth and climb up into heaven, and make reckoning with yourself what must be the heart of God towards us men, seeing the Son of God did all that for our sakes, and seeing He did it of the will and commandment of the Father. Is it not so that your reason will constrain you, so that you have to say: Since God has thus given His only-begotten Son for our sakes, He can never intend evil towards men. He never wills that they should perish, seeing that He seeks and uses the very highest means to help them to life" (*Serm. on Matt.* 20$^{1-16}$ W.A. 52, 140, 28). And with the older Luther we may number Melanchthon: *Nec ex ratione nec ex lege iudicandum est de elcctione, sed ex evangelio. Totus numerus salvandorum proper Christum electus est. Quare nisi complectamur agnitionem Christi, non potest de electione dici. Non aliam iustificationis, aliam electionis causam quaeramus …. Quaeramus ergo promissionem, in qua voluntatem suam expressit Deus et sciamus non esse aliam voluntatem quaerendam de gratia extra verbum, sed mandatum Dei immutabile esse. ut audiamus Filium*^{EN128} (*Loci*, 1559, C.R. 21, 914). Following Melanchthon, the *Formula of Concord* gave the truth in symbolical form: *Praedestinatio non in arcano Dei consilio est scrutanda, sed in verbo Dei*^{EN129} (*Ep.* XI, 6). The Word of God, however, *deducit nos ad Christum, is est liber vitae*^{EN130} (*ib.*, 7). *Vera igitur sententia de praedestinatione ex evangelio Christi discenda est*^{EN131} (*ib.*, 10). *Aeterna Dei*

---

^{EN126} in Him

^{EN127} On the Predestination of Christ

^{EN128} The matter of election is not to be judged according to reason, nor according to law, but according to the gospel. The whole number of those who are to be saved have been chosen on account of Christ. Therefore unless we embrace the knowledge of Christ, it is impossible to speak of election. Let us seek no other ground of justification, nor any other ground of election … So let us seek the promise in which God has expressed his will and let us know that there is no other will to be sought – to find grace – outside of his Word. But the decree of God is unchangeable, so that we may hear the Son

^{EN129} Predestination is not to be examined in the secret counsel of God, but in his Word

^{EN130} leads us to Christ, who is the book of life

^{EN131} Therefore the true opinion of predestination is to be learned from the Gospel of Christ

praedestinatio in Christo et nequaquam extra mediatorem Christum consideranda est[EN132] (*Sol. decl.* XI, 65).

The Lutherans thought that they had to maintain this thesis against Calvin and the Calvinists. But in Calvin himself they might have read the following: *Neque ego sane ad arcanam Dei electionem homines ablego, ut inde salutem hiantes expectent, sed recta ad Christum pergere iubeo, in quo nobis proposita est salus: quae alioqui in Deo abscondita lateret. Nam quisquis plana fidei via non ingreditur, illi Dei electio nihil quam exitialis erit labyrinthus. Itaque ut certa sit nobis peccatorum remissio, ut in vitae aeternae fiducia conscientiae nostrae acquiescant, ut Deum intrepide patrem invocemus, hinc minime faciendum est exordium, quid de nobis ante mundum conditum Deus statuerit, sed quid de paterno eius amort nobis in Christo sit patefactum et quotidie per evangelium Christus ipse praedicet .... Fateor .... Christum unicam esse ianuam, qua in regnum coelorum omnes ingredi opportet ... quicunque inde vel minimum deflectunt, nihil quam per flexuosas ambages errare, et quo quisque in profunda illa divini consilii adyta confidentius irrumpere et penetrare conatur, eo longius a Deo recedere*[EN1323] (*De aet. Dei praed.*, 1552, *C.R.* 8, 306 f.). *Quum nobis in Christo proposita sit salutis certitudo, perperam, nec sine Christi ipsius iniuria, facere qui praeterito hoc vitae fonte, ex quo haurire promptum erat, ex reconditis Dei abyssis vitam eruere moliuntur .... Ne quis ergo aliunde electionis suae fiduciam petat, nisi librum vitae, in quo scriptus est, delere velit .... Christus aeternae et absconditae Dei electionis tum luculentum nobis speculum est, tum arra quoque et pignus. Fide autem, quam Deus in hoc speculo nobis repraesentat, vitam contemplamur: fide pignus hoc arramque amplectimur* (*ib.*, 318). *Ideo manifestare nobis Christus patris nomen dicitur, quia electionis nostrae scientiam, evangelii sui voce testatam, spiritu quoque suo in cordibus nostris obsignat* (*ib.*, 319). *Quod si in Christo sumus electi, non in nobis ipsis reperiemus electionis nostrae certitudinem ac ne in Deo quidem patre, si nudum illum absque filio imaginamur. Christus ergo speculum est, in quo electionem nostram contemplari convenit, et sine fraude licet*[EN134] (*Instit.* III, 24, 5). Bullinger, too, declares most definitely: *Improbamus illos, qui extra Christum quaerunt: An sint electi? Et quid ante omnem aeternitatem de ipsis statuerit Deus? Audienda est enim praedicatio evangelii, eique credendum est et pro indubitato*

[062]

[EN132] The eternal predestination of God is to be considered in Christ, and in no way separately from Christ the mediator

[EN133] I do not rightly take men to the secret election of God in order that they thereby eagerly await their salvation; rather, I rightly command them to go to Christ, in whom our salvation is set forth to us. As for the other – God's secret election – it lies hidden in God. For whoever does not travel upon the plain way of faith, to him election will be nothing other than a deadly labyrinth. Therefore, in order that our forgiveness of sins be certain to us, in order that our consciences rest in the confidence of eternal life, in order that we may fearlessly have confidence in God our Father, there is no other beginning to be made (one which God has established for us before the foundation of the world) but what has been made plain to us in his paternal love in Christ, and which Christ himself proclaims every day in the gospel. I say that Christ is the only gate by which it is possible for all to enter the Kingdom of Heaven ... Whoever diverges from that even in the least wanders only through tortuous windings, and anyone who tries too confidently to break through and penetrate to the deep, secret recesses of the divine counsel, thereby withdraws more distantly from God

[EN134] Since the certainty of our salvation is set forth to us in Christ, those who pass by this fountain of life (from which it is easy to draw) and exert themselves to snatch life from the hidden depths of God, do wrong, and not without injury to Christ himself ... So, may no-one seek confidence in his election from anywhere else, unless he wills to destroy the book of life in which he is written ... For Christ is both a bright, clear mirror of the eternal and hidden election of God, but also the pledge and deposit of it. And we contemplate life in faith, which God represents to us in this mirror: by this faith we embrace the pledge and deposit (318). Therefore, Christ is said to manifest the name of the Father to us, since he seals by his Spirit in our hearts the knowledge of our election witnessed in the word of his Gospel. If we have been chosen in Christ, we do not find the certainty of our election in ourselves, nor even in God the Father, if we think of him separately from the Son. For Christ is the mirror in which it is right to contemplate our election, and we do so quite rightly

habendum: si credis et sis in Christo electum te esse. Pater enim praedestinationis suae aeternam sententiam ... in Christo nobis aperuit. Docendum ergo et considerandum ante omnia, quantus amor patris erga nos in Christo nobis sit revelatus .... Christus itaque sit speculum, in quo praedestinationem nostram contemplemur. Satis perspicuum et firmum habebimus testimonium nos in libro vitae inscriptos esse, si communicaverimus cum Christo et is in vera fide noster sit, nos eius simus[EN135] (*Conf. Helv. post.*, 1566, *art.* 10).

In view of these texts it can hardly be said that the Reformed theology deserved to be reprimanded by Luther and the Lutherans in this respect. The Reformed school knew just as well as the Lutheran what was that biblical centre which must form the object of genuinely theological knowledge in matters of predestination. Indeed, Calvin was not content simply to maintain this line. Following the suggestions of Augustine—to which we will return in their proper context—he tried to show that Christ is the *speculum electionis*[EN136] to the extent that in the incarnation of the divine Word in the man Jesus of Nazareth we have to do with the prototype and essence of, as it were, all divine electing and human election. And in this respect the *Confessio Scotica* (1561) went so far that first of all, in articles 7 and 8, the question *Cur Deus homo?* was answered by a reference to the eternal and immutable divine decree, i.e., predestination, and then later, and most surprisingly, under the title *De electione* there was simply presented the doctrine of the true Godhead and the true manhood of Jesus Christ, and the necessity and reality of both in the unity of the person of the Mediator. In spite of their zealous protestations that predestination is to be known only in Christ, the Lutherans exerted themselves far less for a christological understanding of predestination than did the Reformed school against which they thought themselves bound to make a polemical assertion of that very thesis. However that may be, the Augustinian-Reformed allusion to Christ as the mirror of election does make one thing clear beyond all possible doubt—and its merit in this respect can never be rated too highly. It emphasises in most drastic fashion the singularity of the election, and of the freedom in which God as Elector stands over against the elect. The elect must look always to Jesus Christ in matters of the election because whoever is elected is elected in Christ and only in Christ. But if this is so, then it is settled conclusively that no one can ever seek the basis of election in himself, because no one is ever elected in himself or for the sake of himself or finally of himself. There is no basis for the divine election in man as such, and no such basis may be found in man. When they pointed to our election in Christ, Augustine and the Reformers were undoubtedly right, and faithful to the teaching of the Bible on this matter. But such a reference carries with it an unmistakable call always to magnify in this matter the grace of God, the grace which appeared concretely in the person of the Mediator between God and man. It is not in man himself or in the work of man that the basis of election must be sought. It is in this other person who is the person of God Himself in the flesh. It is in the work of this other person: a work which comes to man and comes upon man from without; a work which is quite different from anything that he himself is or does. Man and his decision follow the decision which is already made before him, without him and against him; the decision which is not made in himself at all, but is

---

[EN135] We condemn those who ask, outside of Christ, whether they are elect, and what God has decreed for them before all eternity. For the preaching of the Gospel must be heard, and it must be believed and held with certainty. If you believe that you are elect in Christ, then you are. For the Father has opened the eternal decree of his predestination to us in Christ. Therefore what must be taught and considered before all things is how great is the love of the Father towards us that has been revealed to us in Christ ... So, Christ is the mirror in which we contemplate our predestination. We will hold clearly and strongly enough to the testimony that we are written in the book of life, if we have participated in Christ, and in true faith, he is ours and we are his

[EN136] mirror of election

made concerning him in this wholly other person. And as he recognises this, he recognises in truth the meaning and nature of the divine election: that it is the essence of divine favour. He recognises, too, the meaning and nature of the doctrine of election: that it is the sum of the Gospel. In the last resort this was how Augustine and Calvin would have it understood. It is good for man and his decision to stand so wholly and utterly under the prior decision of God, as is actually the case according to the doctrine of election. To that extent that christo-logical reference asserts the very thing which we have stated with regard to the biblical basis of the doctrine: *Quos Deus sibi filios assumpsit, non in ipsis eos dicitur elegisse sed in Christo suo, quia nonnisi in eo amare illos poterat, nec regni sui haereditate honorare nisi eius consortes ante factos. Quod si in eo sumus electi, non in nobis ipsis reperiemus electionis nostrae certitudinem*[EN137] (Calvin, *Instit.* III, 24, 5). *En nous-mesmes nous sommes hays et dignes que Dieu nous ait en abomination; mais il nous regarde en sons Fils, et lors il nous aime*[EN138] (*Congr. sur l'élection éternelle*, 1562, C.R. 8, 95). *Sachons donc que nostre salut est certain. Et pourquoy cela? Pource qu'il est en la main de Dieu. Et comment en sommesnous assurez? Pource qu'il l'a mis en la main de nostre Seigneur Jesus, qui nous manifeste que le Pere, qui nous a esleus, veut avancer son conseil à plein effect et perfection*[EN139] (*ib.*, 100). *Apprenons que nous ne pouvons pas nous asseurer de nostre salut que par la foy. Car si un homme dit: Et que say-ie si ie suis sauvé ou damné? par cela il demonstre que iamais il n'a cognu que c'est de foy ne de l'asseurance que nous devons avoir en Dieu, par Jesus Christ. Veux-tu donc bien savoir si tu es eslu? Regarde-toy en Jesus Christ. Car ceux qui, par foy, communiquent vrayement en Jesus Christ, se peuvent bien asseurer, qu'ils appartiennent à l'élection éternelle de Dieu, et qu'ils sont de ses enfans. Quiconque doce se trouve en Jesus Christ, et est membre de son corps par foy, celuy-là est asseuré de son salut, et quand nous le voudrions savoir, il ne faut pas que nous mentions là-haut pour nous enquerir de ce qui nous doit à ceste heure estre caché. Mais voilà Dieu qui s'abaisse à nous; il nous monstre dequoy en son Fils; comme s'il disoit: Me voicy: contemplez-moy, et cognoissez comment ie vous ay adoptez pour mes enfans. Quand donc nous recevons ce tesmoignage de salut qui nous est rendu par l'Evangile, de là nous congnoissons et sommes asseurez que Dieu nous a esleu. Et ainsi il ne faut point que les fideles doutent de leur election, mais qu'ils ayent cela pour tout resolu, que depuis qu'ils sont appelez à la foy par la predication de l'Evangile, ils sont participans de ceste grace de nostre Seigneur Jesus Christ, et de la promesse qu'il leur a faite en son Nom. Car nostre Seigneur Jesus Christ est le fondement de ces deux: c'est assavoir, des promesses de salut et de nostre election gratuite, qui a ésté faite dès la creation du monde*[EN140] (*ib.*, 114).

In all these texts, however, (even those of Luther and the Lutherans) there is something unsatisfactory about the christological reference, factually important though it undoubtedly is. The reason for this is that notwithstanding all these earnest protestations the following

---

[EN137] Those whom God has brought to himself as sons, he is said to have chosen not in themselves, but in his Christ, because he could only love them in him. Nor can he honour them with inheritance in his Kingdom, before he has made them his partners. So, if we are elect in him, we will not find the certainty of our election in our own selves

[EN138] In ourselves, we are hated, and worthy of God holding us in abomination. But He looks upon us in His Son, and then He loves us

[EN139] Let us hold then to the knowledge that our salvation is certain. Why? Because it is in the hand of God. And how can we be assured of that? Because He has put it in the hand of our Lord Jesus, who shows us that the Father who has elected us wills further to put his purpose into full effect and perfection

[EN140] Let us learn that we can be assured of our salvation only by faith. But someone may say, 'How do I know if I am saved or condemned?' In so saying, he shows that he has never known how it is with the faith and assurance that we should have in God. Do you want to know if you are elect? Look at Jesus Christ. For those who by faith truly share in Jesus Christ can certainly be assured that they participate in the eternal election of God, and that they are his children. Whoever, then, is found in Jesus Christ and is a member by faith of his body, is thereby assured of his salvation and when we would want to know it, we must not ascend to the

question still remains unanswered: Is it the intention of these thinkers that serious theological attention should be paid to the assertion that the election is to be known in Jesus Christ? Does this assertion contain the first and last word on this matter, the word by which we must hold conclusively, and beyond which we must not conceive of any further word? Is it a fact that there is no other basis of election outside Jesus Christ? Must the doctrine as such be related to this basis and this basis only? Must it take account only of this basis? In this matter of election are we noetically to hold by Christ and Christ alone because ontically there is no election and no electing God outside Him? Or is it rather the case that we are to understand this assertion merely as an impressively stated pastoral rule, a practical direction regarding the attitude which, *rebus sic stantibus*^{EN141}, we ought to adopt towards this matter if we are not to be plunged into doubt or despair? Is it the case, in fact, that behind the pastoral (and in some measure the historico-psychological) truth that God's election meets us and is revealed to us in Jesus Christ, there stands a higher truth which, for the sake of prudence and charity, must be withdrawn from the practical usage of the Church, a truth which cannot be denied or entirely suppressed, but which is so dangerous that it must be covered over and kept out of the reach of the curious like a kind of poison? Is it the case that, according to this [064] higher and dangerous truth concealed for practical purposes in the background, while Christ is indeed the medium and instrument of the divine activity at the basis of the election, and to that extent He is the revelation of the election by which factually we must hold fast, yet the electing God Himself is not Christ but God the Father, or the triune God, in a decision which precedes the being and will and word of Christ, a hidden God, who as such made, as it were, the actual resolve and decree to save such and such men and to bring them to blessedness, and then later made, as it were, the formal or technical decree and resolve to call the elect and to bring them to that end by means of His Son, by means of His Word and Spirit? Is it the case, then, that in the divine election as such we have to do ultimately, not with a divine decision made in Jesus Christ, but with one which is independent of Jesus Christ and only executed by Him? Is it the case that that decision made in Jesus Christ by which we must hold fast is, in fact, only another and a later and subordinate decision, while the first and true decision of election is to be sought—or if we follow the pastoral direction had better not be sought—in the mystery of the self-existent being of God, and of a decree made in the absolute freedom of this divine being?

If in any sense we are forced to accept this second interpretation, it is inevitable that there should be tension between the theological truth and the pastoral direction which would have us hold fast by Christ. And in this tension it is the latter which will feel the strain the more seriously. It is only those who accidentally have not experienced or suspected the existence of the hidden truth who can really be satisfied with the advice simply to hold fast by the incarnate Son of God and the Word and Spirit of God and not enquire concerning the hidden will of the Father or of the eternal Godhead. For why should they not enquire concerning it, if it is true, and if they know that we have here two very different things and that the decisive word for salvation is spoken at that hidden and secret place? If there does exist

---

heavens to inquire about that which is at this time hidden from us. But lo, God comes down to us; he shows us …. in His Son, and says, 'Here I am! Think on me, and know how I have adopted you as my children'. So when we receive this testimony of salvation which is given to us by the Gospel, it is from there that we know and are assured that God has elected us. So, the faithful should not doubt their election, but should rather have it as a surety that since they have been called to faith by the preaching of the Gospel, they are participants in this grace of our Lord Jesus Christ, and in the promise which He has made to them in His name. For our Lord Jesus Christ is the basis of them both: that is to say, both of the promises of salvation, and of our free election which has been decreed since the creation of the world

^{EN141} as things stand

something like an absolute decree of this nature concerning the salvation and blessedness of individuals, a decree which is independent of and precedes the decision made in Jesus Christ, and if we have to take account of a decree which is absolute in this sense, even if only theoretically, then what right has anyone to suppress the question concerning such a decree as the basis of election? By the power of what *sic volo sic iubeo*[EN142] can this question actually be quashed? In spite of all pastoral intentions, however excellent, is it not a highly relevant and highly necessary question? Is it not a question to which we must pay heed and which in some way we must answer? But of course, when this happens, when the question of the decree which is absolute in this sense crops up again, what an abyss of uncertainty is opened up! The thought of the election becomes necessarily the thought of the will and decision of God which are hidden somewhere in the heights or depths behind Jesus Christ and behind God's revelation. The first and last question in respect of the relationship between God and man brings us face to face with a God who is above and beyond Jesus Christ and with a relationship which is independent of Jesus Christ. How, then, can we attain to any sure know-ledge of God or ourselves? How, then, can we have any sure knowledge of this relationship? How can we be certain that it is good to be so fully in the hands of God as we are proclaimed to be when we assert that God elects? Such an uncertainty is almost inevitably imposed by a presentation like that of Thomas Aquinas. It was against this uncertainty that Reformation theology sought to protect itself by its thesis that Jesus Christ is the *speculum electionis*[EN143]. The reference to the person of the Mediator and the Word and self-revelation of God was intended to liberate reflection on this subject from the inevitable tendency to lose itself in a sphere inaccessible by its very nature to human effort, a sphere which allows only of asser-tions which cannot sustain us because they are never more than our own assertions and are [065] as such hopelessly dialectical. What can sustain us is the declaration which God Himself as Creator and Lord of life and death has made in our favour in Jesus Christ. When we let ourselves be taught by the Word of God and the Spirit of God, then we can and should be sure of the divine election. We can and should be sure of the fact that it is good for us to have an electing God. We can and should rejoice in God and in ourselves because we can see God's electing and our election at the place where God Himself has revealed it, in the Word of God made flesh. By this christological reference Reformation theology did assert and defend the honour and dignity of the divine self-revelation as such against all the attempts of man to be his own instructor in the things concerning God and himself. It did this in a way which had very obviously not been the case with Thomas Aquinas, with detriment to the purity and the power of the Church's doctrine. Reformation theology did have a proper regard for the fact of the biblical witness which must always be the proper starting-point for thinking on the divine election.

If only it could be said that it had so adhered to this line (as correctly perceived) that it had not only combated but completely banished all the uncertainty, and with it the com-promising of the honour and dignity of the divine self-revelation in Jesus Christ. But while we may gratefully acknowledge the right intention expressed in the Reformation allusion to Christ, this is the very thing which we cannot say. The christological reference was warmly and impressively made, but it is left standing in the air. It cannot be carried through theo-logically, and for this reason. It does forbid in practice any glancing away at an absolute decree of God, i.e., a decree which is different from the eternal saving decision of God as made in Jesus Christ. Yet it does not exclude any such glancing away in theory, but more or less expressly permits it. This fact appears incidentally in a passage like *Conf. helv. post.* 10. In his sober ecclesiastical fashion, Bullinger had been content simply to lay down what it is that

---

[EN142] 'as I will, I command'
[EN143] mirror of election

the Church must ask and hear and consider and teach, and he had stated that this is Jesus Christ Himself, and that we ought not to enquire concerning any other basis of election outside of and beyond Christ. *Vestrum non est, de his curiosius inquirere, sed magis anniti, ut per rectam viam coelum ingrediamini*[EN144]. But then his first and decisive statement on the subject ran as follows: *Deus ab aeterno praedestinavit vel elegit libere et mera sua gratia nullo hominum respectu sanctos, quos vult salvos facere in Christo*[EN145]. Even with him, then, it is evident that the *velle salvos facere in Christo*[EN146] is preceded by a *praedestinare vel eligere quos ...* [EN147] and thus by the election itself and as such. It is evident that to Christ must be ascribed not the function of the electing God Himself, but only that of the organ which serves the electing will of God, as a means towards the attainment of the end foreordained for the elect. Now, according to John's Gospel, the electing of the Father and that of the Son are one and the same. And according to Ephesians 1⁴ we are not only called and redeemed in Christ, but are already elected to calling and salvation in Him. Bullinger not only says nothing of all this, but in the formula mentioned he expressly denies it, although he never returns later to this background truth. What, then, is the value of the most praiseworthy pastoral zeal with which he refers us to Christ as the *speculum electionis?*[EN148] Whatever else Christ may be, *speculum electionis*[EN149] is the very thing which on this presupposition He obviously is not. In respect of our election, and therefore of our calling and redemption, all that remains according to Bullinger's formula is secret speculation of quite a different kind, and contrary to Bullinger's own prohibition. That which the pastoral prudence of Bullinger to a large extent conceals is, however, quite palpably revealed elsewhere. And because Luther and the later Lutherans thought that this was one of the matters which they ought particularly to hold against Calvin and the Calvinists, it is very much to the point to recall that, long before Calvin, Luther himself had been foremost in adding to the christological reference the equally definite reference to a divine decision which took place apart from Christ, a decision hidden and unsearchable, but not on that account any the less real. It is to the point to recall [066] that in this hidden and unsearchable but nevertheless real decision Luther had found the true and ultimate reality of the divine election. In his old age Luther, as a rule, made no mention of this side of the matter. In the fragments of his preaching which have come down to us it is impossible to find any further trace of this background. The christological reference became for Luther the one and only thing that mattered. Yet it should not be forgotten that the older Luther ranked the *De servo arbitrio* (1525) as one of his best works. Thus there had not been any theoretical abandonment of the earlier position. And in that work we find already (*W.A.* 18, 689, 18) the most impressive warning: *de secreta illa voluntate maiestatis non esse disputandum et temeritatem humanam, quae perpetua perversitate relictis necessariis illa semper impetit et tentat, esse avocandam et retrahendam, ne occupet sese scrutandis illis secretis maiestatis, quae impossibile est attingere, ut quae habitet lucem inaccessibilem*[EN150]. On the positive side, too, Luther tells the thinking man quite definitely that his concern must be *cum Deo incarnato,*

EN144 It is not for you to inquire with too much curiosity into these things, but rather to take pains to enter heaven through the straight path

EN145 God has predestined from eternity, or has freely chosen by his undiluted grace, with no partiality, the saints whom he wills to save in Christ

EN146 'wills to save in Christ'

EN147 'predestining or choosing those ... '

EN148 mirror of election

EN149 mirror of election

EN150 Concerning that secret will of his majesty, there is to be no disputing, and human rashness (which always – having left aside what is necessary – intrudes and touches upon these things with its constant perversity) must be revoked and checked, lest it occupy itself with scrutinising the secrets of that majesty which it is impossible to reach, as it inhabits inaccessible light *cum Jesu crucifixo*[EN151]. It is this *Deus incarnatus* whom we find weeping over Jerusalem. It is He whom we hear saying: "Ye would not." It is He whom we see offering to all men everything that they need for salvation ... *cum voluntas maiestatis ex proposito aliquos relinquat et reprobet, ut pereant*[EN152]. Luther would reject and suppress the question concerning the nature and content of this *voluntas maiestatis: Nec nobis quaerendum, cur ita faciat sed reverendus Deus, qui talia et possit et velit*[EN153]. But how can this question possibly be rejected, how can there be any confident turning to the *Deus incarnatus*, when behind Him and above Him another and different *voluntas maiestatis*[EN154] is always laid down and maintained? (And it was to the presentation of the omnipotent rule of this *voluntas maiestatis* that Luther devoted the whole work in his controversy with Erasmus.) No matter what warnings or prohibitions may accompany it, does not the establishment of such a *voluntas*[EN156] mean that the revelation of God is only a relative truth about God? In defiance of all such warnings and prohibitions, will not the question of the hidden God emerge one day as the question of the true God? Even where in conformity with the warnings and prohibitions there is still an adherence to the *Deus revelatus*[EN156], will not the question of the electing of this true God always lurk in the background? Is there not something necessarily spasmodic and artificial about the reference to Jesus Christ when in fact it is accompanied by the assertion of a quite different *voluntas maiestatis*[EN157]? And we must ask the same question of Calvin. What are we to think when on one occasion he makes use of this formula: *videmus, ut a se ipso incipiat Deus, quum nos eligere dignatur; sed nos a Christo incipere velit, ut nos sciamus in sacro illo peculio censere*[EN158] (*De aet. Dei praed.*, 1552, *C.R.* 8, 319)? It is obvious what Calvin means by the latter part: Christ is *sic toti mundo ordinatus ad salutem, ut eos servet, qui a Patre illi dati sunt— eorum sit vita, quorum est caput—eos in bonorum suorum societatem recipit, quos sibi Deus gratuito beneplacito haeredes adoptavit*[EN159] (*ib.*, 298). It is in the being and work of Christ accomplished on the basis of the election and for the attainment of its end—that He ministers to certain men, that He is their life, that He adopts them into the fellowship of the benefits which He Himself has and is—it is here that we must know the electing God. And to that extent God wills that in respect of the election we, at any rate, should begin with Christ. But what does Calvin mean when he says that on His side God begins *a se ipso*[EN160] (in contradistinction to *a Christo*[EN161]) when He elects us, i.e., when the Father gives us the Son, when He predestinates us members of the body of this Head and partakers of His inheritance? And what is this *gratuitum beneplacitum*[EN162] which plainly here precedes and is superior to the being and work of Christ? The question of the election is really the question of this *gratuitum*

[EN151] with the incarnate God, with Jesus crucified
[EN152] although according to the decree, his majestic will abandons and rejects them, such that they perish
[EN153] majestic will: It is not for us to ask why he acts in such a way, but it is for us to revere the God who is able and wills to do such things
[EN154] majestic will
[EN155] will
[EN156] revealed God
[EN157] majestic will
[EN158] We see that when he deigns to elect us, God begins from his very self. But he wills us to begin from Christ, so that we know that we assessed among his holy property
[EN159] thus ordained for the salvation of the whole word, in order that he might save those who were given him by the Father – of whom he is life, of whom he is the head. These he received into partnership in his possessions, whom God adopted for himself as his heirs, by his free decree
[EN160] from his very self
[EN161] from Christ
[EN162] free decree

beneplacitum[EN163] as such. And the reference to Christ as the One who executed the *beneplacitum*[EN164] is only an answer to the question of the *beneplacitum*[EN165] if the *beneplacitum*[EN166] as such is understood to be Christ's, if Christ is already thought of not [067] merely as the executive instrument of the divine dealings with man ordained in the election but as the Subject of the election itself. But Calvin was not prepared to think of Him in this way. He did come appreciably near to such an understanding in his exposition of the passages in John (13^8, 15^{19}) which speak of Christ's own election of His disciples. We do find there the words: *Sibi ius eligendi communiter vindicat cum Patre …. Se Christus electionis facit autorem*[EN167]. But the thought is not followed to its conclusion. From other passages in John, however, whose tenor was apparently different, the unequivocal deduction is drawn: *Electi dicuntur ante fuisse Patris, quam eos donaret unigenilo Filio*[EN168] (*Instit.* III, 22, 7). The fact that according to Eph. 1^4 the *electio Patris*[EN169] which preceded the *donatio*[EN170] is to be thought of as taking place *in Christo*[EN171] is something which Calvin will not acknowledge. He says the direct opposite: *Qui ad Christum accedunt, iam filii Dei erant in eius corde … et quia praeordinati erant ad vitam, Christo dati sunt*[EN172] (*De praed. C.R.* 8, 292). It was inevitable, then, that in spite of the christological reference the main emphasis in Calvinistic doctrine should come to rest in effect upon this reference to the secret *electio Patris*[EN173]. But how, then, could the first reference have any force? Assent might be given to it, but it was inevitable that a secret dissatisfaction should lead to its supersession by the real truth to be found *in Deo incipiente a se ipso*[EN174], in the *beneplacitum gratuitum*[EN175] which was before Christ and behind Him and above Him. It was inevitable, then, that little store should be set by the revelation when there was no need to adhere strictly to it. It was inevitable that even within the revelation the main concern should be, not with a relative truth, but quite unreservedly and unhesitatingly with this real and inward truth concerning God.

As is known, at the end of the 16th and beginning of the 17th centuries there arose a lively opposition to the Calvinistic doctrine of the *decretum absolutum*[EN176].

On the one hand, there was the opposition within the Reformed Church itself. This was made by the Dutch Remonstrants named after Jacob Arminius.

This party drew up a series of Articles on the whole complex of questions relating to predestination. These Articles were discussed and condemned at the Synod of Dordrecht (Dort). The fifth of them contains (I, 3) the striking sentence: *Christus mediator non est solum executor electionis, sed ipsius decreti electionis fundamentum*[EN177]. But because of the context in

---

[EN163] free decree

[EN164] decree

[EN165] decree

[EN166] decree

[EN167] He lays claim to the right to elect in common with the Father … Christ makes himself the author of election

[EN168] The elect are said to have belonged to the Father before he gives them to his only begotten Son

[EN169] the election of the Father

[EN170] gift

[EN171] in Christ

[EN172] Those who approach Christ were already sons of God in his heart, and because they were foreordained to life, they were given to Christ

[EN173] election of the Father

[EN174] in God beginning from his very self

[EN175] free decree

[EN176] absolute decree

[EN177] Christ the mediator is not only the executor of election, but is the basis of the decree of election

which it was presented, and the intention which obviously underlay it, we unfortunately cannot find much cause for pleasure in such a statement. We can say only that it would have been good if the orthodox majority at Dort had let the (in any case) remarkable wording remind them of the problem to which the Calvinistic and in particular the Reformation conception of the doctrine had returned so unsatisfactory an answer. But the general tenor of the Remonstrant theology laid down in the Five Articles was so bad that in effect they failed to give the stimulus which they might have given in this respect. The only result was a hardening of the conception inherited from the Reformers. There can be no doubt that the Remonstrants were, in fact, the last exponents of an understanding of the Reformation which Erasmus had once represented against Luther and later Castellio against Calvin; an understanding which can and should be interpreted in the light of the persistence of mediaeval semi-Pelagianism no less than in that of the Renaissance. And as the last exponents of that understanding they were also the first exponents of a modern Christianity which is characterised by the very same ambiguity. They were the first Neo-Protestants of the Church, and it was their basic decision which gave unity to all subsequent developments along this line (from the end of the 17th century onwards). The basic decision which they made was this—that in the understanding of God and His relationship with man, in the question of the formulation of Christian doctrine, the criterion or measure of all things must always be man, i.e., man's conception of that which is right, and rational, and worthy, therefore, of God and

[068] man. It was in the light of this basic decision that the Remonstrants opposed to the Calvinistic doctrine of the *decretum absolutum*[EN178] the assertion that we cannot and must not state that God elects (and rejects) whom He wills solely upon the basis of His own free *beneplacitum*[EN179] and without reference to conduct, and particularly to belief or unbelief, obedience or disobedience. On the contrary, the divine election is made with due consideration of the conduct of men as foreseen by God from all eternity, i.e., of the use which, according to God's foreknowledge, they make of their freedom, whether in belief or unbelief, whether in obedience or disobedience. It is to this context, unfortunately, that there belongs the intrinsically so remarkable statement of the Remonstrants that Christ is the *fundamentum electionis*[EN180], a statement which was obviously meant to outbid and correct the Calvinist statement that Christ is the *speculum electionis*[EN181]. We cannot take the statement to mean that as Christ is the Subject of the saving decree of God, so, too, He is the Subject of the free election which underlies it, an election independent of and preceding and predetermining absolutely all creaturely decisions. It is simply a polemical assertion in the battle against the *servum*[EN182] and for the *liberum arbitrium*[EN183]. It does not mean, unfortunately, what in itself the wording might well mean: that *in concreto*[EN184] the Calvinistic and Reformation magnifying of the freedom of the election of grace must consist in the magnifying of the sovereignty of Jesus Christ, who in His own person is Himself the God who freely elects and then acts towards the creature, the One behind and above whom there is no other God and no other election. As directed against the *decretum absolutum*[EN185] the statement does not contend for the dignity of Jesus Christ, but for the dignity of man standing over against Jesus Christ in an autonomous freedom of decision. Read in the context of the general teaching of the Five Remonstrant Articles it unfortunately means nothing more

---

[EN178] absolute decree
[EN179] decree
[EN180] basis of election
[EN181] mirror of election
[EN182] bondage
[EN183] freedom of the will
[EN184] concretely
[EN185] absolute decree

than that Christ is the essence of the divine order of salvation. It is in Him that the grace of God is offered to men. It is by their belief or unbelief in Him that the decision is made—according to God's foreknowledge, but independently—whether the grace of God profits or does not profit them. The Remonstrants did not say that Christ is the electing God. They can never have wanted to say that. What they did want to say, and what they actually did say in this statement, was that in the distinctive sense of the word there is no divine decision at all. There is only the establishment of a just and reasonable order of salvation, of which Christ must be regarded as the content and the decisive instrument. Above and beyond that, there is no more than a divine foreknowledge of what individuals will become as measured by this order of salvation and on the basis of the use which they make of their creaturely freedom. It might almost be called fate that a statement which is so interesting in its wording should engage the attention of Calvinistic orthodoxy, and the Synod of Dort in particular, only in the form of an argument for so revolutionary an error, and that in the mouth of the Remonstrants it should not be a more accurate or Christian definition of the mystery of the election of grace, but an attempt to deny it altogether; an attempt to make of divine predestination something more akin to a religious world-order.

It was not that the importance of the statement was simply not recognised at Dort. It was not that there was no attempt made to come to grips with it. In the 65th session (Jan. 22, 1619) it was the occasion of a clash between the most resolute champion of Calvinistic orthodoxy, Franz Gomarus, and the leader of the Bremen delegation, Matthias Martini—a clash which nearly assumed dangerous proportions. In modification of the orthodox Calvinistic thesis that the decree of salvation follows the decree of election, and is brought into effect only in Christ, the English expounded Eph. 1^4 to mean that after his human nature Christ is the first of the elect, and the Swiss that He is the basis of those blessings of which the elect are made partakers. But Martini wished to go further, and to say that Christ is the basis of the election itself, on the ground that He is its principal author: the *causa meritoria eligibilitatis*[EN186], i.e., the cause of the election of anyone at all—although we have still to seek elsewhere than in Christ the *causa electionis*[EN187] as such, i.e., the election of this or that particular individual. On this point, the following statement is still to be found amongst the final resolutions of the Bremen delegation: *Hoc decretum est liberrimum, quatenus Deus miseretur cuius vult; est iustissimum utpote factum in Christo mediatore, irae Dei placatore et hominum reconciliatore; benignissimum ut simul dandae salutiferae gratiae et gloriae propositum*[EN188]. It was sheer narrow-mindedness when the Palatinate delegates indignantly rejected the Bremen position simply on the ground that it was out of place to attempt in any way to improve upon the teaching of Calvin. And it rested upon a more adequate but even more malicious recognition of the actual facts of the case when the anti-Remonstrants accused the Bremen party of Arminian tendencies. Unfortunately, it cannot be stated positively that the Bremen delegates were impelled to the point at which their conception, while clearly avoiding the Arminian error, might have taken on the character of a real correction of the Calvinistic teaching. In such a form it might perhaps have struck the Synod as really necessary. The Canons of the Synod did aim, indeed, to take account of the Bremen conception (in the main definition I, 7 often quoted in this connexion). The divine *propositum*[EN189] of the election is there defined as that *quo Deus ... certam hominum multitudinem ... ad salutem elegit in Christo, quem*

[069]

[EN186] meritorious ground for the possibility of election

[EN187] cause of election

[EN188] This is his most free decree, in which God has mercy on whom he wills, inasmuch as it is the most just act in Christ the mediator, who placates the wrath of God and reconciles men. It is most generous, as the proposition of the giving of saving grace and glory

[EN189] proposition

etiam ab aeterno mediatorem ... constituit[EN190]. But the rulings of other foreign delegations and the Dutch provincial synods show that now as ever this passage from Canon I, 7 was, on the whole, to be taken as implying the superiority of a genuine decree of election, which was independent of Christ, over a decree of salvation which was subordinate to it and had Christ as its content. In the last analysis, the English would speak of Christ as the *fundamentum electionis*[EN191] (I, 2) only in the sense that all the benefits ordained in election are conferred upon us *non nisi propter Christum, per Christum et in Christo*[EN192]; the Hessians (I, 3) only in the sense, *quatenus electio accipitur pro ordinatione mediorum ad vitam aeternam tendentium;*[EN193] the Nassau delegates (I, 2) only in so far as *in mediis istis (ad vitam aeternam) primum locum obtinet adeoque reliquorum mediorum fundamentum est Christus mediator, cui Deus electos dedit;*[EN194] the Emden representatives (I, 11) only in so far as Christ is the way *inter electionis decretum et decreti finem*[EN195], etc. And the Swiss delegation (which consisted of J. J. Breitinger of Zurich, Markus Rütimeyer of Berne, Sebastian Beck and Wolfgang Meyer of Basel and J. C. Koch of Schaffhausen) unfortunately had the temerity to reject the phrase altogether: *etsi electio respectum habeat ad Christum mediatorem, in quo omnes ad salutem et gratiam eligimur, tamen nos elegit Deus non velut existentes in illo priusquam eligeremur, sed elegit ut essemus in illo, perque eum servaremur*[EN196] (I, 4). It was fatal that in all these expositions of Eph. 1⁴, or understandings of the concept *fundamentum*[EN197], there was too close an agreement with the Remonstrants in seeking to relate the *ἐν αὐτῷ*[EN198] only to the pre-existent decree of salvation as such, and not to the election properly speaking. This was done by maintaining against the Remonstrants a decree of election different from the decree of salvation. On the one hand, then, the decree of salvation was emptied of meaning, for quite unintentionally it was rendered inevitable that the true divine decision should be sought elsewhere than in the Saviour, Jesus Christ. And, on the other hand, the decree of election was also emptied of meaning, for it was removed to the divine sphere above and behind Christ where it could not in fact be known as Christian truth. And that meant that there could be no sure knowledge of it at all, and that it was set in the light of a purely speculative axiom. Thus the way was made all too easy for future Neo-Protestants some day to set aside the decree of election as too obscure and uncertain, and to understand the decree of salvation, now deprived of its mysterious background, only after the semi-Pelagian fashion of the Remonstrants. Our consideration of the interaction between Calvinism and the Remonstrant thesis that Christ is the *fundamentum electionis*[EN199] can lead us to only one conclusion, that here, too, we stand at one of those points where unwittingly and unwillingly the older Protestant orthodoxy helped to dig its own grave.

[070]

From our present standpoint, the opposition brought against the doctrine of the *decretum absolutum*[EN200] by 17th century Lutheran theology is far more significant. The motive of the

---

[EN190] in which God elected a fixed multitude of men in Christ, the Christ whom he had established as mediator even from eternity

[EN191] basis of election

[EN192] only on account of Christ, through Christ, and in Christ

[EN193] in which election is received by the establishment of means which lead to eternal life

[EN194] among those means (to eternal life) Christ the mediator, to whom God has given the elect, has the first place, and 5hereby is the basis of the other means

[EN195] between the decree of election and the end of the decree

[EN196] even if election is related to Christ the mediator, in whom all are elected to salvation and grace, nevertheless God elected us not as if we were elected pre-existently in him, but he elected us to be in him, and to be saved through him

[EN197] basis

[EN198] in him

[EN199] basis of election

[EN200] absolute decree

opposition was not in this case the mediaeval and humanistic axiom that man is the measure of all things, although it must be asked whether it, too, did not ultimately work itself out in the sense of this axiom. It must be recognised that at least in aim and tendency we have to do here with a genuine and necessary concern to take the common Reformation assertion that the basis of the election is to be found in Jesus Christ (as we are most impressively reminded in the utterances of the later Luther), and so to confirm it that, unlike a direction intended merely for pastoral understanding, it has to be reckoned with quite seriously from the theological standpoint. In this way an attempt was made to intercept the fatal glancing aside at an election which takes place behind and above Christ in the hiddenness of God. The direction was no longer to be construed merely as a prohibition. It was to be understood as a pointer to the real and ultimate truth of the matter, a truth which cannot be supplemented in any other quarter. Yet at this point the Lutheranism of the *Formula of Concord* obviously found itself in the dilemma of not being able to do more than to make mere assertions along these lines, or rather simply to negate the Calvinistic *decretum absolutum*[EN201] (which involved, of course, an abandonment of the 1525 Luther!). At a decisive point (*Sol. decl.* XI, 23) we find this statement: *Deus illo suo consilio, proposito et ordinatione ... omnes et singulas personas electorum (qui per Christum salvandi sunt) clementer praescivit, elegit et decrevit*[EN202]. It will be noted that *praescrivit*[EN203] is given the emphasis of precedence, and that *elegit*[EN204] and *descrevit*[EN205] must obviously be explained largely in the light of it. This shows us at once the direction in which it was intended to move (in the steps of the mediating theologians of the 9th century). It will be seen, however, that if the *electi*[EN206] are defined as those *qui per Christum salvandi sunt*[EN207], there has not been any true or genuine overthrowal of the Calvinistic conception of Christ as merely the *medium salutis*[EN208] or *executor decreti*[EN209]. So long as these terms were used, what advance was there at Kloster Bergen in 1577 upon the position which Dort showed itself determined to maintain in 1619? Was there here any real grounding of the election as such in Jesus Christ? This was clearly the question which rightly disturbed Lutheran theologians even after that great codification of Lutheran belief. Much of their further effort in this matter was devoted to its further elucidation. And whether (in pursuing this legitimate question) it did to any extent attain its object is the standard by which we must measure this activity. In what follows we will confine ourselves to J. Gerhard at the beginning and A. Quenstedt at the end of the "orthodox" period in Lutheran theology.

An outstanding characteristic of the orthodox Lutheran teaching on predestination is that in its initial stages the concept of predestination or election as such is usually replaced by a general heading under which it is introduced later. The common setting in which it is put by the Lutherans is a doctrine *De universali Dei misericordia et benefica erga omnes voluntate*[EN210] (as with J. Gerhard, *Loci theol.*, 1610f. VII, *cap.* 4), or, more briefly (as with Quenstedt, *Theol. did. pol.*, 1685, III, *cap.* 1). *De benevolentia Dei universali*[EN211]. There is a *catholicismus paternae miserationis*[EN212] (Quenstedt, *ib.*, *sect.* I, *th.* 9). Its subject is God the

---

[EN201] absolute decree
[EN202] God has mercifully foreknown, elected and decreed in that will of his, by his proposition and
   arrangement, each and every one of the elect (who is to be saved through Christ)
[EN203] 'foreknown'
[EN204] elected
[EN205] decreed
[EN206] elect
[EN207] those who are to be saved through Christ
[EN208] means of salvation
[EN209] executor of the decree
[EN210] Of the universal mercy of God and his good will toward all
[EN211] On the universal benevolence of God
[EN212] universality of the Father's mercy

Father, *non tamen excluso Filio et Spiritu Sancto, quorum Trium unus erga nos amor est*EN213 (*th.* 8). Its object is the whole of fallen humanity as such: *homines per lapsum miseri facti, illique in universum omnes, ne unico quidem excluso, nemine excepto*EN214 (*th.* 9). Its basis within the Godhead is the *interventio Filii Dei ... qui ab aeterno in arcano S.S. Trinitatis consilio ad perfectissimam salisfactionem ... vice et loco omnium hominum ... sese obtulit et spopondit*EN215 (*th.* 10). It is as such God's *voluntas antecedent*EN216 (*th.* 5). It is meant in all seriousness, i.e., it wills the salvation of men not in appearance only but with an ultimate sincerity and urgency (*th.* 12). It is not a mere wish, not *velleitas*EN217, not *voluntas inefficax*EN218, but *voluntas efficax, qua Deus salutem hominum ardentissime desideratam etiam efficere ac per media sufficientia et efficacia consequi et procurare serio intendit ... quantum in se est, omnes homines ex aequo vult salvi*EN219 (*th.* 6). It is not, of course, *absoluta*EN220 but *ordinata*EN221: *fundatur enim in Christo et determinatur ad finem et media, quibus illa accenditur*EN222 (*th.* 12). *Benignissima haec Dei voluntas primum salutis humanae principium*EN223 (*th.* 13). In the exposition of this basic doctrine appeal could be made to certain passages of Scripture; as 1 Tim. 2[4]: "God willeth that all men should be saved, and come unto the knowledge of the truth"; Rom. 11[32]: "For God hath shut up all unto disobedience, that he might have mercy upon all"; 2 Pet. 3[9]: "He does not will that any should perish, but that all should come to repentance." J. Gerhard (*cap.* 5) further enlarges it by laying down that all men are as such created in the divine image.

[071]

It is only on the ground of this basic doctrine that the Lutherans arrive at the doctrine of predestination properly speaking. By this time it has naturally been decided that the basis and essence of the divine election is not to be sought in any *propositum Dei absolutum*EN224. The will of God is wholly and utterly the will which in Jesus Christ is directed to the salvation of all men. Yet God elects whom He elects in view of the twofold fact present to His foreknowledge from all eternity—the fact of the work of Christ, and the fact of faith directed towards that work: *intuitu satisfactionis in Christo praestandae et per fidem acceptandae*EN225 (J. Gerhard, *cap.* 8, 148). The divine election corresponds exactly with the temporal event in which salvation is provided for men and appropriated by them: *Quae enim in tempore Deus agit, sunt manifestatio eorum quae ab aeterno agere decrevit; quod et quomodo Deus in tempore agit, illud et non aliud, illo et non alio modo ab aeterno agere decrevit*EN226. God's consideration of the work of

---

EN213 but not to the exclusion of the Son and the Holy Spirit, the three of whose love is one towards us

EN214 men made wretched through the fall, all those in the world, without exception, with not even one excluded

EN215 intervention of the Son of God ... who from eternity in the secret counsel of the most Holy Trinity offered and pledged himself as a most perfect satisfaction in the stead and place of all men

EN216 antecedent will

EN217 wish

EN218 inefficacious will

EN219 the efficacious will, by which God intends most fervently to bring about the desired salvation of men, and to continue it with sufficient and efficacious means, and to attend to it in earnest ... all that is in him wills all men equally to be saved

EN220 absolute

EN221 ordained

EN222 For his will was established in Christ and was determined for a goal and for the means by which it would be kindled

EN223 This most kind will of God is the first cause of the salvation of man

EN224 absolute decree of God

EN225 by knowledge of the satisfaction to be demonstrated in Christ and to be received by faith

EN226 For what God does in time is the manifestation of those things which he decreed in eternity to bring about; what and how God brings about in time – that and nothing else, in that way and in no other way – he decreed to bring about from eternity

Christ in time belongs, then, to the divine decree of election itself, so certain is it that that decree is identical with God's eternal resolution to provide salvation for man in that work (*ib.*, 151). But to the divine decree of election there belongs equally God's consideration of the faith in which man meets that work and in which he makes right use of it: the *intuitus fidei*EN227. For: *Christi meritum nemini prodest absque fide*EN228 (*ib.*, *cap.* 9, 161). It is in view of this twofold reality fulfilled in time that God elects from all eternity. We saw that God's *benevolentia*EN229 is indeed *universalis, stria* and *efficax*EN230, but it is not for that reason *absoluta*EN231. As God's *benevolentia*EN232 it is *ordinata*EN233. And the *ordinatio*EN234 in which God's *benevolentia*EN235 is made real and effective for all men is this—that in His answering of the question which men should profit by it, God keeps to the way which He Himself has appointed: the work of Christ, and the faith which meets that work, and in which it becomes profitable to this or that man. According to the Lutheran teaching, the elect from all eternity are those who in faith—by this is meant, of course, a serious and persevering faith (*ib.*, 176)—make a right and proper use of that work, according to the divine foreknowledge. In the characteristic expression of Quenstedt (*cap.* 2, *sect.* 2, *qu.* 4, *Thesis*) there is a *circulus electionis*EN236. God's eternal will to save all men is directed *in concreto*EN237 to those who are called to faith in Jesus Christ and who are obedient to this calling. To that extent it is an electing will. The more detailed statement (*cap.* 2, *sect.* 1) runs as follows. Concretely the gracious will of God to all men is the divine will as determined by the *meritum Christi*EN238 and its appropriation in faith. As such it is an electing will, distinguishing and separating within the totality of men (*th.* 9–11). But God's electing. His πρόθεσις EN239, is determined by His πρόγνωσις EN240, by His *praevisio individuorum finaliter creditorum*EN241 (*th.* 12). These individuals: *quicunque finaliter in Christum, mundi redemptorem credituri sunt, illi electi sunt ad vitam aeternam*EN242 (*th.* 13). The divine will in its election is directed, therefore, by the divine knowledge, and to that extent by the actuality of an object which is distinct from God. But this object is on the one side Christ, and on the other faith wrought by the Holy Spirit. It is still true, then, that in the words of Rom. 9¹⁶ "it is not of him that willeth nor of him that runneth, but of God that sheweth mercy" (*th.* 10). It is still true that we have to do with an eternal, specific, unalterable election of divine grace (*th.* 20). But we do not have to do with an absolute decree. For it is in the *meritum Christi praevisum et praedefinitum*EN243 which He Himself has established that God, its author, finds the good-pleasure in which He elects whom He wills (*sect.* 2, *qu.* 3). And His electing is partly determined by the consideration of the faith which He Himself gives man and in which the *meritum Christi* is appropriated by

[072]

EN227 knowledge of faith
EN228 without faith, the merit of Christ is of no benefit to anyone
EN229 kindness
EN230 universal, serious, and effective
EN231 absolute
EN232 kindness
EN233 ordered
EN234 ordination
EN235 kindness
EN236 circle of election
EN237 concretely
EN238 merit of Christ
EN239 foreordination
EN240 foreknowledge
EN241 foreknowledge of each person who would eventually believe
EN242 whoever eventually are to believe in Christ, the redeemer of the world, are elected to eternal life
EN243 the merit of Christ, foreseen and foreordained

man (*sect.* 2, *qu.* 4). In this way Quenstedt (*qu.* 4, *ekth.* 5) hopes to be able to avoid Pelagianism as well as "Absolutism."

We must recognise at once and unreservedly the seriousness of this effort to reach an understanding of the thought of election which at all points takes account of the ἐν αὐτῷ EN244 of Eph. 1⁴. The basic concern of the Lutheran teaching was to remove the useless blemish of an absolute and meaningless divine freedom behind and above the divine decree of salvation, a blemish which marred all Reformation teaching, and especially the, in this respect, far too orthodox predestinarian doctrine of the Reformed Church. Its aim was to make the reference to the primal decision of God a genuine christological reference. In the accomplishment of this task it was concerned just as basically with the establishment of the fact that the primal decision is really God's grace. Looking back at the predestinarian teaching of the *Formula of Concord*, we must say that in it the problem was at least taken up and advanced energetically. Looking away from it to the doctrine of the Synod of Dort, we are obliged to confess that it compares favourably with it. It does so in virtue of its initial concern for a Christian conception of this article of faith. We can only regret that on the Reformed side this teaching failed to give rise to any effort to make place for such a concern even if in very different fashion. It must always be a matter for surprise that the Reformed Church and Reformed theology so obstinately forbade any following of the Lutherans along this path, preferring to cling to the unsatisfactory and dangerous doctrinal forms of the earlier 16th century rather than to allow of the correction which had been so zealously and carefully made in Lutheranism. And if this is a matter for surprise, then there is certainly cause to regret that the Reformed school never reached the point of attempting what might perhaps have been a better correction. For it must be recognised in any case that the Lutheran solution for its part was not so satisfactory that its success was inevitable or even possible. There are, in fact, reasons which help to explain why the Reformed party, faced with the choice, could still believe that the doctrine of the *decretum absolutum* EN245 offered a relatively better safeguard for Reformed and Christian interests in this whole matter.

The first consideration arises at once in respect of the Lutheran point of departure. We, too, had to understand the doctrine of election at the very outset as the sum of the Gospel. It is the first and decisive expression, belonging to the doctrine of God as such, of the knowledge of the *benevolentia divina erga omnes homines* EN246. But it is one thing to interpret the doctrine in advance from this starting-point and quite another to try to deduce it in advance from this starting-point. And it was the latter which the older Lutherans obviously did. For with them is not that fine *benevolentia Dei universalis* EN247, that *catholicismus paternae miserationis* EN248, simply another general truth, another systematic principle which must be developed and carried through in the doctrine of predestination as such? And such being the case, we cannot but allow to the older Reformed and Calvinistic *decretum absolutum* EN249 at least the merit that it was designed to prevent any over-rash assumption that we can always know the will of God (theology's over-confident control of its subject). For it referred away even from the *paterna miseratio* EN250 of God to God Himself and to the freedom of the divine mercy. We are not overlooking the fact that the Lutherans found the *fundamentum* EN251 of this general redemptive will of God in Jesus Christ, in the self-offering of the Son of God for

[073]

EN244 in him
EN245 absolute decree
EN246 divine kindness towards all men
EN247 universal benevolence of God
EN248 universality of the Father's mercy
EN249 absolute decree
EN250 fatherly mercy
EN251 basis

man's salvation which was determined and made from all eternity in the bosom of the Trinity. But can we take this fact at its face value? Is it really a question of Jesus Christ, and not rather of the divine *benevolentia*[EN252] as such understood as a systematic principle? If in this basic doctrine it really is a question of Jesus Christ and of the eternal and temporal reality of His self-offering for man's salvation, then what place is there in the Lutheran presentation for the judicial character of this self-offering of the Son of God? If it is true that He came to seek and to save that which was lost, and that from all eternity He was destined and empowered to do so, then it is equally true that even in this activity foreordained from all eternity and fulfilled in time He is the One before whom the spirits divide, and that even in this capacity He is no less the One who fulfils the divine will and the divine *benevolentia*[EN253]. The question of the nature of this *benevolentia*[EN254], of this love of God for all men, is, of course, a question which is raised and answered in the reality of Jesus Christ. But the question must not be dissolved in this reality. There must not be any systematisation, or setting up of a principle. There must not be any delimitation by the assertion of the *benevolentia Dei universalis*[EN255] as an assertion which binds God in advance and thus anticipates and secretly controls the reality. The Gospel is the one thing which does not lend itself to be translated or transformed into such a principle. *Quantum in se est, omnes homines ex aequo vult salvi*[EN256]— that is the Gospel translated and transformed into a principle. Yet the Gospel does not permit itself to be translated or transformed even into a principle so excellent in itself as this one. For the Gospel is what it is in the divine-human person of Jesus Christ Himself. And this person does not permit Himself to be translated into a proposition. It is not our task to understand this person in the light of a Gospel abstractly formulated and presupposed. Our task is to understand the concrete Gospel in the light of this person. And this being the case, under the main heading—if there ought to be such a heading at all—the concept of the election in which the Gospel is revealed as person must be considered and prepared and grounded quite otherwise than was the case in the Lutheran constructions. When we have heard that basic doctrine of the Lutherans, there is nothing we expect less than to be told that there is still an election even within the *catholicismus paternae miserationis*[EN257]. Has not the general redemptive will of God already been described as *voluntas universalis, seria et efficax*?[EN258] How, then, can it be an electing will? Is it not bound in advance, and in itself, to its object, and therefore to the totality of men? Where, then, is its freedom? Where, then, is its character as free grace? The Lutherans answer that it is not *voluntas absoluta*[EN259] but *ordinata*[EN260]. That is correct. But when we say that it sets up an order, and itself adheres to that order, and deals with the totality of men within the sphere of that order, we have obviously hardly attained to, let alone exhausted, the concept of divine election, of a differentiation within the totality of men freely controlled and executed by God. The Lutherans, however, imagine that by saying this we actually do exhaust the concept of election as such. This is the great *quid pro quo*[EN261] of their predestinarian doctrine. If we inspect it closely, their teaching has nothing whatever to say about the fact that God elects. It says only that God has determined to actualise, and has actualised, His general redemptive purpose in

---

[EN252] kindness
[EN253] kindness
[EN254] kindness
[EN255] universal kindness of God
[EN256] All that is in him wills all men equally to be saved
[EN257] universality of the Father's mercy
[EN258] universal, earnest, and efficacious will
[EN259] the absolute will
[EN260] the ordered/ordained will
[EN261] something for something

such a form that in its operation it does necessarily give rise to a selection from amongst men. Naturally God knows about this selection from all eternity. He also affirms it by fulfilling His purpose in this particular form. But He affirms it only secondarily, and the fact that He affirms it does not mean that it is His selection in the strict sense of the word. This construction excludes the initiative of a free divine election. And at this point, in spite of all other differences, in spite of its intended and avowed anti-Pelagianism, the Lutheran teaching occupies common ground with the Arminian doctrine rejected at Dort. For this reason, and quite decisively, it can never be acceptable to Calvinists. The divine salvation revealed in Jesus Christ is the place where the basis of the election is to be found. But according to the Lutheran construction this means that the decree of election merges into the decree of salvation and there disappears. What apparently remains, but only apparently, is the idea of the divine foreknowledge: that everything in time is fulfilled in accordance with the eternal redemptive decree by which God gives specific form to His general redemptive will. It is in this way (properly speaking, without any initiative on the part of God) that there arises the question of a selection. From all eternity God has had the *intuitus meriti Christi*[EN262] and the *intuitus fidei*[EN263]. On the basis of this twofold *intuitus*[EN264] He wills from all eternity the salvation of those who present this twofold aspect: that in faith the *meritum Christi*[EN265] avails for them, and that in faith they allow the *meritum Christi* to avail for them. This will of His is the divine election of such men. Between the general benevolence of God towards all on the one hand, and, on the other the *ordinatio*[EN266] by which it is joined with the work of Christ and with faith, it is useless to ask what is the true meaning of the will of God by which He wills to save some. At all events, that will cannot be a free and electing will which differentiates between men. Once we have denied the *decretum absolutum*[EN267], and substituted for it that *catholicismus paternae miserationis*[EN268], we can no longer attribute to God the capacity for such a will. In Lutheran teaching the fact that God elects can mean no more and no less than that God wills and affirms in advance that which He knows will take place within the sphere of His ordained redemptive will. But obviously this is not a free electing on the part of God. Of course the Lutherans did maintain most emphatically that not merely the foreseen work of Christ but also the *praevisa fides*[EN269] in which this work is made available and effective to man must be derived wholly and utterly from the free decision and the personal work of God. But at this point, especially in the concept of *praevisa fides*[EN270], a dangerous dilemma was bound to arise. On the one hand, we may take in all seriousness this deriving of *praevisa fides*[EN271] from the grace of the Holy Spirit and therefore from the will of God. In this case a free electing of God will emerge as the foundation of the whole process. It will be decided that it was altogether of God that in faith the work of Christ availed for some men and that in faith they allowed it to avail for them. We shall then have to understand such men as truly elected by God and not as self-elected to that status. But this being the case, how can we avoid the Calvinistic *decretum absolutum*[EN272], as originally intended? On the other hand, we may have doubts about the freedom of the grace of the Holy Spirit, supposing that the gift of

[074]

EN262 knowledge of the merit of Christ
EN263 knowledge of faith
EN264 knowledge
EN265 merit of Christ
EN266 ordination
EN267 absolute decree
EN268 universality of the Father's mercy
EN269 foreseen faith
EN270 foreseen faith
EN271 foreseen faith
EN272 absolute decree

faith may be conditioned and circumscribed on the human side, at least so far as the lack of opposition to it is concerned. In this case we shall avoid "Absolutism," but what about Pelagianism? The Lutherans did not openly maintain any such circumscribing or conditioning. On the contrary, they rejected it as a scholastic and papistical heresy (Quenstedt, *sect.* 2, *qu.* 4, *antith.* II). But to say that they did not intend to maintain it was the very last thing they could really say in this context. How could they help maintaining it when they would not state the opposite view, that of the unconditioned nature of the divine will over against man, and when they intended by that refusal to steer clear of "Absolutism." The deduction may not be explicit and it may be involuntary, but is it not inevitable that God knows from all eternity that in certain men there will not be any opposition, and that because He knows these men He elects them? The deduction was denied, but it could hardly be evaded, and it was on account of this undeclared deduction that the Calvinists decisively rejected the tenet of *praevisa fides*^{EN273}, and with it the whole Lutheran doctrine of predestination. As they saw it, it is at this decisive point in the whole relationship of God with man that the complete freedom of grace should always be maintained. They thought it better to cling to the *decretum absolutum*^{EN274} than in attempting to avoid it to enter on a path which seemed as though it must ultimately endanger the basic interest of the Reformation. Why was it, they asked, that   [075] at this decisive point the Lutherans allowed the will of God to be conditioned by the knowledge or prescience of God, why was it that they thought it necessary to introduce the concept of *praevisa fides*^{EN275}, if they had no wish to compromise this basic interest, the defence of the free grace of God against every form of Pelagianism? Since the Lutherans could not clearly explain this to the Reformed school, the result was that the latter determined to choose Charybdis rather than Scylla, holding fast by the *decretum absolutum*^{EN276}. And the further result was that the Lutheran teaching did not become the effective stimulus which in virtue of its intention it well deserved to be. It cannot be maintained that there was no foundation for the mistrust with which the Reformed party persisted in their views as against the Lutheran effort, or, indeed, for the defiance with which they clung to the opposing solution of the older Reformation theology. The Lutheran doctrine of predestination was, in fact, a doubtful experiment. The purity of its intention was compromised at least by the fact that the whole of Lutheran orthodoxy thought it justifiable to appropriate the Jesuit doctrine of the divine *scientia media*^{EN277}. It did this partly for the express reason that that doctrine could be of service in combating the Calvinistic *decretum absolutum*^{EN278}, and partly and more positively in order that it might explain the decisive point in Lutheran teaching, the concept of *fides praevisa*^{EN279}. Yet when the Jesuit doctrine deals with the specific form of the divine foreknowledge in which it has as its object the free acts of the creature as such, it does so in a way which allows those acts virtually to precede the decision of the divine will, and thus to limit and determine the divine will itself. If there was any possibility or intention of the divine foreknowledge or its specific object the *fides praevisa*^{EN280} being understood in this way, then it was indeed all up with the basic interest of the Reformation. The Lutheran doctrine could very well become the entrance-gate for a new Pelagianism. And it cannot be denied that the heritage of orthodox Lutheranism on this side—a heritage which dates from as early as Melanchthon—did later work itself out in this direction.

---

^{EN273} foreseen faith
^{EN274} absolute decree
^{EN275} foreseen faith
^{EN276} absolute decree
^{EN277} middle knowledge
^{EN278} absolute decree
^{EN279} foreseen faith
^{EN280} foreseen faith

On the other hand, we must not conceal the fact that some risk had to be taken to improve on the older Reformation solution. We must adopt at least the intention of the Lutheran doctrine in so far as it aimed to establish the christological basis of the election. We must not identify this basis quite so rashly or systematically with the general redemptive will of God. Nor must we reduce God's will concerning individuals to a mere ratification of what He knows from all eternity concerning their salvation in Christ and their faith. On behalf of a truly electing and free will of God we must claim boldly the place maintained for it in the Reformed doctrine of the *decretum absolutum*[EN281]. The assertion of the christological basis should not lead to an ultimate denial of the election as such and therefore of the free grace of God. It must be shown, then, that it is Jesus Christ Himself who occupies this place. It must be shown that in Him we have to do not only with very man but with very God. It must be shown that in Him we have to do not only with elected man but with the electing, the truly and freely electing God. This is the point which must be made clear if in accordance with the correct intention of the Lutherans we are to find in the revealed decree of salvation as such the divine decree of election. The most serious objection to the Lutheran doctrine is that ultimately it does not succeed in making this point clear, any more than does the Calvinistic doctrine. It deduced the election from the basic concept of the *paterna miseratio*[EN282]. True, it did maintain that the eternal self-offering of the Son of God was the basis of this divine attitude. But it hesitated to understand this self-offering of the Son of God as the act of eternal election. It failed to point to the person of the Son, Jesus Christ, as the Subject of that act. If it had done this, it would have overcome the Reformed doctrine of the *decretum absolutum*[EN283] and really improved on the older Reformation solution. And it could then have represented that act quite genuinely as election, the free election of God, the decision of the gracious and merciful Judge, Jesus Christ. In this way it would not of itself have approached so closely the Scylla of Pelagianism. When we stand unequivocally and definitively before Jesus Christ, when we stand before the electing God, all longings of this kind are at an end.

[076]

The historical survey leads us, then, to the following conclusion. We found previously that the doctrine of election must not begin *in abstracto*[EN284] either with the concept of an electing God or with that of elected man. It must begin concretely with the acknowledgment of Jesus Christ as both the electing God and elected man. But, generally speaking, this finding is not really an innovation. It is the confirmation and readoption of something which Reformation theology has always said, and said most emphatically, in this connexion. Unfortunately, it did not say it in a way which stamped it as a tenet for serious theological study rather than a purely pastoral direction. Notwithstanding the Reformation statements, then, there has always lurked in the background the doctrine of a God who elects *in abstracto*[EN285]. The Arminians and Lutherans saw the blemish and attempted to remove it. But what happened was that the concept of the election as such was thereby attacked and set aside. And the result was a fresh approximation to the doctrine of man elected *in abstracto*[EN286], or of man's electing of God. This was palpably the case with the Arminians and implicitly with the Lutherans. The historical survey clearly reveals to us again our own task. We must adopt the Reformation thesis. But we must ground and formulate it in such a way that on both sides it is treated with the seriousness which it deserves. We must do so in such a way that when we

---

[EN281] absolute decree
[EN282] fatherly mercy
[EN283] absolute decree
[EN284] in the abstract
[EN285] in the abstract
[EN286] in the abstract

utter the name of Jesus Christ we really do speak the first and final word not only about the electing God but also about elected man.

3. THE PLACE OF THE DOCTRINE IN DOGMATICS

It is not at all self-evident that the doctrine of election should occupy in dogmatic enquiry the place here accorded to it. We have given it precedence over all the other individual tenets of the Christian faith relating to the work of God, and placed it in the context of the doctrine of God itself. As far as I know, no previous dogmatician has adopted such a course. We must ask then: Is it really the case that the doctrine of election forms a part of the definition of the Subject of all Christian doctrine? May we and must we deal with it before we deal even with the creation of the world and of man, or before we deal with the work of reconciliation and the end of that work in eternal redemption?

We answer this question affirmatively when we maintain of God that in Himself, in the primal and basic decision in which He wills to be and actually is God, in the mystery of what takes place from and to all eternity within Himself, within His triune being, God is none other than the One who in His Son or Word elects Himself, and in and with Himself elects His people. In so far as God not only is love, but loves, in the act of love which determines His whole being God elects. And in so far as this act of love is an election, it is at the same time and as such the act of His freedom. There can be no subsequent knowledge of God, whether from His revelation or from His work as disclosed in that revelation, which is not as such knowledge of this election. There can he no Christian truth which does not from the very first contain within itself as its basis the fact that from and to all eternity God is the electing God. There can be no tenet of Christian doctrine which if it is to be a Christian tenet does not necessarily reflect both in form and content this divine electing—the eternal electing in which and in virtue of which God does not will to be God, and is not God, apart from those who are His, apart from His people. Because this is the case, the doctrine of election occupies a place at the head of all other Christian dogmas. And it belongs to the doctrine of God Himself because God Himself does not will to be God, and is not God, except as the One who elects. There is no height or depth in which God can be God in any other way. We have not perceived or understood aright the Subject of all Christian doctrine if in our doctrine of God there is lacking the moment which is the specific content of the doctrine of election.

[077]

It was and is for these reasons that we introduced the matter at this point, and this point particularly. But this involves us in an innovation for which we must give account in the face of dogmatic tradition. Tradition itself, of course, is not quite so unanimous in this matter as it was for the most part in relation to the doctrine of the Trinity. But it is at least unanimous to this degree, that all the arrangements attempted differ from that planned and carried out in the present work. For this reason it is just and necessary that we should at least

81

mention these other arrangements. By defining our attitude towards them from the standpoint of the considerations we have in mind, we shall defend our own arrangement from any taint of arbitrariness.

1. At a first glance it might seem as though we are in agreement with, or approximate very closely to, the arrangement which became to some extent classical in the Reformed orthodoxy of the 17th century. According to that scheme, the doctrine of predestination followed closely upon the doctrine of God, preceding directly the doctrine of creation and the whole remaining content of confession and dogmatics.

We find this arrangement in the *Irish Articles of Religion* (1615) and the *Westminster Confession* (1647). Amongst dogmaticians we find it in Polanus, Wolleb, Wendelin, H. Alting, A. Heidanus, F. Burmann, F. Turrettini, P. van Mastricht, S. van Til and others. It is in the light of this striking branch of the Reformed tradition, especially as concerns the dogmaticians, that in the modern period the doctrine of predestination has often been called the "central dogma" of Reformed theology. Even some of the older Reformed writers themselves did occasionally speak of it in that way. In this connexion we must draw attention to the fact that the arrangement was not that of Zwingli, or Bullinger, or even Calvin himself. Nor was it the arrangement followed by most of the Reformed confessions. And not quite all the Reformed dogmaticians of the 17th century adopted it. In any case there can be no historical justifica-

[078] tion for taking the concept "central dogma" to mean that the doctrine of predestination was for the older Reformed theologians a kind of speculative key—a basic tenet from which they could deduce all other dogmas. Not even the famous schema of T. Beza (cf. Heppe. *Dogm. d. ev. ref. Kirche*, ed. 1935, 119) was intended in such a sense. Its aim was rather (rightly or wrongly) to show the systematic interconnexion of all other dogmas with that of predestination in the then popular graphic fashion. There was no question of making the latter doctrine a derivative principle for all the rest. And even in the *Westminster Confession* and the theologians mentioned, it was not a matter of deducing all dogmatics from the doctrine of predestination. They did bring the doctrine into direct relationship with the doctrine of God. They placed it at the head of all other doctrines. And this meant, of course, but meant only, that in it they found the first and decisive word which we have to receive and proclaim in respect of the will of God in relation to creation; the word of which we have always to take account in everything that follows. If we read their expositions connectedly we are more likely to get the impression that from the standpoint of its systematic range and importance they gave to the doctrine too little consideration rather than too much.

Our present procedure, however, cannot be identified simply with that followed in this branch of the Reformed tradition. One reason for this is that according to that tradition the main confessional and and dogmatic tenet was not strictly speaking the doctrine of election. It was rather the tenet which took precedence over that of the election—the tenet of the decrees of God in general.

Decretum Dei est interna voluntatis divinae actio, qua de iis, quae in tempore fieri debebant, ab aeterno liberrime et certissime statuit[EN287] (Wolleb, *Chr. Theol. comp.*, 1626, I, 3, 3). It was the

---

[EN287] The decree of God is that internal action of the divine will by which he establishes most freely and most definitely from eternity concerning those things which are to come to pass in time

assertion of this general divine decree which formed the starting-point once the doctrine of God had been completed. And it was explained that the purpose of God in this general *decretum*^{EN288} was to set forth the glory of His power, wisdom and goodness. Only within the context of this general decree could there be any mention of the *speciale decretum*^{EN289}, the purpose of which was defined as the same self-glorification of God *in creaturis rationalibus eligendis aut reprobandis*^{EN290}. And even here the predestination of angels had the precedence over that of men (*ib.*, I, 4, 1 f.). After the model of Thomas Aquinas the doctrine of election was understood as *pars providentiae*^{EN291}. It is a sign of the sure instinct of these theologians that they did not follow out the systematic logic of this view to the point of beginning with the doctrine of providence as such. Consistently and explicitly they introduced the doctrine, of providence only in the context of that of creation. Even so, in the doctrine *De decretis in genere* the doctrine of providence had already been anticipated *in nuce*^{EN292}, and it was under this specific aspect, the absolute world-governance of God, that the doctrine of predestination arose as the specific doctrine of God's purposes with respect to the salvation of men.

We have already stated the reasons why we cannot adopt this line of approach. It takes God in His general relationship with the world as its first datum and understands His electing as one function in this general relationship. As against that, we are commanded by the Bible and our Christian profession to take and to understand first the living God in His electing, in the specific relationship which He has established with man in Jesus Christ. Only from this point can we go on to consider His general relationship with the world and His *decretum generale*^{EN293}. A further difference between us is that with these theologians, so far as I can see, the doctrine of election was never [079] regarded or treated as an integral part of the doctrine of God.

There is a link here with the particular conception of the fathers and Scholastics frequently touched on in the first part of our doctrine of God—a conception now appropriated afresh by the older Protestant orthodoxy. According to this conception God is everything in the way of aseity, simplicity, immutability, infinity, etc., but He is not the living God, that is to say, He is not the God who lives in concrete decision. God lives in this sense only figuratively. It is not something which belongs to His proper and essential life, but only to His relationship with the world. Basically, then, it may only be "ascribed" to Him, while it is believed that His true being and likewise His true Godhead are to be sought in the impassibility which is above and behind His living activity within the universe. It was illogical, but most fortunate, that theologians still dared to speak not only of the *opera Dei ad extra externa*^{EN294} but also, with reference to the divine decrees, of the *opera Dei ad extra interna*^{EN295}. They could speak, then, of the concrete forms and directions and aims of the divine will and the divine being. They could define the concept of the decree as *interna voluntatis divinae actio*^{EN296}, in spite of the fact that God, as *ens simplex et infinitum*^{EN297}, was not properly or by definition capable of

---

EN288 decree
EN289 special decree
EN290 in rational creatures to be elected or rejected
EN291 part of providence
EN292 in germ
EN293 general decree
EN294 external works of God outside of himself
EN295 internal works of God outside of himself
EN296 internal action of the divine will
EN297 simple and infinite being

such *opera ad extra interna*[EN298], of such *interna actio*[EN299]. It was surprising enough that this being should be capable of any such *opera ad extra*[EN300] at all. But how could it be capable of such a concrete decision within itself? It was the Bible which plainly enforced the latter concession not less than the former. But what these theologians did not dare to do was this. From the fact that God is the living God, that He is the living God inwardly as well as outwardly, a quality expressed and attested in concrete decision, they did not dare to deduce the further fact that clearly God does not exist otherwise, and that He does not will to be understood otherwise, than in the concreteness of life, in the determination of His will, which is as such a determination of His being. Strangely enough, they did not feel driven to make such a deduction even by their doctrine of the Trinity. They spoke of the three persons, of their inter-relationship, of their common work *ad extra*[EN301], without ever realising the implications of the fact that this triune being does not exist and cannot be known as a being which rests or moves purely within itself. God is not *in abstracto*[EN302] Father, Son and Holy Ghost, the triune God. He is so with a definite purpose and reference; in virtue of the love and freedom in which in the bosom of His triune being He has foreordained Himself from and to all eternity. And when we treat of the doctrine of election, we have to do with this determination of His will, and *eo ipso*[EN303] of His being and all His perfections. For how can we speak of the being of God without at once speaking of this *interna actio*[EN304] of His being, i.e., the election? And how can we speak of the election without speaking of the concrete life of the very being of God? It is this unity which we would honour by thinking and treating of the doctrine of election as a constituent part of the doctrine of God. Yet at this point even the representatives of the Reformed tradition now under consideration put asunder what ought not to be put asunder—to the detriment of the doctrine of God, and to the detriment of the doctrine of election. For in the case of the doctrine of the being of God the result of this separation was to confirm the fatal picture of a God not living in Himself. And in the case of the doctrine of election there resulted a fatal forgetfulness of the fact that the task of this doctrine is to speak of the election whose Subject is the person of God Himself.

[080] Our intention, then, is to recapture a concern which underlay this particular Reformed tradition. With the tradition, we acknowledge the importance of the doctrine of predestination, not as a derivative principle for all that follows, not as a basic tenet, of which all the rest is only interpretation—we are dealing with much more than a development of the thought of election when we treat later of creation, reconciliation and redemption—but as the Word which together with the revealed and eternal being of God we must accept as the determination of the decision in which God is God. To do justice to this concern we must follow up the two lines indicated, but we must do so far more radically than was the case in this very important Reformed tradition. To that extent, even in relation to this tradition, we shall find ourselves on a path which is characteristically different.

2. All the other methods of arrangement which may now be mentioned have

---

EN298 internal works outside of himself
EN299 internal action
EN300 works outside of himself
EN301 outside of himself
EN302 in the abstract
EN303 by definition
EN304 internal action

one feature in common. As against the Reformed scheme already referred to, they speak first of creation and providence, and only then, in greater or lesser proximity, of the election. It is plain that with these arrangements we depart increasingly from the order which we ourselves believe to be correct. It will be useful, however, to consider in detail how things worked out in such cases. At the outset, we must notice a small but interesting group in which the Christology followed directly upon the doctrine of God, being succeeded by creation and then predestination.

To this class there belongs Zwingli in his *Fidei ratio* (1530). With him the doctrine of election (III) forms the crown and completion of the doctrine of providence (II). This in turn is preceded by the Christology, which is included in the doctrine of God and of the Trinity (I). Among the older Lutherans, L. Hutterus (*Comp. Loc. theol.*, 1610) and J. Gerhard (*Loci theol.*, 1610 f.) belong to the same group. The latter in particular brings out remarkably well the direct sequence God-Christ-providence-predestination. In the case of Hutterus, the arrangement betrays the influence of another tradition which we have yet to mention, for between the doctrines of creation and predestination he has interjected those of sin, the Law, the Gospel and justification. Finally, one of the Reformed Confessions is to be found in this class, the *Consensus Bremensis* (1595), which introduced the polemical articles against Lutheranism in the same sequence, Christ-providence-election (-sacraments).

If we could allow that this arrangement had been determined by some objective consideration, then, as in the case of the classical Reformed sequence, we should have to see in it the correct insight that the work of God (the work of all works!) is not creation, but that which precedes creation both eternally and in effect temporally, the incarnate Word of God, Christ. We ourselves attempted to do justice to this truth by treating the doctrine of the incarnation even earlier, as the central part of the doctrine of the Word of God which introduces all dogmatics. But we must repeat that Christology is more than the doctrine of the incarnation or person of Christ. It is also the doctrine of the work of Christ, His humiliation, His exaltation, His threefold office. And as such it forms the presupposition and substance of our whole doctrine of reconciliation and faith, of justification and sanctification, of the Church and the sacraments. To that extent those who would introduce their Christology at [081] this point might have showed greater perspicacity in their thinking. It is obvious that the doctrine must also be asserted in the place reverently enough allotted to it in this second form of arrangement, i.e., in direct connexion with the doctrine of God and therefore with that of creation. But it can be asserted here only in the form of the doctrine of election, which, if we comprehend it aright, must from its very roots be thought of and developed christologically. Those who advocated this arrangement, however, allowed the Christology to displace the doctrine of election, instead of filling it out and giving it form. The precedence given to Christology might have been justified and illuminating in its effects if the doctrine of election had been grounded upon it and the transition to the doctrine of creation and providence made in that way. But its advocates did not do that. With them the doctrine of election seems to be co-ordinated with that of creation and providence, and even subordinated to it, according to the well-known Thomistic *schema*. In this decisive relationship the precedence given to Christology was thus rendered ineffective. For this reason, although the arrangement is interesting in itself, it is not one which we are tempted to follow.

In view of the fact that the arrangement was never applied effectively, it is probable that its adoption was not based upon any material consideration, but solely upon a regard for the teaching of the early Church, i.e., the Niceno-Chalcedonian sequence. The main intention was to bring out the ecumenical orthodoxy of Protestant doctrine. That is no doubt an interesting consideration. But materially the arrangement was very unsatisfactory and its exponents did not ground or apply it in a very illuminating way. It might surely have been turned to much better account.

3. The specific characteristic of all remaining arrangements is that now the election of grace is quite clearly detached from the doctrine of God and treated after the doctrine of creation and even after that of sin. The result is that it is detached equally clearly from the doctrine of providence, and instead brought into direct connexion with the doctrine of reconciliation. To this doctrine it is in some sort the key, and at every point in its discussion it has to be taken into account. We have this arrangement in its original and basic form when predestination is dealt with quite simply within the context of the doctrine of the Church.

At this point we must again mention Zwingli's *Fidei ratio*, for Zwingli re-introduced the election when he came (VI) to speak of the Church, i.e., of the Church of true believers concealed in the Church visible and as such known only to God and to itself. According to Zwingli, the Church in this most inward sense is identical with the totality of the *electi, qui Dei voluntate destinati sunt ad vitam aeternam*[EN305]. This view is chiefly important because it was also that of the younger Calvin. Thus in the first edition of the *Institutio* (1536), which was openly modelled on the *schema* of Luther's *Smaller Catechism*, the election of grace appeared in the second chapter: *De fide*[EN306], and it came in there in the discussion of the fourth article of the Creed (according to Calvin's reckoning): *Credo ecclesiam*[EN307]. According to Calvin this *ecclesia sancta et catholica*[EN308] of faith is identical with the *universus electorum numerus, sive angeli sint, sive homines, ex hominibus; sive mortui sive adhuc vivant, ex viventibus: quibuscumque in terris agant aut ubivis gentium dispersi sint*[EN309]. It is so because it is undoubtedly identical with the Pauline *ordo misericordiae Dei*[EN310] (Rom. 8[30]): "Whom he did predestinate, them he also called: and whom he called, them he also justified: and whom he justified, them he also glorified." Where there are the called and justified and glorified—and the place where they are is, in fact, the Church—there God proclaims (*declarat*) His eternal election, in which He foreordained them even before they were born. Already, then, Calvin declares quite

[082]

[EN305] the elect, who are destined by the will of God to eternal life
[EN306] On Faith
[EN307] I believe in the Church
[EN308] holy and catholic Church
[EN309] universal number of the elect, be they angels or men from mankind; be they dead or still alive from the living, in whatever lands they may be, or wherever among the nations they are dispersed
[EN310] order of the mercy of God

expressly that this is not a question of the *una illa et incommutabilis Dei providentia*[EN311], but of the basic determination of the existence of those who may be known—at any rate by certain signs—as the children of God, in that they are impelled by the Spirit of God along this course from *vocatio*[EN312] to *glorificatio*[EN313]. We must take account of the fact that within the visible Church there are also the non-elect, those who belong to this place only in appearance. And this is a warning to us to be circumspect. But it should not prevent us from hoping the best for everyone. Above all, it should not prevent us from holding to the unity of election, faith, and the true Church, which is always true and valid. Calvin has expressed in unforgettable terms the Christian assurance which has its basis in this unity: *Cum autem ecclesia sit populus electorum Dei, fieri non potest, ut qui vere eius sunt membra tandem pereant, aut malo exitio perdantur. Nititur enim eorum salus tam certis solidisque fulcris, ut, etiamsi tota orbis machina labefactetur, concidere ipsa et corruere non possit. Primum, stat cum Dei electione, nec nisi cum aeterna illa sapientia variare aut deficere potest. Titubare ergo et fluctuari, cadere etiam possunt, sed non colliduntur, quia Dominus supponit manum suam; id est quod ait Paulus* (Rom. 11[29]): *sine poenitentia esse dona et vocationem Dei. Deinde, quos Dominus elegit, eos Christo filio suo in fidem ac custodiam tradidit, ut neminem ex illis perderet, sed resuscitaret omnes in novissimo die* (Jn. 6[39]). *Sub tam bono custode et errare et labi possunt, perdi certe non possunt*[EN314]. In the *Instruction et confession de foi* of 1537 (the first form of his *Catechism*), and also in the later drafts of the *Institutio*, Calvin abandoned this arrangement in favour of others which we shall consider later. In the final (1542) form of the *Catechism*, however, he did return to it. But now the Lutheran arrangement as a whole had been replaced by one which was more consistent with the Calvinistic conception, for faith was put first and the Law second. Even here, however, predestination appeared in the context of an exposition of the 4th (or 3rd) article of the Creed: *Qu'est ce que l'Eglise catholique? C'est la compagnie des fidèles, que Dieu a ordonné et éleu à la vie éternelle*[EN315]. Rom. 8[30] was again quoted and expounded, and it was again stated that there is also a visible Church of God which may be known by certain marks or notes. But the Church *proprement parlé*[EN316], the Church in which we believe, is the *compagnie de ceux, que Dieu a eleu pour les sauver: laquelle ne se peut pas pleinement voir à l'œil*[EN317]. There is an echo of this teaching in *Qu.* 54 of the *Heidelberg Catechism* (the only place in this document, apart from *Qu.* 52, in which the doctrine of election is expressly dealt with): "What dost thou believe concerning the Holy Catholic Church? Answer: That out of the whole human race, from the beginning to the end of the world, the Son of God, by His Spirit and Word, gathers, defends, and preserves for Himself unto everlasting life, a chosen communion in the unity of the true

---

[EN311] that one unchangeable providence of God
[EN312] calling
[EN313] glorification
[EN314] But since the church is the people of the elect of God, it cannot be that those who are truly his could eventually perish, or be destroyed in the horror of death. For their salvation rests upon sure and solid foundations, such that even if the whole mechanism of the world were to collapse, they could not fall or sink with it. First, it stands with God's election, and cannot change or suffer except by his eternal wisdom. So they can totter or waver – and even fall – but they cannot be bruised, because God has placed his hand under them. That is what Paul says (Rom 11.29): 'The gifts and call of God are irrevocable'. Then, those whom the Lord has chosen, those whom he has handed over to Christ his Son in trust for safekeeping, so that he might lose none of them, but raise them all up on the last day (John 6.39). In such good keeping they may wander or stumble, but they certainly cannot be lost
[EN315] What is the Catholic Church? It is the company of the faithful, which God has ordained and elected to eternal life
[EN316] strictly speaking
[EN317] company of those whom God has elected to salvation; that company cannot fully be seen by the eye

faith; and that I am, and forever shall remain, a living member of the same." At a more distant remove, this conception seems most surprisingly to have engaged and satisfied the older Melanchthon. At any rate in the final edition of the *Loci* (1559, and departing from the 1521 scheme) he let the article on predestination follow immediately that on the Church. And even if after his manner he softened the contours, and under the heading *praedestinatio*EN318 spoke in effect only of *vocatio*EN319, to which we must and ought to restrict ourselves in matters of the election, yet it does emerge to some extent that he, too, would base both belief in the Church and the Church itself on the fact that in reality it is the *ecclesia electorum semper mansura, quam Deus mirabiliter etiam in hac vita servat, defendit et gubernat*EN320. It may be said, then, that there can be no radical development of the doctrine of the Church which does not at least introduce more or less definitely the concept of election.

[083]

In favour of this third arrangement we certainly can and should say this. It is marked out from all others by its direct relationship with the Bible. As we stated in our own introductory observations, in the Bible the concept of election stands decidedly in a direct and indissoluble union with that of the people of God, the people which is called Israel in the Old Testament and the Church in the New. The divine election is the election of and to this people. All the consequences of this election as they concern the relationship between God and man, indeed the relationship itself and as such, are worked out within the framework of the life of this people which is twofold but one and the same. The connexion between the election and the Church is both close and comprehensive, and for this reason constitutive for the whole of Christian doctrine. But because this is so, it is advisable, at any rate when we are attempting a coherent understanding of the whole of Christian doctrine, to consider the election, not when we treat directly and specifically of the Church, but much earlier, when our theme is God Himself as the Creator, Lord and Ruler of this people. It is obvious that before the *populus electus*EN321 there comes the *Deus elector*EN322. Before the assurance of election, described so finely by Calvin and proper to the true Church or the true humanity gathered into the body of Christ, there stand the mercy and righteousness of the true God who has created and who preserves this true humanity as such, and in whom its assurance has both its ground and Subject. There is no such thing as an assurance of faith apart from the electing God. Assurance of faith is only in the knowledge of the electing God. And it is this fact which at the very least this conception can only too easily obscure.

Self-evidently, this was not Calvin's own intention. But something of it does appear in the rather jejune presentation of Melanchthon. It seems there as if the concept of election is ultimately only a kind of reflection of the comfort which we may have in faith. It seems as if it

---

EN318 predestination
EN319 calling
EN320 the church of the elect, that will always remain, which God wonderfully preserves, defends and governs even in this life
EN321 elect people
EN322 electing God

is enough to give to the *ecclesia senescens*[EN323] "in these last and tragic days" the assurance that in the last resort it will always be preserved and sustained by God Himself. The other aspect, that of His free grace God has foreordained it from all eternity to that which it possesses, and that the claim which He has upon it corresponds to this fact, in a word, the transcendence of the electing God in and over His Church—all this remains strangely in the background. When we realise the tenuous nature of Melanchthon's perception of the relationship between predestination and the Church, we shall readily understand why it was that Calvin for his part was impelled in the meantime to move forward to a more comprehensive consideration of the question. We shall also understand why this later consideration could subse-quently be given an even more radical turn by the Reformed school (as described under the first heading).

[084]

If, in our later treatment of the doctrine of the Church, we are to stand on the firm ground which is none other than the Church's eternal divine election, and if we are to do full justice to the aim and intention of this third arrangement, then we must begin our consideration of the divine election at a much earlier point, in the doctrine of God Himself as the Lord and foundation of the Church.

4. Three other arrangements have still to be mentioned. They have this in common, that in different ways they all seek to present predestination as the principle and key to the whole doctrine of reconciliation, or soteriology. This was naturally the opinion of those who related predestination more particularly to the Church as the place where atonement between God and man is actualised. But, of course, there could be many ways of bringing this out. A first possibility was to let predestination follow immediately after Christology. From this point one could then proceed to the work of the Holy Spirit both in individual believers and in the Church as such.

This was the method chosen by Calvin in the first draft of his *Catechism* (1537), and later by Peter Martyr in his *Loci communes* (1576). According to this presentation the doctrine of election brings us, as it were, to the climax of that activity which begins with the gracious God and is completed in sinful man. In it we look backwards from God's electing and man's election to Christ Himself, the basis of the salvation which God has wrought. And in it we look forward to the status of the Christian and to the Church where this salvation is applied to and avails for us. I am aware of only one later presentation in which this conception recurs—the dogmatics of a later disciple of Coccejus, Hermann Witsius, *De oeconomia foedorum* (1693). In the second book of this work Witsius develops the doctrine of the divine origin and the person and work of Christ. In the third he then deals with the doctrine of the economy of personal salvation under the title *De foedere Dei cum electis*. This is a more extended and detailed treatment of the concepts of Rom. 8^{30} and therefore of the election.

5. A second possibility within the sphere of this particular outlook is that of either directly or indirectly conjoining the doctrine of election with that of sin. In this case it will be given precedence over Christology as well as soteriology, occupying the same position in relation to the full doctrine of reconciliation as

---

[EN323] aging church

in the arrangement mentioned under (1) it does in relation to dogmatics as a whole.

Here, again, we must first mention Calvin, this time as the author of the basic text of the *Conf. Gallicana* (1559). The order in this confession became a standard and model for a whole series of Reformed statements: for the *Conf. Scotica* (1560), which was substantially the work of John Knox, and which brought together the doctrines of election and of Christ in the original manner already indicated; for the *Conf. Belgica* (1561); for H. Bullinger's *Conf. Helv. post.* (1562); for the confession of the Markgraf Ernst Friedrich von Baden-Durlach usually known as the *Staffort Book* (1599); and also for the *Waldensian Confession* of 1655. [085] Amongst the Reformed dogmatics the *Leidener Synopsis pur. Theol.* (1642) belongs to this group, although in this case the doctrine of sin was followed by that of the Law and the Gospel and of the relationship between the Old and the New Testament, this doctrine being given the precedence over that of election. Also under this heading we must put the *Loci communes* of Anton Walāus (1640), who, without any explanation, without any attempt even to show its reasonableness or value, adopted a highly original and capricious order. From the doctrine of sin he proceeded at once to that of providence, and only then (it is almost incredible), at the farthest possible remove from the doctrine of God, did he move forward to the doctrine of the Trinity, the Trinity being followed by Christology and Soteriology. To this same group there belongs above all the *Summa Theologiae* of J. Coccejus (1662). In this work *Locus 14: De consilio gratiae et irae*, forms the point of transition from the doctrine of sin to that of grace. And yet here, too, Christology and the doctrine of election seem to be most closely inter-related. The same arrangement was also adopted by a group of Lutheran theologians, e.g., by F. J. König in his *Theologia positiva* (1664.) The order of this work, like everything else, was most closely followed by Quenstedt in his *Theol. did. Pol.* (1685), and in the final stages of Lutheran orthodoxy by D. Hollaz in his *Examen theol. acroam.* (1707). These Lutherans followed J. Gerhard in putting their specific doctrine of the *benevolentia Dei universalis*[EN324] at the head of the doctrine of predestination, but this did not alter the fact that in respect of the place of the doctrine within the *schema* as a whole—and certainly in the avoidance of the federal theology of Coccejus, which was most influential on the Lutheran side—they appropriated the plan of the *Conf. Gallicana*, and therefore one of the plans of the theologian whom, in other respects, they so consistently opposed, Calvin himself.

6. The third possibility within this understanding of the doctrine of election as the key to that of reconciliation is to make the doctrine of election in some degree the consummation of that of reconciliation, introducing it not in the middle or at the beginning, but as the ultimate and decisive word which sheds additional light upon all that has gone before.

This was the function of the doctrine as Melanchthon obviously meant it to be understood in the *schema* of *res theologicae*[EN325] which he put at the head of the first draft of the *Loci communes* (1521), a *schema* to which, of course, he did not himself adhere in the actual work. But, above all, this was the place and function of the doctrine in the editions of Calvin's *Institutio* which appeared between 1539 and 1554, and ultimately in the definitive redaction itself. Here Christology had become the climax and culmination of the second book *De Deo redemptore*, which dealt earlier with sin, the Law and the distinction and unity between the Old Testament and the New. In the third book, *De modo percipiendae Christi gratiae*, we are led

---

[EN324] universal benvolence of God
[EN325] theological items

from the work of the Holy Ghost actualised in faith to repentance and the Christian life, the latter being seen from the standpoint both of its outlook on eternity and also of its conditioning in time. We then proceed to the basis of this life in the justification given by God, to its character as Christian freedom, to its maintenance by prayer, and only finally to its eternal root in the divine election of grace, against which there is counter-balanced in a most effective conclusion its eternal end and purpose in the resurrection of the dead. The doctrine of the Church forms the content of the fourth book, and in relation to the rest it has something of the same self-sufficiency as the first book at the beginning of the work: *De Deo creatore*. We must confess, however, that the very *caesurae*[EN326] serve to bring out more clearly the interconnexion both of the end and the beginning with the main body of the work in the second and third books and with the doctrine of election in which that central section culminates.

In order to appreciate Calvin's own position, we must establish first the following points. It [086] is true that Calvin did partly share and partly inaugurate four different conceptions of the place and function of the doctrine of election. But it is also true that we do not find amongst these the conception which is usually described as classical in Reformed dogmatics. Calvin never connected the doctrine of predestination with that of God, whether directly or indirectly. And we can describe only as a complete and evident delusion the *opinio communis*[EN327], expressed even by serious dogmatic historians, which attributes to Calvin something which even the later Reformed dogmaticians did not do—the establishment of this doctrine as a basic tenet from which all other doctrines may be deduced. W. Niesel (*Die Theologie Calvins*, 1938, 159) is quite right when he says: "If anyone does maintain such a view, then here, as elsewhere, he is constructing the theology of Calvin as for one reason or another best suits himself." But we must still ask whether in combating this traditional error some recent writers have not underestimated the function of the doctrine in Calvin's theology (e.g., P. Barth, "Die Erwählungslehre in Calvins Institutio, 1536," in *Theol. Aufsätze*, 1936, 432 f.; Heinz Otten, *Calvins theol. Anschauung von d. Praed.*, 1938, 26; and even W. Niesel). Can we really say that Calvin spoke of the election at the proper place, "but not more fully than of other matters" (Niesel, *op. cit.*)? Is not the proper place where he does speak of it, and what he says concerning it, far too important and far too prominent for us to be able to say that this doctrine should not be used, and Calvin did not mean it to be used, to shed a decisive light on all that precedes and follows? Undoubtedly Calvin did not understand or handle the doctrine as a basic tenet. But this does not mean that he placed it on the same level as all the rest. Between these two views there is a third. What Calvin did appear to find in the doctrine of election was this—a final (and therefore a first) word on the whole reality of the Christian life, the word which tells us that the existence and the continuance and the future of that life are wholly and utterly of the free grace of God. But all Christian doctrine, even that of God at the beginning and that of the Church at the end, deals substantially with this reality of the Christian life, with the life of the man whom God has claimed for Himself in Jesus Christ. And if this is the case, then how can we help thinking of the doctrine of election as the last or first word of all Christian doctrine? When we consider the place given to the doctrine of election in the later forms of Calvin's *Institutio* and especially in the definitive redaction, it seems that the total picture presented by that work drives us irresistibly to the conclusion that at this point Calvin did intend to find and to say something particularly and appropriately significant both in its substance and also in its consequences.

It is a matter for surprise that the pattern set in the definitive redaction of the *Institutio* did not gain a greater following than was actually the case. It was obviously under its influence,

---

[EN326] divisions
[EN327] consensus view

or under that of one of the earlier post-1539 editions, which followed the same plan, that this arrangement passed both into the *Forty-Two Articles* (later *Thirty-Nine*) which in 1553 became the confessional basis of the Church of England, and also into the *Conf. Rhaetica* (1562). The only Reformed dogmatician to adopt it was W. Bucanus in his *Institutions theol.* (1602). Bucanus also followed Calvin in the interconnexion of predestination with eschatology. As against that, we may again mention a whole series of important Lutherans. Thus in the great *Systema loc. theol.* (1655f.) of A. Calov, the doctrine of predestination forms the conclusion of the great sequence Christ-Church-sacraments-personal salvation according to Rom. 8³⁰ (the content of this sequence should be studied as well as the order). At the head of this sequence, apparently far removed from the doctrine of predestination, but in reality most impressively balanced against it from an architectonic standpoint, Calov introduces the peculiar Lutheran doctrine of the divine *misericordia generalis*EN328. In his *Comp. Theol. pos.*

[087]   (1686), J. W. Baier has a similar arrangement: Christ-personal salvation-sacraments-predestination, but he differs from Calov by removing the Church from this sequence and treating of it independently. With a similar modification J. F. Buddeus, who was of the so-called "rationalist orthodoxy," took up the same arrangement in his *Institutiones theol. dogm.* (1723). It is quite singular to see how in the constructions of later Lutheranism the doctrine of predestination seems to move more and more to the end of the whole dogmatic sequence. In the talented plan of Calov it is followed only by a special doctrine of the cross in Christian life and by the doctrine of the Law and eschatology, while with Baier and Buddeus it is followed only by the doctrine of Church and state. Even with these theologians we are forced to ask whether their intention would not have been realised just as well, and perhaps better, if they had put the doctrine at the very beginning.

It is obvious that one and the same systematic purpose underlies the three attempts last mentioned. In different ways they understand the divine election as the divine reality which controls the particular activity of salvation between God and man. In a developed and comprehensive form they say the very same thing as was already intended when the election was introduced in connexion with the Church. The point must be made that all three of the possibilities which here present themselves were exploited—the doctrine of election was put at the beginning of the full doctrine of reconciliation, in the middle of that doctrine, and at the end. The point must also be made that we meet with Calvin on each of these paths (and also at their point of departure, the interconnexion of election with the Church). To establish these facts is far more important than to decide along which of the three paths the common intention is best fulfilled, or which of the three ways is best adapted to the matter in hand. Equally good reasons may be adduced in favour (and also against) all three of these possibilities.

The doctrine of election is indeed "the final and necessary expression of the evangelical doctrine of grace" (W. Niesel, *op. cit.* p. 161). This fact would seem to favour the third way. In presenting the doctrine of election we look back, characterising again the mystery, and the meaning and purpose of the mystery, of all the reality which is between Christ and the Christian. The necessity of this third way is exclusively upheld and argued by Buddeus: *nec enim aliter quam ex eventu de decretis divinis nobis iudicare licet*EN329 (*op. cit.*, V, 2, 1). Yet in spite of

---

EN328 general mercy
EN329 for it is not permissible for us to judge other than from the outcome of the divine decrees

that, we cannot come to such a decision. At the very place where the doctrine of election may be understood as the final word, it is borne in upon us that it may also be understood as the first word, and that it must indeed be understood in this way. And in the passage so frequently appealed to, Rom. 8^{30}, the election is actually the first word. There can be no doubt that the doctrine of election is more than a mere underlining of the remaining content of the doctrine of grace. There can be no doubt that it is more than a mere heightening of the awareness that grace is free and eternal and divine grace. It does contribute to such a heightening and underlining, but it does far more. And it should never be regarded as a result of our awareness and experience of grace, as a postulate consequent upon such awareness and experience. Here, at any rate, the concept of a *iudicium ex eventu*[EN330] must always be suspect. Some such suspicion might rest even upon Calvin's arrangement in the *Institutio* of 1559, but it is dispersed by the fact that in that same year, in the *Conf. Gallicana*, he adopted the second and opposite arrangement whereby the doctrine of election forms the beginning of the whole sequence. There can be no doubt that Calvin, too, regarded that last [088] word as also the first. If this fact ought to find expression in the ordering of the material, then it might be asked whether Calvin's first attempt at a solution (1537) was not the best (cf. 4). There the doctrine of the election was placed between Christology and the doctrine of personal salvation. This helped to bring out more clearly than any of the other works both the connexion of the election with Christ and also the order of Rom. 8^{30}. But in the light of this we have to reinterpret the solution of the *Conf. Gallicana* (1559) and all the other solutions which, obviously following the thought of Eph. 1^4, aim at a proper introduction, substantiation and effective application of Christology, and also aim to set the doctrine of reconciliation in clear relief against the preceding doctrines of sin, original sin and the *servum arbitrium*[EN331], to that end giving precedence to the doctrine of election over every other doctrine except Christology itself (cf. 5). Along all three paths, however, there is a clear recognition of the outstanding character of the doctrine of election in relation to all other aspects of the doctrine of reconciliation. If we had to choose between them, then we should prefer the first solution advocated by Calvin in 1537, on the ground that this solution best expresses the intention underlying all these attempts: to understand the decision of the divine election as an event which works itself out between Christ and the Christian.

But we do not need to choose between these three possibilities. The doctrine of election is the last or first or central word in the whole doctrine of reconciliation, as all of them rightly perceive. But the doctrine of reconciliation is itself the first or last or central word in the whole Christian confession or the whole of Christian dogma. Dogmatics has no more exalted or profound word—essentially, indeed, it has no other word—than this: that God was in Christ reconciling the world unto Himself (2 Cor. 5^{19}). As the doctrine of the Word of God it can describe the Christian knowledge of God upon the basis of God's self-revelation only with a constant and wholehearted reference to the event which as such is both the source of truth and the truth itself. It can understand and present the divine work revealed to us in God's Word, whether creation or redemption, only in the light of the mystery of this event. It must already have dealt with the mystery of this event, and only with the mystery of this event, at the very outset, if it is ever to treat of it directly and in

---

[EN330] judgment after the outcome
[EN331] bondage of the will

detail at its real centre, in the specific doctrine of grace. How, indeed, could we ever speak of God at all, as the Subject of the whole divine work, the Creator, Reconciler and Redeemer, if in our teaching about His being and perfections we were not ready to acknowledge that which is the centre of this work, which contains within itself its beginning and end, which alone makes possible the knowledge of it? It is here that we make the decisive step, the transition from the knowledge of God to the knowledge of all His work. Is it not necessary, then, that first of all we should show what is the centre, and as such the beginning and end of this work? Is it not necessary that we should first show who and what God is in His dealings with His creation, who and what the God is whose dealings correspond to what does actually take place and is made known at this [089] centre? How can we speak rightly of God unless we deal first with this word of decision, unless we point first to the mystery of this doctrine of reconciliation? Does not this word of decision belong necessarily at this point? Must not this mystery be considered at the very outset? How can we possibly take cognisance of this word and this mystery in a merely secondary and supplementary capacity? But, according to the right insight of all the theologians who advocated the three (or four) solutions last mentioned, it is the doctrine of election itself which is this decisive word, this mystery of the doctrine of reconciliation. And all the attempts based upon these arrangements suffer from the fact that their order necessarily gives to the doctrine of election the character of teaching which is purely supplementary and secondary.

This means that when we come to treat of Christ and the Christian (or the Church), it may well appear as though we suddenly remember something which hitherto we have for the most part forgotten. We make amends by enlarging upon what for some reason has hitherto been suppressed, i.e., the fact that in all His work as the One who reconciles the world to Himself, God is the One who acts in Jesus Christ; and not only the One who acts in Jesus Christ, but the One who from all eternity has willed and ordained that He should act in Jesus Christ. In this whole conception the discussion of the eternity, freedom and immutability of God as the basis, meaning and dynamic of what takes place between Christ and His people, between Christ and the Church, comes in a sense too late. And when it is a matter of God's eternity, we obviously cannot afford to let the discussion come too late. The happening which is the meaning and purpose of all the divine work is grounded in God's election and decision. It is, therefore, glorious beyond measure. It is absolutely different from all other happenings. For this reason, we can never speak of it too soon. We cannot be too insistent in the recognition and introduction of it as the presupposition of all God's perfect work (as that which is truly and properly perfect in its perfection). It is because of this that we put the doctrine of election—meaning, of course, this decisive word, this mystery of the doctrine of reconciliation, the doctrine of the election which took place in Jesus Christ—at the very beginning, and indeed before the beginning, of what we have to say concerning God's dealings with His creation. It is for this reason that we

94

understand the election as ordination, as God's self-ordaining of Himself. And it is for this reason, then, that we regard the doctrine of election as a constituent part of the doctrine of God.

Again, if the doctrine of election is treated as something secondary and supplementary along the lines of the three possibilities mentioned, this means that it may well appear as if we could deal at least with creation and sin without any previous consideration of this decisive word, this mystery of the doctrine of reconciliation. But in this case creation takes on the character of a presupposition relatively independent of reconciliation and redemption. It [090] becomes self-sufficient. It has its own reality and must be considered in and for itself. But this makes it appear as if the universe and man might well have been created and sustained without any inner necessity of the continuation and completion of the divine work in reconciliation and redemption. They may, then, be considered directly, apart from the divine election and decision, apart from the kingdom of Christ. But in this case there arises the concept of a realm whose existence allows us at least to question the infinity and divinity of this kingdom, opposing to it the parallel kingdom of nature. But this means that sin, the mishap which takes place in this separate kingdom of nature, acquires the character of an unforeseen incident which suddenly transforms the good creation of God into something problematical, breaking and shattering it in such a way that only a few traces of the original remain and what virtually amounts to a different world is brought into being. On this view God Himself appears in a sense to be halted and baffled by sin, being pressed back into a kind of special "world of God." From this it might easily appear as if reconciliation is the corresponding escape from this dilemma, a mysterious wrestling with what is almost a rival God, a reaction against a different power, something not at all in keeping with the unity and omnipotence of God. In the whole of the divine work, however, it is really a question of only a single act of divine rule. This act is, of course, differentiated and flexible within itself. But it is not arrested or broken. It fulfils itself step by step, and at each step it is irresistible. We can and should recognise that in His unbroken grace and truth the one and omnipotent God is the One in whom there is neither error nor mistake, neither weakness nor compromise, but who in and through everything lets His own goodwill be done. We can and should recognise that the *regnum Christi*[EN332] is not one kingdom with others, for in that case it might well be merely hypothetical. On the contrary, it is the kingdom of all kingdoms. We can and should recognise the fact that however we regard man, as creature, sinner or Christian, we must always regard him and understand him as one who is sustained by the hand of God. Neither in the height of creation nor in the depth of sin is he outside the sphere of the divine decision. And if we see in this decision the divine election, this means that he is not outside the sphere of the election of grace. At no time and in no way is he neutral in the face of the

---

[EN332] kingdom of Christ

95

resolve and determination which are proper to the will of God in virtue of the decision made between Father and Son from all eternity. For this reason we must see the election at the beginning of all the ways of God, and treat of the doctrine accordingly. We believe that in so doing we shall not be disloyal to the intention which activated Calvin especially as he drew up those different outlines. We shall rather be taking up and realising this very same intention.

[091]   When we give to the doctrine the position suggested, it assumes in Church dogmatics its necessary function; the function proper to the concept of election in the biblical testimony to God and to the work and revelation of God. That God elects man, that He determines man for Himself, having first determined Himself for man, is not one moment with others in the prophetic and apostolic testimony. Enclosed within the testimony to God Himself, it is the moment which is the substance and basis of all other moments in that testimony. The biblical witness to God is itself wholly characterised by the fact that this God has determined Himself the Lord of Israel and the Church, and as such the Lord of the universe and man in general. It is for this reason and to this end that He wills the calling of Israel and the Church and the creation of the universe and man. It is only in this self-determination, and in the indestructible order which results from it, that the Bible bears witness to God, and that according to that biblical witness God can be truly known as God. It is, then, only upon the basis of this divine self-determination that, according to this witness, all the works of God are what they are. In this self-determination and only in this self-determination does God will to be known, to be loved and feard, to be believed in and worshipped as Creator, Reconciler and Redeemer. There is no single moment in the biblical witness that must not be understood in the light of it. There is no single moment in this witness that can be understood in the light of anything else, whether out of religious or philosophical caprice or perversity. It is in virtue of this self-determination that God wills to be God solely in Jesus Christ. And it is as such that He is the Lord of Israel and the Church, and as such, and not otherwise, that He is the Creator, Reconciler and Redeemer of the universe and man. But it is with this primal decision of God that the doctrine of election deals.

In the first sub-section we established the fact that inasmuch as the doctrine does deal with this decision it contains and expresses the sum of the Gospel. It does so because it is the good news, the best news, the wholly redemptive news, that from all eternity God has decided to be God only in this way, and in the movement towards man which takes on this form. Then in the second sub-section we established the fact that the basis of our knowledge of this doctrine cannot be any other than its basis in actuality, i.e., Jesus Christ Himself, who because He is the Head of Israel and the Church is the content of this primal decision of God, and as such the authentic revelation of it. We treat of the doctrine as understood in this way within the context of the doctrine of God. And as an integral part of this doctrine we put it at the head of all other doctrines. Thus placed, it is in relation to all that follows a necessary witness to the fact that all God's works and ways have their origin in His grace. In virtue of this self-determination of His, God is from the very first the gracious God. For this self-determination is identical with the decree of His movement towards [092] man. This movement is always the very best thing that could happen to man. The reality and revelation of this movement is Jesus Christ Himself. This movement is an eternal movement, and therefore one which encloses man in his finitude and temporality. It is free, and therefore it is entirely grounded in the good-pleasure and the will of God. It is constant, and therefore it cannot deceive, nor can it be withdrawn or rejected. In virtue of the self-determination which is to be presented in the doctrine of election, God is, as the gracious God, the constantly self-asserting Subject which calls always for renewed thought and consideration. He is *Deus ipse*[EN333] at the beginning of all His ways and works. From the standpoint of this beginning and this Subject these ways and works are *per se*, in all circumstances and in all forms and stages, the ways and works of grace. Since it is the divine self-determination, the primal decision from which they derive cannot be over-ridden, abrogated, weakened or altered by any other decision. Always and from every point of view they derive from the fact that from and to all eternity God has moved towards man freely and therefore definitively. Always and from every point of view they derive from Jesus Christ, the One who in the will of God was to be, was, is, and will be both very man and very God. Always and from every point of view they are what from all eternity they were necessarily foreordained to be. And that applies to all God's works without exception. There is no such thing as a created nature which has its purpose, being or continuance apart from grace, or which may be known in this purpose, being and continuance except through grace. Even sin, death, the devil and hell—works of God's permissive will which are negative in their effects—even these works do not constitute any exception to the general rule. For even in these God's knowing and willing are gracious, even though they take effect as negation (and in that sense are permissive). Even the enemies of God are the servants of God and the servants of His grace. Thus God and the enemies of God cannot be known at all unless both they and their negative character and whole work of negation are known in the service which they render as instruments of the eternal, free and immutable grace of God. God is gracious and continues gracious even where there is no grace. And it is only by grace that the lack of grace can be recognised as such. For in the beginning, in His primal decision, in Jesus Christ, at the place where alone He can be known as God, where alone He can be known at all, known as the *Deus ipse*[EN334] which He is still even in His permitting of sin and the devil, even in the terrors of death and hell, God is gracious and not ungracious. To know Him always means to know the gracious God, even in sin and death, even under the dominion of the devil, even in the abyss of hell. And

---

EN333 God himself
EN334 God himself

97

conversely, where can there be any true or serious knowledge of sin and the devil, of death and hell, if there is not also a knowledge of the gracious God? But, above all, the blessings and triumphs of His work as Creator, Reconciler and Redeemer do not constitute any exception to this general rule. For except with grace, and through grace, and to the glory of grace, there can be no rejoicing and praise of creation, no receiving of the Holy Spirit and of the enlightenment and guidance of the Holy Spirit, no glory of saints and angels in the consummation of His kingdom, no height and no depth. Church doctrine must speak not only of God Himself, but also of all His ways and works, of all the ways and works of God. But in so doing it must be aware that in their very origin these ways and works have been determined, and at all times and in all places it must make mention of their determination. It must never speak as though it had to do with someone other than the gracious God. It must always give glory to God and bear witness to God as the gracious God. But the gracious God is the One who is God in the beginning, and therefore in the self-determination which is the specific concern of the doctrine of election. This doctrine is the basic witness to the fact that the gracious God is the beginning of all the ways and works of God. It defines grace as the starting-point for all reflection and utterance, the common denominator which should never be omitted in any statements which follow, and which should, if possible, be asserted in some form in these statements. The specific function of the doctrine is, in fact, to bear this basic witness. It is to enable it to fulfil this function that we have given to it its present position. To do this we have had to part company with tradition to a more or less noticeable degree. Yet we have also taken up the concern or aim of tradition, doing justice to it in a very different form.

THE ELECTION OF JESUS CHRIST

The election of grace is the eternal beginning of all the ways and works of God in Jesus Christ. In Jesus Christ God in His free grace determines Himself for sinful man and sinful man for Himself. He therefore takes upon Himself the rejection of man with all its consequences, and elects man to participation in His own glory.

1. JESUS CHRIST, ELECTING AND ELECTED

Between God and man there stands the person of Jesus Christ, Himself God and Himself man, and so mediating between the two. In Him God reveals Himself to man. In Him man sees and knows God. In Him God stands before man and man stands before God, as is the eternal will of God, and the eternal ordination of man in accordance with this will. In Him God's plan for man is disclosed, God's judgment on man fulfilled, God's deliverance of man accomplished, God's gift to man present in fulness, God's claim and promise to man declared. In Him God has joined Himself to man. And so man exists for His sake. It is by Him, Jesus Christ, and for Him and to Him, that the universe is created as a theatre for God's dealings with man and man's dealings with God. The being of God is His being, and similarly the being of man is originally His being. And there is nothing that is not from Him and by Him and to Him. He is the Word of God in whose truth everything is disclosed and whose truth cannot be over-reached or conditioned by any other word. He is the decree of God behind and above which there can be no earlier or higher decree and beside which there can be no other, since all others serve only the fulfilment of this decree. He is the beginning of God before which there is no other beginning apart from that of God within Himself. Except, then, for God Himself, nothing can derive from any other source or look back to any other starting-point. He is the election of God before which and without which and beside which God cannot make any other choices. Before Him and without Him and beside Him God does not, then, elect or will anything. And He is the election (and on that account the beginning and the decree and the Word) of the free grace of God. For it is God's free grace that in Him He elects to be man and to have dealings with man and to join Himself to man. He, Jesus Christ, is the free [095] grace of God as not content simply to remain identical with the inward and eternal being of God, but operating *ad extra*[EN1] in the ways and works of God.

[EN1] outside himself

And for this reason, before Him and above Him and beside Him and apart from Him there is no election, no beginning, no decree, no Word of God. Free grace is the only basis and meaning of all God's ways and works *ad extra*[EN2]. For what *extra* is there that the ways and works could serve, or necessitate, or evoke? There is no *extra* except that which is first willed and posited by God in the presupposing of all His ways and works. There is no *extra* except that which has its basis and meaning as such in the divine election of grace. But Jesus Christ is Himself the divine election of grace. For this reason He is God's Word, God's decree and God's beginning. He is so all-inclusively, comprehending absolutely within Himself all things and everything, enclosing within Himself the autonomy of all other words, decrees and beginnings.

We shall elucidate these statements by a short exegesis of the passage Jn. 1^{1-2}: Ἐν ἀρχῇ ἦν ὁ λόγος, καὶ ὁ λόγος ἦν πρὸς τὸν θεόν, καὶ θεὸς ἦν ὁ λόγος. οὗτος ἦν ἐν ἀρχῇ πρὸς τὸν θεόν[EN3].

"*In the beginning* was the Word"—this is the emphasis according to the order of the sentence. The sentence does tell us, of course, what was in the beginning. But it does so in the form of a declaration about the Word. The Word was in the beginning. It did not arise later. It did not enter in as one moment with others in the totality of the world created by God and differentiated from Him. Again, it was not merely the first and original link in the development of this totality. It was not merely (as Philo said of his Logos): πρεσβύτατος τῶν γένεσιν εἰληφότων[EN4]. And we certainly must not understand in this sense what Prov. 8^{22} says concerning wisdom: "The Lord possessed me in the beginning of his way, before his works of old;" for the continuation in v. 23 tells us: "I was set up from everlasting, from the beginning, or ever the earth was." Again we cannot understand in this sense the statement in Col. 1^{15}, πρωτότοκος τῆς κτίσεως[EN5], for it continues: ὅτι ἐν αὐτῷ ἐκτίσθη τὰ πάντα[EN6]. The First-begotten is thus clearly removed from the series of created realities. What is said in these passages, and in the Johannine ἐν ἀρχῇ[EN7] (or ἀπ' ἀρχῆς[EN8], 1 Jn. 1^1) is this. The Word as such is before and above all created realities. It stands completely outside the series of created things. It precedes all being and all time. It is like God Himself. As was rightly said concerning it in the expositions of the 4th century: "There was no time when it was not." And this Word was in the beginning and at the beginning of all that which, being created by Him, is distinct from God. Within the sphere of this creation there is, then, no time which is not enclosed by the eternity of this Word, no space which does not have its origin in its omnipresence and which is not for this reason conditioned by it. There is, in fact, no possibility of escaping or avoiding this Word. But the question arises, where, except in or with God, can there be any being which is "in the beginning" in this sense.

The answer to this question is given in the second statement. "And the Word was *with God*." Here the emphasis falls beyond all doubt upon the two final words. This statement too, then, constitutes an assertion concerning the Word. It declares that there was, in fact, no being "in the beginning" in this sense except in and with God. But the Word itself was in and with God.

[EN2] outside himself
[EN3] In the beginning was the Word, and the Word was with God, and the Word was God. He was with God in the beginning
[EN4] that oldest of created things
[EN5] the first-born over all creation
[EN6] because in him all things were created
[EN7] in the beginning
[EN8] from the beginning

1. *Jesus Christ, Electing and Elected*

Πρὸς θεόν[EN9] does not mean "for God," as in the famous saying of Augustine: *Ad te me creasti*[EN10]; nor does it mean "in communication with God" (T. Zahn). These statements could both be made of a being which was not "in the beginning" in this sense. Strictly speaking, they could be made only of such a being. If the second assertion is to elucidate and not to contradict the first, then the πρός[EN11] must be understood quite plainly and simply to mean this: That He could be "in the beginning" who was with God, who is beyond all created reality, because He belongs to God, because His being is as the being of God Himself. It was because the Word was "with God" in this sense that it could also be "in the beginning." But how could it be "with God" in this sense? What do we mean when we say that it belongs to God, or that its being is as the being of God Himself?

[096]

The answer to this question is given in the third statement; and as in the first two, we must again find our subject in "the Word": "And the Word was *God*." The sentence tells us, then, that the Word was itself God; it participated absolutely in the divine mode of being, in the divine being itself. The fact that there is no article before "God" does not mean that deity is not ascribed to the Word in the strictest and most proper sense. What is done is simply this. The mode of being, and being, of a second "He," the Logos, is identified with the mode of being and being of the first "He," God. Thus the deity of ὁ θεός[EN12] is also ascribed to ὁ λόγος[EN13]. In saying this, we are at once presupposing that in view of the definite article "the Word" ought to be characterised as a "He" in exactly the same way as "the God." That this presupposition is correct is forcibly demonstrated by what follows. And if it is correct, then here, too, the exegesis of the 4th century must have been on the right track with its doctrine of the *homoousion*, or unity of substance of the three distinctive divine persons, prosopa or hypostases. The step taken in the third sentence is this—that the Word can be with God, and it can be "in the beginning," because as person (that of the Son) it participates in its own way with the person of "God" (the Father) in the same dignity and perfection of the one divine being. It must be conceded that read in this way, after the manner of so-called "orthodoxy," the verse is at any rate meaningful within itself, each word being intelligible in its own place.

But who or what is the Word whose predicates are declared in Jn. 1¹? As is well known, in the Johannine Prologue the concept recurs only once (v. 14), and in the rest of the Gospel it does not recur at all in this sense. In the presentation as a whole its character is obviously that of a stop-gap. It is a preliminary indication of the place where later something or someone quite different will be disclosed. The same is true of the only other place in the whole of the New Testament where the concept is unequivocally used in the same sense as in Jn. 1¹. In Rev. 19¹³ it is said of the Rider on the white horse that one of the diadems on His head bears a name which no one knows (i.e., understands) but He Himself. And this name, which can be read but which only He can understand, this ideogram which only He can decipher, is as follows: ὁ λόγος τοῦ θεοῦ[EN14]. Here, too, the concept is used as a stop-gap. It is a preliminary and veiling concept for that other and true concept which the Rider on the white horse has of Himself, which, as it were, consists and is expressed in His very existence. In Jn. 1¹ the reference is very clear: ὁ λόγος[EN15] is unmistakably substituted for Jesus. His is the place which the predicates attributed to the Logos are meant at once to mark off, to clear and to reserve. It is He, Jesus, who is in the beginning with God. It is He who by nature is God. This

---

EN 9 with God
EN10 You have created me for yourself
EN11 with
EN12 God
EN13 the Word
EN14 the Word of God
EN15 the Word

is what is guaranteed in Jn. 1¹. But why specifically by means of this concept? If we ask this as a question in historical genetics, we are faced by a whole host of possibilities, ranging from the Logos of Philo to the personal, semi-personal and impersonal essences of Mandaistic theory. Within this medley it will probably always be a waste of time to look for that unknown quantity, the source used by the writer of the Fourth Gospel; for we do not know in what form the author took over this widespread and variously used concept, nor do we know in [097] what way he transformed this concept, nor finally can we be absolutely certain of the fact that he did take over the concept from some other source. What is certain is that he had no intention of honouring Jesus by investing Him with the title of Logos, but rather that he honoured the title itself by applying it a few lines later as a predicate of Jesus. He offered no other exegesis of the concept apart from that in which he made this predication. We can only say that by offering this exegesis he rejects all other possible interpretations of the concept in this context, interpretations which would define it primarily and essentially as the principle of an epistemology or of a metaphysical explanation of the universe. There is no doubt that in Jn. 1³ (and 1¹⁰) a cosmogenic function is ascribed to the Logos. But there is also no doubt that the Evangelist did not adopt the concept for the sake of this interpretation of it. It is rather that in vv. 3 and 10 he recalls this interpretation in order to emphasise and elucidate what he has said in vv. 1 and 2. And he leaves it at once without construing anything more out of it. Having touched lightly on this aspect of the concept he moves forward quickly to his own conclusion: the Word was the bearer of life (v. 4), the life which was the light of men in their age-long battle with darkness (vv. 5, 9); the Word became flesh; the Word is the μονογενὴς θεός EN16, which was in the bosom of the Father; and as such the Word has made known to us the unknown God (v. 18). Such is the Johannine Logos so far as we can define it at all apart from the recognition that the Logos is Jesus. It is the principle, the intrinsically divine basis of God's revelation, God's supernatural communication to man. And this was what the author of the Fourth Gospel found in Jesus. Jesus was the life which was light, the revelation of God, the saying, or address, or communication in which God declares Himself to us. But as this revelation He was not something other outside and along-side God. He was God Himself within the revelation. He was not revelation alone, then, but in the revelation He was the principle, the intrinsically divine basis of revelation. He was revelation in its complete and absolute form. It was to show this that the Evangelist—no matter where he derived the concept, or what else it conveyed to him—made use of the term Logos. We can be satisfied with the translation "Word." In German the word *Spruch* (saying) might be better, since it would proclaim the contents of v. 2 in the masculine as is done in the Greek. As is well known, Goethe's *Faust* found it difficult to rate the concept "word" so highly, and he thought that the term should be translated differently. "Suddenly I see the way and boldly write: In the beginning was the deed." But the moment he had boldly written it, the devil appeared! "Word" or "saying" is the simple but genuine form in which person communicates with person. It is by the Word that God communicates with man. Because it is God's Word it is not called "a" word but "the" Word, the Word of all words. There is no need to import into this Word reason, signification, power, etc., for it contains all these within itself in virtue of the fact that it is Word, the divine self-communication proceeding from person to person and uniting God and man. It may be noticed that the Evangelist presup-poses that the Word is there, that it has been given or spoken. This is not something which must be proved, or inferred from anything else. The force of the threefold ἦν EN17 in Jn. 1¹ is more than axiomatic. It points to an eternal happening and to a temporal: to an eternal in the form of time, and to a temporal with the content of eternity. For this reason no stress is

---

EN16 the one and only God
EN17 was

laid upon the threefold ὁ λόγος EN18, and there can be no point in attaching oneself to this or that signification of the concept as authenticated elsewhere. It is there as an ideogram, like the inscription on the diadem of the Rider of the Apocalypse. It is something which we can read but not comprehend. It is the *x* in an equation whose value we can know only when the equation has been solved. Of this solution Jn. 1¹⁹ is the beginning. But the Prologue states the equation, giving the unknown factor its place in relation to those which are known, God, the universe, man, the testimony (of John the Baptist) and the believer. The beginning of this presentation is Jn. 1¹: Where God is, that is, in the beginning, there is the Word. It   [098] must, therefore, belong to God, and by nature it must itself be God. If the Word of God is to be there in the beginning, the God Himself is required, no more and no less. But the Word is there, and therefore God Himself must be there with it. Thus far v. 1.

The Prologue continues: "The same was in the beginning with God." The supposition that these words are a recapitulation of v. 1 is quite unconvincing. For one thing, v. 1 does not stand in need of any such recapitulation. For another, there is no clear reason why it should be given in v. 2. And since the third assertion in v. 1 is itself the elucidation of the first two, we can hardly hold (with T. Zahn) that the repetition of the first two in v. 2 is meant, for its part, to be an elucidation of the third. We ought rather to follow A. Schlatter on this point: that the οὗτος EN19 must be understood as a reference forward and not backward. The expression οὗτος ἦν EN20 occurs again in the Prologue, at the climax of the most important record of the witness of the Baptist (v. 15 f.): "This was he of whom I said, He that cometh after me is preferred before me: for he was before me. And of his fulness have all we received, and grace for grace." The remaining contents of the Prologue all show clearly enough that the Evangelist has appropriated this attestation of the Baptist, and that he has identified himself with the testimony which he bore. This first becomes apparent in the significant anticipation in v. 2. The Evangelist himself (also a "John") points to οὗτος ἦν EN21. And this reference in v. 2 shows us that v. 1 is meant as the marking off or reservation of a place, for it points us to that which fills the place indicated by the concept Logos. The statement tells us, then, that "the same," the One who no more needs to be made known as a person than the One described as ὁ θεός EN22, the One whom we all know because He has come forth to all of us, "the same" was in the beginning with God, and "the same" was Jesus. For this reason, when we think of the Word which was in the beginning with God and which belongs to God, we may count upon the fact that it has been spoken with a certitude which is far more than axiomatic. And for this reason, too, we have no need to project anything into eternity, for at this point eternity is time, i.e., the eternal name has become a temporal name, and the divine name a human. It is of this name that we speak. V. 2 is, then, a part of the third assertion of v. 1, but it is not a repetition of it. What v. 2 does tell us, with backward reference to v. 1, is that "the same," Jesus, is the Word which partakes of the divine essence. What it tells us is that "the same," Jesus, was in the beginning because as this same divine Word he belongs legitimately to God. Thus this witness of the Evangelist, this οὗτος ἦν EN23, answers two of our questions at the same time: Who was in the beginning with God, sharing His divine nature? and: Is it true that there was anyone in the beginning with God, sharing the divine essence? The answer to both questions is that it was He, Jesus. The naming of this name (and for the moment it is only indicated) is at once a thesis and a proof in relation to that which was in the beginning with God. And as v. 2 is to be understood in this way, as a reference to the

---

EN18 the Word
EN19 he
EN20 he was
EN21 he was
EN22 God
EN23 he was

name and person of Jesus, we are forced to the following exposition of the third statement in v. 1, with its identification of two distinctive persons in respect of their divine essence: that side by side with the One described as ὁ θεός EN24, and itself partaker of the same θεότης EN25, there has entered in the Word (that Word which is "the same," οὗτος EN26).

It is to Him, then, "the same," that the αὐτοῦ EN27 refers in vv. 3 and 10, where we are told that τὰ πάντα EN28, the κόσμος EN29, was made by Him, and that without Him was not anything made that was made. And here the unique statement of Jn. 1¹⁻² issues in a reflection which is quite familiar in the witness of the New Testament. Thus in Col. 1¹⁷ we read that the Son of God—the Son *in concreto* and not *in abstracto*, Jesus Christ, who is the Head of His body, the Church—this Son is "before all things," and "in Him all things consist." It was, in fact, "the good pleasure of the fulness of the Godhead" (and here the concept of election is quite clear) to take form, or to take up residence in Him (κατοικῆσαι ... σωματικῶς EN30, Col. 1¹⁹, 2⁹). For this reason we must understand the passages 2 Cor. 4⁴, Col. 1¹⁵ and Hebrews 1³ exclusively: He is the one "image of God," "the effulgence of his glory," "the image of his substance," and therefore "before all things" He is "the mystery of God ... in whom are hid all the treasures of wisdom and knowledge," "the mystery which from the beginning of the world hath been hid in God, who created all things" (Eph. 3⁹). For this reason He Himself is categorical and exclusive: He is "the first-born of every creature" (Col. 1¹⁵), and in order "that in all things he might have the pre-eminence" He is affirmed to be such by the fact that "he is the beginning, the first-born from the dead" (1 Cor. 15²⁰, Col. 1¹⁸). For this reason He is the κεφαλή EN31 of all principality and power (Col. 2¹⁰), so that in the revelation and reconciliation which He has accomplished there can be only an ἀνακεφαλαιοῦσθαι EN32 of all things, "both which are in heavens, and which are on the earth" (Eph. 1¹⁰). For this reason He is "the fulness of him that filleth all in all" (Eph. 1²³), so that His temporal manifestation and work must necessarily be called "the fulness of time(s)" (Gal. 4⁴, Eph. 1¹⁰). It is, then, only by way of explanation of His being as the God who is conceived of in this primal, original and basic movement towards man that Heb. 1² (like Jn. 1³ ¹⁰) says concerning Him that He whom God "appointed heir of all things" is the one "by whom also he made the worlds," and Heb. 1³ that He "upholds all things (φέρων EN33) by the word of his power," and Col. 1¹⁶ that "by him were all things created, that are in heavens, and that are in earth, visible and invisible ... all things were created by him and for him."

If that is true, then in the name and person of Jesus Christ we are called upon to recognise the Word of God, the decree of God and the election of God at the beginning of all things, at the beginning of our own being and thinking, at the basis of our faith in the ways and works of God. Or, to put it the other way, in this person we are called upon to recognise the beginning of the Word and decree and election of God, the conclusive and absolute authority in respect of the aim and origin of all things. And this authority we must acknowledge not merely as something which is like God, but as God Himself, since God Himself in all His ways and works willed wholly and utterly to bear this name, and actually does bear it: the Father of our Lord Jesus Christ, the Son of the Father, the Holy Spirit of the Father and the Son. There

[099]

EN24 God
EN25 Godhead
EN26 he
EN27 his
EN28 all things
EN29 world
EN30 to dwell ... bodily
EN31 head
EN32 a bringing together
EN33 upholds

is given to man under heaven no ἕτερον ὄνομα ... ἐν ᾧ δεῖ σωθῆναι ἡμᾶς EN34 (Ac. 4¹²), and if this is the case, it is decided even more comprehensively that "at the name of Jesus every knee should bow, of things in heaven, and things in earth, and things under the earth" (Phil. 2¹⁰). If this is so, then there is no higher place at which our thinking and speaking of the works of God can begin than this name. We are not thinking or speaking rightly of God Himself if we do not take as our starting-point the fact which should be both "first and last": that from all eternity God elected to bear this name. Over against all that is really outside God, Jesus Christ is the eternal will of God, the eternal decree of God and the eternal beginning of God.

It is as God's election that we must understand the Word and decree and beginning of God over against the reality which is distinct from Himself. When we say this, we say that in His decision all God's works, both "inward" and "outward," rest upon His freedom. We say, too, that in so far as these works are done in time, they rest upon the eternal decision of God by which time is founded and governed. God elects. It is this that precedes absolutely all other being and happening. And at this point both subject and predicate clearly lead us beyond time and beyond the nexus of the created world and its history. [100] They lead us to the sphere where God is with Himself, the sphere of His free will and pleasure. And this sphere is His eternity, which gives to the world and time and all that is in them their origin, their direction and their destiny.

But there is a temptation here, and we have already seen something of the part played by it in the history of the doctrine. It is the temptation to think of this sphere as at once empty and undetermined. It is the temptation to think of God the Father, Son and Holy Spirit merely as a Subject which can and does elect, a Subject which is furnished, of course, with supereminent divine attributes, but which differs from other such subjects only by the fact that in its election it is absolutely free. It is not responsible to any other being for the nature or direction of this election. It must be acknowledged, then, as the Subject whose election is always absolutely right. And it follows that its election is absolutely unconditioned, or is conditioned only by the Subject in and for itself and as such. And this means that the choice actually made must be regarded as a *decretum absolutum*EN35. This construction has been very influential in the history of the doctrine. And it can still actually be a temptation, and a temptation which we must recognise and resist. And first, we must ask a question of its exponents. In respect of the whole attitude and being of God *ad extra*EN36, in His relationship with the order created by Him, can there be anything higher or more distinctive and essential in God than His electing? Must we not say that in His confrontation of the creature, in His relationship with everything which is outside Himself, God is God absolutely in the fact that from all eternity He elects, He decides one way or the other concerning the being and nature of the creature (with all that this involves)? And if so, how are

EN34 other name by which we might be saved
EN35 absolute decree
EN36 outside of himself

105

we to distinguish God's electing from His Word and decree in the beginning?
Are we not forced to say that the electing consists in this Word and decree in
the beginning; and conversely, that this Word and decree in the beginning are
God's electing, His free, subjective self-determination, the primal act of lordship over everything else, independently of all outward constraint, conditioning or compulsion? And if we agree in this with the exponents of the
construction referred to, we must ask further whether we can agree in saying
that God's Word and decree in the beginning consist in the fact that He has
assumed and bears the name of Jesus Christ, that this name itself is God's Word
and decree in the beginning. But if this is so, how can we avoid the all-
important assertion that in its origin, in its real truth and power as that which
is decisive for all that follows, the election of God consists in the fact that from
all eternity, in an act of unconditional self-determination, He has ordained
Himself the bearer of this name? If this is not God's election, then what else
can it be? What choice can precede the choice by which God has of Himself
[101]   chosen to have with Himself in the beginning of all things the Word which is
Jesus? What *decretum absolutum*[EN37] is there that secretly or openly can over-ride
or challenge this *decretum absolutum*[EN38]? What room is there even for the
notion of a *decretum absolutum*[EN39]? In face of this choice, how can we regard as
absolute and autonomous the choice by which God decides for the existence
and nature of the creature? How can we even understand this choice except as
it is included in the choice by which God (obviously first) decides for Himself,
i.e., for this self-ordination, this being under the name of Jesus, this being in
Jesus Christ?

The choice or election of God is basically and properly God's decision that
as described in Jn. 1^{1-2} the Word which is "the same," and is called Jesus,
should really be in the beginning, with Himself, like Himself, one with Himself
in His deity. And for this reason it is *per se*[EN40] an election of grace. This is not,
of course, self-evidently the case. God would not be God, He would not be free,
if this had to be so. "What is man, that thou art mindful of him? and the son of
man, that thou visitest him?" (Ps. 8^5). The eternal God was not under an obligation to man to be in Himself the God whose nature and property it is to bear
this name. That He is, in fact, such a God is grace, something which is not
merited by man but can only be given to him. And that God is gracious, that in
assuming this name He gives Himself to the man who has not merited it, is His
election, His free decree. It is the divine election of grace. In a free act of
determination God has ordained concerning Himself; He has determined
Himself. Without any obligation, God has put Himself under an obligation to
man, willing that that should be so which according to Jn. 1^{1-2} actually is so. It
is grace that it is so, and it is grace that God willed it to be so.

EN37 absolute decree
EN38 absolute decree
EN39 absolute decree
EN40 in itself

In the beginning, before time and space as we know them, before creation, before there was any reality distinct from God which could be the object of the love of God or the setting for His acts of freedom, God anticipated and determined within Himself (in the power of His love and freedom, of His knowing and willing) that the goal and meaning of all His dealings with the as yet non-existent universe should be the fact that in His Son He would be gracious towards man, uniting Himself with him. In the beginning it was the choice of the Father Himself to establish this covenant with man by giving up His Son for him, that He Himself might become man in the fulfilment of His grace. In the beginning it was the choice of the Son to be obedient to grace, and therefore to offer up Himself and to become man in order that this covenant might be made a reality. In the beginning it was the resolve of the Holy Spirit that the unity of God, of Father and Son should not be disturbed or rent by this covenant with man, but that it should be made the more glorious, the deity of God, the divinity of His love and freedom, being confirmed and demonstrated by [102] this offering of the Father and this self-offering of the Son. This choice was in the beginning. As the subject and object of this choice, Jesus Christ was at the beginning. He was not at the beginning of God, for God has indeed no beginning. But He was at the beginning of all things, at the beginning of God's dealings with the reality which is distinct from Himself. Jesus Christ was the choice or election of God in respect of this reality. He was the election of God's grace as directed towards man. He was the election of God's covenant with man.

We are following an important insight of J. Coccejus (*S. Theol.*, 1662, *c.* 37, 2) when we trace back the concept of predestination to the biblical concept of the covenant or testament, the self-committal first revealed to Noah (Gen. 9^{14}) as God's covenant with "every living creature of all flesh that is upon the earth," then (Gen. $17^{7f.}$) as His covenant with Abraham and his posterity, and later (Is. 55^3, Jer. 32^{40}, Ezek. 16^{60}, 37^{26} and cf. Jer. 50^5) as His covenant with Israel. By its definition as *b'rith 'olam* [EN41] this self-committal is characterised (no matter what time-concepts may be presupposed) as a relationship which is not haphazard and transitory, but which derives its necessity from God Himself. It is more steadfast than the hills (Is. 54^{10}). God has sworn it by Himself (Gen. 22^{16}, Ex. 32^{13}, Is. 45^{23}, 54^9, 62^8, Ps. 110^4, Heb. 6^{13}). In Mic. 5^2 (cf., too. Is. 9^7, Dan. $7^{13f.}$) it can be said of the Messiah that "his goings forth have been from of old, from everlasting." As the Jews are aware in Jn. 12^{34}, He "abideth" for ever. According to Heb. $7^{16f.}$ (cf. Ps. 110^4), He "is a priest for ever" "after the power of an endless life." "Through the eternal Spirit he offered himself without spot to God" (Heb. 9^{14}). "Before Abraham was," He was, and "Abraham rejoiced to see his day" (Jn. $8^{56f.}$). We also find references to this divine past in the $\epsilon \dot{v} \delta \acute{o} \kappa \eta \sigma a$ [EN42] of Mt. 3^{17}, the $\epsilon \dot{v} \delta \acute{o} \kappa \eta \sigma \epsilon v$ [EN43] of Col. 1^{19}, the $\delta \iota \acute{\epsilon} \theta \epsilon \tau o$ [EN44] of Lk. 22^{29}, and the $\pi \rho o \acute{\epsilon} \theta \epsilon \tau o$ [EN45] of Eph. 1^9. Now it is quite impossible to distinguish all these from the reality which is treated of in the New Testament passages which speak of the election in express connexion with the name

---

[EN41] everlasting covenant
[EN42] I am pleased
[EN43] he was pleased
[EN44] he assigned
[EN45] he purposed

and person of Jesus. In Eph. 1^{3-5} the one follows directly on the other: there is a general mention of the blessings with which we have been blessed "in heavenly places" in Christ εὐλογήσας ἡμᾶς ... ἐν Χριστῷ EN46, and then there is the particular statement: ἐξελέξατο ἡμᾶς ἐν αὐτῷ πρὸ καταβολῆς κόσμου ... προορίσας ἡμᾶς εἰς υἱοθεσίαν διὰ Ἰησοῦ Χριστοῦ εἰς αὐτόν, κατὰ τὴν εὐδοκίαν τοῦ θελήματος αὐτοῦ EN47. Again, in Eph. 1^{9-11} there is the general: προέθετο εὐδοκίαν ... ἀνακεφαλαιώσασθαι τὰ πάντα ἐν τῷ Χριστῷ EN48, and the particular ἐν αὐτῷ, ἐν ᾧ καὶ ἐκληρώθημεν προορισθέντες κατὰ πρόθεσιν τοῦ τὰ πάντα ἐνεργοῦντος κατὰ τὴν βουλὴν τοῦ θελήματος αὐτοῦ EN49. From these passages, and from Eph. 3^4, we gather that the concrete form of the divine εὐλογία EN50, and of the εὐδοκία EN51 of the eternal πρόθεσις EN52 is in fact that προορίζειν EN53 which will be made known by the existence of the Church (Eph. 3^{10}), so assuredly did God "purpose his eternal πρόθεσις EN54 in Jesus Christ our Lord." And conversely, what we now experience as our deliverance and calling takes place only because it is gifted to us as God's own purpose (πρόθεσις EN55) and grace: ἐν τῷ Χριστῷ Ἰησοῦ πρὸ χρόνων αἰωνίων EN56 (2 Tim. 1^{19}); because Christ as the Lamb without blemish and without spot was προεγνωσμένος πρὸ καταβολῆς κόσμου EN57 (1 Pet. 1^{20}, cf. Rev. 13^8); because ἀπὸ καταβολῆς κόσμου EN58 His high-priestly suffering was necessary (ἔδει) (Heb. 9^{26}). "Him, being delivered by the determinate counsel and foreknowledge (πρόγνωσις) of God, ye have taken, and by wicked hands have crucified and slain" (Ac. 2^{23}). "For to do whatsoever thy hand and thy counsel determined before to come to pass," both Herod and Pilate, with the Gentiles and the peoples of Israel, were gathered together against thy holy servant Jesus

[103]

(Ac. $4^{27f.}$). Again, the glory with which Jesus prayed that He might be glorified (in Jn. 17^5) is none other than that glory which He had with the Father before the world was. In these texts it is not of any importance whether the mention of God's will and purpose preceding the history, or more specifically the expressions πρὸ χρόνων αἰωνίων EN59 and πρὸ EN60 or ἀπὸ καταβολῆς κόσμου EN61, are meant to refer to the eternity of God in itself, or "only" to the beginning of the creation, and therefore of the universe and time. What is certain is that in all the passages the reference is to the beginning of all God's ways and works *ad extra* EN62. And it is also certain that all these passages describe this beginning under the name of Jesus Christ, whose person is that of the executor within the universe and time of the primal decision of divine grace, the person itself being obviously the content of this decision.

In its simplest and most comprehensive form the dogma of predestination

---

EN46 he has blessed us in Christ
EN47 he chose us in Him before the foundation of the world, having predestined us for adoption through Jesus Christ, and for him, according to the good pleasure of his will
EN48 he purposed his will ... to bring all things together in Christ
EN49 in him, in whom we were appointed, having been predestined according to the purpose of the one who works all things according to the counsel of his will
EN50 blessing
EN51 will
EN52 purpose
EN53 predestination
EN54 purpose
EN55 purpose
EN56 in Christ before all ages
EN57 foreknown before the foundation of the world
EN58 from the foundation of the world
EN59 before all ages
EN60 before
EN61 from the foundation of the world
EN62 outside of himself

consists, then, in the assertion that the divine predestination is the election of Jesus Christ. But the concept of election has a double reference—to the elector and to the elected. And so, too, the name of Jesus Christ has within itself the double reference: the One called by this name is both very God and very man. Thus the simplest form of the dogma may be divided at once into the two assertions that Jesus Christ is the electing God, and that He is also elected man.

In so far as He is the electing God, we must obviously—and above all—ascribe to Him the active determination of electing. It is not that He does not also elect as man, i.e., elect God in faith. But this election can only follow His prior election, and that means that it follows the divine electing which is the basic and proper determination of His existence.

In so far as He is man, the passive determination of election is also and necessarily proper to Him. It is true, of course, that even as God He is elected; the Elected of His Father. But because as the Son of the Father He has no need of any special election, we must add at once that He is the Son of God elected in His oneness with man, and in fulfilment of God's covenant with man. Primarily, then, electing is the divine determination of the existence of Jesus Christ, and election (being elected) the human.

Jesus Christ is the electing God. We must begin with this assertion because by its content it has the character and dignity of a basic principle, and because the other assertion, that Jesus Christ is elected man, can be understood only in the light of it.

We may notice at once the critical significance of this first assertion in its relation to the traditional understanding of the doctrine. In particular, it crowds out and replaces the idea of a *decretum absolutum*[EN63]. That idea does, of course, give us an answer to the question about the electing God. It speaks of a good-pleasure of God which in basis and direction is unknown to man and to all beings outside God Himself. This good-pleasure is omnipotent and incontrovertible in its decisions. If we are asked concerning its nature, then ultimately no more can be said than that it is divine, and therefore absolutely supreme and authoritative. But now in the place of this blank, this unknown quantity, we are to put the name of Jesus Christ. According to the witness of the Bible, when we are called upon to define and name the first and decisive decision which transcends and includes all others, it is definitely not in order to answer with a mysterious shrug of the shoulders. How can the doctrine of predestination be anything but "dark" and obscure if in its very first tenet, the tenet which determines all the rest, it can speak only of a *decretum absolutum*[EN64]? In trying to understand Jesus Christ as the electing God we abandon this tradition, but we hold fast by Jn. 1$^{1-2}$.   [104]

[EN63] absolute decree
[EN64] absolute decree

109

Jesus Christ was in the beginning with God. He was so not merely in the sense that in view of God's eternal knowing and willing all things may be said to have been in the beginning with God, in His plan and decree. For these are two separate things: the Son of God in His oneness with the Son of Man, as foreordained from all eternity; and the universe which was created, and universal history which was willed for the sake of this oneness, in their communion with God, as foreordained from all eternity. On the one hand, there is the Word of God by which all things were made, and, on the other, the things fashioned by that Word. On the one hand, there is God's eternal election of grace, and, on the other, God's creation, reconciliation and redemption grounded in that election and ordained with reference to it. On the one hand, there is the eternal election which as it concerns man God made within Himself in His pre-temporal eternity, and, on the other, the covenant of grace between God and man whose establishment and fulfilment in time were determined by that election. We can and must say that Jesus Christ was in the beginning with God in the sense that all creation and its history was in God's plan and decree with God. But He was so not merely in that way. He was also in the beginning with God as "the first-born of every creature" (Col. 1¹⁵), Himself the plan and decree of God, Himself the divine decision with respect to all creation and its history whose content is already determined. All that is embraced and signified in God's election of grace as His movement towards man, all that results from that election and all that is presupposed in such results—all these are determined and conditioned by the fact that that election is the divine decision whose content is already determined, that Jesus Christ is the divine election of grace.

Thus Jesus Christ is not merely one object of the divine good-pleasure side by side with others. On the contrary, He is the sole object of this good-pleasure, for in the first instance He Himself is this good-pleasure, the will of God in action. He is not merely the standard or instrument of the divine freedom. He is Himself primarily and properly the divine freedom itself in its operation *ad extra*[EN65]. He is not merely the revelation of the mystery of God. He is the thing concealed within this mystery, and the revelation of it is the revelation of Himself and not of something else. He is not merely the Reconciler between God and man. First, He is Himself the reconciliation between them. And so He is not only the Elected. He is also Himself the Elector, and in the first instance His election must be understood as active. It is true that as the Son of God given by the Father to be one with man, and to take to Himself the form of man, He is elected. It is also true that He does not elect alone, but in company with the electing of the Father and the Holy Spirit. But He does elect. The obedience which He renders as the Son of God is, as genuine obedience, His own decision and electing, a decision and electing no less divinely free than the electing and decision of the Father and the Holy Spirit. Even the fact

[105]

[EN65] outside of himself

that He is elected corresponds as closely as possible to His own electing. In the harmony of the triune God He is no less the original Subject of this electing than He is its original object. And only in this harmony can He really be its object, i.e., completely fulfil not His own will but the will of the Father, and thus confirm and to some extent repeat as elected man the election of God. This all rests on the fact that from the very first He participates in the divine election; that that election is also His election; that it is He Himself who posits this beginning of all things; that it is He Himself who executes the decision which issues in the establishment of the covenant between God and man; that He too, with the Father and the Holy Spirit, is the electing God. If this is not the case, then in respect of the election, in respect of this primal and basic decision of God, we shall have to pass by Jesus Christ, asking of God the Father, or perhaps of the Holy Spirit, how there can be any disclosure of this decision at all. For where can it ever be disclosed to us except where it is executed? The result will be, of course, that we shall be driven to speculating about a *decretum absolutum*[EN66] instead of grasping and affirming in God's electing the manifest grace of God. And that means that we shall not know into whose hands we are committing ourselves when we believe in the divine predestination. So much depends upon our acknowledgment of the Son, of the Son of God, as the Subject of this predestination, because it is only in the Son that it is revealed to us as the predestination of God, and therefore of the Father and the Holy Spirit, because it is only as we believe in the Son that we can also believe in the Father and the Holy Spirit, and therefore in the one divine election. If Jesus Christ is only elected, and not also and primarily the Elector, what shall we really know at all of a divine electing and our election? But of Jesus Christ we know nothing more surely and definitely than this—that in free obedience to His Father He elected to be man, and as man, to do the will of God. If God elects us too, then it is in and with this election of Jesus Christ, in and with this free act of obedience on the part of His Son. It is He who is manifestly the concrete and manifest form of the divine decision—the decision of Father, Son and Holy Spirit—in favour of the covenant to be established between Him and us. It is in Him that the eternal election becomes immediately and directly [106] the promise of our own election as it is enacted in time, our calling, our summoning to faith, our assent to the divine intervention on our behalf, the revelation of ourselves as the sons of God and of God as our Father, the communication of the Holy Spirit who is none other than the Spirit of this act of obedience, the Spirit of obedience itself, and for us the Spirit of adoption. When we ask concerning the reality of the divine election, what can we do but look at the One who performs this act of obedience, who is Himself this act of obedience, who is Himself in the first instance the Subject of this election.

The passages in Jn. 13[18] and 15[16 19], in which Jesus points to Himself as the One who elects His disciples, are not to be understood loosely but in their strictest and most proper sense. It

---

[EN66] absolute decree

is clear that at this point John knows nothing of a rivalry which can and should be dissolved by subordination. If Jesus does nothing "of himself" (ἀφ' ἑαυτοῦ, Jn. 5¹⁹, ³⁰), there is the closely corresponding verse: "Without me ye can do nothing" (Jn. 15⁵). The statement "All mine are thine," is balanced by the further statement: "Thine are mine" (Jn. 17¹⁰). Jesus was "sent," but He also "came." As He is in the Father, the Father is also in Him (Jn. 14¹⁰). "As the Father hath life in himself, so hath he given to the Son to have life in himself" (Jn. 5²⁶). The Father glorifies Him, but He, too, glorifies the Father (Jn. 17¹⁻⁵). It is Jesus' "meat to do the will of him that sent him" (Jn. 4³⁴), but the Father abiding in Him doeth His works (Jn. 14¹⁰). The Father is greater than He (Jn. 14²⁸), but "he hath given all things into his hand" (Jn. 3³⁵), and "hath given him power over all flesh" (Jn. 17²). In the same breath He says: "Believe in God, and believe also in me" (Jn. 14¹). No man can come unto Jesus except it be given unto him of the Father (Jn. 6⁶⁵). He who comes must have "heard and learned of the Father" (Jn. 6⁴⁵). He must have been "drawn" by the Father (Jn. 6⁴⁴). He must have been given Jesus by the Father (Jn. 6³⁷, 17⁶ ⁹ ²⁴). But again, He, Jesus, is the way, the truth and the life, and no one cometh unto the Father but by Him (Jn. 14⁶). The Father is the husbandman, but He, Jesus, is the true vine (Jn. 15¹ᶠ·). And for this reason He prays(!): "Father, I will that they also, whom thou hast given me, be with me where I am; that they may behold my glory, which thou hast given me" (Jn. 17²⁴). In the light of these passages the electing of the disciples ascribed to Jesus must be understood not merely as a function undertaken by Him in an instrumental and representative capacity, but rather as an act of divine sovereignty, in which there is seen in a particular way the primal and basic decision of God which is also that of Jesus Christ. And so, too, behind that summons to "discipleship" which is so frequent in the Synoptics, there stands the statement of Mt. 11²⁷: "Neither knoweth any man the Father, save ... he to whomsoever the Son will reveal him." And that other statement in Mt. 16¹⁷, that the Son may be known only by revelation of the Father, does not in any way restrict this truth, but rather expounds it according to its true sense. Even in those places where it is said of Christ that He "emptied" Himself and "humbled" Himself (Phil. 2⁷ᶠ·), or that He "gave" Himself (Gal. 1⁴, 1 Tim. 2⁶), or that He "offered" Himself (Gal. 2²⁰, Eph. 5²), or that He "sacrificed" Himself (Heb. 7²⁷, 9¹⁴); even in those passages which treat of His obedience (Phil. 2⁸, Heb. 5⁸), we cannot but see the reflection of the divine spontaneity and activity in which His own existence is grounded, and together with it the covenant between God and man.

It is not sufficient, then, to say with Thomas Aquinas: *ipsa unio naturarum in persona Christi cadit sub aeterna Dei praedestinatione: et ratione huius Christus dicitur esse praedestinatus*[EN67] (*S. Theol.* III, *qu.* 24, *art.* 1 *c*). It is also true, of course, that in His divinity, as in His humanity, Jesus Christ is indeed *praedestinatus*[EN68], the first of the elect. But Thomas would restrict the election of Christ to this passive relationship, and thus to His human nature: *Praedestinatio attribuitur personae Christi non quidem secundum se vel secundum quod subsistit in divina natura sed secundum quod subsistit in humana natura*[EN69] (*ib., ad.* 2). *Solum ratione humanae naturae praedestinatio competit Christo*[EN70] (*ib., art.* 2 *c*). *Dicitur lumen praedestinationis et gratiae, in quantum per eius praedestinationem et gratiam manifestatur nostra praedestinatio*[EN71] (*ib., art.* 3 *s.c.*). The

[107]

[EN67] The very union of the natures in the person of Christ falls under the eternal predestination of God: and by reason of this, Christ is said to be predestined

[EN68] predestined

[EN69] Predestination is attributed to the person of Christ not indeed according to himself, or according to what subsists in the divine nature, but according to what subsists in human nature

[EN70] Predestination applies to Christ only by reason of his human nature

[EN71] The light of predestination and grace means the extent to which our predestination is manifested through his predestination and grace

limitation implied in these sentences is one which cannot be sustained, especially in the light of the Johannine relationship between the Father and the Son. Of course, the fact that Jesus Christ is the Son of God does not rest on the election. What does rest on it is the fact that as such He also becomes man, that as such (to use the Johannine concept) He is "sent," that as such He is the bearer of the divine name of the Father in the world. Between the eternal Godhead of Christ which needs no election and His elected humanity, there is a third possibility which was overlooked by Thomas. And that is the being of Christ in the beginning with God, the act of the good-pleasure of God by which the fulness of the Godhead is allowed to dwell in Him, the covenant which God made with Himself and which is for that reason eternal, the oath which God sware by Himself in the interests of man. But this third possibility does not belong only passively to the *aeterna Dei praedestinatio*[EN72]. That is, of course, one side of the truth, for the man Jesus can only suffer, receive and accept the divine election, and in that act of the good-pleasure of God, in that covenant of God with Himself, even the eternal Son is elected, ordained and sent by the Father to be its executor. But if He and the Father are one in this unity of the divine name and glory, a unity in which there can be no question of rivalry, then it is clear that the Son, too, is an active Subject of the *aeterna Dei praedestinatio*[EN73] as Son of Man, that He is Himself the electing God, and that only in this way, and therefore in an unlimited divine sovereignty, is He the Elect, the One who is subjected to the divine predestination, the Son who is voluntarily obedient to the Father; that only in this way and for this reason is He the Son of Man establishing and fulfilling the will of God in the world. If we say only what Thomas would say, then we have knowledge only of the election of the man Jesus as such, and not of the election and personal electing of the Son of God which precedes this election. And once again we make the election of grace a divine mystery detached from the person of Jesus Christ. And of the reality of that mystery we know nothing. We cannot even believe it. In face of it we can only attempt to create the necessary knowledge by constructing a *decretum absolutum*[EN74]. In such circumstances predestination is not only a higher something behind and above the covenant effected and revealed in the divine-human person of Jesus Christ. In its very essence it is something quite different from this person. It is a hidden decree which we can never recognise as divine and to which we cannot possibly be required or advised to entrust ourselves. For trust in the divine decision depends upon whether that decision can be and actually is manifested to us as God's decision. And this is impossible unless it can be and actually is manifested to us as the decision of Jesus Christ. But how can it really be manifested to us as the decision of Jesus Christ if this is not actually the case, as according to the doctrine of Thomas and many others it is not? How can it really be manifested to us as the decision of Jesus Christ if we can think of the reality of the divine-human person of Jesus Christ only as one of those divine works which come about under the divine foreordination, and not as the work of works, not as the content of the Word and decree of God at the beginning of all things, not as the revelation of the mystery of predestination itself? Our own election by the grace of God directed towards us is revealed in the election of Jesus Christ. The election of that man is for us the *lumen praedestinationis*[EN75]. But we can only believe this if we can find in that election the eternal election (both passive and also active) of the Son of God Himself, if we can be absolutely certain that in Jesus Christ   [108] we have to do immediately and directly with the electing God. If this is not the case, we are exposed always to the doubt that in the election we have to do perhaps with the will of a God who has not bound Himself in covenant with us and who is not gracious towards us. If our

---

[EN72] eternal predestination of God
[EN73] eternal predestination of God
[EN74] absolute decree
[EN75] light of predestination

own election is truly revealed to us in the election of the man Jesus—and that is the meaning of the New Testament when it speaks of this man's election as our Saviour, Head and Priest, and of the foreordination of His passion and death—it is because in Him we have to do not merely with elected man, but with the electing God, with the Word and decree which was in the beginning with God; not, then, with a messenger or angel (Is. 63⁹), but with God Himself, with our Saviour, with the One who alone can be a true and faithful witness to our election.

Thomas, and many others after him, spoke of the election of Jesus Christ only in this second and passive sense, and with reference only to the man Jesus. Augustine, too, had spoken of it in this way, and we ourselves must do the same. But Augustine—and in this we must at once follow him—also looked upwards to the place where the incarnation, the reality of the divine-human person of Jesus Christ before the foundation of the world and all other reality, is identical with the eternal purpose of the good-pleasure of God, and where the eternal purpose of the good-pleasure of God which precedes all created reality is identical with the reality of the divine-human person of Jesus Christ. He looked upwards to the place where the eternal God not only foresees and foreordains this person, but where He Himself, as the presupposition of its revelation in time, actually is this person. The text Tit. 1² speaks of "the hope of eternal life, which God, that cannot lie, promised before times eternal." And in face of this text Augustine asks how God can make a promise "before times eternal" to men who did not exist "before times eternal." He answers: *In (Dei) ipsius aeternitate atque in Verbo eius coaeterno iam praedestinatione fixum erat, quod suo tempore futurum erat*[EN76] (*De civ. Dei* XII, 16). When he described it as an ultimate authority in which there is established already what was later to be in time, Augustine can hardly have been thinking of the eternal Word of God in itself and as such. If he had been, he would have been doing something very far from his purpose (and expressly contested by him at a later point in the passage), i.e., defining temporal existence as something externally pre-existent in God. His statement is, however, understandable, and valid and important, if by the eternal Word he understands the Word and decree which was in the beginning with God as maintained in Jn. 1¹⁻², and if he identifies this Word with Jesus, and regards *in Verbo eius coaeterno*[EN77] as an equivalent of *in Verbo eius incarnando*[EN78]. It is in this Word that before times eternal life eternal could be and actually was promised to man, even before man himself existed at all.

But Augustine was not the only father whose witness should be summoned and heard on this point. Nor was he the first. Before Augustine, and much more fully, Athanasius had expressed himself as follows (*Or. II c. Arianos, cap.* 75–77): "As the apostle has said (Tit. 2¹¹), the grace of God brought by the Saviour hath appeared, and hath been conveyed to us by His coming; but it was prepared long before we ourselves or even the world was in being. And the reason is indeed good and admirable. For it would be unworthy of God to think of Him as taking counsel to provide for us only later, lest it should appear as though our circumstances were not previously known to Him. The God of all things, who created us by His Word, knew what should befall us better than we ourselves, and He foreknew that after our first righteousness we should transgress His commandment, and that because of our disobedience we should be expelled from paradise. For that reason in His loving-kindness and goodness He prepared beforehand in His Word by whom He created us a provision for our salvation (προετοιμάζει ἐν τῷ ἰδίῳ λόγῳ, δι᾽ οὗ καὶ ἔκτισεν ἡμᾶς τὴν περὶ τῆς σωτηρίας ἡμῶν οἰκονομίαν). He did this so that even if we fell, deceived by the serpent, we

---

[EN76] In the eternity of (God) himself and in his co-eternal word, it has already been fixed by predestination what was to come to pass in his time
[EN77] in his co-eternal Word
[EN78] in his to-be-incarnate Word

should not finally be destroyed, but possessing the redemption and salvation prepared   [109]
beforehand in the Word, should rise again and live for ever. For the Word Himself was created for our sakes 'the beginning of His ways,' and 'the First-born of the brethren,' and He
Himself rose again as the first-fruits from the dead .... How, then, has He chosen us before
we came into existence, unless, as He Himself says, we were typified and represented in Him?
And how could He have predestined us to sonship before man was created, unless the Son
Himself had been laid as a foundation before time was, and had undertaken to provide a way
of salvation for us (πρὸ τοῦ αἰῶνος τεθεμελίωτο, ἀναδεξάμενος τὴν ὑπὲρ ἡμῶν
οἰκονομίαν)? Or how could we, as the Apostle goes on to say, 'have an inheritance being
predestinated' (Eph. 1¹¹), unless the Lord Himself had been laid as a foundation before
time was, and had thus been able to purpose in Himself (πρὸ τοῦ αἰῶνος ἦν θεμελιωθείς,
ὥστε αὐτὸν πρόθεσιν ἔχειν ὑπὲρ ἡμῶν) to take upon Himself in His flesh the sentence
decreed against Him, so that in Him we might finally attain to sonship? And how could we
receive anything before times eternal, we, the creatures of time, who did not then exist,
unless the grace appointed for us had already been deposited in Christ (εἰ μὴ ἐν τῷ Χριστῷ
ἦν ἀποκειμένη ἡ εἰς ἡμᾶς φθάνουσα χάρις). For that reason, on the day of judgment,
when everyone receives according to his works, He says: 'Come, ye blessed of my Father,
inherit the kingdom prepared for you from the foundation of the world' (Mt. 25³⁴). But
how, or in whom, could this kingdom be prepared for us before our existence, unless it were
in the Lord who was laid as the foundation of it before the world (ἐν τῷ κυρίῳ τῷ πρὸ
αἰῶνος εἰς τοῦτο θεμελιωθέντι), in order that built up upon Him we might be partakers of
His life and grace as stones fitly framed together? And all this happened ... that, as has been
said before, we may rise again shortly after our death and live for ever. For this would be
impossible for us as men formed of earth unless before time there had been prepared for us
in Christ the hope of life and salvation (εἰ μὴ πρὸ τοῦ αἰῶνος ἦν προετοιμασθεῖσα ἡμῖν ἐν
Χριστῷ ἡ τῆς ζωῆς καὶ σωτηρίας ἐλπίς). Obviously the Word which dwelt in our flesh,
set there as a beginning of God's ways for His works, was Himself laid as a foundation even as
the will of the Father fulfilled in Him ... that is to say, 'before time,' 'before the earth was,'
'before the mountains were settled' and 'before the fountains burst forth,' so that when the
earth and the mountains and the forms of the phenomenal world pass at the end of the
present age, we should not decay as they do, but live on, possessing the life and spiritual
blessings prepared for us in the Word Himself according to the election even before these
things were. And thus it is granted to us not to live only for the moment, but to live for ever in
Christ, our life having been grounded and prepared in Christ Jesus long before (ἐπειδὴ καὶ
πρὸ τούτων ἡ ζωὴ ἡμῶν τεθεμελίωτο καὶ ἡτοίμαστο ἐν Χριστῷ Ἰησοῦ). Nor was it
possible for our life to be grounded in any other, but only in the Lord who was before all
time and by whom time was, in order that we might inherit eternal life as it was in Him; for
God is good. And being always good, He willed this, He who saw that our weak nature stood
in need of His help and salvation. Now a wise master-builder, when he undertakes to build a
house, considers at the same time how he may repair that house should it fall into decay after
its erection, and weighs up what preparations must be made for that purpose, supplying the
foreman with the materials necessary for such repair, and thus making all the preparations
for renovation even before the house is built. In like manner, the renewing of our salvation is
grounded in Christ even before we were created (τὸν αὐτὸν τρόπον πρὸ ἡμῶν ἡ τῆς
ἡμετέρας σωτηρίας ἀνανέωσις θεμελιοῦται ἐν τῷ Χριστῷ), in order that it might be
possible for us to be created afresh in Him. The decree and purpose of this fresh creation
was formed before time was, but it was only as the need required it that the work was executed and the Saviour came. For in heaven the Lord Himself will represent us all, receiving

[110] us to everlasting life." It should be quite clear that Athanasius had a very powerful perception of the third possibility which lies between the being of the eternal Word or Son as such and the reality of the elected man Jesus, together with the election of those who believe in Him as this election is bound up with His election. He saw that the election of the man Jesus and our election, with all the grace and gifts of grace which this includes, have their "foundation," as he himself says, in the eternity of the Word or Son, an eternity which differs not at all from that of the Father. Without prejudice to His eternity, then, he ascribed to the eternal Word or Son of God a determination towards the elected man Jesus and towards the election of believers in Him as they are enclosed in Him. As against Thomas, he not only had a conception of the pure being of the triune God on the one hand, and a conception of the concrete temporal history of salvation willed and fulfilled by God on the other, but over and above that he had also a conception of the concrete decree of salvation made in the bosom of the triune Godhead, and a conception of the Johannine Logos which was identical with Jesus and which was in the beginning with God. He had, then, a truly Christian conception of the divine decree. With Athanasius the decree, or predestination, or election, was, in fact, the decision reached at the beginning of all things, at the beginning of the relationship between God and the reality which is distinct from Him. The Subject of this decision is the triune God—the Son of God no less than the Father and the Holy Spirit. And the specific object of it is the Son of God in His determination as the Son of Man, the God-Man, Jesus Christ, who is as such the eternal basis of the whole divine election.

We can conclude only that in spite of its great richness this insight had little or no influence upon the later development of the doctrine of predestination, to which it might well have given a completely different aspect. Not only Thomas, but the Reformers too, ignored it altogether. They did state that Jesus Christ is for us the *lumen*[EN79] or *speculum electionis*[EN80]. But they thought it sufficient to base this belief upon the reference to Jesus Christ as the first of the elect according to His human nature. They restricted themselves to this basis with the same exclusiveness as Thomas. They missed the fact that this basis is quite insufficient to explain the ἐν αὐτῷ[EN81] of Eph. 1⁴. And they also missed the fact that to establish the certainty of a belief in our own salvation it is not sufficient merely to say that in respect of our election we must cleave only to Jesus Christ on the ground that He must be regarded as the first of the elect, the Head of all others, the means chosen by the electing God for the execution of that which He determined concerning those elected by Him. A statement of this kind will hardly serve even as a truly effective or penetrating pastoral admonition. For when we tackle that question which is no mere quibble, but decisive for each of us, the question whether we ourselves belong to those who profit by what God has ordained to be of benefit to His elect in and through the means which He first elected, in other words, whether we ourselves are of the number of the elect, what is the value of an answer of this type? If in regard to the decisive factor, the election itself, or the electing God, we cannot fix our gaze and keep it fixed on Jesus Christ, because the electing God is not identical with Christ but behind and above Him, because in the beginning with God we have to reckon with someone or something other than the οὗτος[EN82] of Jn. 1², a decision of the divine good-pleasure quite unrelated to and not determined by Him, what useful purpose can such an answer serve? Of what avail is it to exhort us, as did the Reformers, and after them orthodox Protestants of both confessions, that we must acquiesce in the hidden decision of that ultimate authority, respecting it as a secret? Of what avail is it for the Calvinists to protest that

---

[EN79] light
[EN80] mirror of election
[EN81] in him
[EN82] he

as God's decision it is based on grounds which are just and adequate although beyond our comprehension, or for the Lutherans to assist us with the comforting assurance that this decision is determined by the general loving-kindness of God towards us? If it is not true that Jesus Christ Himself is for us the electing God, then all these attempts at consolation point us elsewhere than to the Word of God. We are directed to a different mystery from that of the [111] cradle and cross of Christ, a different revelation from that of His resurrection. And all the earnest statements concerning the majesty and mystery of God, all the well-meaning protest-ations of His fatherly loving-kindness, cannot in any way alter the fact that we necessarily remain anxious in respect of our election. For with statements of this kind we neither can nor ought to let ourselves be appeased. How can we have assurance in respect of our own election except by the Word of God? And how can even the Word of God give us assurance on this point if this Word, if Jesus Christ, is not really the electing God, not the election itself, not our election, but only an elected means whereby the electing God—electing elsewhere and in some other way—executes that which He has decreed concerning those whom He has—elsewhere and in some other way—elected? The fact that Calvin in particular not only did not answer but did not even perceive this question is the decisive objection which we have to bring against his whole doctrine of predestination. The electing God of Calvin is a *Deus nudus absconditus*[EN83]. It is not the *Deus revelatus*[EN84] who is as such the *Deus absconditus*[EN85], the eternal God. All the dubious features of Calvin's doctrine result from the basic failing that in the last analysis he separates God and Jesus Christ, thinking that what was in the beginning with God must be sought elsewhere than in Jesus Christ. Thus with all his forceful and impressive acknowledgment of the divine election of grace, ultimately he still passes by the grace of God as it has appeared in Jesus Christ. We have seen already how the Synod of Dort failed to answer this same question. It merely repeated, more harshly if any-thing, the unsatisfactory answer already given by Calvin. We have shown, too, that the Dutch Remonstrants on the one hand and the Lutherans on the other, while they did perceive and answer the question, unfortunately answered it in such a way as to alter the concept of the divine election, of the free and eternal decision of God, replacing it by the quite different concept of a divinely established religious world-order. In the last resort, then, they denied that the election of grace was God's election; and with the Remonstrants there was the quite unmistakeable introduction of a new and humanistic Pelagianism from which Neo-Protestantism was later to derive. In general, the theology of 17th century Protestantism could find no escape from this dilemma, apart from the attempt made in Coccejus.

Amongst the orthodox dogmaticians known to me I can think of only one in whom we find passages which point a way past the dilemma, and that is Polanus. With reference to Eph. 1⁴, he sees first: *Elegit nos Pater non ut Pater, quia electio non est opus personae Patris prop-rium, sed ut Deus, quandoquidem electio est totius sacrosanctae Trinitatis commune opus, cuius princi-pium est Pater*[EN86] (*Synt. Theol. chr.*, 1609, *col.* 1574). To this statement he adds the further statement *Electionis subiectum ἐν ᾧ in quo electi sumus, est Christus, non quatenus Deus, nec quate-nus nudus homo, sed quatenus θεάνθρωπος et mediator noster. Medio enim, in quo eligeremur, opus erat, quia sine illo non poterat fieri unto inter Deum eligentem et homines electos. Ita Christus est vinculum, quo Deus et electi coniunguntur*[EN87] (*col.* 1596). For this reason, Polanus accepts as

---

[EN83] purely hidden God
[EN84] revealed God
[EN85] hidden God
[EN86] The Father has chosen us not as Father, because election is not the personal work of the person of the Father, but as God, since election is the common work of the whole most Holy Trinity, of whom the Father is the beginning
[EN87] The subject of election 'in Him', in whom we have been elected, is Christ. Not because he is God, nor because he is simply a man, but because he is the God-man, and our mediator. This

self-evident the assertion which Dort in part contested and in part blatantly reinterpreted: *Electio Christi est fundamentum et firmamentum electionis angelorum et hominum*[EN88]. (*col.* 1570). His main definition can then read as follows: *Aeterna electio Christi est praedestinatio qua Deus Filium suum unigenitum designavit ab aeterno, ut etiam quoad suam humanam naturam esset Filius Dei et caput angelorum et hominum et mediator inter Deum et angelos hominesque*[EN89] (*col.* 1568 f.). We cannot say quite simply that in these passages the loftiness of Athanasius' teaching has again been attained. They are too general and indeterminate for that. Yet at the same time Polanus did know the passage of Athanasius. Indeed, he expressly reproduced it (*col.* 1596 f.). And in Jesus Christ the Mediator (with characteristic boldness he contrasted this concept with that of Redeemer, *col.* 1596 f.) he found the true and primary object of the divine

[112] election (which he characterised expressly as the work of the whole Trinity). In view of these facts we are forced to the conclusion that he was at least aware of the loftiness of Athanasius' conception, and that he did make some effort to direct his own thinking into similar channels.

If we except the doubtful efforts of the Lutherans and Coccejus and his school, the same cannot be said of the doctrine as held and taught by other orthodox dogmaticians, any more than it can of that of Thomas and the Reformers. The Reformed party were right to safeguard against the Remonstrants and Lutherans the tenet that the *causa efficiens impulsiva electionis*[EN90], that which motivates the will of God, is not to be sought outside of God Himself, but solely in His free good-pleasure. Thus it is not to be sought in a created reality foreseen by God. Nor is it to be sought in the good will of man, or the use which he makes of divine grace, or the meritorious work of faith, or even faith itself, or prayer, or perseverance, or the dignity and worth of the race. Nor is it to be sought even in the *meritum Christi*[EN91]; the obedience as such which was rendered by the man Jesus. All that is an effect and result of the divine election, but not its basis. The election itself is grace, free grace, having its origin and basis in God alone and not elsewhere: *Itaque electionis nostrae omniumque beneficiorum, quae cum ea coniuncta sunt, causam in Deo solum ab aeterno exsistere necesse est*[EN92] (as Polanus clearly has it, *ib. col.* 1575 f.). What was not seen, however, was that the correctness of this necessary thesis, and the power of the proclamation of free grace, are bound up with the fact that grace in its origin is concretely determined and fulfilled in God. Thus when we think of the origin of grace and the beginning of all things, we cannot and must not think either of divine caprice or divine loving-kindness, for these are both general and therefore without real content. What we must think of is Jesus Christ. To define and explain the election as free grace, it is not enough simply to keep on speaking of it as the unique work of God. Yet when the Reformed doctrine comes to speak of that which motivates the will of the electing God, all that it can tell us is this: *antecessit voluntas in Patre quosdam eligendi antequam Filium elegit*[EN93] (Walaeus, *Loci comm.*, 1640, 381, cf. *Syn. pur. Theol.* of Leiden, 1624, *Disp.* 24, 25). It is only because this *voluntas antecedens per iustitiam suam impediebatur* (!) *quoniam illis actu complete*

---

means, in whom we were elected, was required, since without him there could not be a union between the electing God and elect men. Thus, Christ is the chain by which God and his elect are joined

[EN88] The election of Christ is the foundation and firmament of the election of men and angels

[EN89] the eternal election of Christ is the predestination by which God designated his only Son from eternity, so that even with respect to his human nature he might be the Son of God, and head of the angels and of men, and mediator between God and the angels and men

[EN90] the efficient motive cause of election

[EN91] merit of Christ

[EN92] Therefore, it is necessary that there exist in God only in eternity a cause of our election and all the benefits which are joined to it

[EN93] The will in the Father to elect individuals precedes his election of the Son *salutem aeternam destinaret, ideo illis destinavit mediatorem, qui iustitiae Dei satisfaceret*[EN94], and only in so far as our election is in fact determined by the election of this Mediator, that our election follows His and we are elected "in Christ." It is true that these theologians did speak of a *certus aliquis respectus, a mutua relatio inter Christum tanquam caput et electos*[EN95] (*Leiden Synopsis*, 25, 27). But they made, too, the express distinction: *Decretum de nobis seruandis est praedestinatio ad finem, decretum vero de Christo tanquam capite nobis dando est praedestinatio ad media*[EN96] (Wolleb, *Theol. chr. comp.*, 1626, I *cap.* 4, 9). It could even be said: *Christum substratum esse electioni tanquam fundamentum conferendae salutis, ad quam electi eramus, adeo ut Christus demum electus consideretur post nostram electionem*[EN97] (Walaeus, *ib.*, p. 380). *Electi erant Patris, antequam Christi erant*[EN98] (p. 381). Of what avail was it, then, to append the philosophical observation that this was merely a question of a *prioritas ordinis, non temporis: nam et electi Christo et Christus electis datus in caput eodem eligendi actu*[EN99] (*ib.*, p. 382)? If in this order the higher authority is the general choice of the Father, and the election of Jesus Christ is only His election in execution of the decree of the Father, if the order is not to be understood as meaning that the divine election is as such the election of Jesus Christ, the passive and active election of the Son of God to be the Son of Man, and in Him the election of those who believe in Him, then it is inevitable that we should enquire concerning the decision of this higher authority, and certainly we cannot be described as elected "in Christ," but at very best only "for Christ." Jesus Christ is not in any sense, then, the *fundamentum electionis*[EN100]— at the Synod of Dort this was disputed on all sides and in all kinds of ways, with the exception of the timid and easily quashed suggestion of the Bremen delegation—but at very best [113] He is only the *fundamentum salutis*[EN101]. And the question is whether this "very best" is actually the case, i.e., whether it is the case with us. Is Christ really the *fundamentum salutis*[EN102] for us, because we belong to those whom the Father has given Him in fulfilment of the decree of election, and who now have Him as their Head? This question is absolutely decisive for the whole relationship between God and man, but there is no answer to it in the Reformed dogma of predestination. On the contrary, the question is raised there in its most acute form, raised in such a way as apparently to exclude all possibility of a positive answer unless recourse is had either to a pretended knowledge of the secret divine decree, or to personal faith, some inward testimony of the Spirit, or indeed (with the assistance of the much misunderstood *syllogismus practicus*[EN103]) to certain works of faith whose existence is supposed to give direct confirmation of faith and indirect confirmation of election. Certainly in this matter, in regard to the election and the electing God Himself, recourse cannot be had to Jesus Christ, of whom we are necessarily told that He is only the *primum medium*

[EN 94] antecedent will is hindered (!) by his justice, since when the act is complete, he destines them to eternal salvation, therefore he destines for them the mediator who satisfies the justice of God

[EN 95] definite other respect, mutual relation between Christ as head, and the elect

[EN 96] The decree concerning our salvation is the predestination to the end; the decree to give Christ to us as our head is the predestination to the means

[EN 97] that Christ is the substratum of election as much as of the salvation to be conferred – that salvation to which we were elected, such that Christ was considered finally elect after our election

[EN 98] The elect belonged to the Father before they belonged to Christ

[EN 99] priority of order, not of time; for both the elect were given to Christ, and Christ to the elect, in the same act of the election of the head

[EN100] foundation of election

[EN101] basis of salvation

[EN102] basis of salvation

[EN103] practical syllogism

electionis^{EN104}. A zeal for the free divinity of the *causa efficient impulsiva electionis*^{EN105} has led to the obscuring of the election itself (and the electing God) by the clouds of a divine good-pleasure which does not yield to more exact definition. And in proportion to the growing secrecy which was demanded in the face of this unknown factor, and the ever greater impressiveness and mysteriousness with which the name of God came to be uttered, the danger became ever more acute that in one way or another the emphasis would and could be laid again upon "man," with theologians concerning themselves more and more with the affairs of the very enemy that they had set out to fight—semi-Pelagianism both old and new. The refusal to speak of Christ in order to speak rightly of grace prevented any proper discernment of the fact that the complement of election is faith. And the inevitable result was an experimenting with those other "complements" which are always in the offing when it is thought that there can be dealings with God apart from Jesus Christ, and consequently the call to faith cannot be heard. On the one hand, it was only to be expected that in the shadow of such a Christless doctrine of predestination there should develop a Reformed mysticism. G. Tersteegen bore classical witness to this trend when in his last words he could glorify God as "omnipresent" and "all-sufficient being" without even so much as an allusion to the name of Jesus Christ. On the other hand, it was quite understandable that in the shadow of this same doctrine there should develop a Reformed ethic of "secular" asceticism and industry, an ethic which did for a time—as embodied to some extent in a Benjamin Franklin—enable Calvinism to play so triumphant a part in world affairs. What there was of goodness and greatness in these developments, from the Christian standpoint, did not in any case derive from the orthodox Reformed doctrine of predestination as such, but from those elements of a Christian and biblical doctrine of predestination which were suppressed and yet in spite of the suppression still lived on in the orthodox teaching. There can be no doubt that even in the abbreviated form of a doctrine of the elected Mediator the Pauline ἐν αὐτῷ ^{EN106} could in practice be presented in such a way as, in fact, to cover over the mysterious background of the *decretum absolutum*^{EN107}. To that extent men would be constrained to cleave directly to Christ in respect of their election and salvation, and thus headed off—or at any rate many of them—from the flight into mysticism or moralism which is apparently an unavoidable consequence of the doctrine of the *decretum absolutum*^{EN108}. But for this happy inconsistency, there is no telling what fate might not have overtaken the Reformed Church. But this Church has no cause to pride itself on manifestations which can be explained only as the results of a false start, i.e., the results of the doctrine of a *decretum absolutum*^{EN198}. And the possibility of such a happy inconsistency should not prevent us from recognising this false

[114] start for what it was. Nor must it encourage us to perpetuate the error. It must encourage us rather to correct it, replacing the doctrine of the *decretum absolutum*^{EN110} by that of the Word which was in the beginning with God.

As early as the beginning of the 17th century an important attempt was made in this direction even within the older Reformed dogmatics. This attempt was by J. Coccejus and his disciples. It is no mere accident that Coccejus came from the theological school of Bremen, from which there had already originated at Dort a protest which was at first quite ineffective. The merit of Coccejus consists primarily in something which we have already mentioned—that he reunites two things which would never have been separated if the Bible had been

---

EN104 first means of election
EN105 the efficient motive cause of election
EN106 in him
EN107 absolute decree
EN108 absolute decree
EN109 absolute decree
EN110 absolute decree

properly studied: the eternal election of grace and the eternal decree of salvation, the testament or covenant-decree of God which is His *voluntas ultima, qua apud se ipsum designavit haeredes iustitiae et salutis per fidem non sine mediatore testamenti*[EN111] (*S. Theol.*, 1662, *cap.* 33, 7). Coccejus thought of that decree as identical with the decree of predestination (*ib.*, 37, 2). So, too, did F. Burmann, *Syn. Theol.*, 1678, I, 38, 23: *Consilium exercendae gratiae a Deo dispositum est per modum testamenti. Testamentum autem de haeredibus Deo sine mediatore et sponsore testamenti factum non est, cut primo dispositum est regnum*[EN112]. It is true that at a first glance these statements seem to leave the question open whether the direct object of salvation is not sought in the elect themselves predestinated the heirs of righteousness and salvation; whether it is not held that the election of Jesus Christ belongs to this primary election with a necessity which is only relative and not absolute: *non sine mediatore testamenti. Simul constituit Christum caput et primogenitum et illos membra et fratres Christi*[EN113] (Coccejus 37, 31). Later writers like F. Burmann (*op. cit.*) and P. van Mastricht (*Theor. Pract. Theol.*, 1698, III, 3, 8) identified the *obiectum electionis*[EN114] with the *totus Christus mysticus, h. e. Christus cum omnibus suis*[EN115]. In reality the true sequence of thought is quite plain both with Coccejus and his disciples: *primum Christum electum fuisse ut caput, deinde nos ut membra in ipso*[EN116] (Burmann, *op. cit.*). Coccejus himself (*ib.*, 33, 16 f.) developed the doctrine of the covenant under three heads. *Prima pars testamenti est, quod Deus decrevit Filium suum unigenitum dare, eumque mittere in carne ut esset caro, semen Abrahae et mulieris, frater servandorum, atque ita sanctificans et qui sanctificantur ex uno essent omnes*[EN117] (Jn. 3^{16}, Heb. 2^{11}). The second part of the covenant is the divine *voluntas iustificandi per fidem in sponsor em*[EN118], i.e., the dispensation indicated in Jn. 3^{16}, that those that believe in Him should not perish but have everlasting life, the *communio peccatoris et spontoris per spiritum sponsoris, qui peccatorem unit sponsori*[EN119] and whose first work is faith. It is only in the third part of the covenant that we come to the *designatio haeredum iustitiae*[EN120], the eternal separating out of those who according to Jn. 3^{17} are to be saved by the coming into the world of the Son of God, and who according to Rom. 8^{29} are to belong to the brethren of the first-born, and according to Gal. 3^8 to the Gentiles justified by faith. At the decisive point, then, Coccejus can say quite unequivocally: *Patet, hoc consilio introductam esse illam plenum ut consolationis et amabilitatis ita gloriae oeconomiam, qua Pater se constituit vindicem sanctitatis et nominis divini, regnumque ac indicium Filio dedit, Filius autem ut Sapientia (h. e. in quo sapientia Dei creotoris, volentis glorificari in homine, potuit explicari) unctus est et designatus princeps salutis, sacerdos populi sui, eiusque rex et dominus et uno verbo, angelus Jehovae assertor,*

[EN111] final will, by which he designated before his very self the heirs of his righteousness and salvation through faith, and not without the mediator of the covenant

[EN112] the counsel of the grace to be worked by God is granted through the means of the covenant. But the covenant is not made without a mediator and sponsor of the covenant, to whom first the Kingdom is granted

[EN113] not without the mediator of the covenant. He established Christ as the head and the first-born at the same time as the members and brothers of Christ

[EN114] object of election

[EN115] the whole mystical Christ, that is Christ with all his own

[EN116] that Christ was chosen first as the head, and then us as the members in him

[EN117] The first part of the covenant is that in which God decreed to give his only Son, and to send him in the flesh to be flesh, the seed of Abraham and of the woman, as brother of those who were to be saved. And thus the sanctifier and those who are sanctified are all from the same

[EN118] will for justifying by faith in the one who promises

[EN119] fellowship of the one who sins with the one who promises, but the spirit of the one who promises, who unites sinner to promissor

[EN120] designation of the heirs of righteousness

Patris gloriae restitutor et manifestator[EN121] (*ib.*, 34, 22). According to Coccejus (37, 31), then, the ἐν αὐτῷ[EN122] of Eph. 1⁴ must be understood in a twofold sense: *cum Christo ut praecognito*[EN123] and *per Christum et cum Christo ut eligente: quod est sponsoris*[EN124]. The same applies to the ἐποίησεν πρόθεσιν ἐν τῷ Χριστῷ Ἰησοῦ[EN125] of Eph. 3¹¹; to the passages in John which relate to the election of Jesus; to Ps. 2⁸: "Ask of me, and I shall give thee the heathen for thine inheritance, and the uttermost parts of the earth for thy possession"; to Jn. 5²¹: "For as the Father raiseth up the dead and quickeneth them; even so the Son quickeneth whom he will"; and strangely enough to Mt. 11¹⁷: "We have piped unto you, and ye have not danced

[115]   ..." To sum up, Coccejus saw three things: (1) that the decree of election is identical with that of salvation; (2) that the decree of salvation relates primarily to the mission and people of the Son; and (3) that, like the Father and the Holy Spirit, the Son participates in the decree as divine Subject, so that He is both *electus*[EN126] and *eligens*[EN127]. These three things enable us to overcome and set aside the Calvinistic *decretum absolutum*[EN128] (the notion that the true basis of election is an indeterminate and abstract good-pleasure of God), and to attain to a genuinely Christian understanding of the doctrine of predestination. This is especially the case if the first assertion in particular is meant and carried through with all strictness. The defect of Coccejus and his followers consists in the fact that while they did maintain the identity of the two decrees they did not exploit this identity as they might have done in relation to the whole doctrine of election. The discovery which they made is like a light shining above the doctrine of this particular school, but not interpenetrating it in such a way as to mark off its outlines clearly and effectively from those of the older Calvinistic teaching held by the other orthodox dogmaticians of the Reformed Church. The result is that in the development of theology Coccejus has gained a name and played his part as a pioneer of the so-called soteriological understanding of the divine covenant of grace actualised in time, but not as a pioneer of this important correction of the Reformed doctrine of predestination. Hence it is possible and even understandable that on the one hand a Coccejus specialist like G. Schrenk (*Gottesreich und Bund im älteren Protestantismus*, 1923) should hardly have been aware of the scope of Coccejus' reflections on the doctrine of predestination, and that on the other a specialist on the history of the doctrine like A. Schweitzer should completely overlook and ignore Coccejus and his disciples. It is true that the suggestions of the school did not, in fact, change the aspect of 17th century Reformed theology in this respect, but we must conclude that within those suggestions there was always present at least the possibility of such a change.

The election of Jesus Christ is the eternal choice and decision of God. And our first assertion tells us that Jesus Christ is the electing God. We must not ask concerning any other but Him. In no depth of the Godhead shall we encoun-

---

[EN121] It is plain that in this plan, that full economy of his comfort, his love, and his glory has been introduced. In this economy, the Father establishes himself as the vindicator of his holiness and his divine name, and he gives his Kingdom and his judgment to his Son, and his Son is anointed as wisdom. That is, in the Son, the wisdom of God the creator, who wills to be glorified in man, can be explicated. He is also designated the captain of salvation, the priest of his people, and its king and Lord, and in short the protecting angel of Yahweh, restorer and revealer of the glory of the Father

[EN122] in him

[EN123] with Christ as the one who is foreknown

[EN124] through Christ and with Christ as the electing one: because he is the one who promises

[EN125] he effected his purpose in Christ Jesus

[EN126] elected

[EN127] electing

[EN128] absolute decree

ter any other but Him. There is no such thing as Godhead in itself. Godhead is always the Godhead of the Father, the Son and the Holy Spirit. But the Father is the Father of Jesus Christ and the Holy Spirit is the Spirit of the Father and the Spirit of Jesus Christ. There is no such thing as a *decretum absolutum*[EN129]. There is no such thing as a will of God apart from the will of Jesus Christ. Thus Jesus Christ is not only the *manifestatio*[EN130] and *speculum nostrae praedestinationis*[EN131]. And He is this not simply in the sense that our election can be known to us and contemplated by us only through His election, as an election which, like His and with His, is made (or not made) by a secret and hidden will of God. On the contrary, Jesus Christ reveals to us our election as an election which is made by Him, by His will which is also the will of God. He tells us that He Himself is the One who elects us. In the very foreground of our existence in history we can and should cleave wholly and with full assurance to Him because in the eternal background of history, in the beginning with God, the only decree which was passed, the only Word which was spoken and which prevails, was the decision which was executed by Him. As we believe in Him and hear His Word and hold fast by His decision, we can know with a certainty   [116] which nothing can ever shake that we are the elect of God.

Jesus Christ is elected man. In making this second assertion we are again at one with the traditional teaching. But the christological assertion of tradition tells us no more than that in His humanity Jesus Christ was one of the elect. It was in virtue of His divinity that He was ordained and appointed Lord and Head of all others, the organ and instrument of the whole election of God and the revelation and reflection of the election of those who were elected with Him.

Now without our first assertion we cannot maintain such a position. For where can Jesus Christ derive the authority and power to be Lord and Head of all others, and how can these others be elected "in Him," and how can they see their election in Him the first of the elect, and how can they find in His election the assurance of their own, if He is only the object of election and not Himself its Subject, if He is only an elect creature and not primarily and supremely the electing Creator? Obviously in a strict and serious sense we can never say of any creature that other creatures are elect "in it," that it is their Lord and Head, and that in its election they can and should have assurance of their own. How can a mere creature ever come to the point of standing in this way before God, above and on behalf of others? If the testimony of Holy Scripture concerning the man Jesus Christ is true, that this man does stand before God above and on behalf of others, then this man is no mere creature but He is also the Creator, and His own electing as Creator must have preceded His election as creature. In one and the same person He must be both elected man

---

[EN129] absolute decree
[EN130] manifestation
[EN131] mirror of our predestination

123

and the electing God. Thus the second assertion rests on the first, and for the sake of the second the first ought never to be denied or passed over.

Because of this interconnexion we must now formulate the second statement with rather more precision. It tells us that before all created reality, before all being and becoming in time, before time itself, in the pre-temporal eternity of God, the eternal divine decision as such has as its object and content the existence of this one created being, the man Jesus of Nazareth, and the work of this man in His life and death, His humiliation and exaltation, His obedience and merit. It tells us further that in and with the existence of this man the eternal divine decision has as its object and content the execution of the divine covenant with man, the salvation of all men. In this function this man is the object of the eternal divine decision and foreordination. Jesus Christ, then, is not merely one of the elect but *the* elect of God. From the very beginning (from eternity itself), as elected man He does not stand alongside the rest of the elect, but before and above them as the One who is originally and properly the Elect. From the very beginning (from eternity itself), there are no other elect together with or apart from Him, but, as Eph. 1^4 tells us, only "in" Him. "In Him" does not simply mean with Him, together with Him,

[117] in His company. Nor does it mean only through Him, by means of that which He as elected man can be and do for them. "In Him" means in His person, in His will, in His own divine choice, in the basic decision of God which He fulfils over against every man. What singles Him out from the rest of the elect, and yet also, and for the first time, unites Him with them, is the fact that as elected man He is also the electing God, electing them in His own humanity. In that He (as God) wills Himself (as man), He also wills them. And so they are elect "in Him," in and with His own election. And so, too, His election must be distinguished from theirs. It must not be distinguished from theirs merely as the example and type, the revelation and reflection of their election. All this can, of course, be said quite truly of the election of Jesus Christ. But it must be said further that His election is the original and all-inclusive election; the election which is absolutely unique, but which in this very uniqueness is universally meaningful and efficacious, because it is the election of Him who Himself elects. Of none other of the elect can it be said that his election carries in it and with it the election of the rest. But that is what we must say of Jesus Christ when we think of Him in relation to the rest. And for this reason, as elected man. He is the Lord and Head of all the elect, the revelation and reflection of their election, and the organ and instrument of all divine electing. For this reason His election is indeed the type of all election. For this reason we must now learn really to recognise in Him not only the electing God but also elected man.

The basic passage in Jn. 1^{1-2} speaks of the man Jesus. In so doing, it contains self-evidently this second assertion, that Jesus Christ is elected man. All the Johannine passages which speak of His mission, of His doing the will and works of His Father, of His submission, and of the submission of His people to the rule of the Father, really point to this aspect of the matter. Indeed, all the New Testament passages so far quoted find in Jesus Christ this elected man and therefore in a creature distinct from God the divine decree in the very beginning. To that extent do they not all testify to a second and passive meaning of the election of Jesus Christ? More specific testimony is given in the words of Jn. 17^{24}: "Thou lovedst me before the foundation of the world"; and quite expressly in Lk. 9^{35} and 23^{35}. It is common to the verses from Luke "that Jesus is identified as the Christ in the immediate context of His sufferings. He was declared υἱός μου ὁ ἐκλελεγμένος EN132 at the transfiguration, just before His entry on the way of suffering. His declaration as ὁ Χριστὸς τοῦ θεοῦ ὁ ἐκλεκτός EN133 came when He had already taken the form of the crucified. He is elected man not only in His passion and in spite of His passion, but for His passion" (G. Schrenk in *Theol. W.B. zum N.T.* IV, 194, 11 f.). There is little room for doubt that in Jn. 17^{24}, too, there is a specific reference to the story of the passion. If we compare with it Ac. 2^{23}, 4$^{27f.}$, 1 Pet. 1^{20}, Heb. 9^{14} and Rev. 13^{8}, we can hardly make too much of this aspect of it. Deutero-Isaiah speaks of the Servant whom Yahweh upholds; of the Elect in whom His soul delighteth and upon whom He has set His Spirit, that he may bring forth judgment to the Gentiles (Is. 42^{1}); of the One who was given as a covenant for the people, for a light of the Gentiles (Is. 42^{6}, 49^{8}). And it is of this One that he tells us, at the very climax of his presentation, that "they made his grave with the wicked, and with the rich in his death; although he had done no violence, neither was any deceit in his mouth. Yet it pleased the Lord to bruise him; he hath put him to grief: when thou shalt make his soul an offering for sin, he shall see his seed, he shall prolong his days, and the pleasure of the Lord shall prosper in his hand" (Is. 53$^{9f.}$). And it is in the light of this climax—election for suffering—that the relevant passage in Heb. 2$^{11f.}$ must certainly be understood: "For both he that sanctifieth and they that are sanctified are all of one: for which cause he is not ashamed to call them brethren, saying, I will declare thy name unto my brethren, in the midst of the church will I sing praise unto thee. And again, I will put my trust in him. And again, Behold I and the children which God hath given me. Forasmuch then as the children are partakers in flesh and blood, he also himself likewise took part of the same; that through death he might destroy him that had the power of death, that is, the devil." Ἰδοὺ ὁ ἄνθρωπος EN134 (Jn. 19^{5}). [118]

In relation to this passive election of Jesus Christ the great exponents of the traditional doctrine of predestination developed an insight which we too must take as our starting-point, because, rightly understood, it contains within itself everything else that must be noted and said in this connexion. The insight is this: that in the predestination of the man Jesus we see what predestination is always and everywhere—the acceptance and reception of man only by the free grace of God. Even in the man Jesus there is indeed no merit, no prior and self-sufficient goodness, which can precede His election to divine sonship. Neither prayer nor the life of faith can command or compel His election. It is by the work of the Word of God, by the Holy Spirit, that He is conceived and born without sin, that He is what He is, the Son of God; by grace alone. And as He became Christ, so we become Christians. As He became our Head, so we become His body and members. As He became the object of our faith, so we become believers in Him. What we have to consider in the elected man Jesus is, then, the destiny of human nature, its exaltation to fellowship with God,

---

EN132 my chosen son
EN133 the Christ of God, the chosen one
EN134 Behold, the man

and the manner of its participation in this exaltation by the free grace of God. But more, it is in this man that the exaltation itself is revealed and proclaimed. For with His decree concerning this man, God decreed too that this man should be the cause and the instrument of our exaltation.

It was along this line that Augustine (*De praed. sanct.* 15) made his second important contribution to the christological understanding of predestination. The *praeclarissimum lumen praedestinationis el gratiae is ipse salvator, ipse mediator Dei et hominum homo Jesus Christus*EN135. What works of His own, what prior faith, could ever have given this man, as man, the right to be the Son of God, our Mediator and Redeemer? *Respondeatur quaeso: ille homo, ut a Verbo Patri coaeterno in unitatem personae assumptus Filius Dei esset, unde hoc meruit? Quod eius bonum qualecumque praecessit? Quid egit ante, quid credidit, quid petivit, ut ad hanc ineffabilem excellentiam perveniret? Nonne faciente ac suscipiente Verbo ipse homo ex quo esse coepit, Filius Dei unicus esse coepit?*EN136 At this point we are forced to ask in all seriousness: "O man, who art thou that repliest against God?" (Rom. 9²⁰) and we receive the answer: "Thou art man as He. Jesus, is man." *At enim gratia ille talis ac tantus est. Appareat itaque nobis in nostro capite ipse fons gratiae, unde secundum unius cuiusque mensuram se per cuncta eius membra diffundit. Ea gratia fit ab initio fidei suae homo quicumque christianus, qua gratia homo ille ab initio suo factus est Christus: de ipso Spiritu et hic renatus, de quo est ille natus; eodem Spiritu fit in nobis remissio peccatorum, quo Spiritu factum est, ut nullum haberet ille peccatum ... ipsa est igitur praedestinatio sanctorum quae in Sancto sanctorum maxime claruit: quam negare quis potest recte intelligentium eloquia veritatis? Nam et ipsum dominum gloriae, in quantum homo factus est Dei Filius, praedestinatum esse didicimus*EN137. Augustine's reference here to Rom. 1¹⁴ is not a very happy one, for he relied upon the Vulgate translation of ὁρισθέντος υἱοῦ θεοῦ EN138 as *qui praedestinatus est Filius Dei*EN139, which can hardly be the correct rendering. But in the light of those passages of Scripture which are really relevant he is quite right when he continues: *Preadestinatus est ergo Jesus, ut qui futurus erat secundum carnem Filius David, esset tamen in virtute Filius Dei secundum Spiritum sanctificationis .... Praedestinata est ista naturae humanae tanta et tam celsa et summa subvectio, ut quo attolleretur altius non haberet, sicut pro nobis ipsa divinitas quo usque se deponeret humilius non habuit quam suscepta natura hominis cum infirmitate carnis usque ad mortem cruets*EN140. When we

[119]

EN135 brightest light of predestination and grace, the saviour himself, the mediator between God and men, the man Jesus Christ

EN136 Who can answer this: whence did that man merit that he be the Son of God, assumed by the Word of the coeternal Father into the unity of personhood? What possible good of his was so excellent? What did he do, what did he believe, what did he seek beforehand, that he should arrive at this ineffable excellence? Surely it is not by the action and undertaking of the Word whereby man himself began to exist, that the only Son of God began to exist?

EN137 But he is so abounding and excelling in grace. Thus, may he appear to us in our heads as the very fountain of grace, from which according to the measure of each one he pours himself through all his members. By this grace each man becomes from the beginning of his faith a Christian, and by this grace that man was made from the beginning the Christ. By the same Spirit through which a man is reborn, he is also born; by that same Spirit the forgiveness of sins comes to us, and by that Spirit it was established that he would have no sin ... Therefore it is the same predestination of the saints which is most greatly clear in the predestination of the Saint of Saints. Who, who rightly understands the words of truth, could deny this? For we have learned that the Lord of glory himself, inasmuch as he as Son of God became man, was predestined

EN138 designated Son of God

EN139 the Son of God who was predestined

EN140 Therefore Jesus was predestined, as the one who would be the Son of David according to the flesh, nevertheless to be the Son of God in power, according to the Spirit of holiness ... For that so great and so noble and most high transportation of human nature is predestined such

consider Jesus, how else can we understand the grace which comes to us except as grace and therefore as predestination? *Sicut ergo praedestinatus est ille unus, ut caput nostrum esset, ita multi praedestinati sumus, ut membra eius essemus .... Ille quippe nos fecit credere in Christum, qui nobis fecit in quern credimus Christum; ille facit in hominibus principium et perfectiunem in Jesum, qui fecit hominem principem fidei et perfectorem Jesum*[EN141] (Heb. 12²). Augustine expressed himself to the same effect in *De dono perseu.* 24, 67 (cf. too *Tract, in Joann.* 105, 5–7, and *Sermo* 175, 2): *Nullum est illustrius praedestinationis exemplum quam ipse Jesus ... ipse mediator. Quisquis fidelis vult eam bene intelligere, attendat ipsum, atque in illo inveniat et seipsum: fidelis, inquam, qui in eo veram naturam credit et confitetur humanam, id est nostrum quamvis singulariter suscipiente Deo Verbo in unicum Filium Dei sublimatam .... Et ilium ergo et nos praedestinavit; quia et in illo, ut esset caput nostrum et in nobis, ut eius corpus essemus, non praecessura merita nostra sed opera sua futura praescivit*[EN142].

All this was said by Augustine against Pelagius and the Pelagians. It is of a piece, then, that as he saw it the significance of the predestination of Jesus Christ for us should lie essentially in the fact that in it we are forced to see clearly the freedom of grace as against all human claims to merit. Yet it was not an inversion of the teaching of Augustine, but only a making explicit of what was already implicit within it, when Thomas Aquinas gave to this thought a positive turn: *Dicitur (Christus) lumen praedestinationis et gratiae in quantum per eius praedestinationem et gratiam manifestatur nostra praedestinatio*[EN143] (*S. theol.* III, *qu.* 24, *art.* 3 *s.c.*). We have had occasion to contest Thomas' qualifying of this statement, but even as qualified by Thomas it is still correct, and as an expansion of the polemical teaching of Augustine it is most important. The election of Jesus Christ is, in fact, the revelation of our election. In His election we can and should recognise our own. *Praedestinatio Christi est exemplum nostrae praedestinationis secundum illud ad quod aliquis praedestinatur .... Ipse enim est praedestinatus ad hoc quod esset Dei Filius naturalis; nos autem praedestinamur ad filiationem adoptionis, quae est quaedam participata similitude filiationis naturalis*[EN144] (*ib., qu.* 24, *art.* 3 *c.*). And if it might be asked whether the words *manifestatio*[EN145] and *exemplum*[EN146] are not inadequate in this connexion, we are taught in *qu.* 24, *art.* 4 that the *praedestinatio Christi*[EN147]

---

that there could be no higher place to which it could be elevated, just as for us, that divinity had no lower place to which it could be degraded, than assuming human nature with the weakness of the flesh, even to death on a cross

[EN141] Therefore, just as that one man was predestined to be our head, so many of us were predestined to be his members ... Evidently, the one who made for us the Christ in whom we believe, also made us believe in Christ. The one who made the man Jesus the author and perfector of our faith (Heb. 12.2) also made beginning and perfection among men in Jesus

[EN142] There is no more graphic example of example of predestination than Jesus himself ... the mediator himself. Whoever wishes to understand predestination well should attend to him, and in him he will also find himself. The believing man, I say, who believes and confesses that in Him is true human nature, that is, our human nature however uniquely assumed by the Word of God and sublimated into the unique Son of God. Therefore God has predestined both him and us; since he foreknew not our already meritorious works, but his works to come, in order that he might be our head and in us, and we might be his body

[EN143] Christ is said to be the light of predestination and grace inasmuch as our predestination is manifested through his predestination and grace

[EN144] The predestination of Christ is the example of our predestination, according to which anyone is predestined. For he himself is predestined to this – to be the natural Son of God. But we were predestined to the sonship of adoption, which is something of a likeness in common with natural sonship

[EN145] manifestation

[EN146] example

[EN147] predestination of Christ

may indeed be called the *causa nostrae praedestinationis*[EN148] to the extent that God did decree our salvation from all eternity together with the attainment of it through Jesus Christ and therefore with the incarnation of Jesus Christ. It was because God decreed the incarnation of Christ that He also and at the same time (*simul*) decreed *ut esset nostrae salutis causa*[EN149]. But that, too, is surely inadequate. Thomas rests, unfortunately, upon a basic assertion which he made in due form and with complete clarity: *praedestinatio nostra ex simplici voluntate Dei dependet*[EN150] (*qu.* 24, *vid.* 2). And this means that he rests like Calvin

[120] upon the *decretum absolutum*[EN151]. He can even hazard the outrageous statement: *Si Christus non fuisset incarnandus, Deus praeordinasset homines salvari per aliam causam*[EN152] (*ib.*, *ad.* 3). As against that, we reaffirm the necessity of our first assertion, that only if Jesus Christ is the true and incontestable basis of our election can He be the basis of our knowledge of the election according to the second assertion, and only then can we have any assurance of our own election. But once again, within these limits Thomas did perceive and state quite correctly that the election of Jesus Christ, understood as the election of the man Jesus, has for us the positive significance that it carried with it (we should say, in it) from all eternity the reality and discernible truth of our own election.

On the same line as Augustine and Thomas, we now arrive at Calvin. *Jesus Christ est le miroir et le patron où Dieu a declaré les thresors infinis de sa bonté; car il est le chef de l'Eglise. Aussi nous faudra il commencer par luy, quand nous voudrons cognoistre comment Dieu besongne en ses membres inferieurs. Voila Jesus Christ, vray Dieu et vray homme. Or ceste nature humaine a esté exaltée en une dignité merveilleuse; car Jesus Christ estant Dieu et homme, est toutesfois Fils de Dieu: je dy, Fils unique, Fils naturel. Qu'est-ce qu'a merité la nature humaine qui est en Jesus Christ? Car elle procede de la race d'Adam; il falloit qu'il fust de la semence de David, ou autrement il n'eust point esté nostre Sauveur. Il a esté conceu de sa mere d'une façon miraculeuse, mais tant y a qu'il est venu de la race de David, d'Abraham et d'Adam. Ce qu'il a esté sanctifié et qu'il n'a point esté subiet à mesme corruption que nous, cela est venu de la grace admirable de Dieu et excellente. Mais tant y a, que si nous considerons la nature humaine de Jesus Christ, elle n'avoit point merité d'estre exaltée en ce degré d'honneur, pour dire: Voila celuy qui dominera par dessus les Anges, devant lequel tout genouil se ployera. Quand nous considerons une telle grace de Dieu en nostre Chef, ne faut-il pas qu'un chacun de nous entre en soy-mesme pour cognoistre: Dieu m'a esleu, moy qui estoye banny et rejetté de son Royaume. Je n'avoye aucune chose en moy qui luy peust estre agreable, et neantmoins il m'a choisi pour estre des siens. Ne faut-il pas bien que nous cognoissions une telle grace, pour la magnifier?*[EN153] (*Congrég. sur l'élect. ét.*, 1562, C.R. 8, 108 f.; cf. *De aet. Dei praed.*, 1552, *ib.*, 306 f.; *Instit.* III, 22, 1).

This insight is a true and important one. Yet we cannot say that in the form

---

[EN148] cause of our predestination
[EN149] in order that he might be the basis of our salvation
[EN150] our predestination depends upon the simple will of God
[EN151] absolute decree
[EN152] If Christ was not to be incarnate, then God would have ordained another means for men to be saved
[EN153] Jesus Christ is the mirror and the sponsor where God has declared the infinite treasures of his goodness; for he is the head of the Church. We must also begin with him when we would know how God cares for his lesser members. Behold Jesus Christ, very God and very man. To this wonderful dignity has human nature been elevated, for Jesus Christ being God and man is ever the Son of God. I say, only Son, natural Son. What has the human nature which is in Jesus Christ merited? For it proceeds from the root of Adam; he must come from the seed of David, or else he would not be our Saviour. He was conceived by his mother in a miraculous way, but still he came from the root of David, Abraham and Adam. The fact that he has been sanctified and has by no means been subject to the same corruption as we, comes from the admirable and excellent grace of God. But when we consider the human nature of Jesus Christ, it did not deserve to be exalted with this degree of honour as this: Behold the one

given to it by the great exponents of the doctrine of election it exhausts or embraces everything that is to be perceived and remembered in relation to this topic. Even as the object of predestination, even as elected man, Jesus Christ must still be understood as truly the beginning of all God's ways and works. That is the first thing which we have to bring out more clearly in this connexion. The second is that the election of the man Jesus is specifically His election to suffering, and that it is for this reason and in this form that it is the basic act of the divine election of grace. And the third is that we have to see our own election in that of the man Jesus because His election includes ours within itself and because ours is grounded in His. We are elected together with Him in so far as we are elected "in Him," i.e., through Him who is not merely the object but also and primarily the Subject of the divine election. We must attempt so to think of the reality of the passive election of Christ, of Jesus Christ as the object of the divine predestination, that in all our further discussion of this topic we may turn to good account the insight handed down to us by tradition.

Augustine and his followers emphasised quite rightly that the man Jesus as [121] such has nothing to bring before the electing God which would make Him worthy of the divine election or make His election necessary. He is the Son of God only by the grace of God. That this is indeed the case may be proved conclusively by the absoluteness of the gratitude and obedience with which this man stands before God and submits Himself to Him. It is thus that the creature lives before God, its freedom consisting in the fact that in its autonomy it recognises and acknowledges that it is wholly and utterly responsible to God. And so this man Jesus, as the object of the divine decree, is the beginning of all God's ways and works, the first-born of all creation. In Him it comes to pass for the first time that God wills and posits another being different from Himself, His creature. Be it noted that this determination of the will of God, this content of predestination, is already grace, for God did not stand in need of any particular ways or works *ad extra*EN154. He had no need of a creation. He might well have been satisfied with the inner glory of His threefold being, His freedom, and His love. The fact that He is not satisfied, but that His inner glory overflows and becomes outward, the fact that He wills the creation, and the man Jesus as the first-born of all creation, is grace, sovereign grace, a condescension inconceivably tender. But this determination of the will of God is eminently grace to the extent that in relation to this other, the creation of God, God's first thought and decree consists in the fact that in His Son He makes the being of this other His own being, that He allows the Son of Man

---

who has reigned above the angels, before whom every knee bows. When we consider such such grace of God in our Head, is it not necessary that each one of us embarks to know this: God has chosen me, me, who was banished and rejected from his kingdom. I have nothing in me which could be likeable, but nevertheless he has chosen me to be his own. Is it not necessary that we know such a great grace, in order to magnify it?

EN154 outside of himself

Jesus to be called and actually to be His own Son. In and with His lordship over this other, in and with the creaturely autonomy of this other—and even that is grace—God wills and decrees and posits in the beginning both His own fatherhood and also the sonship of the creature. This is more than mere kindness and condescension. It is self-giving. And that is how the inner glory of God overflows. From all eternity it purports and wills its own impartation to the creature, the closest possible union with it, a fellowship which is not to its own advantage but to that of the creature. It is in being gracious in this way that God sets forth His own glory. It is in the election of the man Jesus that His decision to be gracious is made. "God so loved the world, that he gave his only begotten Son" (Jn. 3^{16}). In a first and most important way we can now understand the extent to which, in the light of the election of the man Jesus, all election can be described only as free grace. The man Jesus is the elect of God. Those whom God elects He elects "in Him," not merely "like Him," but in His person, by His will, and by His election. Those whom God elects, the One blessed of God elects also. What can this election be, then, but more grace, a participation in the grace of the One who elects, a participation in His creatureliness (which is already grace), and a participation in His sonship [122] (which is eminently grace)? From its very source the election derives from the man Jesus. And as election by Him it is indirectly identical with that beginning willed and posited by the condescension and self-suffering of God. It is "the grace of our Lord Jesus Christ."

But the elected man Jesus was foreordained to suffer and to die. That is how His selection, and sending, and, as we have seen, His election, are understood in the New Testament. The free grace of God directed in Him towards the creature took on this form from the very first (from all eternity). According to Phil. 2$^{6f.}$ it is obedience unto death, even unto the death of the cross, to which the Son of God predestines Himself when He empties Himself of His divine form of being. And this predestining is the content of the divine decree at the beginning of all things. "The Word became flesh" (Jn. 1^{14}). This formulation of the message of Christmas already includes within itself the message of Good Friday. For "all flesh is as grass." The election of the man Jesus means, then, that a wrath is kindled, a sentence pronounced and finally executed, a rejection actualised. It has been determined thus from all eternity. From all eternity judgment has been foreseen—even in the overflowing of God's inner glory, even in the ineffable condescension of God's embracing of the creature, even in the fulness of self-giving by which God Himself wills to become a creature. For teleologically the election of the man Jesus carries within itself the election of a creation which is good according to the positive will of God and of man as fashioned after the divine image and foreordained to the divine likeness (reflection). But this involves necessarily the rejection of Satan, the rebel angel who is the very sum and substance of the possibility which is not chosen by God (and which exists only in virtue of this negation); the very essence of the creature in its misunderstanding and misuse of its creation and destiny and in its desire to be as God, to be itself a god. Satan (and the whole kingdom of evil, i.e., the demonic, which has its basis in him) is the shadow which accompanies the light of the election of Jesus Christ (and in Him of the good creation in which man is in the divine image). And in the divine counsel the shadow itself is necessary as the object of rejection. To the reality of its existence and might and activity (only, of course, in the power of the divine negation, but to that extent grounded in the divine will and counsel) testimony is given by the fall of man, in which man appropriates to himself the satanic desire. When confronted by Satan and his kingdom, man in himself and as such has in his creaturely freedom no power to reject that which in His divine freedom God rejects. Face to face with temptation he cannot maintain the goodness of his creation in the divine image and foreordination to the divine likeness. This is done by the elected man Jesus (Mt. 4^{1-11}). In himself and as such man will always do as Adam did in Gen. 3. And for this reason, according to the will and counsel of God, man in himself and as such incurs the rejection which rests upon his temptation and corruption. He stands under the wrath [123] which is God's only answer to the creature which abuses and dishonours its creatureliness. Exposed to the power of the divine negation, he is guilty of death. But it is this very man in himself and as such who in and with the election of the man Jesus is loved of God from all eternity and elected to fellowship with Him: he who was powerless against the insinuations of the tempter and seducer; he who in his actual temptation and seduction became the enemy of God; he who incurred rejection and became guilty of death. In this one man Jesus, God puts at the head and in the place of all other men the One who has the same power as Himself to reject Satan and to maintain and not surrender the goodness of man's divine creation and destiny; the One who according to Mt. 4 actually does this, and does it for all who are elected in Him, for man in himself and as such who does not and cannot do it of himself. The rejection which all men incurred, the wrath of God under which all men lie, the death which all men must die, God in His love for men transfers from all eternity to Him in whom He loves and elects them, and whom He elects at their head and in their place. God from all eternity ordains this obedient One in order that He might bear the suffering which the disobedient have deserved and which for the sake of God's righteousness must necessarily be borne. Indeed, the very obedience which was exacted of Him and attained by Him was His willingness to take upon Himself the divine rejection of all others and to suffer that which they ought to have suffered. He is elected, and He maintains the goodness of man's divine creation and destiny, not for His own sake but for their sake, for the sake of man in himself and as such. He, the Elect, is appointed to check and defeat Satan on behalf of all those that are elected "in Him," on behalf of the descendants and confederates of Adam now beloved of God. And this checking and defeating of Satan must consist in His allowing the righteousness of God to proceed against Himself instead of them. For this reason, He is the Lamb slain, and the Lamb slain from the foundation of the world.

For this reason, the *crucified* Jesus is the "image of the invisible God." If, then, there is an election of others on the basis of the election of this man Jesus, we can see that that election is to be understood only as free grace, and we can also see why this is so. The ones who "in Him," i.e., through Him, are elected and made partakers of His grace are those who could see in themselves only lost sinners "oppressed of the devil" (Ac. 10^{38}). If He did not stand at their head, if they were not elected "in Him," without Him and outside Him they would be for ever rejected. They have nothing which they can call their own except their transgression. Yet these transgressors are the ones on whose behalf the eternal love of God for Jesus Christ is willed and extended. They knew nothing of this love. They did not even desire it. But for His part the Elect who stands at the head of the rejected elects only the rejected. The Gos-

[124] pel tells us unequivocally in this connexion that "the Son of man is come to seek and to save that which is lost" (Lk. 19^{10}), that the sick have need of Him and not the whole (Mk. 2^{17}), and that in heaven there is more joy over one sinner that repenteth than over ninety and nine just persons which have no need of repentance (Lk. 15^7). Who is the Elect? He is always the one who "was dead and is alive again," who "was lost and is found" (Lk. 15^{24}). That the elected man Jesus had to suffer and die means no more and no less than that in becoming man God makes Himself responsible for man who became His enemy, and that He takes upon Himself all the consequences of man's action—his rejection and his death. This is what is involved in the self-giving of God. This is the radicalness of His grace. God must let righteousness reign, and He wills to do so. Against the aggression of the shadow-world of Satan which is negated by Him and which exists only in virtue of this negation, God must and will maintain the honour of His creation, the honour of man as created and ordained for Him, and His own honour. God cannot and will not acquiesce in the encroachment of this shadow-world upon the sphere of His positive will, an encroachment made with the fall of man. On the contrary, it must be His pleasure to see that Satan and all that has its source and origin in him are rejected. But this means that God must and will reject man as he is in himself. And He does so. But He does it in the person of the elected man Jesus. And in Him He loves man as he is in himself. He elects Jesus, then, at the head and in the place of all others. The wrath of God, the judgment and the penalty, fall, then, upon Him. And this means upon His own Son, upon Himself: upon Him, and not upon those whom He loves and elects "in Him;" upon Him, and not upon the disobedient. Why not upon the disobedient? Why this interposition of the just for the unjust by which in some incomprehensible manner the eternal Judge becomes Himself the judged? Because His justice is a merciful and for this reason a perfect justice. Because the sin of the disobedient is also their need, and even while it affronts Him it also moves Him to pity. Because He knows quite well the basis of Satan's existence and the might and force with which sinners were overthrown and fell in the negative power of His own counsel and will. Because in the powerlessness of sinners against Satan He sees their

guilt, but in their guilt He sees also their powerlessness. Because He knows quite well that those who had no strength to resist Satan are even less able to bear and suffer the rejection which those who hear Satan and obey him merit together with him. Because from all eternity He knows "whereof we are made" (Ps. 103^{14}). That is why He intervened on our behalf in His Son. That is why He did no less. He did not owe it to us to do it. For it was not He but we ourselves in out culpable weakness who delivered us up to Satan and to the divine wrath and rejection. And yet God does it because from all eternity He loves and elects us in His Son, because from all eternity He sees us in His Son   [125] as sinners to whom He is gracious. For all those, then, whom God elects in His Son, the essence of the free grace of God consists in the fact that in this same Jesus God who is the Judge takes the place of the judged, and they are fully acquitted, therefore, from sin and its guilt and penalty. Thus the wrath of God and the rejection of Satan and his kingdom no longer have any relevance for them. On the contrary, the wrath of God and the rejection of Satan, the free course of divine justice to which God Himself has subjected Himself on their behalf, has brought them to freedom. In the One in whom they are elected, that is to say, in the death which the Son of God has died for them, they them- selves have died as sinners. And that means their radical sanctification, separ- ation and purification for participation in a true creaturely independence, and more than that, for the divine sonship of the creature which is the grace for which from all eternity they are elected in the election of the man Jesus.

And now we must say, too, of the elected man Jesus (apart from the fact that He is what He is by grace, and that His grace consists in bringing many to freedom) that in His mercy God remains just as faithful to Him as He in His readiness to do God's will remains faithful to God. There is steadfastness on both sides. On God's side, it is the steadfastness of grace even in the judgment to which He condemns the Elect. It is the constancy of love even in the fire of the wrath which consumes Him. It is the steadfastness of election even in the midst of the rejection which overtakes Him. And on the side of the Elect, it is the steadfastness of obedience to God, and of calling only upon Him, and of confidence in the righteousness of His will. It is in the unity of this steadfast- ness both divine and human that we shall find the peculiar secret of the elec- tion of the man Jesus. In this twofold steadfastness there is to be seen both the glorifying of God and also the salvation of men, the two things which together constitute the aim and meaning of the covenant willed by God and the elec- tion of this man. In this steadfastness Satan is resisted, defied and defeated both by the God against whom he revolted and also by the man against whom he had triumphed. In this steadfastness the Word of God is spoken and the answer of man is given, and together the Word and the answer represent the decision willed by God in all His ways and works, and therefore constitute the content of the will and counsel of God in the beginning. The Word of the divine steadfastness is the resurrection of Jesus from the dead, His exaltation, His session at the right hand of the Father. By these events God confirms the fact that the Elect is the only-begotten Son of God who can suffer death but cannot be holden of death, who by His death must destroy death. By these events God makes manifest the vindication of His positive will as Creator against the assault of Satan, a vindication which He made by the offering up of His Elect. There takes place here the decisive act of history, which is the actual-[126] isation of the overflowing of the inner glory of God. The kingdom of God is here set up as the consummation towards which all God's ways and works are moving. And the answer of human steadfastness is the prayer which is the assent of Jesus to the will of God as it confronts His own will. This prayer is His intercession with God on behalf of His people. And yet it is also a prayer which He teaches His people and places on the lips of His people. With this prayer He proves Himself to be the Son of God who is rejected for their sakes and yet who is still the Elect of God even in His rejection. With this prayer He undertakes to be both priest and victim, thus affirming for His part the salutariness of the holy wrath of God. In this prayer He fulfils His creaturely office in the history of creation as it was determined and prepared by God. In this prayer He affirms the fact that He is the King who was appointed by God to be at the head and in the place of the elect as their Lord and Head. In this prayer He affirms that He Himself in His own person is the kingdom of God. This divine and human steadfastness (reflected in the resurrection and the prayer of Jesus) constitutes the meaning and purpose of the election of Jesus. And so, too, this election itself is the content of the divine decree which obviously precedes not only creation but that whole complex of problems which accompany and threaten creation. The real concern in the resurrection and prayer of the man Jesus is that those problems should be overcome and solved, the divine lordship over Satan actualised and the positive will of God as Creator vindicated and enthroned. Looking at it from that standpoint, we can never be too comprehensive as we attempt to understand the election of Jesus as the beginning of all things. If it is true that this man is the Elect of God, if it is true that the free grace which is the basis of all election is the reality of the divine and human steadfastness determined and actualised in this man, the reality of the resurrection and the prayer of Jesus, then in respect of those who are elected "in Him" it follows that their election consists concretely in their faith in Him. The mystery of the elected man Jesus is the divine and human steadfastness which is the end of all God's ways and works and therefore the object and content of the divine predestination. And the fact that it is actualised in Him and on their behalf is the fact to which those who are elected "in Him" must cling, the fact in which their confidence must repose, the fact from which their joy and consolation must be derived. And this fact is one which is ever new, and one which is their strength and wisdom in all circumstances. Being elected "in Him," they are elected only to believe in Him, i.e., to love in Him the Son of God who died and rose again for them, to laud in Him the priest and victim of their reconciliation with God, to recognise in Him the justification of God (which is also their own justification), to honour in Him their Leader and

Representative, their Lord and Head, and the kingdom of God which is a kingdom above all other kingdoms. It is as they love Him and laud Him and recog- [127]
nise Him and honour Him in this way that they can have their own life, their
rejection being put behind them and beneath them, rejected with His rejection. To believe in Jesus means to have His resurrection and prayer both in the
mind and in the heart. And this means to be elected. For it is the man that
does this who "in Him" is the object of the divine election of grace.

This is perhaps the place to make a statement and to come to some decision on a notable
controversy which took place within the orthodox Reformed theology of the 17th century:
the so-called Supralapsarian–Infralapsarian controversy. It has been recognised and
accepted fairly generally, and quite correctly, that this controversy was not fundamental and
not therefore a controversy which (like that between the Calvinists and Arminians) disrupted the Church. It was rather a difference which could form the subject of purely academic disputation *sine ullo mutuae caritatis et fraternitatis dispendio*^{EN155} (as A. Heidanus put it,
Corp. Theol. chr., 1686, I, 217). And as such it was left an open question at the Synod of Dort
(although with a clear bias towards Infralapsarianism). Later it found gradual settlement in
the form of various compromises. At a first glance it does not seem to have anything to do
with the specific question of the election of Jesus Christ. But to recall it may well shed light
upon the path which we have to tread, and it will itself be illuminated by the conclusions
which result from our own sequence of thought. There is good reason, then, to introduce it
at this juncture.

In the controversy between the 17th century Supralapsarians and Infralapsarians the
point at issue is the *obiectum praedestinationis*^{EN156} (for what follows, cf. H. Heppe: *Dogm. d. ev.
ref. Kirche*, 1935, 129 f.; A. Schweizer, *Protest. Centraldogmen*, 1856. II. 43 f., 181 f.). The question is put in this way: What do we mean when we say that from all eternity man was elected
by God, or, as we should have to say with equal emphasis according to the presuppositions of
their theology, rejected by God? Is it that in His eternal election God was thinking simply of
man, man as not yet created but still to be created, man as not yet fallen but still to fall by
divine permission and human action? Or is it that He was thinking of man as already created
and already fallen in virtue of this divine permission and human action? In other words, is
the one elected or rejected *homo creabilis et labilis*^{EN157}, or is he *homo creatus et lapsus?*^{EN158} The
whole difference of opinion narrows down ultimately to this formula.

We will consider first the Supralapsarian position. Its best known exponents were Beza,
Bucanus, Gomarus, Maccovius, Heidanus and Burmann. About the turn of the 17th century
it was readopted most forcefully by the mathematician Philip Naudaeus. It is difficult to
prove whether Calvin himself can be claimed as a Supralapsarian (cf. on this point Heinz
Otten, *op. cit.*, p. 91 f.). To be sure, his basic definition (*Instit.* III, 21, 5) can be understood in
this sense: *Non enim pari conditione creantur omnes; sed aliis vita aeterna, aliis damnatio aeterna
praeordinatur. Itaque prout in alterutrum finem quisque conditus est, ita vel ad vitam vel ad mortem
praedestinatum dicimus*^{EN159}. And the passage in *Instit.* III, 23, 7 seems to point even more
clearly in the same direction: *Inficiari nemo potest, quin praesciverit Deus quem exitum esset*

---

^{EN155} without any loss of mutual love and brotherhood
^{EN156} object of predestination
^{EN157} man to be created and fallible
^{EN158} man created and fallen
^{EN159} For not all are created in the same state; rather, eternal life is foreordained for some, and
 eternal damnation for others. Therefore, just as each is created for one or other of these
 ends, so we say that they are predestined either for life or for death

habiturus homo antequam ipsum conderet et idea praesciverit quia decreto suo sic ordinarat[EN160]. But it is difficult and even impossible to judge whether he had clearly in mind the alternatives as formulated in the later controversy. The same is true of Zwingli, who is usually cited in this connexion, especially in view of the opening section of Chapter 5 of his *De providentia*. The probability of consequence supports the view that if they could have been questioned further on the matter Zwingli and Calvin (but also the Luther of the *De servo arbitrio*[EN161]) would have been found on the Supralapsarian side. The thesis of the genuine 17th century Supralapsarian is stated by W. Bucanus (*Instit. theol.*, 1605, *Loc.* 36, 8 f.) in the following way: *Quid est praedestinationis decretum? Quo Deus homines a se creandos, antequam eos conderet, iam tum quorsum eos conderet constituens, sic ipsius gloriae inservire pro suo iure et mera voluntate decrevit, ut eorum alii essent vasa et exempla ipsius bonitatis et misericordiae, alii autem vasa et ὑποκείμενα ipsius irae, iustae in scelera ultionis atque potentiae .... Estque hoc decretum eiusmodi, quod ipsas exequutionis causas disponit, nedum ut ab iis pendeat*[EN162]. But the only cause is *quod sic velit glorificari Dominus summe misericors et summe iustus*[EN163]. The sequence of thought in the Supralapsarian scheme is this. God had and has a primal and basic purpose which has to be considered and taken into account quite apart from all His other specific purposes, and therefore quite apart from His purpose to create the world and quite apart from the further purpose to permit the fall of man. The original and proper purpose of God consists quite simply in this: that He Himself, and His glory, and more particularly His mercy and justice, should be revealed among men and to men by means of the salvation of some and the damnation of others. To this proper divine will and decree of God everything else that God wills is subordinate, as an interrelated means to its accomplishment. Because He has decreed this self-revelation, and in decreeing it, God has also decreed that man should be created to serve this end. It was also necessary that man should be created in such a way that by his own fault but with unfailing certainty he should fall into sin, thus arriving at the status and situation which would be a means to reveal the mercy of God in the salvation of some men and the justice of God in the damnation of others. For the purpose of executing the one divine decree it was necessary, then, that Adam, and all men in Adam, should in actual fact be brought to this situation and status. It was necessary, then, that they should in actual fact fall into sin. And for the purpose of executing this one divine decree it was also necessary that individual men should be willed either to salvation or to damnation and thus for one possibility or the other of divine self-revelation—as already predestinated thereto by God even before He decided to allow the fall of all men in the one man Adam, even before He decided on the original being of Adam in a state of innocence, even before He decided on the creation of Adam and the universe and all men. *Quod primum est in intentione, ultimum est in executione*[EN164]. And conversely: *Quod ultimum est in executione, primum est in intentione*[EN165]. The revelation of the mercy of God in the salvation of the elect and the justice of God in the damnation of the reprobate is last in execution. But for this reason it

[128]

[EN160] No-one can deny that God foreknew which end a man would take before he created him; therefore he knew because he had ordained it so in his decree

[EN161] On the Bondage of the Will

[EN162] What is the decree of predestination? It is that by which God establishes those men to be created by himself, having then already created them for a certain end before he created them. Thus he decrees by his law and pure will that they serve his glory, such that some of them are to be vessels which are examples of his goodness and mercy, and others vessels which are subject to his wrath – his power and righteous vengeance upon their crimes ... And this decree is such that it determines the very causes for its execution, so that it is in no way dependent upon them

[EN163] Because the Lord, utterly merciful, and utterly just, wills thus to be glorified

[EN164] What is first in intention is last in execution

[EN165] What is last in execution is first in intention

must have been first in the decree and purpose of God. What the Supralapsarian says, then, is that the fall had inevitably to take place, not apart from but in accordance with the will of God. But he also knows why it was that the fall and even creation had to take place. He tells us that the fall and creation had to have a place in God's plan and purpose, and that they had to take place, because God willed to reveal His mercy and justice. He knows that in God's primal and basic will as such there was decreed all that was necessary to such a revelation: the election of some men and the reprobation of others; the creation and the fall. He knows, in fact, that for the sake of His own glory God from all eternity predestinated each individual man either to the one alternative or to the other, either to election or to reprobation. And he knows that God created man, and each individual man, and allowed him to sin in the person of Adam, in order that he might fulfil either the one destiny or the other, and therefore be a means to the revelation of God's glory, whether of His mercy or of His justice.

It must be noted that on the Supralapsarian view evil does not cease to be evil, sin does not cease to be sin, and the guilt of man does not cease to be real guilt. But the Supralapsarian does know why it is that God has allowed these things, and why it is that He has to that extent willed these things. As he sees it, God's over-ruling of evil is not to be presented or explained as a later and additional struggle in which God is dealing with a new and to some extent [129] disruptive feature in His original plan. On the contrary, it must be thought of as an element in that original plan itself. As the Supralapsarian considers the details of the execution of the divine plan, i.e., in the course of created history as controlled by God, and as he considers the corresponding details in the whole eternal purpose of God, he does not regard these details individually or even in their relationships the one to the other. He regards them wholly and utterly in the light of the one divine plan which is the plan of all plans. In all the details it is the one basic plan which the Supralapsarian would have known and honoured. According to him, we cannot say simply that God created man to allow him to fall into sin. Nor can we say that He allowed him to fall into sin in order to damn him, or in His mercy to save some. Rather, all these individual *media*^{EN166} combine to form one single *medium*^{EN167}. And to know this *medium* as such, and the basis and meaning of all individual *media*, we must see them in the light of their ultimate purpose: that God created the universe and man, that He allowed the fall of man, that He allowed a general condemnation of sin to follow, and that in mercy He delivered some men from the general condemnation, in order that in and through this whole process He Himself might be glorified as the God of mercy and justice. Not one of the details is an end in itself—not even the eternal salvation or damnation of individuals which is the final link in the chain. On the contrary: *Omnia fecit propter se ipsum*^{EN168}, a much quoted verse in Prov. 16^{14} which was understood to mean that God made all things, and from all eternity He willed all things for Himself. *Est enim Deus ipse summum et amabile bonum, in quod fertur necessitate naturae. Ita Deus fertur non nisi in seipsum et gloriam suam. Qua cum voluerit misericordiam et iustitiam suam effulgere, non potuit id effectum dare, nisi in salute vel damnatione peccatoris*^{EN169} (Heidan, *op. cit.*, p. 221). That is the function and the only function of the eternal salvation or damnation of men in the counsel of God. And it was

---

^{EN166} plans
^{EN167} plan
^{EN168} He made all things for his very self
^{EN169} For God himself is the highest and delectable good, to which he is driven by the necessity of his nature ... Thus God is driven only for himself and for his own glory. Since by this he has willed his mercy and righteousness to shine out, he cannot bring it to effect by the salvation and condemnation of the sinner

because his eternal salvation or damnation had this necessary function (but only this function) in the counsel of God that man had to become *peccator*[EN170]. And it was because he had to become *peccator*[EN171] that he had to be created *homo*[EN172]. The *obiectum praedestinationis*[EN173] is, then, man as he is seen by God in His eternal election, i.e., *homo creabilis et labilis*[EN174].

Such are the main features of Supralapsarianism. At the outset we may characterise it as a system of consistent theistic monism. In view of its bold consistency and outstanding clarity we surely cannot withhold our admiration from this system.

Against it we may set the position of the Infralapsarians. Amongst strict Calvinists, at the furthest possible remove from any concessions to Arminianism and Lutheranism, this has always been the dominant view right up to our own day. At the Synod of Dort in particular, Supralapsarianism, while not rejected, was accepted only as a private opinion over against and distinct from the orthodox teaching. The Infralapsarian, too, knows of a primal and basic plan of God. God's eternal purpose is to reveal and to glorify Himself. According to him, too, creation and evil do not enter into this plan by chance, but by the efficient will of God in the one case, and by His permissive will in the other. For him, too, the fall is inevitable because it is an event decreed by God. Unlike the Supralapsarian, however, the Infralapsarian does not think that he has any exact knowledge either of the content of God's primal and basic plan or of the reasons for the divine decree in respect of creation and the fall. On the contrary, he holds that the reasons for this decree are ultimately unknown and unknowable. And, in any case, he does not say that creation and the fall were necessary in order to reveal the divine mercy and justice. He does not explain the creation of man and the universe in relation to this twofold revelation, but more generally as *communicatio et velut* ἔκστασις *potentiae, sapientiae et bonitatis creatoris*[EN175] (F. Turrettini, *Instit. Theol. el.*, 1679, L. IV, *qu.* g, 22). And he would have the decree of predestination as such subordinated as a decree of creation and the fall which has its basis elsewhere (and not in this specific plan). Only in the decree of predestination as such does he come across the particular divine purpose to reveal God's mercy and justice by the salvation of some and the damnation of others. But the existence of sin, and the existence of man as a sinner, and his existence at all, cannot be explained by this purpose. We cannot say that because God willed to reveal His mercy and justice by election and reprobation, therefore He willed creation and the fall. All that we can say is that the same God who willed men who would necessarily fall into sin, and who as Creator willed the existence of men at all, wills also that of those men some should of His mercy be saved, and the rest abandoned to the punishment which all have merited. It is true that God is absolutely free in His choice of the elect and reprobate. It is true that there can be no question of grounding this choice in the greater or lesser sins of the one group or the other. It is true that it is not a matter of the merit of good works which the one group has earned and the other has not earned. Elect and reprobate, they are all sinners, and they are such by the will and counsel of God. But the fact that they are sinners and the fact that they are created ought not to be connected with the decree of predestination as such, nor deduced from that decree. We must understand the decree of predestination as an independent entity, related to the decree of creation and the fall only to the extent that in an inconceivable unity they are both the eternal decree of God. And in order, although not of

[130]

[EN170] sinner
[EN171] sinner
[EN172] man
[EN173] object of predestination
[EN174] man to be created and fallible
[EN175] the communication and, as it were, displacement, of the power, wisdom and goodness of the creator

course in time, the decree of predestination must be thought of as subsequent to that of creation and the fall. It must be thought of, then, as referring to and presupposing that prior decree. The revelation of the *misericordia Dei*[EN176] presupposes an already existent *miser*[EN177], and the revelation of the *iustitia Dei*[EN178] presupposes an already existent *iniustitia*[EN179]. And both these presuppose an existent creature to whom that twofold revelation can apply, and also the creation of this creature. We may say that the revelation is made by a means already appointed, Christ Himself, and that it takes place by way of a calling and justification and sanctification which are efficacious either to life or to death. But the means already presuppose the existence of sin and the existence of sinful, guilty and wicked men. Creation and sin are then *conditioner in obiecto praerequisitae. Nisi enim homo conditus esset et lapsus praedestinatio non posset venire in executionem*[EN180] (F. Turrettini, *op. cit.*, IV, *qu.* 9, 20 f.). Against the Supra-lapsarian application of the assertion: *Quod ultimum est in executione, debet esse primum in intentione*[EN181], it is objected that the *illustratio misericordiae et iustitiae in hominum salute vel damnatione*[EN182] is not absolutely the *finis ultimus, quoad hominis gubernationem in genere*[EN183], but only *secundum quid et relate, quoad gubernationem hominis lapsi. Finis ultimus fuit manifestatio gloriae Dei in communi per hominis creationem et lapsum*[EN184]. The decree of election is the first and chief of those decrees which relate to the destiny of sinful man, but it is not the first and chief of all the divine decrees. Between creation and the fall on the one hand and salvation on the other there is no *necessaria connexio et subordinatio*[EN185]. For: *Nemo non videt hiatum et* μέγα χάσμα *propter peccatum quod creationis ordinem abrupit et redemptionis oeconomiae locum dedit: peccatum est contra naturam, nec medium vel respectu salutis, nisi per accidens*[EN186] (F. Turret-tini, *op., cit.*, IV, *qu.* 9, 23). Only to this extent do one or two think that they may speak of the unity of the divine purpose in respect of both dispensations—that God willed first to show *quid in homine possit liberum arbitrium*[EN187], and then *quid possit suae gratiae beneficium*[EN188] (*Syn. pur. Theol.*, 1624, *Disp.* 24, 23). Or else, it is a question of the revelation of the twofold majesty of God, first in the Law and then in the Gospel (H. Heidegger, *Corp. Theol.*, 1700, V, 34, as quoted by Heppe, 130).

The attack on the Supralapsarians was conducted along the following lines (cf. F. Turret-tini, *op. cit.*, IV, *qu.* 9, 9–14). (1) *Homo creabilis et labilis*[EN189] is a *Non-ens*[EN190]. But predestin-ation has to do with a being which has already been raised from non-being to being. It has to

---

[EN176] mercy of God (on the wretched)
[EN177] wretchedness
[EN178] righteousness of God
[EN179] unrighteousness
[EN180] required conditions for the matter. For unless man has been created and has fallen, predes-tination could not come into operation
[EN181] What is last in execution, should be first in intention
[EN182] demonstration of righteousness and mercy in the salvation and condemnation of the sinner
[EN183] final end concerning the governance of man in general
[EN184] according to that related sense, concerning the governance of fallen man. The final end was the manifestation of the glory of God alike through the creation, and fall of man
[EN185] necessary connection and subordination
[EN186] For anyone can see the gap, indeed the great chasm by virtue of the sin which has broken the order of creation and which makes a place for the economy of redemption. For sin is against nature, and is not a means either in respect of salvation (except by accident) or in respect of condemnation
[EN187] what the free will in man could do
[EN188] what the blessing of his grace could do
[EN189] creatable and fallible man
[EN190] non-being

[131] do with an already existent being, and with a specific form of the existence of this being. (2) The concept *homo creabilis el labilis* would, in fact, include all men, even those who were never created and never fell. It would apply to all those whose existence was at least a possibility. But predestination has to do with men as really created and fallen. Its object, then, cannot be *homo creabilis et labilis*. (3) *Homo creabilis et labilis* is neither *eligibilis*[EN191] nor *reprobabilis*[EN192]. For to be a possible object of election or reprobation presupposes qualities corresponding to the electing mercy and reprobating justice of God. And such qualities belong only to *homo creatus et lapsus*. *Homo creabilis et labilis*[EN193] cannot, then, be the *obiectum praedestinationis*[EN194]. (4) If *homo creabilis et labilis* were indeed the object of predestination, then creation and the fall would be instruments of predestination. But they are not defined as such in Scripture. Man might well have been created and have fallen into sin without the question of election or reprobation ever arising. Creation and the fall belong to the *ordo naturalis providentiae*[EN195]. Salvation and damnation form the specific content of the *ordo supernaturalis praedestinationis*[EN196]. It is absurd to suppose that first of all God arranged the eternal salvation or damnation of men and only then arranged their actual existence and fall. Creation and the fall must be regarded as necessary from the standpoint of predestination not as a *medium per quod*[EN197] but as a *conditio sine qua non*[EN198]. Obviously the sick man cannot be cured unless he exists as a man and is sick. But obviously, too, his existence as a man and his sickness cannot be regarded as means to cure him. (5) The Supralapsarian view of *homo creabilis et labilis* is ἐνδιάβλητος[EN199] and open to the severest criticism because it implies the impossible belief that God rejected some men even before they existed in His own consciousness as reprobates, and that He allowed them to become worthy of rejection simply in order that He might as such reject them.

As against this view the Infralapsarians advance positively the following propositions (cf. F. Turrettini, *op. cit.*, IV, *qu.* 9, 15–19). (1) Man is the object of the eternal predestination precisely in the situation in which God knows him as the one whom He will encounter in time. As Jn. 15[19] tells us: "I have chosen you out of the world." *Homo peccator*[EN200], the object of temporal calling, is also the object of eternal election. (2) The election of men takes place in Christ. The elect in Christ from all eternity are, however, the *redimendi et sanctificandi per ipsum*[EN201]. Thus the elected man is *homo lapsus*[EN202] as such. (3) In Rom. 9[21] Paul speaks of a φύραμα[EN203], the one lump from which the potter, according to his own pleasure, makes some vessels to honour and some to dishonour. Isaac and Ishmael, Jacob and Esau belonged equally to that one lump. And since God's varied dealings with them are determined by mercy and wrath, it is clear that they are a lump of sin and misery, a *massa corrupta*[EN204]. It is also clear, then, that the object of God's twofold predestination is *homo lapsus*[EN205]. Rom. 9[22] does not tell us that God created but that He prepared some to salvation and others to

---

[EN191] electable
[EN192] rejectable
[EN193] man, created and fallen, Man to be created, and fallible
[EN194] object of predestination
[EN195] natural order of providence
[EN196] supernatural order of predestination
[EN197] means by which
[EN198] lit 'a condition without which it could not be' i.e., 'a prerequisite and essential condition'
[EN199] reprehensible
[EN200] sinful man
[EN201] (ones) to be redeemed and sanctified through Him
[EN202] fallen man
[EN203] lump
[EN204] corrupt mass
[EN205] fallen man

damnation. And that means that God's choice between men was made not according to a physical predetermination but according to an (admittedly inconceivable) ethical judgment. He made that choice from all eternity, but with reference to man as already created and fallen. (4) According to the common understanding of Rom. 9^{22} the mercy and justice of God are the decisive motives in the divine predestination. But these must have fallen man as their object, not merely in temporal fulfilment, but in eternal purpose. Otherwise mercy would not be mercy, but *quaedam immensa bonitas*[EN206]. And justice would not be justice, but *absoluta potestas*[EN207]. As an act of mercy and justice predestination relates necessarily to *homo creatus et lapsus*[EN208].

Such, then, is the Infralapsarian view. At a first glance we cannot deny it one definite advantage—that even at the cost of a general systematic coherence and clarity in detail it does do greater justice than its Supralapsarian counterpart to the logical and moral difficulties of the common doctrine. If we consider the ever-recurring problem of the ecclesiastical utility of the doctrine we can readily understand why it was that the Infralapsarian and not the Supralapsarian view was adopted and retained as an official interpretation of the Calvinistic dogma. We can also understand why it was that the Supralapsarian view was more sharply attacked and repudiated by the Romanist, Lutheran, Arminian and other opponents of that dogma. And we can understand, too, why it was that the Infralapsarian arguments could be and actually were applied by these common enemies in their struggle against the particularly obnoxious Supralapsarian understanding. But this does not mean that the Infralapsarians did, in fact, approximate even in the slightest degree towards these common foes. The Infralapsarian interpretation did not involve the slightest concession to these enemies, and in relation to them we can regard it only as a variation which was based upon the same confessional position. Alongside the friendly words of the Supralapsarian A. Heidanus we may place the equally friendly statement of the Infralapsarian F. Turrettini: *Qualiscunque sit theologorum hac in parte diversitas, manet tamen apud utrosque salvum fidei fundamentum et ex aequo isti opponuntur exitiali Pelagianorum et Semipelagianorum errori .... In eo omnes conveniunt, quod homines Deo pares, non impares obiiciunt, et tales quorum discretio a solo Deo pendeat, a quo fundamento recedunt omnes sectarii*[EN209] (*op. cit.*, IV, *qu.* 9, 4). Unfortunately we must add that from the standpoint of the present context the Supralapsarians and Infralapsarians had a further point in common. They were concerned—as we are—with the question of the *obiectum praedestinationis*[EN210], but they both of them missed the decisive insight into the heart of the matter.

It will be instructive, finally, to investigate one of the compromise theories which settled the controversy towards the end of the 17th century. For this purpose we will choose the presentation of P. van Mastricht (*Theor. Pract. Theol.*, 1699, III, *cap.* 2, 12 f.). As van Mastricht sees it, if we are to arrive at any true understanding and decision in this controversy, we must distinguish in our minds four different divine acts which characterise the one decree of God in relation to man. The first is the *propositum manifestandi gloriam misericordiae et iustitiae vindicantis*[EN211]. In respect of this first act the object of predestination must undoubtedly be

[132]

[EN206] some immeasurable good
[EN207] absolute power
[EN208] man, created and fallen
[EN209] Whatever difference there may be among the theologians in this matter, among all of them there nevertheless remains the saving foundation that is faith, and they are equally opposed to the deadly error of Pelagianism and Semi-Pelagianism ... All agree on this point: they present men as equal, not unequal, before God, and the difference between them depends solely upon God. This is the basis from which all heretics depart
[EN210] object of predestination
[EN211] decree of manifesting the glory of mercy and of judicial righteousness

identified with *homo creabilis et labilis*[EN212] as in the Supralapsarian scheme. For there can be no doubt that in this purpose the decree of creation and the fall is not yet presupposed. It is impossible then, that *homo creatus et lapsus*[EN213] should be the object. The second is the *statutum creandi et in lapsum permittendi homines*[EN214] which applies to all men equally. In respect of this second act the object of predestination must be identified as *homo creandus et lapsurus*[EN215]—again in the Supralapsarian sense. For this second act is indeed identical with the decree of creation and the fall as such, but for that very reason we cannot think of *homo creatus et lapsus*[EN216] as its object, but only of the future reality in time of *homo creatus et lapsus*[EN217]. The third is the decree of election properly speaking, on the basis of which some are foreordained and separated to the glorifying of God's mercy and others to the glorifying of His justice. It is in respect of this third act that the Infralapsarians are in the right. Only *homo creatus et lapsus*[EN218] can be the object of the divine will and purpose in the decree of election properly speaking and as such. The fourth is the divine purpose in respect of the ways and means appropriate to the *electio*[EN219] of some and the *reprobatio*[EN220] of others. In so far as these ways and means are intended and ordained for man, man as envisaged in this fourth act can only be *homo electus et reprobatus*[EN221], and as such, according to the third, he is *homo creatus et lapsus*[EN222]. Here too, then, the Infralapsarians are in the right. In arriving at his decision van Mastricht presents the arguments of the two parties as follows. Against the Supralapsarians the Infralapsarians adduce Jn. 15^{19} and Rom. 9^{21} in proof of the assertion that it is *homo creatus et lapsus*[EN223] who is elected or rejected. Against this it may be argued that while the assertion is true in relation to the third and fourth of the acts above mentioned, to which the texts quoted refer, and more particularly in relation to the narrower

[133] understanding of *electio*[EN224] and *reprobatio*[EN225], yet this understanding of predestination is far too narrow, for predestination includes the first and second acts as well, and in relation to these the assertion is not true. As against that, the Supralapsarian complains that the Infralapsarian understanding of creation and the fall leaves no place for the divine purpose. It must be allowed that he is right when he speaks of the *manifestatio gratiae et iustitiae*[EN226] as the divine purpose which lies behind predestination in its wider and more comprehensive sense. He is also right when he claims that *homo creabilis et labilis*[EN227] is the object of this purpose. Nevertheless the object of election properly speaking, of *electio et reprobatio*[EN228], is not *homo creabilis et labilis*[EN229] but *homo creatus et lapsus*[EN230], as the Infralapsarian rightly maintains. As an acute piece of work this compromise rightly deserves credit. Yet it must be

---

[EN212] creatable and fallible man
[EN213] man, created and fallen
[EN214] decree of creating and permitting men to fall
[EN215] man to be created and to fall
[EN216] man, created and fallen
[EN217] man, created and fallen
[EN218] man, created and fallen
[EN219] election
[EN220] reprobation
[EN221] elect and reprobate man
[EN222] man, created and fallen
[EN223] man, created and fallen
[EN224] election
[EN225] reprobation
[EN226] manifestation of grace and righteousness
[EN227] man to be created, and fallible
[EN228] election and reprobation
[EN229] man to be created, and fallible
[EN230] man, created and fallen

asked whether the older and genuine exponents of the two trends could ever have accepted a judgment which reconciled and corrected them after this fashion. After all, both parties were proved wrong, the Supralapsarians in respect of the decisive concepts of election and reprobation, the Infralapsarians in respect of the equally decisive question of the distinction between the two dispensations. They were proved right, in fact, only by telling them that in their most important convictions they were wrong. In the light of this fact we must at least recognise that Mastricht was an honest mediator. He did not simplify the issue either for himself or for the two schools. And his proposal certainly has the merit that it brings out clearly and systematically the interrelatedness and indeed the unity of the two trends, a unity which was not challenged by either party. It proves, in fact, that there can be no question of finding any confessional difference between the two schools, or any disruptive significance in the controversy.

We may now attempt an estimate of the controversy. And first of all it will be well clearly to remind ourselves what were the common presuppositions underlying the two positions, and also the attempted compromise between them, as they are revealed in this attempted compromise. There can be no doubt that all the orthodox Reformed trends of that period shared the same earnest desire to serve the main interest of Calvinistic dogma—to extol the free grace of God and the sovereignty of the freely gracious God as the beginning of all Christian truth and of all Christian apprehension of truth. It should be noted in this respect that not only the Supralapsarians but such avowed Infralapsarians as Polanus and Wolleb, and at the end of the century F. Turrettini, gave to the doctrine of predestination a place immediately after the doctrine of God and before all the remaining *Loci*, although according to the Infralapsarian understanding of predestination it ought not to have been introduced prior to the doctrine of sin at the very earliest. Obviously they felt very strongly the need to treat this doctrine before everything else, so that all that followed could be set against the one background of the sovereignty of divine grace. But quite apart from this indisputably Christian kernel of Calvinistic dogma, there are other and equally unassailable presuppositions common to all the trends of the period.

Supralapsarians, Infralapsarians and mediators all agreed that the controverted *obiectum praedestinationis*[EN231], elected or rejected man, must be identified directly and independently with the partly elected and partly rejected individual descendants of Adam, both in the mass and also in detail. The interest of both parties, and of the older Reformed theology as a whole (and indeed of all the older theology), centred exclusively upon these individuals as such. It is in the election of some of these individuals that the man Jesus Christ plays a specific and indispensable part as the first of the elect. With the rejection of the others He has nothing whatever to do. Yet when the question of the *obiectum praedestinationis*[EN232] arises, then in one way or another He is quickly passed over, and a proper solution is found in the individual *x* or *y*. It may be as *creabilis*[EN233] or *creatus*[EN234], it may be as *labilis*[EN235] or *lapsus*[EN236], but this *homo*[EN237] *x* or *y* is always the *obiectum praedestinationis*[EN238].

Second, all parties were at one in thinking that in God's eternal decree predestination (and therefore the election or rejection of individuals) implies the setting up of a fixed system which the temporal life and history of individuals can only fulfil and affirm. The [134]

[EN231] object of predestination
[EN232] object of predestination
[EN233] creatable
[EN234] created
[EN235] fallible
[EN236] fallen
[EN237] man
[EN238] object of predestination

doctrine of predestination does not proclaim the free grace of God as glad tidings, but as the neutral impartation of the message that from all eternity God is gracious to whom He will be gracious, and whom He will He hardeneth, and that this constitutes the limit within which each individual must run his course. The Supralapsarian maintains that this system of the eternal election or reprobation of individuals is the system above every other system, being identical with the primal and basic plan of God besides which there is none other. The Infralapsarian allows the existence of another plan or system either alongside or prior to it, in the form of the decree of creation and the fall. But both parties presuppose and maintain that that system is in any case from all eternity, and that it is indeed fixed and unalterable, so that not merely individuals, but God Himself as its eternal author is bound by it in time, and (in relation to that pattern of all things, which is itself thought of as fixed) there can be nothing new under the sun, whether on man's part or on God's.

Third, all parties were agreed that when God set up this fixed system which anticipated the life-history and destiny of every individual as such, then in the same way, in the same sense, with the same emphasis, and in an exact equilibrium in every respect, God uttered both a Yes and a No, accepting some and rejecting others. In respect of the decree of creation the Infralapsarians do speak in some sense of a general purpose of God in the revelation of His glory, although without attempting to define this purpose more exactly. But when they come to the decree of predestination as such, they too speak of God's purpose in respect of created and fallen man in a way which is absolutely symmetrical. This purpose is to demonstrate His mercy to some and His justice to others. From the general mass of corruption the mercy of God infallibly inclines and guides a certain fixed number of individuals to election, and in the same way the justice of God infallibly inclines and guides a certain fixed number to perdition. There can be no more question of a disturbance or upsetting of the equilibrium of these two attitudes in God than there can be of any subsequent alteration within the system which has been established by the twofold will of God. The two attitudes together, the one balancing the other, constitute the divine will to self-glorification, and God is glorified equally in the eternal blessedness of the elect and the eternal damnation of the reprobate.

Fourth and above all—the hidden basis of all other agreement—all parties were agreed in their understanding of the divine good-pleasure which decided between election and rejection and thus determined the concrete structure of the system appointed from all eternity for time. They agreed, then, in thinking that this good-pleasure must be understood wholly and utterly as *decretum absolutum*[EN239]. It is an act of divine freedom whose basis and meaning are completely hidden, and in their hiddenness must be regarded and reverenced as holy. This *decretum absolutum*[EN240] is (according to the Infralapsarian view) the divine disposition in respect of *homo creatus et lapsus*[EN241], or (according to the Supralapsarian view) the divine disposition in respect of *homo creabilis et labilis*[EN242]. Behind both these views (at a different point, but with the same effect in practice), there stands the picture of the absolute God in Himself who is neither conditioned nor self-conditioning, and not the picture of the Son of God who is self-conditioned and therefore conditioned in His union with the Son of David; not the picture of God in Jesus Christ.

Such, then, are the common presuppositions of Supralapsarianism and Infralapsarianism, presuppositions which our earlier deliberations have shown to be not at all self-evident but most doubtful from a Christian standpoint. To do justice to the two trends we must take into

---

[EN239] absolute decree
[EN240] absolute decree
[EN241] creatable and fallible man
[EN242] man to be created, and fallible

account the doubtful presuppositions. And the first question which we must ask in relation [135] to them is to what extent, upon the basis and within the limits of these presuppositions, the two views did or did not serve the undoubtedly Christian interest or concern of Calvinistic dogma.

Now first it must be admitted that the Supralapsarian construction has a good deal to be said in its favour, for it puts the divine decision between mercy towards some and justice towards others—the free grace of God—so consistently and definitely at the head of all Christian knowledge and understanding. A clear light is shed upon all God's work—and indirectly upon all His being—when His will to reveal His glory is understood concretely as His will to reveal His mercy and justice, when we construe the *Omnia fecit propter seipsum*[EN243] in the light of that understanding, when *Deus ipse*[EN244] is thought of in advance as a God of mercy and justice. In its choice of this starting-point Supralapsarianism is not quite so specu-lative as a first and general glance would suggest. And we cannot but recognise that in its choice and unconditional assertion of this starting-point it did aim to treat of the God of Holy Scripture. To consider the eternally electing and rejecting One from the standpoint of the specific qualities of the God of Holy Scripture, to seek to understand the causative will of the Creator and the permissive will of the One who over-rules even the fall as the will of this God of mercy and justice, is not an undertaking of speculative theology, but it is rather (and especially when we consider the conception of God dominant in the orthodoxy of the cen-tury) something in the nature of a sally against speculative theology in general. If we are to think of the Supralapsarians as theistic monists, we must at least admit that it was a biblical and Christian monism which they envisaged. Can we really blame them for wanting to know too much at this point? Should we not blame them rather because there was something more which they ought to have known in their obvious attempt to make the biblical concep-tion of God their starting-point? They became speculative in the bad sense only in the abstract use which they permitted themselves to make of the biblical concepts of mercy and justice. They became speculative only when they looked for God Himself in the mysterious choice which governed the application of these two qualities. They were speculative in that they did not start with the concrete biblical form of these qualities and of God Himself. But when they chose this starting-point, when they sought to assert their *oeconomia supernaturalis praedestinationis*[EN245], and therefore the order of God's mercy and justice, as the first and chief order which is normative and decisive for all others and for the realisation of all others in time, there can be no doubt—and we must not forget this—that they were advancing in the direction of a penetration to the Christian understanding of the doctrine of predestin-ation. As against that, the Infralapsarian isolation of a specific and prior *oeconomia naturalis providentiae*[EN246] is undoubtedly weaker, redounding less to the credit of free grace, and relativising and contracting it in an unfortunate manner. Speaking of God, the Creator of heaven and earth, *qu.* 26 of the *Heidelberg Catechism* tells us that "the eternal Father of our Lord Jesus Christ ... is my God and my Father for the sake of His Son Jesus Christ." Those who summarise and confess their faith in God in these words cannot isolate the dispensation of creation and providence from the later dispensation of grace and predestination. At any rate, they cannot hide the first dispensation in the obscurity which enfolds it in Infralapsar-ian teaching. The logico-empirical objections of the Infralapsarians sound well enough.

[EN243] He made all things on his own account
[EN244] God himself
[EN245] the supernatural economy of predestination
[EN246] the natural economy of providence

Before God could decide in mercy and justice, there must have been a corresponding consti-
tution of individuals and an actualisation of their existence. And there is a show of sound-
ness and plausibility in their indignation at the very absurdity of the assumption that God
could first arrange the salvation or damnation of men and only later their existence and fall.
But we cannot deny that these are not spiritual objections. They are not the arguments of
faith. They do not take into account the deity of the eternal God, and the possibility that with
Him the last could actually be the first. Only too self-evidently they apply to God standards
taken from the order of human reason. But the history of Israel and of Jesus Christ and of
the Church is not played out within the framework of a prior and already preceding history
of nature and the universe. That is not the picture of the world and history as it is given us in
the Bible. According to the Bible, the framework and basis of all temporal occurrence is the
history of the covenant between God and man, from Adam to Noah and Abraham, from
Abraham and Jacob to David, from David to Jesus Christ and believers in Him. It is within
this framework that the whole history of nature and the universe plays its specific role, and
not the reverse, although logically and empirically the course of things ought to have been
the reverse. At this point the Supralapsarians had the courage to draw from the biblical
picture of the universe and history the logical deduction in respect of the eternal divine
decree. The Infralapsarians did maintain the sequence of the biblical picture in respect of
the realisation of salvation, but they shrank from the deduction. In respect of the eternal
divine decree they maintained a supposedly more rational order, isolating the two dispensations and subordinating the order of predestination to that of providence. In so doing, they
shrank from defining more closely the *oeconomia naturalis providentiae*[EN247]. The result was
that at a central point in their teaching, side by side with the still obscure *decretum
absolutum*[EN248], there arose necessarily a further obscurity which overshadowed their whole
doctrine of the second dispensation. This was the obscurity of the question with whom or
with what we really have to do in the God who created man and the universe, and who
permitted the fall of man. Where the distinction was thought of as a major one, and one that
must be maintained, it was inevitable that a later age should ask for more information. And it
was also inevitable that they should find such information in the belief that in the works of
creation and providence (we may say, too, in nature and reason) there is a certain general
goodness and power and wisdom of God which corresponds to the specific mercy and justice
of God in the work of salvation. It was inevitable, then, that the Infralapsarian construction
could at least help towards the later cleavage between natural and revealed theology. It is
that which (within the framework of the common presuppositions) makes it appear the less
happy of the two.

But within this framework we must not deny to the Infralapsarian view some particular
advantages. Two things call for notice in this respect.

1. If we start with the position that predestination must be thought of as the decree of the
free good-pleasure of God by which the election or rejection of individuals is foreordained
with the fixity and equilibrium of the two systems, then from the standpoint first of God but
also of man this means that on the Infralapsarian view there is a certain mitigation in the fact
that this decree is not the first and primary decree, not the decree which is above all other
decrees, not the absolute decree of God in respect of the distinct reality of the universe and
man. We recall the affirmation made by the Supralapsarians on the basis of the same presupposition: that in so far as the divine concern is not self-concern, or a concern with the revelation of the divine glory, it is directed wholly and utterly to individuals as such, and to their
eternal destiny of salvation or perdition, and to their progress towards this end. It is to serve

[EN247] the natural economy of providence
[EN248] absolute decree

this one end, the bringing of individual x to heaven and of individual y to hell, that there is brought into being the monstrous apparatus of the creation of heaven and earth, the sinister contrivance of a permitted fall and the resultant dominion of evil in the world, the appearance of Jesus Christ in the world, and His work, and the founding and maintaining of His Church, and all the operations of effectual calling and hardening which are involved in this redemptive work. This and this alone is the concern of the triune God (apart, of course, from His prior concern with Himself) in His movement towards the universe and man. But that means (with the constant proviso that the whole process and the end itself are necessary $\quad$ [137] and are made actual only for the self-glorification of God) that man, and indeed the individuals x and y are made the measure and centre of all things to a degree which could hardly be surpassed. What vistas open up and what extremes meet at this point! Is it an accident that A. Heidanus, and even so pronounced a disciple of Coccejus as his son-in-law F. Burmann, were at one and the same time Supralapsarians—and also Cartesians? And supposing the theological basis of this whole outlook and system were shaken! Supposing an anthropological basis were disclosed, and openly or secretly it replaced the theological! Heidanus and Burmann were amongst the older Reformed theologians in whom we have advance warning of a movement in this direction. We can hardly deny that with its surprisingly direct relationship between the totality of the divine work and the individual, Supralapsarianism could, and in fact did, prepare the way for such a movement. As against that, Infralapsarianism—which in other ways contributed to the same development—could at least exercise a certain restraint by refusing to allow the divine rule over and in the world to be identified quite so dominantly or fully with the attainment of this one end. Its subordination of the decree of predestination to that of creation and the fall did at least achieve the negative result of preventing the individual's every possible thought about God from degenerating automatically into thought about himself. It prevented the reverence for the holy self-seeking whereby God is zealous for His own honour from carrying with it the immediate and direct stimulation of an equally holy self-seeking on the part of the predestinated man, whether in his desire to attain heaven or in his fear of being cast into hell. In such an understanding there lurks always the possibility of a reversal of the relationship. God may well come to be thought of as the One who is God for man's sake, for the sake of the individual x or y, and who is at the disposal of this individual in order that he may attain that which he desires and escape that which he fears. The Infralapsarians could at least hold such a tendency in check, for they remembered that the decree of creation and the fall preceded that of predestination, thus leaving a place for thought about God and His lordship and work which does not stand in any direct relationship with thought about our own interests, which cannot be deduced from such thought, but which stands over against it as something independent and even superior. It is true that the way in which the Infralapsarians introduced this safeguard cannot be regarded as a happy one. In the long run the threat of anthropologism could not be warded off by a safeguard which consisted in the reference to a supposedly independent realm of creation and providence over and above that of redemption. On the contrary, the more strongly the autonomy of that realm was emphasised, the more surely was the foundation laid for a later proclamation of the self-glorification of the individual with divine help. Within the framework of the common presuppositions there is no effective safeguard against aberration in this direction. It must be allowed, however, that within these common presuppositions the Infralapsarian recollection of the first and independent divine decree, and the Infralapsarian loosening of the rigid relationship between God and the salvation or perdition of the individual, did exercise a retarding function in face of the threatened aberration. But such a loosening could also mean a certain mitigation in respect of man. According to Supralapsarian opinion man was nothing more than the elect or reprobate in whose whole existence there was only the one prospect of the fulfilment of a course already mapped out either one way or the other. But the Infralapsarians knew of another secret of God side by side with the decree of predestination. Theoretically at least, then, they knew of another secret of man apart from the fact that he is either elect or reprobate. For them man was also (and indeed primarily) the creature of God, and as such responsible to God. This view involved a softening in the understanding of God which is both dangerous and doubtful. And in the long run it could not have any really effective results. For practical purposes the Infralapsarians knew of man only in his twofold destiny. But they needed only to let that slip, they needed only to let the theoretically possible modification take practical shape as a specific anthropology deriving from the first article, and they were well on the way to a naturalistic doctrine of man which would relativise and finally replace the Christian doctrine. For that reason the theoretically possible modification was never made in practice before the end of the 17th century. It can only be said that within the common presuppositions the Infralapsarians had the advantage of leaving open the question of how or in what respect man is elect or reprobate. They had, then, the advantage of pointing (although not from a very well-chosen standpoint) to something which lies beyond the determination of man as either the one thing or the other, thus calling in question the rigidity of the determination.

2. The second obvious advantage of Infralapsarianism consists naturally in its greater reserve with respect to the reality of the fall and the presence of evil in the world. The Infralapsarians, too, attributed this reality to God's eternal will and counsel. They could not be accused of dualism at this point. But they distinguished between the decree which permitted evil and the decree of predestination. The permitting of evil was not thought of as a means which God willed and posited in execution of His electing and rejecting, but rather as a means of which He actually made use in this activity. God's permitting of evil was a very different matter, as was His creating of the universe and man. But He then made use of the creation and the fall of man, acting on the man created by His will and fallen in accordance with it, according to the measure of this twofold predestination. In accordance with this fact the decrees of God must be considered and understood together in spite of the difference between them. In God they are one. But they must not be interfused the one with the other nor deduced the one from the other. On the Infralapsarian view the fact that these decrees stand alongside one another and together constitute the one holy will of God is—along with the freedom of the good-pleasure of God in respect of His decisions—the divine secret. The corresponding statements of the Supralapsarians were far bolder, but harsh and dangerous, giving occasion at least to the constant reproach made against the Calvinists that they think of God as the *auctor peccati*[EN249]. The Supralapsarians so exalted the sovereignty of God above everything else that they did not sufficiently appreciate the danger of trying to solve the problem of evil and to rationalise the irrational by making it a constituent element in the divine world-order and therefore a necessity, a part of nature. In their eyes the more pressing danger was that of opening up the slightest chink to dualism. But the Infralapsarians obviously thought the other danger the more serious. That is why in their system evil (like creation itself) assumes a more enigmatical character, being enfolded in an impenetrable darkness. The enemy is the Evil One, and his power is a real power, and consequently our redemption is a real redemption. By separating instead of uniting the economies of evil and redemption the Infralapsarian can bring out these truths better, or at any rate more clearly. They can state much more decidedly that in our redemption a moral judgment is executed and a victory won for the almightiness of God. They can also state that God has not foreordained any one for evil, not even the reprobate. It must be conceded that within the common presuppositions Infralapsarianism is better able to show that that which takes place between God and man is not a natural, let alone a mechanical process. The Supralapsarians

---

[EN249] author of sin

had no desire to maintain a view of this kind. But the Infralapsarians were better able to show why it ought not to be maintained. By leaving to God Himself a mystery which has nothing whatever to do with the revelation of His mercy and justice (the mystery of the divine permitting of evil), they were better able to safeguard the respect which is owed to God by the man who is enslaved to evil and does it. They were better able to avoid the temptation to find an excuse in the fact that the divine purpose includes evil for the sake of election or reprobation. This legitimate interest was better safeguarded, although we cannot, of course, say more. [139]

When we weigh the pros and contras together, our first inclination is to take up an attitude of radical neutrality or indifference. Within the presuppositions common to both parties the reasons and counter-reasons seem to be more or less equally balanced. We could, of course, concentrate upon the theological points which both parties held in common, as has been done since the end of the 17th century. This would leave us perfectly free to decide in favour of the one or the other according to taste or sentiment. It would also give the assurance that the two standpoints are not irreconcilable, as the compromise of van Mastricht has shown, but that at a pinch they can be fused into one. I do not think that this course is really possible. If the controversy is rightly understood, the indecision cannot be radical; it cannot mean a renunciation of decision, but only the conclusion (inevitable, of course) that on the ground on which it was fought out the controversy was one which could not be decided, and one which we, too, cannot satisfactorily decide. But that does not mean that the controversy does not concern us and that we are not called at this point to decision. The question of the *obiectum praedestinationis*[EN250], the elect man, is still a question which we have to face, and we cannot very well maintain that it was satisfactorily answered in the 16th century. We are not in any position to dismiss the 17th century problem as superfluous, or to abandon the problem to merely capricious solution. Again, we are not in any position to concentrate upon what was common to both trends, for this common element has itself become a problem from the standpoint of the normative and central concern of Calvinistic dogma, and in the light of our own understanding of this concern. When on the basis of quite different presuppositions we are seeking an answer to the same question, we may not be able to accept the answers already given, but we cannot dismiss them as a matter of indifference. We are obliged to ask which side had relatively the greater truth at that age and within the now shattered theological unity of that age. We have no reason to assume that we can judge freely in this matter according to taste or sentiment, nor have we any reason to content ourselves with the fact that at a pinch some kind of compromise could be arranged. To know that at a pinch both standpoints could be accepted on the basis then adopted does not help us to learn from this tract of history. We are fully convinced that on that basis both standpoints were in their way necessary. But we are also convinced that it was only at a pinch, i.e., under all kinds of difficulties, that the two could be accepted and fused the one with the other. What we do really need to know is this: Granted the doubtful nature of the common presuppositions, which of the two standpoints has more in its favour in the sense of clearing the ground for the answer which, on quite different presuppositions, we ourselves must give to a question no less legitimate to-day than it was then? In other words, when we adopt this quite different basis, to which of the two opposing standpoints can we attach ourselves, so that we not only reach a decision in the then controversy, but also think out the matter, not in an indifferent discontinuity, but in continuity with this section of the Church's theological history (not breaking off the threads but gathering them together)?

[EN250] object of predestination

When we put it in this way, the answer is unavoidable. The greater right (*praemissis praemittendis*[EN251] and *omissis omittendis*[EN252]) lay then on the side of the Supralapsarians. The objections against them, and our own objections against them (which constitute the relative correctness of Infralapsarianism), do not amount finally to anything more than a demonstration of the specific dangers in their position. Behind their rigid theocentricity there lurks somewhere the menace of a swing over to an equally rigid anthropocentricity. We may describe it as highly probable that Supralapsarianism did help to prepare the way for this swing over as it actually took place. Again, behind their consideration of creation, sin and redemption only from the standpoint of the revelation of God's glory, there lurks somewhere the relativisation of the problem of evil, the resolving of the whole relationship between God and man into a kind of natural process which admits of no contradictions. But the fact that a position is dangerous is not to say that it is wrong, even less that the contrary position is right. And when we examine more closely the undoubted and unavoidable dangers of Supralapsarianism, it becomes evident that they are real dangers, and that they could and did help to pave the way for the unfortunate developments later, only because Supralapsarianism rested on the fatal basis of the four common presuppositions. If the *obiectum praedestinationis*[EN253] is the individual abstractly understood, then it is most dangerous to seek God's primal and basic purpose in election and reprobation. If predestination consists in the eternal setting up of that fixed system which governs all temporal reality, and if within that system election and reprobation are evenly balanced, then it is most dangerous so unconditionally to carry through the thought of the divine sovereignty that the fall and evil are understood as means foreseen and foreordained by God to the attainment of the finally good purpose which He has willed. If the *decretum absolutum*[EN254] is the last possible word concerning the basis of divine predestination, then it is most dangerous to think of God as the One who sees and plans and achieves His own glory in the foreordaining of a certain number of individuals irresistibly to heaven and of a certain number of individuals no less irresistibly to hell. And it is most dangerous to believe that for this purpose God created the world, and permitted and to that extent willed the existence of sin and the devil, and then of course, in line as it were with these prior acts, accomplished the work of redemption. It is most dangerous to believe that, in virtue of His over-all determination, this redemptive work must itself mean both calling and also hardening, that it must be a means of election and also a means of rejection—and both with that unshakeable fixity, both in that indestructible equilibrium, both as the fulfilment of that secret good-pleasure of God which is wholly anonymous and completely closed in upon itself. It is quite true—and the relative truth of Infralapsarianism is based upon the fact—that if the presuppositions hold, the Supralapsarian God threatens to take on the appearance of a demon, and in the light of this fact we may well understand the horror with which Roman Catholics, Lutherans, Arminians and even many of the Reformed themselves recoiled from the doctrine. It must be made quite clear, however, that the danger and the corresponding horror arise only as Supralapsarianism is attempted on the basis of these presuppositions. On this basis Supralapsarianism is an enterprise which attracts and strikes us by what amounts almost to its intellectual audacity. It did, in fact, have something of this character and even more (as we see for example in the school of Maccovius). But the danger tells against Supralapsarianism as such only if the presuppositions are as necessary and unshakeable in themselves as they were for all the older theology and for the Supralapsarians of the 17th century.

[140]

[EN251] saying what needs to be said in advance
[EN252] omitting what needs to be omitted
[EN253] object of predestination
[EN254] absolute decree

Let us try for a moment to think of the Supralapsarian teaching as detached from this background and freed from all the influences which there affected it. Let us try to understand what happens in and to the universe and for and to man, the origin and purpose and meaning of the universe and man, in terms of the eternal counsel of a God who in His love is sovereign. The primal and basic purpose of this God in relation to the world is to impart and reveal Himself—and with Himself His glory. He Himself being the very essence of glory. And because all things are His creation, because He is the Lord of all things, this primal and basic purpose is the beginning of all things, the eternal reality in which everything future is already determined and comprehended. And in this purpose which is the beginning of all things God does not will at random. He wills man: not the idea of man, not humanity, not human individuals in the mass or in particular; or rather all these, but *in concreto*EN255 and not *in abstracto*EN256. He wills man, His man, elected man, man predestined as the witness to His glory and the object of His love. In this man, but only in him. He wills humanity and every individual man and what we may describe as the idea of humanity. But first and specifically and immediately He wills man, His man, man elected by Him. His intention is that this man should testify to His glory and thus reveal and confirm and verify both positively what He is and wills, and negatively what He is not and does not will. The latter part of the intention is not positive but negative; a marking off, a separating, a setting aside. It is not a second Yes on God's part, but a No which is of God only to the extent that it corresponds and is opposed to the Yes, a No which forms the necessary boundary of the Yes: so assuredly is God God and not not God; so assuredly does He live in eternal self-differentiation from all that is not God and is not willed by God. In this sense God is and is not; He wills and does not will. And for this reason He intends and ordains that the object of His love and the witness to His glory in the universe which He has created should testify in a twofold manner—he should testify to His Yes and to what He wills, and he should also testify to His No and to what He does not will. In this way the witness can truly exist and live in covenant with God. In this way there may be manifest to him the fulness of the divine glory. It is not God's will that elected man should fall into sin. But it is His will that sin, that which God does not will, should be repudiated and rejected and excluded by him. It is God's will that elected man should repudiate what He repudiates, and that thereby the Yes of God should be revealed and proclaimed. God does not will and affirm evil and the fall and an act of sin on the part of this man (it will never come to that, so assuredly is he elected man), but for the sake of the fulness of His glory, for the sake of the completeness of His covenant with man, for the sake of the perfection of His love, He wills and affirms this man as sinful man, i.e., as man laden with sins and afflicted by their curse and misery, and He wills and affirms this man as one who stands like Himself in opposition to sin, as His companion in the necessity of repudiating it, as the one foreordained to utter the same No and thus to corroborate the divine Yes. But for this purpose it was necessary that this man should really be confronted with what God Himself repudiates, even as God Himself is confronted with it in that self-differentiation, in that disavowal of what He is not, and does not will. And it is inevitable that this confrontation with what God repudiates, with evil, should mean for man, who is certainly not God and not almighty, that evil confronts him as a hostile power, a power which is, in fact, greater than his own power. In his case, then, the defeat of this evil power cannot be so self-evident as it was in God's case. In his case it must take on the character of an event. It must become the content of a history: the history of an obstacle and its removing; the history of a death and a resurrection; the history of a judgment and a pardon; the history of a defeat and a victory. In God Himself there is a simple and immediate victory of light over darkness,

[141]

EN255 concretely
EN256 in the abstract

with the issue never for one moment in doubt. In the creaturely sphere and for man—as man is to be the witness to the divine glory—this victory must take on historical form, thus becoming an event in time. In willing man. His man, elected man, God wills that this should be the case. He wills the confrontation of man by the power of evil. He wills man as the one assailed by this power. He wills him as the one who, as man and not God, has not evolved this power of himself but is subjected to it. He wills Himself as the One who must and will come to the help of man in this subjection, who alone in this subjection can and will give to man the victory. He wills Himself as the One by whose grace alone man must live. He wills man as the one who is thrown wholly and utterly upon the resources of His grace. He does so in order that man should proclaim His glory as the one who is freed by Him from the domin-ion of sin, the one who is saved by Him from death the consequence of sin, the one for whom He Himself must and will and does act as Pledge and Substitute if he is really to take

[142] this path. God wills *homo labilis*EN257, not in order that he may fall, but in order that when he has fallen he may testify to the fulness of God's glory. And His willing and election of *homo labilis*EN258, not for the fall, but for uplifting and restitution by an act of divine power; the demonstration in time, in the creaturely sphere, of His eternal self-differentiation: this fore-ordination of elected man is God's eternal election of grace, the content of all the blessings which from all eternity and before the work of creation was ever begun God intended and determined in Himself for man, for humanity, for each individual, and for all creation. The existence of this man, the predestined bearer and representative of the divine Yes and the divine No, foreordained to victory over sin and death but also to the bearing of the divine penalty, is the divine promise, the divine Word, in which the God who elects from all eternity confronts all humanity and each individual, in which His electing will encounters us and through which He Himself has dealings with us.

Such, then, is the Supralapsarian theory as detached and purified from the doubtful pre-suppositions of the older theology. For a moment, at least, we may picture it to ourselves as thus detached from its background. Its distinctive aims and tenets are brought into relief. No despite can be done to the sovereignty of God as the first and last Word in all matters con-cerning the relationship between Him and us. And this sovereignty is to be thought of as the sovereignty of the God of the Bible, the God who is Judge and yet also merciful, the God who is Judge just because He is merciful. The thought of this sovereignty should be our first and last and only and very real consolation and warning. Sinful man must, in fact, see himself as the object of God's love and witness to His glory. He must do so to the point of understand-ing that He must live wholly and utterly by the grace of God. And the life which is of grace should signify that God Himself represents him against the sin which he cannot overcome but which God has guaranteed to overcome in him by the existence of His Elect. He must live, then, by the promise which is given him in and with this Elect.

Of the Supralapsarian theory as detached from the doubtful presuppositions it must at least be said that in a positive way it does appropriate and respect the Calvinistic concern common to both trends. And it cannot be objected that it is exposed to the dangers which surround Supralapsarianism in its historical form. The God of this purified Supralapsarianism is not the God who in holy self-seeking is so preoccupied with Himself and the revelation of His own glory. He is not the God in face of whom man becomes no more than a means to accomplish the divine purpose. He is the God who loves man. He is the God who in love makes man a companion. He is the God who gives man a share in the divine Yes, and for the sake of the Yes in the divine No. He is the God who puts man in this antithesis and Himself overcomes it. The God of this Supralapsarianism does not demand a

---

EN257 fallible man
EN258 fallible man

holy self-seeking on the part of man or of the individual, because there is no question of the individual as such ever being the final end of the revelation of the divine glory. It remains to the individual only to grasp the promise which is given in the one Elect, and to seek and find his salvation, not as a private end, but as a participation in the victory and blessedness of this other, the Elect of God. Again, we cannot accuse the God of this Supralapsarianism of having a demonic aspect. Indeed, in that His purpose and will aims at the negation of evil accomplished in elect man, and in that He gives to creation its meaning and goal in that man, there can be no question of His having abandoned creation or a part of creation to the dominion of evil. In the Elect He negated in advance the rule of evil, even in the sphere of creation. In the Elect He revealed evil only as a power already vanquished, a kingdom of darkness already destroyed. And, again, the God of this Supralapsarianism cannot give rise to the much feared levity of mind which in the face of evil committed finds comfort and excuse in the fact that even evil is willed by God. God did indeed will evil, but only in the just and holy non-willing to which His Elect is created and summoned to testify and which human history occurs in order to fulfil, in correspondence with the eternal self-determination by which [143] God is God and not not God. And if this is how evil is willed, what excuse is there for doing it, whether consciously or unconsciously? Who is not accused and judged by the existence, posited by God, of the One in whom evil is negated on our behalf? Surely the grace of God that blots out our sin cannot permit us to continue in sin.

For these points to be valid, Supralapsarianism has to be understood in this way, and its historical form has to be drastically corrected and supplemented. We have to remove completely from our minds the thought of an individual purpose in predestination. We have to remove completely from our minds the thought of the foreordination of a rigid and balanced system of election and reprobation. Above all, we have to expunge completely the idolatrous concept of a *decretum absolutum*EN259. In place of these we have to introduce the knowledge of the elect man Jesus Christ as the true object of the divine predestination. But the decisive advantage of Supralapsarianism as compared with Infralapsarianism is that these presuppositions can be removed without setting aside the basic thought. With no material alteration the thesis concerning *homo labilis*EN260 can be developed in a christo-logical direction. Indeed, the thesis has to be corrected and supplemented in this way if the Supralapsarian position is to be established beyond all possibility of reproach. Supralapsarianism is itself a threat to these doubtful presuppositions because upon the basis of them it says something which we must admire for its boldness, which we must recognise as the logical vindication of the main interest and concern of Calvinism, but which—on this basis—we must reject as quite impossible by reason of its harsh and dangerous character. On this basis Supralapsarianism was bound to be at a disadvantage. It could have a place only as the private opinion of radicals and "outsiders" who were more feared than loved. Its success and recognition would have meant far too urgent a summons to the refounding of the whole structure. But this very fact could materially—and in the long run historically—work out in its favour. Its whole impulse was forwards, although in its then form, bound by those presup-positions, it could neither move nor lead in this forward direction.

The same cannot be said of Infralapsarianism. Infralapsarianism was an opposition fed by the dangers of Supralapsarianism. Its merit was to expose those dangers, and to that extent its opposition was justified. We have already noted, however, that its decisive arguments were not arguments of faith but of logic and morality. That is of a piece with the fact that what it says about *homo creatus et lapsus*EN261 does not emulate or improve but weakens what the

---

EN259 absolute decree
EN260 fallible man
EN261 man, created and fallen

Supralapsarians tried to say in their progressive representation of the common interest. By pointing to the dangers and rejecting their thesis, it defended against the Supralapsarians something which in the long run could not be defended. What Supralapsarianism was trying to say was that in the beginning of all things, in the eternal purpose of God before the world and before history, there was the electing God and elected man, the merciful and just God, and over against that God from all eternity *homo labilis*[EN262], man sinful and lost. It is true that it did not and, on the basis of those presuppositions, could not say what it can say when detached from those presuppositions—that Jesus Christ is the merciful and just God who elects from all eternity, and also *homo labilis*[EN263] who is elected from all eternity. It cannot be denied, however, that Supralapsarianism can be understood as pointing in this direction, and can therefore be corrected and supplemented. It cannot be denied that it calls for correction and supplementation in this direction. The same cannot be said of Infralapsarianism. On the contrary, Infralapsarianism closes all doors which might open in this direction. It ordains another decree over and above that of predestination; the decree of creation and providence, and then of the fall. It offers to see and to understand the two

[144] decrees in their inward relationships with each other. According to this view there were two divine decrees at the beginning of all things. In respect of the relationship later revealed as actually and definitely willed of God, these decrees are obscure and indeterminate and neutral. In them we must indeed respect God as God. But it is a mere assertion when we say that we recognise in them the God who is later manifested and revealed in this actual and definitive relationship as the true God. We remember from what we saw earlier how the understanding of predestination was constantly hampered by the placing of predestination within the framework of a general divine world-order. As Thomas Aquinas stated expressly, the aim was to understand predestination as *pars providentiae*[EN264]. Now Calvinism, and Reformation theology in general, had certainly meant that side by side with the whole question of the appropriation of salvation, *this pars providentiae*[EN265] (with its particular significance) had been given an emphasis which it had never had in mediaeval theology. But Supralapsarianism meant that a hopeful attempt was at last made to burst out of the framework which had been a limiting concept from the time of Thomas onwards. It meant that an attempt was made to reverse the relationship between predestination and providence, to understand providence in the light of predestination and not *vice versa*. As against that, Infralapsarianism stood for the tradition which Reformation theology had questioned but not overcome. It canonised to some extent the statement of Thomas; and in so doing it ceased to co-operate in the task of winning through to a deeper and more effective understanding of the Calvinistic dogma. It had, indeed, no contribution to make towards such a better understanding. All that it could do was to repeat the dogma in its traditional form. Fundamentally this was what happened at the Synod of Dort. It had plenty of apprehensions and warnings and assurances to put forward, but nothing of positive value in helping towards a better understanding of the common faith. It was conservative, and nothing more. And for that reason its arguments against Supralapsarianism could never truly be the arguments of faith. And while Supralapsarianism did at least give a jolt to the common theological presuppositions by involuntarily questioning and compromising them, Infralapsarianism could not, in fact, do more than confirm them. As we have seen,

---

[EN262] fallible man
[EN263] fallible man
[EN264] part of providence
[EN265] part of providence

Infralapsarianism did soften the individualistic end of predestination, the rigidity of its system, the equilibrium of its twofold content, the mystery of its origin in the *decretum absolutum*[EN266]. It did this by its reference to the *oeconomia naturalis providentiae*[EN267] preceding the economy of predestination, a reference which theoretically at least made it possible to think of the will of God as something above the whole economy of predestination. Where it took practical effect this softening could only do harm, i.e., by leading to natural theology. As a theory, however, it could result only in a concealing of the questionable nature of the presuppositions, staying the outbreak of disease and rendering superfluous any further discussion of fundamentals. But that is not the best kind of medicine. Reformed theology was pacified, and it determined to hold on to these presuppositions until it could do so no longer. But when that time came it was too late, for here, as elsewhere, the Enlightenment had now shown that the conservative anxiety to hold on to the traditional form of the dogma had resulted in the forfeiture of its substance, concerning which there had for so long been a hesitation to think constructively. In other words, the dogma had now become so alien even to its exponents that in its theological form they could no longer take it seriously and did not dare attempt its defence. The whole process of rejecting Supralapsarianism must, in fact, be numbered as one of the signs of exhaustion which characterise 17th century theology—an exhaustion which made it powerless to resist the Enlightenment at the beginning of the 18th century, since it carried within it the seed of theological Enlightenment and its own dissolution. The theological Enlightenment was nothing more than the exhaustion of thinking upon a basis of faith, for in proportion as such thinking was exhausted it was inevitably replaced by thinking upon a basis of unbelief. Whatever objections we may have to bring against its assertions, in objective content Supralapsarianism provides us with thinking upon a basis of faith which was not yet exhausted, and in this respect the offer which it made was full of hope for the theology of the 17th century. Had it carried that theology with it then things might have been different at the beginning of the 18th century, and the dissolution of that theology might have been averted. But to do that the offer would have had to be pressed in a way which was not actually the case. In that it involuntarily shook the traditional presuppositions but did not consciously dispute or burst through them, Supralapsarianism itself shared in the general exhaustion. In the face of its enemies it could never be wholly convincing. It had to content itself with the position of one intellectual trend tolerated side by side with others. In the history of the doctrine of predestination it could never make an advance commensurate with its initial impetus. For theology as a whole it could never have the significance of a salutary stimulus as it might well have done in the light of that initial impetus. Yet it is still the case that in that initial impetus it did make some advance upon the substance of Calvinistic dogma, an advance which is instructive and which repays a closer acquaintance. The same cannot be said of the thinking of the Infralapsarians. In the long run the Infralapsarians have nothing to tell us which was not said just as well or better by Calvin and other theological masters of the 16th century. The Infralapsarians did nothing to answer the questions which still had to be asked in this matter. They did nothing to answer better the question of the *obiectum praedestinationis*[EN268]. All that they did was to show that by holding fast the common presuppositions the Supralapsarian answer was too dangerous to be satisfying. They made no attempt to improve on it by producing a better answer.

[145]

[EN266] absolute decree
[EN267] natural economy of providence
[EN268] object of predestination

2. THE ETERNAL WILL OF GOD IN THE ELECTION OF JESUS CHRIST

Starting from Jn. 1$^{1f.}$, we have laid down and developed two statements concerning the election of Jesus Christ. The first is that Jesus Christ is the electing God. This statement answers the question of the Subject of the eternal election of grace. And the second is that Jesus Christ is elected man. This statement answers the question of the object of the eternal election of grace. Strictly speaking, the whole dogma of predestination is contained in these two statements. Everything else that we have to say about it must consist in the development and application of what is said in these two statements taken together. The statements belong together in a unity which is indissoluble, for both of them speak of the one Jesus Christ, and God and man in Jesus Christ are both Elector and Elect, belonging together in a relationship which cannot be broken and the perfection of which can never be exhausted. In the beginning with God was this One, Jesus Christ. And that is predestination. All that this concept contains and comprehends is to be found originally in Him and must be understood in relation to Him. But already we have gone far enough from the traditional paths to make necessary a most careful explanation of the necessity and scope of the christological basis and starting-point for the doctrine as it is here expounded.

[146]   1. We may begin with an epistemological observation. Our thesis is that God's eternal will is the election of Jesus Christ. At this point we part company with all previous interpretations of the doctrine of predestination. In these the Subject and object of predestination (the electing God and elected man) are determined ultimately by the fact that both quantities are treated as unknown. We may say that the electing God is a supreme being who disposes freely according to His own omnipotence, righteousness and mercy. We may say that to Him may be ascribed the lordship over all things, and above all the absolute right and absolute power to determine the destiny of man. But when we say that, then ultimately and fundamentally the electing God is an unknown quantity. On the other hand, we may say that elected man is the man who has come under the eternal good-pleasure of God, the man whom from all eternity God has foreordained to fellowship with Himself. But when we say that, then ultimately and fundamentally elected man is also an unknown quantity. At this point obscurity has undoubtedly enveloped the theories of even the most prominent representatives and exponents of the doctrine of predestination. Indeed, in the most consistently developed forms of the dogma we are told openly that on both sides we have to do, necessarily, with a great mystery. In the sharpest contrast to this view our thesis that the eternal will of God is the election of Jesus Christ means that we deny the existence of any such twofold mystery.

In this antithesis it is not a matter of the mystery of God's freedom in His eternal will concerning man. We have to do with this mystery too—the mystery of God, and the mystery of man which arises as man is caught up by the eternal will of God into God's own mystery. But what matters here is really the nature of this one and twofold mystery, whether it is incomprehensible light or incomprehensible darkness. What matters is whether at this point we have to recognise and respect the majesty of a God who is known to us or whether we have to recognise and respect the majesty of a God who is not known to us. Again, what matters is whether the man confronted by the majesty of that God is known or not known to us. The history of the dogma is shot through with a great struggle for the affirmation of the fact that in the mystery of election we have to do with light and not darkness, that the electing God and elected man are known quantities and not unknown. But this affirmation could not and cannot be made as long as the step is not taken which we are now taking and have already taken in the present thesis; as long as it is not admitted that in the eternal predestination of God we have to do on both sides with only one name and one person, the same name and the same person, Jesus Christ. Unless this is done, either the Subject of the concept or its object, and in practice both, will be lost in the all-prevailing obscurity, and the assertion of the obscurity itself becomes necessarily the last and decisive word on the whole subject. For our part we can no longer agree to such a procedure. No doubt it does and [147] often has kindled sensations of a fearful or pleasurable awe, but in the long run its effect is not to build up but to scatter and destroy. For as long as we are left in obscurity on the one side or the other, and in practice both, as long as we cannot ultimately know, and ought not to know, and ought not even to ask, who is the electing God and elected man, it does not avail us in the least to be assured and reassured that in face of this mystery we ought to be silent and to humble ourselves and to adore. For truly to be silent and to humble ourselves and to adore we must know with whom and with what we have to do. The mystery must be manifest to us as such, i.e., it must have a definite character. It must have the power and dignity to provoke in us an equally definite silence and humility and adoration. Otherwise it is inevitable that we ourselves should try to fill in the gap, that of ourselves we should try to make known the unknown. It is inevitable that we should arbitrarily ascribe to this unknown this or that name or concept. It is inevitable that we should seek in Him this or that reality. It is inevitable that we should humble ourselves before this or that self-projected image of God in a silence and adoration which is certainly not intended by those who plunge us into that obscurity, but from which we can hardly restrain ourselves so long as they refuse, like the traditional exponents of the dogma, to point us to the genuine form of the mystery which we could and should approach with genuine silence, humility and adoration.

It is one of the great puzzles of history that the step which we are now taking towards a true form of the electing God and elected man was not taken long ago, although, as we have seen, many thinkers did come near enough to taking it. It is no puzzle, of course, that in these circumstances the doctrine of predestination could not be asserted or carried through with the fundamental importance generally ascribed to it, but was the occasion of so many fatal developments to the right hand or to the left, and was even pushed on one side as a kind of offence—to the great detriment of thinking upon the basis of the Christian faith, which could never move radically enough in this matter, but was inevitably imperilled at the very roots as long as the only ultimate possibility was the mystification of an unknown God and unknown man.

But the fact that the step which we are taking is a step forward, an innovation, is sufficient to justify us in asking yet again whether such a step can be made, whether we are right to make it, or whether our thesis that the election of Jesus Christ is the substance of the dogma is not merely another arbitrary movement, an encroachment. The thesis does avoid this twofold obscurity. It does give a single and known form to the unknown God and unknown man. The two together acquire one name and the name of one person, so that we may know before whom and what we must be silent and humble ourselves and adore. But (as we look back over the history of the doctrine) this very fact sheds so clear a light that we must ask whether there is not something uncanny

[148] about it, whether we are not exceeding our prerogatives. How do we know that Jesus Christ is the electing God and elected man? How do we know that all that is to be said concerning this mystery must be grounded in His name? We may ask the older exponents of the doctrine how they on their side know about a God and man who in the last analysis are unknown. If we do, we shall be brought up against constructs which more closely resemble philosophical reflection on the origin and development of being than they do the confession of a Christian understanding of God and man. The older teachers think first of cause and effect, of the infinite and the finite, of eternity and time, of idea and phenomenon. And obviously such thinking, or the result and application of such thinking, leads them first and above all to the sovereignly determinative will of the unknown God, and then finally and at the very lowest level to the predestination of unknown man. We must not overlook the fact that these older theologians did read their Bibles carefully, and that in the teaching they did intend to comment as we do on Rom. 9–11 and other passages in the scriptural witness. We must not overlook the fact that the Bible did not impel or constrain them to take the step which we are now taking, but confirmed them rather (even Eph. 1^4 and similar passages) in their positing of a twofold obscurity in respect of God and man at the beginning of all things. The reasons why they did and could posit this obscurity, and the counter-reasons why we can no longer do so, must lie very deep. And they are not to be found, or at any rate not to be found decisively, merely in the fact that they, on the one hand, were committed to a definite *schema* of thought which did not derive from the Bible but with the help of which they read their Bibles, while we, on the other, have now freed ourselves from this *schema*. The decisive point is the reading of the Bible itself. It is the question where and how we find in the Bible itself the electing God and elected man, and therefore that reality of the divine election as a whole which must shape our thinking about the election and form the object of all our individual reflection and speech concerning it.

Proportionately the passages in the Bible which speak expressly and directly of the divine election and predestination are not very numerous. We must always take these as a starting-point. But what is it that these passages speak of, and in what direction do they constrain us to look? Moreover, is it not the case that once we have recognised the subject with which they deal we have to take it into consideration as a necessary background to everything else that is said of the transactions between God and man? Is it not the case that all God's dealings attested in the Bible can be understood only against this background, as the dealings of the elected God with elected man? In exegetical consider-ations of this kind we may well be in full agreement with all the classical expo-nents of the doctrine. As regards the content of this concept it could hardly be otherwise: it is one of those comprehensive concepts which underlies all that [149] the Bible says about God and man, and of which account must always and everywhere be taken even where it does not appear directly. In the Bible the eternal God is the electing God. It is as the electing God that He acts. This is so even when He passes over in wrath and rejection, even when He simply uses man to fulfil His own purposes. And (in one way or another) temporal man is man elected by God. Ishmael and Esau, Pharaoh, too, and Saul and Cyrus, even Judas Iscariot, and the heathen both far and near, all these are elected, at least potentially, at least as witnesses to God's electing and man's election. In their own way even the reprobate and those whom God merely uses are elected. Again, in respect of the divine work of creation, reconciliation and redemption as attested in the Bible, we are in agreement with the classical exponents of the doctrine in that to a greater or less degree of distinctness all of us understand the name and person of Jesus Christ as the keypoint and consummation, the true meaning of all that God says and does, and the true goal of all the divine purposes. In this respect it is hard to put Jesus Christ higher or to give greater prominence to His central and ideological office than did Calvin or in his own way Thomas Aquinas. Where the parting of the ways comes is in the question of the relationship between predestination and Christology. Is there any continuity between the two? Is there a continuity between the christological centre and *telos* of the temporal work of God which was so clearly recognised by the older theologians, and the eternal presuppos-ing of that work in the divine election which was no less clearly recognised by them? Is there the continuity which would mean necessarily the expounding of predestination in the light of Christology and the understanding of Jesus Christ as the substance of predestination? If the witness of divine revelation is rightly received, is it possible to understand the eternal presupposing of God's temporal work in the light of the central point in that work? The older expo-nents of the doctrine did not see any such continuity and they had no desire to bring together the two doctrines in this way. The work of God which had its central point in Jesus Christ was one thing; the eternal presupposing of that work was quite another. Certainly in that eternal presupposing they did aim to acknowledge the true and triune God and none other. But they did not acknowledge Him as they saw Him in His work, or with the distinctness and form of His temporal activity. They separated Him from that one name and that one person. They did not acknowledge Him as the One who is identical with Jesus Christ. Quite naturally, too, they thought of man as the specific object of the eternal predestination. But it was man in general, or the race as a whole, or the sum total of individuals. It was not man as the one who is identical with Jesus Christ. Certainly they found a continuity between the eternal presupposing of the divine work and its centre and *telos* in Jesus Christ. But as

[150] they understood Scripture the relationship between the two was reversed. The eternal predestination was set up as a first and independent entity standing over against the centre and *telos* of the divine work and of time: a different encounter between God and man from that which became temporal event in Jesus Christ. As they saw it, the second decision and all that it involved followed on the first. Now clearly if this view is taken it is impossible to give a concrete answer to the question: Who is the electing God and elected man? The twofold obscurity in the doctrine of predestination is thus made inevitable. The triune God neither appears nor speaks to us except in the form of Jesus Christ, but He is always the unknown God. And if we do not know the electing God, where can we turn when it is a question of elected man? How can elected man be anything else but unknown? However that may be, this was the actual state of affairs as the older theology thought to see it in the light of the testimony of Holy Scripture.

If we undertake to oppose this view, we do so because we believe that their exegesis in this matter was in line with a highly questionable general hermeneutical principle which we ourselves cannot follow. The very best of the older theologians have taught us that in the word which calls and justifies and sanctifies us, the word which forms the content of the biblical witness, we must recognise in all seriousness the Word of God. Beside and above and behind this Word there is none other. To this Word then we have good cause to hold fast both for time and eternity. This Word binds us to itself both for time and eternity, and in it all our confidence must be placed. This Word does not allow us to go beyond it. It allows us no other view of God or man that that which it reveals itself. It focuses all our thoughts upon this view and keeps them focused there. It warns us against any distraction. This Word alone must satisfy all our questioning because it alone can do so. The work of God is revealed in this Word in its totality, being there revealed in such a way that there can be no depth of the knowledge of the divine work except in God's Word, and the knowledge of the divine work cannot lead us to any depth which is not that of God's Word. Again, the very best of the older theologians, who were also the classical exponents of the doctrine of predestination, have taught us that we must seek and will assuredly find (the in every respect) perfect and insurpassable Word of God in the name and person of Jesus Christ, in the unity of true deity and true humanity fulfilled in Him, and in the work accomplished by Him in that unity. Again, they have warned us most seriously that in respect of the knowledge of God and man we must not turn aside in the slightest degree from the knowledge of Jesus Christ, either to the right hand or to the left. We must not dream of any other God or any other man. We must not seek to know about God or man except as we look on Jesus Christ. The New Testament is full of statements about Jesus Christ which cast a penetrating light [151] on the Old as well: that to Him is given all power in heaven and on earth; that God has purposed in Him to gather up all things in heaven and on earth; that in Him are hid all the treasures of knowledge and wisdom; that outside of Him there is salvation in none other; that none other name is given to men whereby they must be saved; that He is the author and perfecter of our faith. And we should find it difficult to take more seriously or to expound more impressively both the individual testimonies and the whole Messianic witness of the Old and New Testaments than did the older theologians when they applied themselves to texts of this kind.

Yet we must still ask whether they did apply themselves to these passages as constantly and continuously as they should have done, whether they were always as faithful to their own insights as we should expect, especially in this matter of predestination. And while we cannot be sufficiently grateful for these insights or pay sufficient attention to them, yet we must still answer these questions in the negative. When they came across the passages in the Bible which treat expressly of the electing God, or elected man, or both, when they read there of God's eternal and unshakable decree and of the foreordination of man by that decree, then in some inexplicable way there suddenly seemed to open up before them the vista of heights and depths beyond and behind the Word which calls and justifies and sanctifies us, the Word which they could never extol enough as the source and standard of all our knowledge of God and man. Suddenly there seemed to be some other eternity apart from the eternity of the eternal life whose revelation and promise and gift in the promised and temporally incarnate Word they elsewhere attest loudly and impressively enough. And in this eternity there seemed to be some other mystery apart from the mystery whose proclamation and disclosure they can confirm elsewhere with clear texts from the New Testament. In respect of the electing God and elected man there was supposed to be some other reality and knowledge apart from the reality and knowledge of which it could elsewhere be said that the Church is built upon it and wholly bound up with it. In the sphere of predestination there arose all at once a different order, even though it had appeared elsewhere that according to the biblical testimony upon which the Church is founded there can be no question of the recognition of any such order. And at this point the question was not merely an incidental question, as the older theologians knew only too well. It was the question of the beginning of all things. It was the question of the knowledge of God's absolutely decisive disposing which takes place in the eternity before time was, and which legislates for salvation or damnation, for life or death, both in time and in the eternity when time shall have ceased to be. It was the question of the knowledge of the specific order of the kingdom or rule of God, with all that that

[152]   means for the existence, the preservation, the history and the destiny of creation and man. The question was in fact the actual and burning question:
What is to become of us at the hand of God? It was, and still is, immeasurably
important that in answering this question the older theology thought itself
dispensed, and let itself be forced away, from the hermeneutical principle
which elsewhere it had so rigidly proclaimed and the application of which it
had elsewhere so scrupulously regarded. But that is undoubtedly what took
place. And it is astonishing how the older theologians thought it self-evident
that there was no further need to adhere to the coherent whole of scriptural
witness which they themselves had revealed and proclaimed, boldly taking it
for granted that they could go beyond this whole and present as the doctrine
of predestination a construction which was quite foreign to it and to their
otherwise Christian witness, thus vitiating that witness at its most sensitive
point, the point of departure. It can hardly be maintained that such a course
was necessitated by the exegesis of the scriptural passages which speak directly
of predestination. Like all other passages, these must be read in the context of
the whole Bible, and that means with an understanding that the Word of God
is the content of the Bible. The exegesis of these passages depends upon
whether or not we have determined that our exposition should be true to the
context in which they stand and are intended to be read. Even the attempt to
philosophise did not compel the older theologians to take this course. At
other points they resisted firmly enough. It was not necessary that they should
be vanquished by it here. And even here the thought-scheme introduced
could be dangerous only because a prior decision had already been made to
depart from the whole meaning and context of Scripture.

From such a decision everything else results inevitably, and did in fact result.
And that is the step which we cannot consent to take. At this juncture we cannot pursue further the reasons which led up to that decision. Nor do we need
to discover its ultimate basis. We can only maintain that the decision was made,
and that once made it was not altered, and that it passed unnoticed even by so
large a company of penetrating thinkers. And we can only maintain that we for
our part cannot approve that decision, but must decide differently. Against the
general hermeneutical decision of the older theology we set up our own—that
in the exegesis of the biblical passages which treat directly of the election we
have to look in the same direction as we must always look in biblical exegesis.
We must hold by the fact that the Word which calls us, the Word which forms
the content of Scripture, is itself and as such the (in every respect) perfect and
insurpassable Word of God, the Word which exhausts and reveals our whole
knowledge of God, and from which we must not turn one step, because in
itself it is the fulness of all the information that we either need or desire con-

[153]   cerning God and man, and the relationship between them, and the ordering
of that relationship. At no point, then, and on no pretext, can we afford either
to dispense with, or to be turned aside from, the knowledge of Jesus Christ.
And why indeed should we do so at this particular point? We should be in full

accord with the majority of those theologians if we were to defend the assertion that what the Bible calls the salvation of man is nothing other than the
salvation once for all accomplished by Jesus Christ, or that what the Bible calls
the Church is nothing other than the life of the earthly body which has in Jesus
Christ its heavenly Head and Subject, or that what the Bible calls our hope can
be nothing other than the return of Jesus Christ to the just judgment by which
those who believe in Him will go to eternal life. We ask then: When it is a
question of the understanding and exposition of what the Bible calls predestination or election, why and on what authority are we suddenly to formulate a
statement which leaves out all mention of Jesus Christ? How is it that at this
point there suddenly arises the possibility of looking elsewhere? How do we
arrive at the position where we are able to do this, when we know that we
cannot do it at any other point without parting company with the older theologians? Is it that when we come to pre-temporal eternity, the sphere of predestination, that which was in the beginning with God, we are suddenly to
think of these apart from Jesus Christ—something which quite rightly we are
not allowed to do when we deal with supra-temporal and post-temporal eternity, with what is and will be? Is Jesus Christ really the One who was, and is, and
is to come, or is He not? And if He is, what constraint or authority is there that
we should not think through to the ultimate meaning of the "He was," not go
back to the real beginning of all things in God, i.e., not think of the divine
foreordination, the divine election of grace, as something which takes place in
Him and through Him? How is it that the concept of eternal election can be
referred to some other reality and not Jesus Christ, who as our salvation and
the Head of the Church and our hope must also be the electing God and
elected man in one and the same person? As presented to us in the Bible, what
can the election be at all, and what can it mean, if it is divorced from the name
and person to which the whole content of the Bible relates as to the exhaustive
self-revelation of God, here with the forward look of expectation and there
with the backward look of recollection? Only in some other context than that
of Holy Scripture can the concept of election, of foreordination, of the eternal
divine decree, refer elsewhere, to the twofold mystery of an unknown God and
unknown man. We cannot understand the hermeneutical decision which the
older theologians made in relation to this question. But in arriving at a different decision we do not believe that we are doing anything out of the ordinary,
but something obvious and straightforward. We believe, in fact, that we are
doing the only possible thing in accordance with the method with which those   [154]
theologians were conversant in other matters. And for this reason we do not
accept the criticism that at this point we have been betrayed into an innovation
which is purely capricious, wanting to know what by its very nature cannot be
known. We know that Jesus Christ is the electing God and elected man from
the same source which fed the older theology, and would have fed it at this
point too, but obviously could not do so because the theologians themselves
arbitrarily turned aside from it. The purpose of our thesis is to make good the

arbitrary act of our predecessors. And if it is calculated to shed light upon a doctrine where obscurity has hitherto prevailed, the light is not one which we ourselves have arbitrarily kindled, but the same light as is given everywhere else. We have no cause to put that light under a bushel merely at this point.

In this thesis of ours we are taking up again the intention which was unequivocally disclosed but not developed by John Knox and his fellow-workers in the *Conf. Scotica* of 1560, Arts. 7–8. In this confession Christology and predestination were regarded as in some sort parallel, and for that reason were treated together. On the one hand, there is the miraculous union of Godhead and manhood in Jesus Christ, and, on the other, our redemption; and both these have their origin and basis in the one eternal and unalterable decree of God. Thus in Art. 7 the answer to the question *Cur Deus homo?* is a concise and simple reference to this decree. And Art. 8 shows to what extent the election of Jesus Christ dominates this reference, for under the heading "Of the Election" the remaining content of the Calvinistic doctrine of predestination, even to the election or rejection of individuals, is introduced only in the form of a citation of Eph. 1[4]. And in the place of a longer exposition there is a detailed development and explanation of the fact that to be our Head, our Brother and our Shepherd, to be the Messiah and Saviour, to bear the punishment which we had merited and to destroy death on our behalf, Jesus Christ had to become both very God and very man. According to the intention of this confession, what should have been said of our election or rejection as the second element in this eternal and unalterable decree has obviously been said already in the statement concerning the nature of Jesus Christ and His being as very God and very man as determined by that eternal and unalterable decree. It is surely no accident that in Arts. 2 and 3, instead of working out in the usual way an independent doctrine of sin, this same confession introduces the problem of the fall only as a postscript to the doctrine of the original foreordination of man, the problem of original sin only as a preface to the doctrine of faith in Jesus Christ as effected by the Holy Ghost. Obviously it is only in that context and not in and for itself that John Knox would have the fact of sin understood. That man is against God is important and must be taken seriously. But what is far more important and must be taken far more seriously is that in Jesus Christ God is for man. And it is only in the light of the second fact that the importance and seriousness of the first can be seen. It can hardly be denied that in the *Conf. Scotica* the specific conception of sin is intimately connected with the peculiar christological conception of predestination.

The christological meaning and basis of the doctrine of election have been brought out afresh in our own time, and with an impressive treatment of Jesus Christ as the original and decisive object of the divine election and rejection. This service has been rendered by Pierre Maury in the fine lecture which he gave on "Election et Foi" at the *Congrès international de théologie calviniste* in Geneva, 1936 (published in *Foi et Vie*, April–May 1936, and in German under the title *Erwählung und Glaube* in *Theol. Studien*, Heft 8, 1940). That Congress dealt exclusively with the problem of predestination, and its records will easily show how instructive was Maury's contribution, and how it stood out from the other papers, which were interesting historically but in content moved entirely within the circle of the traditional formulations, and were almost hopelessly embarrassed by their difficulties.

Apart from these two voices, the one from the period of the Reformation and the other from our own, we can appeal in support of our thesis only (1) to the (in their own context highly significant) passages quoted in the first section from Athanasius and Augustine, together with occasional sentences from Coccejus; (2) to the inevitability of such a solution in the light of the Supralapsarian controversy; and (3) to the general Reformation assertion

[155]

164

that Christ is the *speculum electionis*[EN269], an assertion which obviously stands in need of more profound and comprehensive treatment. Historically there are to hand all kinds of important materials which should encourage and even necessitate an adoption of this thesis, but it cannot be denied that in formulating it as we have done we have exposed ourselves to the risk of a certain isolation. And we may repeat that it is most singular that this should be the case, and that the obvious should have to be stated and defended in the apparent form of an innovation.

2. With the traditional teaching and the testimony of Scripture, we think of predestination as eternal, preceding time and all the contents of time. We also think of it as divine, a disposing of time and its contents which is based on the omnipotence of God and characterised by His constancy (or "immutability"). With the strict exponents of tradition, and especially with the Supralapsarians of the 17th century, we think of it as the beginning of all things, i.e., the beginning which has no beginning except in God's eternal being in Himself; the beginning which in respect of God's relationship with the reality which is distinct from Himself is preceded by no other beginning; the beginning which is itself the beginning of this relationship as such; the beginning which everything else included or occurring within this relationship can only follow, proceeding from it and pointing back to it. We know God's will apart from predestination only as the act in which from all eternity and in all eternity God affirms and confirms Himself. We must guard against disputing the eternal will of God which precedes even predestination. We must not allow God to be submerged in His relationship to the universe or think of Him as tied in Himself to the universe. Under the concept of predestination, or the election of grace, we say that in freedom (its affirmation and not its loss) God tied Himself to the universe. Under the concept of predestination we confess the eternal will of the God who is free in Himself, even in the sense that originally and properly He wills and affirms and confirms Himself. But we can confess this will of God only under the concept of predestination. For it is only in the act of God which it denotes, only in the act by which God's relationship with the universe and ourselves is determined and ordered, that we can truly see this will and see God Himself in the sovereignty and glory which He has in Himself before all worlds. Under the concept of predestination, in full accord with tradition, we acknowledge the unsearchable majesty of the good-pleasure with [156] which God has from all eternity and in all eternity both the right and the power to dispose of the world and us, in which as God He has in fact disposed of us and the world, so that His eternal will is the Alpha and Omega with which all our thinking about the world and ourselves must begin and end.

But we depart from tradition when we say that for us there is no obscurity about this good-pleasure of the eternal will of God. It is not a good-pleasure which we have to admire and reverence as divine in virtue of such obscurity. For us it is not a question-mark to which we can make answer only with an

---

[EN269] mirror of election

empty and question-begging assertion. When we assert the wisdom and mercy and righteousness of this good-pleasure, we do not need to do so merely as a bald statement of fact. We negative this whole understanding because positively we must affirm that at the beginning of all things God's eternal plan and decree was identical with what is disclosed to us in time as the revelation of God and of the truth about all things. This is the light of the divine good-pleasure. This is the content of the statement which not only destroys the question-mark but answers the question. This is the wisdom and mercy and righteousness of God which not only asserts itself but discloses itself so fully and clearly that we may know what it is we do when we have to subordinate ourselves unreservedly to the good-pleasure of this wise and merciful and righteous God, and when in fact we can subordinate and surrender ourselves to this good-pleasure. As we understand the freedom of the predestinating God, it does not deny but opens up itself to our knowledge. And it is this positive understanding which constitutes our deviation from tradition, the "innovation" made in our thesis. The core of this thesis is to be found in the perception that in respect of predestination we must not and need not separate ourselves from the revelation of God as such, because in that revelation predestination is revealed as well, because predestination is not hidden but disclosed. God is the self-revealing God, and as such He is the electing God. The eternal will of God which is before time is the same as the eternal will of God which is above time, and which reveals itself as such and operates as such in time. In fact, we perceive the one in the other. For God's eternity is one. God Himself is one. He may only be known either altogether or not at all. When He is known He is known all at once and altogether. But these are secondary and derivative considerations which would have no force at all unless they were supported by the fact of the revelation of God. This fact has as such the character of completeness. Revealing to us the fulness of the one God, it discloses to us not only what the will of God is, but also what it was and what it will be. And it does so in such a way that we are satisfied as well as God. If we do not lazily close our eyes to this revelation, if we do not try to evade it, wantonly seeking instruction elsewhere, then there is nothing which is not told us concerning the meaning and direction and nature of God's will for us. Certainly, it is the secret of God's good-pleasure that it should take this form and not another, and that it should be revealed to us as such; that in all its fulness it should have the character and form and content displayed to us in God's revelation, and that it should really be disclosed in this revelation and not hidden. Certainly, there corresponds to this secret the secret of faith, in the question whether we do know and know fully its character and form and content, whether the good-pleasure of God does find our confidence and obedience. This is, indeed, the secret of God's good-pleasure, and even in the secret of the decision of faith it is still a question of our relationship to this secret. It is a question of revelation. It is a question of the knowledge of the will of God; of all His will, of His will which is before time, of His predestinating will. Even

[157]

166

under this aspect it is still a matter of the intelligent reverence and worship and love of God. Even under this aspect it is still a matter of our being brought out of darkness into light, and not plunged into a new and ostensibly divine darkness. If we hold fast the revelation of God as the revelation of His eternal will and good-pleasure, if we acknowledge God's freedom in the revelation in which He has proclaimed and enacted it, then as the beginning of all things with God we find the decree that He Himself in person, in the person of His eternal Son, should give Himself to the son of man, the lost son of man, indeed that He Himself in the person of the eternal Son should *be* the lost Son of Man. In the beginning with God, i.e., in the resolve of God which precedes the existence, the possibility and the reality of all His creatures, the very first thing is the decree whose realisation means and is Jesus Christ. This decree is perfect both in subject and object. It is the electing God and also the elected man Jesus Christ, and both together in the unity the one with the other. It is the Son of God in His whole giving of Himself to the Son of Man, and the Son of Man in his utter oneness with the Son of God. This is the covenant of grace which is perfected and sealed in the power of God's free love, established openly and unconditionally by God Himself and confirmed with a faithfulness which has no reserve. And this decree is really the first of all things. It is the decision between God and the reality distinct from Himself. It is a decision which is the basis of all that follows. And this decree is itself the sum and substance of all the wisdom and power with which God has willed this reality and called it into being. It is the standard and source of all order and all authority within God's relationship to this reality. It is the fixing of an end for this reality, foreordained, valid without question, unfailing in efficacy. It is itself the eternal will of God. The will of God is Jesus Christ, and this will is known to us in the revelation of Jesus Christ. If we acknowledge this, if we seriously accept Jesus Christ as the content of this will, then we cannot seek any other will of God, either in heaven or earth, either in time or eternity. This will is God's will. We must abide by it because God Himself abides by it; because God Himself [158] allows us and commands us to abide by it. And this decree of God is not obscure, but clear. In this decree we do not have to assert a God of omnipotence and to cower down before Him. In all His incomprehensibility we may know Him and love Him and praise Him as the One who has truly revealed to us His wisdom and mercy and righteousness, and who has revealed Himself as the One who is Himself all these things. God's glory overflows in this the supreme act of His freedom: illuminating, and convincing, and glorifying itself; not therefore demanding a *sacrificium intellectus*[EN270] but awakening faith. The Son of God determined to give Himself from all eternity. With the Father and the Holy Spirit He chose to unite Himself with the lost Son of Man. This Son of Man was from all eternity the object of the election of Father, Son and Holy Spirit. And the reality of this eternal being together of God and man

---

[EN270] sacrifice of the intellect

is a concrete decree. It has as its content one name and one person. This decree is Jesus Christ, and for this very reason it cannot be a *decretum absolutum*[EN271].

It cannot be said that this understanding of the divine election involves an illegitimate rationalisation and simplification of its mystery.

On the one hand, it is surely true that the idea of the unsearchable freedom of a pre-destinating God and of a man predestinated for unsearchable reasons cannot be that right conception of the mystery of the Christian life which we must be careful not to dissolve. On the contrary, we have to say that while such an idea of God and man is no doubt very mysterious and exciting and in its way consoling, it has nothing whatever to do with the Christian understanding. At bottom, it is an idea which belongs to natural theology, and is only too current in the history of non-Christian "religion." There is no difficulty in abandoning ourselves to the horror, or peace, of the thought of an unknown being disposing of and fixing our destiny in an unknown way. The thought is one which does so little to commit us, comfortably releasing our minds and wills from claims which might seriously tie us. For this reason it does to some extent commend itself as a background for the most diverse conceptions and modes of life as taste or inclination may direct. It is a thought which is so close to us all that to lay hold of it a divine revelation is not really necessary. At bottom, even to describe it as a secret or mystery is itself much too exaggerated if we take the word in its strictest sense. That this thought should take the position of a key-thought in the Christian doctrine of predestination and Christian theology in general is at root quite paradoxical, and that it should consistently be allowed to maintain this position, that it should be defended and honoured as something specifically sacred to Christianity, is a demand which cannot conceivably be represented as right and just. Ought we not, indeed, to expect and to demand the very opposite? When we set this thought in the light of serious Christian reflection, is it not one which we ought to attack and destroy? At root, can there ever be anything more unchristian or anti-christian than the horror or the peace which is given by the thought of the *decretum absolutum*[EN272] as the first and last truth from which everything else proceeds?

On the other hand, it is also true that what our thesis puts in the place of the *decretum absolutum*[EN273], the knowledge of God in Jesus Christ, is still a mystery, so that our proposal to correct and to give greater precision to the traditional teaching cannot be thought of as an attempt to rationalise that teaching. As we see it, our life is hid with Christ in God. In the [159] beginning (the beginning of all things and our own beginning) we find only the one Jesus Christ as the electing God and elected man. The whole relationship between God and man (and the whole relationship between God and the reality which is distinct from Him) consists originally and properly in the relationship between God and man in Jesus Christ. We must seek and find our own part in this relationship only in Him. Our communion with God, God's choice of us, and our election by God, is faith in Jesus Christ. And that is a clear enough idea. It allows and even offers us some knowledge of the divine predestination: a knowledge of the electing God and elected man; a knowledge of our own election and of the whole Whence? and Whither? of our life; not merely the reflection of this knowledge but its substance; not this knowledge with the menacing reservation that in some dark background everything is perhaps quite different, but with the certainty that in this matter background and foreground are one and the same, and that as the foreground may be known the background may also be known. And yet the light shed by this understanding is not a natural

---

[EN271] absolute decree
[EN272] absolute decree
[EN273] absolute decree

light. It is not the light of the logical or ethical deliberation of the human reason engaged in self-discussion. It is the light of revelation, the light of God. It is not something close to us but worlds removed It is not something given to man by his own capacities or energies. Of all ideas, it is the one which is in itself unthinkable, the one which is thinkable only in faith and by the miraculous power of the Holy Spirit: that God Himself should Himself become the Son of Man in His eternal Son; that He should will to take up the cause of the Son of Man as His own cause; that the will by which He did this should be the eternal will of God which constitutes the beginning of all things and our own beginning; that we should stand under the foreordination of this will even before we were born and before the world was; that from the very beginning in God's willing of the world the love of God should be God's rule over everything and all things. If there is any mystery of God, if there is any secret which, even as we know it and it is revealed to us and manifest before us, still proclaims and characterises itself more and more as a secret, then this is it. Here, if anywhere, good care is taken that we should not let slip this mystery in any attempt to rationalise. Here, if anywhere, we are challenged by this mystery itself in all our thinking and willing, so that there is no room for irresponsibility, and we are jolted out of all those conceptions or modes of life which we had freely selected or discovered for ourselves. Here, if anywhere, we can and must say that it is with the Christian mystery that we have to do; not with a riddle of life or thought, but with the very core of the Christian Gospel and the Christian faith. We stand before the mystery to which worship and reverence belong because we know it, the mystery which is worthy to be regarded and treated as a mystery for this very reason. From this standpoint, too, there is no cause for anxiety if we adopt the view that where the traditional *decretum absolutum*[EN274] used to stand there belongs the *decretum absolutum*[EN275] of the election of Jesus Christ.

But if a footing can be gained for this view, if of the presuppositions which controlled the older doctrine the first and fundamental one is corrected—the specific doctrine of the character of the divine decree—then this means that at least we are not led into the void when we ask concerning the divine election, concerning that eternal will which predetermines and over-rules both time and all that is in time. Fundamentally, this question is not unanswerable. It is not one of the questions which are destined always to remain questions. In face of it there is no place for that mysterious shaking of the head or shrugging of the shoulders or wringing of the hands which some perhaps regard as particularly pious in this connexion. Within the framework of the older theology it is the peculiarity and the peculiar scandal of the doctrine of the *decretum absolutum*[EN276] that at the first and last and culminating point in all our thinking and reflection it confronts us with a factor—the unsearchable freedom of God as such—which can only put an end to our questioning, and in face of which our thinking loses itself and is reduced to mere wandering. Face to face with the absolute decree, if we would pursue the matter further, there remains only, as we have seen, the escape into mysticism or moralism, i.e., a self-chosen salvation, idolatry, the righteousness of works. The only fire which a knowledge of the *decretum absolutum*[EN277] can kindle—if it does not extinguish all fires—is that of religion and not of faith. But the *decretum absolutum*[EN278] of the election of Jesus Christ means directly that we are summoned to faith. As the content of the divine revelation itself, it makes of our questioning a questioning which is ordained and fulfilled and accomplished in advance. As the true and Christian mystery—compared with which the alleged mystery of the *decretum absolutum*[EN279] is only a platitude, a truism of man's sound or

[160]

[EN274] absolute decree
[EN275] absolute decree
[EN276] absolute decree
[EN277] absolute decree
[EN278] absolute decree
[EN279] absolute decree

not so sound understanding—it makes us begin to question and to question in good earnest. Those who come to rest in the *decretum absolutum*[EN280] abandon all questioning. They think they know that we cannot know. But that knowledge, with the horror or peace that it brings, destroys all desire to know, all genuine and open questioning. Genuine and open questioning begins with the knowledge of the mystery of the election of Jesus Christ, for in this mystery we are confronted with an authority concerning which we cannot teach ourselves but must let ourselves be taught, and are taught, and can expect continually to be taught. The mystery of the election of Jesus Christ is the genuine answer; and it is for this reason that it makes possible and indeed demands and kindles a genuine questioning, a genuine desire to know. When we say "genuine" we mean necessary, inescapable, claiming and controlling us wholly and utterly, so that we stand or fall by our questions, so that we are no longer free to question or not to question, to desire to know or not to desire to know. "Genuine" means non-academic. And questioning of that sort can arise only when we are confronted by the answer, only when we begin to ask in the light of an answer already given, only when the questioning, once begun, can never end. Ultimately only the election of Jesus Christ has the character of an answer which thus demands and kindles a genuine questioning. Only the election of Jesus Christ—for all the other mysteries which might provoke such questioning eventually lead back to the mystery of the *decretum absolutum*[EN281], the mystery of the unknown God and unknown man, and before this mystery our questioning can only wilt and die. The election of Jesus Christ is the one matter about which we always know and must always ask, for in this election an absolute decision is made in respect of all things, and not least ourselves. This election is the beginning from which everything else proceeds. Our being or non-being, our life or death, is foreordained in the light of it. It is the predestination which in one way or another we must all fulfil. Everything else that happens to us is openly or secretly characterised by the fact that first and fundamentally this election has already taken place. There is much we do not need to know, but one thing we must know is the basic nature and meaning of God's electing and our election. There is much we do not need to ask about, but about this one thing we must ask. This is indeed the one thing about which we are, in fact, always ignorant. This one thing is, in fact, the mystery which always confronts us as such and which we shall weary ourselves in attempting to reduce or to solve. In this matter no teaching can ever reach an end and then be dispensed with. If the teaching is successful, we need it all the more. When it ends, it brings us back again to the beginning. Again, the election of Jesus Christ is the subject about which we know and about which we can therefore ask. This election takes away the idle horror or peace of the knowledge that we cannot know. Notwithstanding its eternity, it is history. It stands in the midst of all history. It is one history with other histories. It is the self-attestation of eternity. And it is also a Word, a Word which is spoken, and can be heard and received and learned. It is not silent but vocal. It is not formless but has form. It is the eternal decree of God which bears one name and consists in the existence of one person. And for this reason it is an answer: not a dark and empty answer, but an eternal divine answer; not a repetition of the question, but its fulfilment. Who and what was in the beginning with God? This decree, this answer tells us. And in face of this answer our thoughts need not lose themselves or be reduced to mere wandering, and the escape into mysticism or moralism is rendered superfluous. This answer itself instructs us, and in so doing it automatically excludes all the self-instruction which we might otherwise inflict upon ourselves, and which could only result in the death of all our questioning.

[161]

The questioning and knowledge, the teaching and instruction of which we are now speak-

---

[EN280] absolute decree
[EN281] absolute decree

ing is that of faith. It is the questioning of faith which is genuine questioning: the questioning which never ends and is never futile; the questioning which from the very first, and again and again, is ordained and fulfilled and accomplished in terms of the answer already given. And the deepest and distinctive difference between the *decretum absolutum*EN282 and the election of Jesus Christ is the fact that we can believe in the latter. What the election of Jesus Christ necessarily demands and evokes is faith, a confidence in God which is itself obedience to God. We cannot believe in the *decretum absolutum*EN283. We can only look at it and then forget it, turning elsewhere for the arbitrary satisfaction of religious needs. We cannot place any confidence at all in the *decretum absolutum*EN284, and obedience to it is quite inconceivable. The substitution of the election of Jesus Christ for the *decretum absolutum*EN285 is, then, the decisive point in the amendment of the doctrine of predestination. It enables us for the first time to show and to say that we can really believe in the divine election. It will not be overlooked that if we presuppose the *decretum absolutum*EN286 the first and decisive link in the *catena aurea*EN287 of Rom. 8³⁰f. could only become even at the very best the object of a mystery-cult or mystery-drama, but certainly not the object of faith. The fact that election and faith belong together, or in Luther's phrase are jumbled together, in the same way as calling and faith, or justification and faith, or sanctification and faith, or God and faith, is made clear only when we understand the election originally and decisively as the election of Jesus Christ.

3. The eternal will of God in the election of Jesus Christ is His will to give Himself for the sake of man as created by Him and fallen from Him. According to the Bible this was what took place in the incarnation of the Son of God, in His death and passion, in His resurrection from the dead. We must think of this as the content of the eternal divine predestination. The election of grace in the beginning of all things is God's self-giving in His eternal purpose. His self-giving: God gave—not only as an actual event but as something eternally foreordained—God gave His only begotten Son. God sent forth His own Word. And in so doing He gave Himself. He gave Himself up. He hazarded Himself. He did not do this for nothing, but for man as created by Him and fallen away from Him. This is God's eternal will. And our next task is to arrive at a radical understanding of the fact and extent that this will, as recognised and expressed in the history of the doctrine, is a twofold will, containing within itself both a Yes and a No. We must consider how and how far the eternal divine predestination is a quality, a *praedestinatio gemina*EN288.

What was it that God elected in the eternal election of Jesus Christ? When we asked concerning the content of predestination in our previous expositions we could never give a single answer but only a double. Primarily God [162] elected or predestinated Himself. God determined to give and to send forth His Son. God determined to speak His Word. The beginning in which the Son

---

EN282 absolute decree
EN283 absolute decree
EN284 absolute decree
EN285 absolute decree
EN286 absolute decree
EN287 golden chain
EN288 double predestination

became obedient to the Father was with Himself. The form and concretion of His will, the determination of His whole being, was reached in Himself. All God's freedom and love were identical with this decree, with the election of Jesus Christ. That is the one side of the matter. And the other is that God elected man, this man. God's decision and ordination concerned this man. He predestinated His own Son to existence as the son of David. He decreed that His Word should be sounded forth in the world of man. And so it was this man, the same, Jesus Christ, who was in the beginning with God. The divine will took on a form and concretion in and with which God was no longer alone with Himself, but this man Jesus Christ was taken up into the will of God and made a new object of the divine decree, distinct from God. To the election of Jesus Christ there belongs, then, elected man as well as the electing God. There are two sides to the will of God in the election of Jesus Christ. And since this will is identical with predestination, from the very first and in itself it is a double predestination. We must return later to the distinction between the first and second aspects and the relationship between them. For the present we must be content with the simple assertion that there is already, in origin and from all eternity, this twofold reference, a double predestination. It is obvious that when we confess that God has elected fellowship with man for Himself we are stating one thing, and when we confess that God has elected fellowship with Himself for man we are stating quite another. Both things together are the divine election. But obviously if its object is twofold so too is its content. It is one thing for God to elect and predestinate Himself to fellowship with man, and quite another for God to predestinate man to fellowship with Himself. Both are God's self-giving to man. But if the latter means unequivocally that a gift is made to man, the former certainly does not mean that God gives or procures Himself anything—for what could God give or procure Himself in giving to man a share in His own being? What we have to consider under this aspect is simply God's hazarding of His Godhead and power and status. For man it means an infinite gain, an unheard of advancement, that God should give Himself to him as his own possession, that God should be his God. But for God it means inevitably a certain compromising of Himself that He should determine to enter into this covenant. Where man stands only to gain, God stands only to lose. And because the eternal divine predestination is identical with the election of Jesus Christ, its twofold content is that God wills to lose in order that man may gain. There is a sure and certain salvation for man, and a sure and certain risk for God.

[163]   If the teachers of predestination were right when they spoke always of a duality, of election and reprobation, of predestination to salvation or perdition, to life or death, then we may say already that in the election of Jesus Christ which is the eternal will of God, God has ascribed to man the former, election, salvation and life; and to Himself He has ascribed the latter, reprobation, perdition and death. If it is indeed the case that the divine good-pleasure which was the beginning of all things with God carries with it the risk and

threat of negation, then it is so because the Son of God incarnate represents and Himself is this divine good-pleasure. The risk and threat is the portion which the Son of God, i.e., God Himself, has chosen for His own.

In the present connexion we must speak first of this negative side. For in the eternal predestination of God the first thing is that God has elected Himself as man's Friend and Partner, that He has elected fellowship with man for Himself. What was involved, then, when God elected to become the Son of Man in Jesus Christ? In giving Himself to this act He ordained the surrender of something, i.e., of His own impassibility in face of the whole world which because it is not willed by Him can only be the world of evil. In Himself God cannot be affected either by the possibility or by the reality of that will which opposes Him. He cannot be affected by any potentiality of evil. In Him is light and no darkness at all. But when God of His own will raised up man to be a covenant-member with Himself, when from all eternity He elected to be one with man in Jesus Christ, He did it with a being which was not merely affected by evil but actually mastered by it. Man was tempted by evil. Man became guilty of evil. Man did evil. Man fell victim to all the consequences of evil. The very fact that man was not God but a creature, even though he was a good creature, had meant already a certain jeopardising of the honour of God as whose instrument man had been created. Would this good instrument extol God's honour as was meet, as God Himself extolled it, as a good instrument ought to extol it? Man was in any case an extremely unreliable champion of this cause, an extremely compromised servant of the divine will, compromising even God Himself. What can it have meant for God to commit Himself to such a creature? If for a moment we attempted the impossible task of picturing to ourselves man unfallen and sinless, we should at any rate have to say this concerning him. He is not God. The fulfilment of his calling to live to God's glory is in any case a matter of his creaturely freedom and decision. For he is quite different from God. He is at least challenged and not sovereign like God. And because of this, man stands on the frontier of that which is impossible, of that which is excluded, of that which is contradictory to the will of God. In so far as he can and should live by the Word of God, participation in this contradiction is impossible for him. It is excluded, forbidden. But will he live by the Word of God? What a risk God ran when He willed to take up the cause of created man even in his original righteousness, when He constituted Himself his God and ordained Himself to solidarity with him! If even the man whose [164] existence we cannot in the least imagine had everything to gain by such a covenant, God Himself had everything to lose by it. But the man with whom the eternal will of God has to do is not this man; or rather, it is this man, not good as God created him, but fallen away from God. In fact, then, the risk taken by God was far greater. His partner in this covenant is not man on the brink of danger but man already overtaken by it; man for whom the impossible has become possible, and the unreal real, and the fulfilment of evil an actual occurrence. It is the man who gave a hearing to Satan, who did not guard the frontier, who did not keep the divine commandment, who lived otherwise than by the will of God, who thus willed to surrender the whole meaning of his existence, who brought dishonour upon God instead of honour, who became a traitor to God, an enemy and an adversary, who could be visited only by the wrath of God. It was the man whose wife was Eve and first son Cain, who answered a long series of special visitations by an equally long series of fresh aggressions, who finally drove the Messiah of God to the cross, whose name is at very best Peter and at worst Judas. And God has chosen this man and fellowship with this man in the election of Jesus Christ. It is the lost son of man who is partner of the electing God in this covenant. We are not so far speaking of what this means for man. What is quite certain is that for God it means severe self-commitment. God does not merely give Himself up to the risk and menace, but He exposes Himself to the actual onslaught and grasp of evil. For if God Himself became man, this man, what else can this mean but that He declared Himself guilty of the contradiction against Himself in which man was involved; that He submitted Himself to the law of creation by which such a contradiction could be accompanied only by loss and destruction; that He made Himself the object of the wrath and judgment to which man had brought himself; that He took upon Himself the rejection which man had deserved; that He tasted Himself the damnation, death and hell which ought to have been the portion of fallen man? What did God choose of glory or of joy or of triumph when in Jesus Christ He elected man? What could this election bring except something of which God is free in Himself and for which He cannot truly have any desire: darkness, and the impossibility of our existence before Him as sinners, as those who have fallen victim to His penalties? If we would know what it was that God elected for Himself when He elected fellowship with man, then we can answer only that He elected our rejection. He made it His own. He bore it and suffered it with all its most bitter consequences. For the sake of this choice and for the sake of man He hazarded Himself wholly and utterly. He elected our suffering (what we as sinners must suffer towards Him and before Him and from Him). He elected it as His own suffering. This is the extent to which His election is an election of grace, an

[165]   election of love, an election to give Himself, an election to empty and abase Himself for the sake of the elect. Judas who betrays Him He elects as an apostle. The sentence of Pilate He elects as a revelation of His judgment on the world. He elects the cross of Golgotha as His kingly throne. He elects the tomb in the garden as the scene of His being as the living God. That is how God loved the world. That is how from all eternity His love was so selfless and genuine. And, conversely, if we would know what rejection is as determined in God's eternal counsel, the rejection of which we cannot but speak even in our doctrine of predestination, then we must look in the same direction. We must look to what God elected for Himself in His Son when in that Son He elected for Himself fellowship with man. We must look simply and solely to what God

took upon Himself when He ordained His Son as Son of Man. We must look to His own portion in His Son, to what He Himself gained by this covenant between Himself and man. What could He expect to gain by this covenant, and what did He actually gain by it, except that there fell upon Him that which ought to have fallen upon man, except that He took to Himself shame and prepared for Himself distress? In the very fact that He did this we must see what was willed by Him from all eternity. In the very fact that from all eternity He willed to suffer for us, we must consider the negative aspect of the divine predestination. Where else should we see it but here? Where else should it be revealed to us but here? For here we see it as God Himself determined it, as He determined it, indeed, from all eternity. Here it is revealed as it is grounded in God's good-pleasure itself, as it actually is from all eternity.

We may remark in passing that the fact that from all eternity God resolved to take to Himself and to bear man's rejection is a prior justification of God in respect of the risk to which He resolved to expose man by creation—and in respect of the far greater risk to which He committed him by His permitting of the fall. We cannot complain because God put a creaturely being on this frontier, a being unlike Himself in that it was subject to temptation. We cannot blame God for confronting man with evil, an evil which in His own case was excluded by the divine nature, but which in man's case could be excluded only by the divine Word and commandment. We cannot hold it against God that He did not prevent but permitted the fall of man, i.e., his succumbing to the temptation of the devil and his incurring of actual guilt. In God's eternal decree these things did not involve any injustice to the creature, for by this same decree God decided that the risk which He allowed to threaten the creature and the plight into which He allowed it to plunge itself should be His own risk and His own plight. God created man. In that sense He exposed him to the risk. Yet from all eternity God did not let him fall, but He upheld him even when Satan's temptation and his own culpability resulted in a fall into sin. Thus even when we think of man in this negative determination, we still think of him as the one whom God loved from all eternity in His Son, as the one to whom He gave Himself from all eternity in His Son, gave Himself that He might represent him, gave Himself that He might bear and suffer on his behalf what man himself had to suffer. We must insist upon man's responsibility for his failure to do on that frontier what he ought to have done as a creature of God and hearer of the Word of God. But much more, we must insist upon the responsibility which God Himself shouldered when He created man and permitted the fall of man. Man cannot evade his own responsibility by complaining that God required too much of him, for what God required of Himself on man's behalf is infinitely greater than what He required of man. In the last analysis what God required of man consists only in the demand that he should live as the one on whose behalf God required the very uttermost of Himself. "Thou wilt say then unto me, Why doth he yet find fault? For who hath resisted his will? Nay but, O man, who art thou that repliest against God?" (Rom. 9$^{19f.}$). And the answer is: The man to whom God Himself turned from all eternity in His Son, even in the subordination to His will which is so strange to you; the man at whose strange need and danger God estranged Himself from all eternity, making it His own; the man who has no cause to reproach God, but if he will reproach anyone can reproach only himself; the man who is justly reproached by God if he attempts to reply against Him, if he does not live as the one on whose behalf God has taken to Himself every reproach, if he does not live in a state of thankfulness towards God.

[166]

175

When we say that God elected as His own portion the negative side of the divine predestination, the reckoning with man's weakness and sin and inevitable punishment, we say implicitly that this portion is not man's portion. In so far, then, as predestination does contain a No, it is not a No spoken against man. In so far as it does involve exclusion and rejection, it is not the exclusion and rejection of man. In so far as it is directed to perdition and death, it is not directed to the perdition and death of man. All these things could come upon man and should come upon him, because by his unreliability as a creature, and more particularly by his demonstrated disloyalty as a sinful creature, he has clearly shown that he is quite unusable in the hands of God. He has clearly shown that he is not worthy of trust as a covenant-partner with God. From all eternity God could have excluded man from this covenant. He could have delivered him up to himself and allowed him to fall. He could have refused to will him at all. He could have avoided the compromising of His freedom by not willing to create him. He could have remained satisfied with Himself and with the impassible glory and blessedness of His own inner life. But He did not do so. He elected man as a covenant-partner. In His Son He elected Himself as the covenant-partner of man. This does not mean, of course, that He willed to overlook or to accept man's unreliability and disloyalty. It does not mean that He reconciled Himself to the outbreak of evil in the creaturely sphere as actualised in the existence of man. What it does mean is that He willed to make good this affronting and disturbing of His majesty, this devastating of His work, not by avenging Himself on its author, but by Himself bearing the inevitable wrath and perdition, by Himself mediating on behalf of the one who must necessarily be rejected, who had necessarily fallen victim to damnation and death, by allowing His own heart to be wounded by the wrath which, if it had

[167] fallen upon man, could only have obliterated and destroyed him. God's eternal decree in the beginning was the decree of the just and merciful God, of the God who was merciful in His justice and just in His mercy. He was just in that He willed to treat evil seriously, to judge it and to sentence it, to reject and to condemn its author, delivering him over to death. But He was merciful in that He took the author of evil to His bosom, and willed that the rejection and condemnation and death should be His own. In this decree of the just and merciful God is grounded the justification of the sinner in Christ and the forgiveness of sins. It does not mean that God does not treat sins seriously, or that He does not summon man their author to render an account. What it does mean is that in doing this God declares His solidarity with their author, taking his place in respect of their necessary consequence, suffering in Himself what man ought to have suffered. It does not mean that God finds excuse. What it does mean is that God takes to Himself the torment that that which is inexcusable must inevitably carry with it. The justification of the sinner in Jesus Christ is the content of predestination in so far as predestination is a No and signifies rejection. On this side, too, it is eternal. It cannot be overthrown or reversed. Rejection cannot again become the portion or affair of man. The exchange

which took place on Golgotha, when God chose as His throne the malefactor's cross, when the Son of God bore what the son of man ought to have borne, took place once and for all in fulfilment of God's eternal will, and it can never be reversed. There is no condemnation—literally none—for those that are in Christ Jesus. For this reason faith in the divine predestination as such and *per se* means faith in the non-rejection of man, or disbelief in his rejection. Man is not rejected. In God's eternal purpose it is God Himself who is rejected in His Son. The self-giving of God consists, the giving and sending of His Son is fulfilled, in the fact that He is rejected in order that we might not be rejected. Predestination means that from all eternity God has determined upon man's acquittal at His own cost. It means that God has ordained that in the place of the one acquitted He Himself should be perishing and abandoned and rejected—the Lamb slain from the foundation of the world. There is, then, no background, no *decretum absolutum*[EN289], no mystery of the divine good-pleasure, in which predestination might just as well be man's rejection. On the contrary, when we look into the innermost recesses of the divine good-pleasure, predestination is the non-rejection of man. It is so because it is the rejection of the Son of God. It is so because it is indeed a foreordination of the necessary revelation of divine wrath—but a revelation whose reality was God's own suffering in Jesus Christ. Only if we are unbelieving or disobedient or unthankful in face of what is ordained for us, only if we misunderstand completely the divine predestination, can we think of this revelation as something which has to do with our own suffering. If in face of the divine predestination we are believing and obedient and thankful, if we have a right understanding of its mystery, we shall never find there the decreed rejection either of ourselves or of any other men. This is not because we did not deserve rejection, but because God did not will it, because God willed the rejection of His Son in our stead.

[168]

That in faith it is impossible to believe in our rejection is an insight which we share with all the more penetrating exponents of the doctrine. Even Augustine, even Calvin and the Calvinists, always said that in faith we must and can hold by the fact that we are elected and not rejected. But it is hard to see how, or how far, there is any real basis for this insight, or any real possibility of carrying out the advice, unless it is quite clear that in believing in the divine predestination we have to believe in the election of Jesus Christ. We cannot believe in the *decretum absolutum*[EN290], and "faith" in it certainly cannot give or allow us the assurance that we are elected and not rejected. Even a general faith in God, or more concretely, in a God of mercy and justice, cannot be of any help in this matter. For by what logic or morality can we ascribe to God a justice and mercy which in their exercise would lead to the exclusion of rejection from the divine purpose? We can maintain that this is the case only if the divine decree is identical with the divine self-giving in Jesus Christ, or, rather, if it is made and comprised wholly within this self-giving. And if this is so, then we must maintain it. For the confession of God and of God's justice and mercy results necessarily in the further confession that there is neither cause nor authorisation for the fear of possible rejection. For in

---

[EN289] absolute decree
[EN290] absolute decree

God's self-giving in Jesus Christ it is clear that rejection does not concern us because God willed that it should concern Himself. We are not called upon to bear the suffering of rejection because God has taken this suffering upon Himself. And if it is the case that in believing in the divine self-giving in Jesus Christ we can and should believe in the divine predestination, then we can believe in our own non-rejection and the non-rejection of all men. We can think of the rejection of man only as the dark background of unbelief, or the objective correlative of false belief: belief in what God has not revealed because it is not true; perverse belief in what God has not decreed but excluded by His decree. If, then, we would maintain what the older theologians rightly intended to maintain with regard to the necessarily positive character of predestination, and certainly not its negative character, then we must not attempt to separate the eternal will of God and the election of Jesus Christ. In this respect we differ from the older theology.

We now turn to the other aspect of this same reality. What did God elect in the election of Jesus Christ? We have said already that not only did He elect fellowship with man for Himself, but He also elected fellowship with Himself for man. By the one decree of self-giving He decreed His own abandonment to rejection and also the wonderful exaltation and endowment of man to existence in covenant with Himself; that man should be enriched and saved and glorified in the living fellowship of that covenant. In this primal decision God did not remain satisfied with His own being in Himself. He reached out to something beyond, willing something more than His own being. He willed and posited the beginning of all things with Himself. But this decision can mean only an overflowing of His glory. It can consist only in a revelation and communication of the good which God has and also is in Himself. If this were not so, [169] God would not be God. Because there is no darkness in God, there can be no darkness in what He chooses and wills. Nor is there anything midway, anything neutral, between light and darkness. In aim and purpose God is only light, unbroken light. What God does is well done. Our starting-point must always be that in all His willing and choosing what God ultimately wills is Himself. All God's willing is primarily a determination of the love of the Father and the Son in the fellowship of the Holy Ghost. How, then, can its content be otherwise than good? How can it be anything else but glory—a glory which is new and distinctive and divine? But in this primal decision God does not choose only Himself. In this choice of self He also chooses another, that other which is man. Man is the outward cause and object of this overflowing of the divine glory. God's goodness and favour are directed towards him. In this movement God has not chosen and willed a second god side by side with Himself, but a being distinct from Himself. And in all its otherness, as His creature and antithesis, this being has been ordained to participation in His own glory, the glory to which it owes its origin. It has been ordained to exist in the brightness of this glory and as the bearer of its image. In all its otherness it is predestined to receive the divine good which has been revealed and communicated. This is what is ordained for man in the primal decision of the divine decree. The portion which God willed and chose for him was an ordination to blessedness. For to be able to attest the overflowing glory of the Creator is blessedness. God willed man and elected man with the promise of eternal life. Life as a witness to the overflowing glory of God is eternal life. In this foreordination man exists in the beginning of all things, in the decree of God with God.

We state at once that we have to do here with the positive content, the Yes of predestination. We have to do with what is primary and proper to it, its meaning and end. For the fact that God willed and chose man with this ordination, the fact that He predestinated him to be a witness of His glory, and therefore to blessedness and eternal life, meant inevitably that he was foreordained to danger and trouble. Man was willed and chosen by God with his limitations, as a creature which could and would do harm to God by the application, or rather the misuse, of its freedom. The danger-point of man's susceptibility to temptation, and the zero-point of his fall, were thus included in the divine decree. In their own way they were even the object of the divine will and choice. This is also true. This second aspect accompanies the first like a shadow preceding and following. In ordaining the overflowing of His glory God also and necessarily ordains that this glory, which in Himself, in His inner life as Father, Son and Holy Spirit, cannot be subjected to attack or disturbance, which in Himself cannot be opposed, should enter the sphere of contradiction where light and darkness are marked off from each other, where what God wills, the good, stands out distinctively from what He does not will, the [170] evil, where by the very existence of good there is conceded to evil and created for it a kind of possibility and reality of existence, where it can and does enter in as a kind of autonomous power, as Satan. The possibility of existence which evil can have is only that of the impossible, the reality of existence only that of the unreal, the autonomous power only that of impotence. But these as such it can and must have. How can God ordain the overflowing of His glory, how can He choose the creature man as witness to this glory, without also willing and choosing its shadow, without conceding to and creating for that shadow—not in Himself, but in the sphere of the outward overflowing of His glory—an existence as something yielding and defeated, without including the existence of that shadow in His decree? Without evil as "permitted" in this sense there can be no universe or man, and without the inclusion of this "permission" God's decree would be something other than it actually is. It should be perfectly clear, however, that the overflowing and the shadow are the will of God at a completely different level and in a completely different sense. The positive will and choice of God is only the overflowing of His glory and the blessedness and eternal life of man. Even in His permitting of man's liability to temptation and fall, even in His permitting of evil, this is always what God wills. The divine willing of evil has, then, no proper or autonomous basis in God. It is not, as it were, an independent light in God which shines or is suddenly kindled at this point. God wills evil only because He wills not to keep to Himself the light of His glory but to let it shine outside Himself, because He wills to ordain man the witness of this glory. There is nothing in God and nothing in His willing and choosing *ad extra*[EN291] to which either evil or the doer of evil can appeal, as though evil too were divinely created, as though evil too had in God a divine origin and counterpart. God wills it only as a shadow which yields and flees. And He wills it only because He wills the shining of only the one true light, His own light, and because He wills to reveal and impart this light. Thus we cannot present as proportionate but only as disproportionate the relationship between the good which God intended for man and allotted to him from all eternity, and the danger and distress of the evil which He "permitted" and to that extent willed in the same eternal decree. We are saying too much and speaking inexactly even when we describe the one as primarily and properly God's will and the other as that will only secondarily and improperly; for when we speak in this way evil can easily come to be thought of as having an autonomy and status within the divine economy which cannot be conceded to it. The only autonomy and status that evil can have is that of a being and essence excluded from the divine economy and rejected by it—the autonomy and status of the non-being which necessarily confronts and opposes being in the [171] realm of creation, but which has its basis and meaning only in this confrontation and opposition, only as the spirit of constant negation. If we ask about the content of divine predestination, at no level do we come upon a foreordination of man which is a foreordination to evil, to the dominion of this spirit of negation, to the distress which results from this dominion. The real foreordination of man is to attestation of the divine glory, to blessedness and to eternal life. It is true that this foreordination cannot be fulfilled except on the brink of the abyss of foreordination to evil. But it is also true that evil can only be the abyss of negation in order at once to be opposed and overcome by the Yes of divine predestination. And the negation itself is revealed and is raised up to its own dreadful life by this Yes. When we say God we say Creator, Reconciler and Redeemer, not the opposite. We say the same and not the opposite even when we say Judge, even when we speak of the holiness and wrath of God. We cannot say that God ordains equally and symmetrically as man's end both good and evil, both life and death, both His own glory and the darkening of this glory. In fear and trembling we can and must and will speak of this abyss. We will take evil seriously for what in its own way—but only in its own way—it is allowed to be on the basis of the eternal divine decree. But we will not make of the two-fold nature of this decree a dualism. Without overlooking or denying the accompanying shadow we will, in fact, speak of God only as Creator, Reconciler and Redeemer; as the One from whom we can always expect good and only good. The concept which so hampered the traditional doctrine was that of an equilibrium or balance in which blessedness was ordained and declared on the right hand and perdition on the left. This concept we must oppose with all the emphasis of which we are capable.

But the emphatic nature of our opposition does not derive from any precon-

---

[EN291] outside of himself

ceived idea that the love of God prevents His equal willing of both, thus excluding any such symmetrical understanding of double predestination. What right have we to tell God that in His love, which is certainly quite different from ours, He cannot equally seriously, and from the very beginning, from all eternity, condemn as well as acquit, kill as well as make alive, reject as well as elect? Even to-day we must still defend the older doctrine against this kind of objection. But we cannot defend it against the objection that while the will of God in the election of Jesus Christ is indeed double it is not dual. It is not a will directed equally towards man's life and man's death, towards salvation and its opposite. If we look at it from the standpoint of the election of Jesus Christ, and if we are consistent in finding the will and choice of God only in this election, then a "love" of God directed equally towards human salvation and human damnation would have to be described as a quite arbitrary construct— just as arbitrary, in fact, as that which would deny to God all right to a love of this kind. We must ask one thing of those who would ascribe to God this rather [172] sinister type of love: What is their supposed source of information on this matter? Certainly this source is not to be found in the consideration or the knowledge of Jesus Christ. Certainly it is not to be found in the knowledge of God's eternal will in the election of Jesus Christ. If we maintain the contrary we must oppose all those theories which presume an equilibrium of God's twofold will. For the only knowledge which we have of man's foreordination to evil and death is in the form in which God of His great mercy accepted it as His own portion and burden, removing it from us and refusing to let it be our foreordination in any form. That removing and refusing took place in Jesus Christ. On our behalf the Son of God took the form of a servant and became obedient unto death, even the death of the cross. In this fact we see the eternal will of God. We know nothing above or beyond the will of God as it is thus realised in time. And for this reason we do not find a proportion but a disproportion between the positive will of God which purposes the life and blessedness of man and the permissive will of God which ordains him to seduction by Satan and guilt before God. In this disproportion the first element is always predominant, the second subordinate. The first is an authoritative Yes, the second a No which is determined only by the Yes, thus losing its authority from the very outset. The first is the coming form of the divine work, the second the perishing. This would, indeed, be an arrogant and quite impossible presentation of the matter if we reached such a conclusion from an arbitrarily formed judgment of our own about God or man. But this presentation is the correct and indeed the only possible one, because all others are excluded by the judgment which God Himself has pronounced on man—excluded, that is to say, if we recognise in this judgment God's original and definitive decree, and if we acknowledge it as such. We are no longer free, then, to think of God's eternal election as bifurcating into a rightward and a leftward election. There is a leftward election. But God willed that the object of this election should be Himself and not man. God removed from man and took upon Himself the burden of the evil which unavoidably threatened and actually achieved and exercised dominion in the world that He had ordained as the theatre of His glory. God removed from man and took upon Himself the suffering which resulted from this dominion, including the condemnation of sinful man. For this reason we cannot ascribe any autonomy to the world of evil, or to the will of God as it is directed towards and assents to it in a permissive form. In Jesus Christ we can see and know this whole sphere of evil as something which has already been overcome, something which yields, something which has been destroyed by the positive will of God's overflowing glory. And what it is in Jesus Christ it is also in the beginning with God. And for this reason in God's decree at the beginning there is for man only a predestination which corresponds to the perfect being of God Himself; a predestination to His kingdom and to blessedness and life. Any other predestination is merely presumed and unreal: a predestination arising from sin and error and opposed by the revelation of God; not the divine predestination fulfilled in God's eternal decree. Man takes upon him something which God has reserved for Himself if he tries to enter into this predestination or to think of himself as predestined to sin and death. If God has reserved for Himself the reckoning with evil, all that man can do is to take what is allotted to him by God. But this is nothing more or less than God's own glory. Unequivocally, and without reserve or diminution, God has elected and ordained man to bear the image of this glory. That and that alone is what we see and know in Jesus Christ in relation to man. The suffering borne on the cross of Golgotha by the son of man in unity with the Son of God, who is as such a sacrifice for the sins of the world, is a stage on the road, an unavoidable point of transition, to the glory of the resurrection, ascension and session. But it is not the Son of God who is glorified. He who humbled Himself according to the decree of God had no need of glorifying. He does not experience glorifying, but rather, in the power of His deity, He realises and accomplishes it. The glorification is of the Son of David. His is the justification, His the salvation from death, His the exaltation to fellowship with God, His the clothing upon with that form of existence predestined for Him, eternal life, His the foretaste of blessedness. This is man's portion in the amazing exchange between God and man as it was realised in time in Jesus Christ because already it was the beginning of all things. And we must recognise this as man's portion in the divine predestination if we trust that God's will revealed in Jesus Christ is the eternal will of God. It is evident that by an act of renunciation God diverts to man the portion which rightly belongs to Himself. If we may put it in this way, the glory and goodness and blessedness which we find in the sphere of creation is no longer God's own. He has given away what is His. He has given away Himself and all the prerogatives of His Godhead. He has given them to the man Jesus, and in Him to the creature. To put it more exactly, in the sphere of creation God has His glory and goodness and blessedness in what He reveals and communicates to the man Jesus and in Him to the creature. There can be no doubt that in His overflowing glory God is sacrificial love; love which

[173]

seeks not her own but the things of others. This corresponds to the humiliation which the Son of God accepted on behalf of the lost son of man, and to the whole exaltation conferred upon the son of man by this divine favour. And the latter is clearly the decisive element in the work of God accomplished in Jesus Christ and therefore in God's eternal decree. Obviously God wills the former: His own humiliation on man's behalf, that judgment might be taken away, all righteousness fulfilled, and the road trodden to the very end. But He wills the former only in connexion with and for the sake of the one thing: that [174] by right man might be heir of His own glory, goodness and blessedness, entering into fellowship with Himself. The order proclaimed in the work of revelation and atonement must be regarded and respected as also the order of the divine predestination. Naturally we must know what it is that God wills to remove from us. But much more we must know what it is that He wills to give to us. And we can know this only in terms of what God has put behind us because He willed to take it from us and has in fact done so. We can know it only in terms of the abyss on whose brink we are held. We cannot look at this abyss as though it were still the place to which we belong. We know that our place is in heaven where Christ sits as our Representative on the right hand of God. We cannot balance the fact that Adam fell, or David sinned, or Peter denied, or Judas betrayed, against the resurrection of Jesus Christ. The facts are true, but it is also true that they are far outweighed by the resurrection of Jesus Christ and that as the result of this resurrection they belong already to the vanished past. The thought of God's predestination cannot, then, awaken in us the mixture of terror and joy which would be in order if we were confronted partly by promise and partly by threat. It can awaken only joy, pure joy. For this order is found in the divine predestination itself, and it cannot be revoked. It is not a system whose component parts must each be considered separately. It is a way willed by God Himself. At the end of this way God's glory is revealed in the fact that He Himself removed the threat and became our salvation. In the light of this end there is no place for anything but joy. And only the end affects us, only grace, not what God had to take away and willed to take away and did take away from us, taking it upon Himself. For this reason, in relation to the divine predestination we must look always to that end. This is not a matter of optimism. It is a matter of being obedient and not disobedient, of being thankful and not self-willed. In obedience and thankfulness we can only rejoice at the double predestination of God.

This interpretation of double predestination stands or falls, of course, with the view that the divine predestination is to be understood only within the election of Jesus Christ. It stands or falls with the view that in regard to the electing God and elected man we must look and continue to look neither to the right hand nor to the left but directly at Jesus Christ. In other words, the question is this: Is the electing God the Son beloved of the Father and Himself loving the Father, the Son who as such is the subject of the beginning and predestination of all things? And is elected man, the object of this beginning and predestination of all things, the man Jesus of Nazareth who was born in the cradle of Bethlehem and died on the cross of Golgotha and on the third day rose again from the dead? If this is so, then double predestination can be understood only in this order, only in this disproportionate relation between the divine taking away and the divine giving, between the humiliation of God and the exaltation of man, between rejection and election. It can hardly be questioned that, according to the witness of the New Testament, this is the relation as seen in the revelation and atonement made in Jesus Christ. But can we see and recognise in this relation the same relation as exists within the divine predestination itself? Or must we really look elsewhere at this point? The teaching of tradition has accustomed us to looking elsewhere. It did not see predestination or think of it as something held within the election of Jesus Christ. And on such a view it is self-evident that the relation between the decrees of election and rejection will take on quite a different character, that it will relapse more or less automatically into a relation of proportion or equilibrium. Now apart from our consideration of the revelation and atonement made in Jesus Christ we have no reason whatever to present the relation within God's double predestination in the form in which we have actually done so. But all we need ask is whether this one reason is not also a command, a command which we must obey regardless of all other considerations. We must ask what considerations can constitute a sufficient reason to release us from the stringency of the command of this one reason. If no satisfactory answer to this question is forthcoming, then for good or evil the above understanding of double predestination must be adopted.

[175]

4. Because it is identical with the election of Jesus Christ, the eternal will of God is a divine activity in the form of the history, encounter and decision between God and man. In God's eternal predestination we have to do already with the living God. From all eternity God is within Himself the living God. The fact that God is means that from all eternity God is active in His inner relationships as Father, Son and Holy Ghost, that He wills Himself and knows of Himself, that He loves, that He makes use of His sovereign freedom, that He maintains and exercises this freedom, and in so doing maintains and demonstrates Himself. In Himself God is rest, but this fact does not exclude but includes the fact that His being is decision. God does not, therefore, become the living God when He works or decides to work *ad extra*[EN292]—in His being *ad extra*[EN293] He is, of course, the living God in a different way—but His being and activity *ad extra*[EN294] is merely an overflowing of His inward activity and being, of the inward vitality which He has in Himself. It is a proclamation of the decision in which in Himself He is who He is. The origin of this proclamation within God Himself is predestination. This is no less activity than in His own way God in Himself is activity and in a different way His whole work in the world is activity. It is the transition from the one to the other: from God's being in and for Himself to His being as Lord of creation. And what else can that be but activity and event? What right have we to think of God at this point except as the living God? The eternal will of God which is the predestination of all things is God's life in the form of the history, encounter and decision between Himself and man, a history, encounter and decision which are already willed

---

EN292 outside of himself
EN293 outside of himself
EN294 outside of himself

and known from all eternity, and to that extent, prior to all external events, are already actual before Him and for Him.

If we are correct in saying this, we must say that the name and person of Jesus Christ was in the beginning with God. The will of God was His self-giving on behalf of man in the concrete form of the union of His own Son or Word [176] with the man Jesus of Nazareth. And as such this beginning is life, the life of a history, encounter and decision. With God, in God's eternal will, a decision was made whose result is manifest to us in the existence of this man as attested by Holy Scripture. This man was the object of the divine good-pleasure. But why this man? It is here surely that we come to the place where we must respect the freedom of the divine election. God's choice was made and fulfilled in such a way that its result confronts us as an unequivocal witness to the purpose and the holiness and the righteousness of this choice. What is demanded is respect for God's free disposing, but such respect is possible only if there is knowledge, not ignorance; knowledge of the free will of God which is the subject of this choice. This is the respect for the divine good-pleasure which is demanded and authorised at this point. When we look at the content of the divine predestination, at once we can and must say that the divine life which was actively expressed in this predestination at the very beginning is the life of God's love. And the fact that God's love was there at the very beginning of all things, as the purpose and power of this overflowing of God's inward being as the living God, is not in any way limited or questioned but rather confirmed by the truth that the divine predestinating is done in freedom. What else can we say when the elect Son of Man is God's own Son, God Himself in His own self-giving? The One elected testifies unequivocally to the nature and being of the One who elects. He speaks for that One: *a posteriori*[EN295], of course; and only in virtue of the fact that that One first speaks for him, that the son of man is taken up into union with the Son of God. The Son of Man speaks, in fact, for the grace of God which stoops down to man and lifts up man to itself. He speaks not for Himself but for the mercy of God. He attests, therefore, the freedom of God's love, but obviously and far more the depth and uniqueness of that love. He testifies that what takes place between God and man according to God's predestination has its source wholly and utterly in the divine initiative. It is not that God and man begin to have dealings with each other, but that God begins to have dealings with man. Without any qualification the precedence is with God. There can be no question of any activity on man's part except upon the basis of the prior activity of God, and in the obvious form of a human response to this prior activity. God is the Lord both in His eternal decree and in all its execution. God decides, and the possibility and actuality of man's decision follow on this decision of God. But that does not mean that God's initiative is obscure even in its sovereignty. Its meaning and bearing are both clear. God does not need man, yet He wills not to be without him, to interest Himself in

---

[EN295] after the fact

[177]

him. God is the presupposition both of Himself and of man. He has caught up man into the sovereign presupposing of Himself. This is the unqualified precedence of God's work, qualified only in so far as it is not a precedence over nothing—for how could it then be precedence ?—but over man. From all eternity God posits His whole majesty (and this is the meaning and purpose of the act of eternal predestination) in this particular relationship to this particular being over against Himself. God pledges and commits Himself to be the God of man.

Such is God's activity in predestination in so far as He is its Subject. But it is not the whole of this activity. In it there begins the history, encounter and decision between Himself and man. For the fulfilment of the election involves the affirmation of the existence of elected man and its counterpart in man's election, in which God's election evokes and awakens faith, and meets and answers that faith as human decision. The electing God creates for Himself as such man over against Himself. And this means that for his part man can and actually does elect God, thus attesting and activating himself as elected man. He can and actually does accept the self-giving of God in its twofold sense, and on the basis of this self-giving he has his true life. There is, then, a simple but comprehensive autonomy of the creature which is constituted originally by the act of eternal divine election and which has in this act its ultimate reality. We cannot overemphasise God's freedom and sovereignty in this act. We cannot assert too strongly that in the election of grace it is a matter of the decision and initiative of the divine good-pleasure, that as the One who elects God has absolute precedence over the One who is elected. We can hardly go too far or say too much along these lines, more particularly when we remember that the theme of the divine election is primarily the relationship between God and man in the person of Jesus Christ. Who has the initiative in this relationship? Who has the precedence? Who decides? Who rules? God, always God. God founds and maintains the union between Himself and man. God awakens man to existence before Him and summons him to His service. God in His Son is Himself the person of man. God knows and confirms and blesses Him as His Son. God creates Him for His own Word. God vouchsafes to grant Him a part in His own suffering for man's frailty and sin and for the discord and judgment which inevitably result from them. God justifies Him, raises Him from the dead, gives Him a part in His own glory. All that man can and will do is to pray, to follow and to obey. The honour of the Son of Man adopted to union with the Son of God can and will consist only in promoting the honour of His heavenly Father. Only as the Son of Man is adopted into this union can He receive, receive His own task, receive the co-operation in suffering which is laid upon Him, receive finally the attestation from above and His own exaltation and glorification. "Not my will, but thine, be done." And this certainly means theonomy, the lordship of God at every point. Jesus Christ is Himself the established kingdom of God. And the establishment of this kingdom, the restoration of the relationship between Himself and the creature, was the will of God [178] from the beginning, the content of divine predestination. Yet we must not emphasise any less strongly that the motive for this establishment of the kingdom is not in any sense an autocratic self-seeking, but a love which directs itself outwards, a self-giving to the creature. It is still true that God wills to be Himself even in His relationship with the reality distinct from Himself (and primarily in His relationship with man). It is still true that in this will it is His own glory which ordains for itself this overflowing as the predestination of all things. The goodness of God's will and work *ad extra*EN296 depends upon the fact that in the smallest things as in the greatest God wholly and utterly wills and fulfils and reveals Himself. But He wills and fulfils and reveals Himself not only in Himself but in giving Himself, in willing and recognising the distinct reality of the creature, granting and conceding to it an individual and autonomous place side by side with Himself. Naturally the individuality and autonomy are only of such a kind as His own goodness can concede and grant. God could not be God if He willed and permitted any other individuality or autonomy side by side with His own. An independent individuality or autonomy could be only devilish in character. It could belong only to evil. Evil as such does not and cannot receive any individuality or autonomy from God. From all eternity this gift is denied to evil. But to the creature God willed from all eternity to give, to communicate, and to reveal Himself. To the creature God determined, therefore, to give an individuality and autonomy, not that these gifts should be possessed outside Him, let alone against Him, but for Him, and within His kingdom; not in rivalry with His sovereignty but for its confirming and glorifying. But the sovereignty which was to be confirmed and glorified was the sovereignty of His love, which did not will to exercise mechanical force, to move the immobile from without, to rule over puppets or slaves, but willed rather to triumph in faithful servants and friends, not in their overthrow, but in their obedience, in their own free decision for Him. The purpose and meaning of the eternal divine election of grace consists in the fact that the one who is elected from all eternity can and does elect God in return. And on these lines, too, we cannot say too much or speak too definitely, especially when we remember that at the beginning of all God's ways and works, in the eternal decree of God, there stands the relationship between Himself and the creature which became event and revelation in Jesus Christ. In this event and revelation, what is it that takes place on God's side? It is not a fatalistic overruling and disposing, but a deciding, a deciding which in a single and truly sovereign decision takes on the form and outward appearance of creation and the man Jesus. The man Jesus is not a mere puppet moved this way and that by God. He is not a mere reed used by God as the instrument of His Word. The man Jesus prays. He speaks and acts. And as He does so He makes an unheard [179] of claim, a claim which makes Him appear the victim of delusion and finally

---

EN296 outside of himself

187

brings down upon Him the charge of blasphemy. He thinks of Himself as the Messiah, the Son of God. He allows Himself to be called *Kyrios*[EN297], and, in fact, conducts Himself as such. He speaks of His suffering, not as a necessity laid upon Him from without, but as something which He Himself wills. His glorifying is for Him not a matter of vague expectancy and hope, but the goal to which He strides with the same sober certainty as to the preceding fulfilment of His humiliation. In His wholehearted obedience, in His electing of God alone, He is wholly free. He is the witness to the kingdom of God whose establishment cannot be withheld. And as such He, the man Jesus, can and should and must be the true King, hidden at first but later manifest, a King over men's hearts, but a King, too, over demons and sicknesses, over waves and storm, over death itself, always a King, even before Pilate, even and most of all on the cross. The truly astounding feature about the person of Jesus Christ is this, that here is a man who not only testified to God's rule by His Word and deeds. In the last analysis all the prophets had done that. Jesus did that, too, but in doing it He did more. He actually claimed and exercised lordship, even the lordship of God. The perfection of God's giving of Himself to man in the person of Jesus Christ consists in the fact that far from merely playing with man, far from merely moving or using him, far from merely dealing with him as an object, this self-giving sets man up as a subject, awakens him to genuine individuality and autonomy, frees him, makes him a king, so that in his rule the kingly rule of God Himself attains form and revelation. How can there be any possible rivalry here, let alone usurpation? How can there be any question of a conflict between theonomy and autonomy? How can God be jealous or man self-assertive? It was in this light, of course, that the Jewish contemporaries of Jesus immediately saw the matter, and they charged and condemned Him in the name of the offended God. They did so because in the King who stood before them they did not recognise the servant of God. They did so because in the form of the servant they did not recognise the King. They did so because they did not recognise in Jesus Christ either very God or very man. They did so because the will of God was hidden from them. For what took place in Jesus Christ—and we shall have to take this further step if we are to see and confess in God's revelation God's eternal decree—was not merely a temporal event, but the eternal will of God temporally actualised and revealed in that event. God's eternal will is man: man who is the wholehearted witness to God's kingdom and enjoys as such a kingly freedom—the Lamb of God which taketh away the sin of the world, but also the Lion of Judah which has gained the victory—man in a state of utter and most abject responsibility over against God, who even in this responsibility, even in the acknowledgment of the absolute pre-eminence of God Himself, is and become; an individual, and autonomous, and in the sphere of creation a sovereign being, and as such the image of God. God's eternal will is the act of prayer (in which confidence in self gives

[180]

[EN297] Lord

way before confidence in God). This act is the birth of a genuine human self-awareness, in which knowledge and action can and must be attempted; in which there drops away all fear of what is above or beside or below man, of what might assault or threaten him; in which man becomes heir to a legitimate and necessary and therefore an effective and triumphant claim; in which man may rule in that he is willing to serve. If Jesus Christ was that man, if from the very beginning He was elected man, then we have to say that God's eternal will has as its end the life of this man of prayer. This is the man who was in the beginning with God. This is the man who was marked and sought out by God's love. This is the man to whom and to the existence of whom the whole work of God applied as it was predetermined from all eternity.

And if we consider God's eternal decree in its entirety, we see that as it is the decree of the living God it is itself divine and living. It is, in fact, the living God Himself in the beginning of all His ways. It is so in virtue of the fact that in the bosom of God it is itself this one event—the history, encounter and decision between God and man. God elects man. On man's side this election becomes actual in man's own electing of God, by which he is made free to do the will of God, and achieves and possesses individuality and autonomy before God. Everywhere we see the divine sovereignty and the divine initiative. This decree is wholly and utterly an election of grace. And yet the decision of the sovereign God, His election of grace (in the understanding of which we cannot be allowed to reverse or even to compare the two partners), has as its sole content the fact that God elects man in order that man may be awakened and summoned to elect God, and to pray that he may give himself to Him, and that in this act of electing and prayer he may exist in freedom before God: the reality *in nuce*[EN298] which is distinct from God and yet united with Him in joy and peace; man who is the meaning and purpose of the whole creation; man who in his own sphere can and should have autonomy and a kingdom.

In this context we must stress the fact that the divine predestination as thus understood is a living act. We can only understand and describe it as an act because in itself it is solely and entirely an act: the theonomy of God which wills and decrees as such the autonomy of man; the electing of God and election of man which take on historical form as a human electing in which man can and should elect and affirm and activate himself. In this chain it is impossible to pick out any one link and to consider it in and for itself. But it is also impossible to make of it a single system and to consider it as such. We can view it as a whole only as we view the living person of Jesus Christ. We can understand it as a whole only if we understand it as an event which in its entirety is as such the [181] will of God and encloses as such man and the will and decision of man and the autonomous existence of man. This divine will in its entirety was in the beginning with God. This divine act of will is predestination.

EN298 in a nutshell

It is now possible and necessary for us to make the controversial assertion that predestination is the divine act of will itself and not an abstraction from or fixed and static result of it. It is not the case, then, that while the predetermined process of the world and life of man are living history, encounter and decision, predestination itself stands over against them as something unchanged and unchangeable. It is not the case that in the form of predestination a kind of death has become the divine law of creaturely life.

We are confronted at this point by a further limitation of the traditional teaching. On the basis of a doctrine of God which was pagan rather than Christian, it thought of predestination as an isolated and given enactment which God had decreed from all eternity and which to some extent pledged and committed even God Himself in time. Because of His immutability, even God could not alter this enactment once it had been determined. It is obvious that in the older Protestantism the reigning concept of the *decretum praedestinationis*[EN299] could be and actually was misunderstood, with very serious consequences. The very concept "decree" reminds us inevitably of a military or political ordinance, a law, a statute, a rule which lays down in black and white and preserves and expresses in definitive form the will of a regnant power. Yet the decree of a human ruler has always the characteristic that notwithstanding respect to the letter, in its exposition and application regard is always and necessarily had, and can actually be had, to the living will of the lawgiver. And this decree has a further characteristic that it can always be corrected or suspended or replaced by another decree, and that sooner or later it will actually be corrected or suspended or replaced in this way. A human decree need not be a dead letter which kills. It can be a living organ of life. When we speak of a divine decree, however, it can easily happen that we conceive of it as our duty to deny to it the two characteristics in virtue of which a human decree can within certain limits be a living organ. The divinity of the decree is then sought in the fact that the will of God has in some measure taken on hard and fast form in that decree, so that there is no possibility of an appeal from the wording of the decree to the will of God, and all thought of an alteration or suspension of the decree is excluded. This could mean, however, that there was only one occasion when God willed, in the pre-temporal eternity when the decree was conceived and established. It was then that God elected. It was then that in the matter of salvation and perdition, of life and death, He decided either to the right or to the left according to His own good-pleasure. The living quality of this action is something *perfectum*[EN300], belonging to the eternal past. It is not an action, an electing and deciding, which is still continued in time. God's living action in the present consists only in the execution of this decree, the fulfilment of an election and decision already made. For us, then, who exist in time, the living God is perceptible and meaningful and active only in the execution and fulfilment of His predestination, not in predestination itself. What we may see in predestination itself and as such is in some degree the monument of the living God, of the God who is meaningful and active in practice. In it God is no longer for us the living God. He surrendered this quality by translating it into act. In His work in time He is the living God for us only to the extent that He is no longer the living God in that pre-temporal eternity. His speech and activity in the temporal present are only an echo of the note which was struck in [182] His eternal decree. That note cannot ring out independently in time. It can only be repeated. As the eternally electing God, God was. He is and will be only in so far as the decree has been made by which He precedes all that is and will be, only in so far as all that is and will be is determined by that decree. God did predestinate. In time He predestinates no

---

EN299 decree of predestination
EN300 completed

longer. In time there is only the predestination of all being and history by an act of pre-destinating which is past. There is no new or additional predestinating. On this view, then, it is the case that the law of creaturely life is a death which is absolutised in the form of a decision reached and an election made by God from all eternity. That which was in the beginning with God is an authoritative and all-powerful letter. The eternal God did all that was needed when He promulgated this letter and gave it authority and power over the whole realm of creaturely life in time. All that now lives derives its life from God only in the sense that it derives it from the authority and power of this letter. After that first and all-embracing act of life, God Himself, the living God, retired behind this letter, taking His rest and satisfy-ing Himself again with His own inner life. He delivered up creaturely life to the rule of this letter. As far as concerned the creature He committed Himself by this letter. Such is the picture which might result, and has in fact resulted, from an application of the concept *decretum*[EN301] to the divine predestination.

There can be no doubt that understood in this way the concept could and did help for-ward the cause of Deism. Deism separated the Creator of the world from the world-process. The Godhead was thought of as quite inactive in relation to this predetermined process. World development took place according to its own divinely established law. Now if God's will and decree in the beginning are regarded as an isolated and self-contained predestin-ation, preceding the life of the creature but no longer present in it, then in the last resort it is hardly possible to maintain seriously that God is the Lord of all that evolves from that first decree. If predestination as such is no longer actual, then in fact God Himself is no longer actual. There is no point in asking us to believe in God at our stage in that development. We may still think of God as the principle of the mysterious authority and power which controls the stream of events in which we actually find ourselves. We may still recognise that at the beginning of that stream the letter must have been established under whose law the world and our own life continues. But we shall prefer to look within that development for other relative but at any rate actual quantities in which we may put the faith which we have no cause to put in that letter and its execution and Him who once perhaps conceived and elected it. Certainly the object of that faith cannot be a God who was once the electing and predestinating God, but is so no longer. Obviously, we can have faith only in a God who is present in His decision and election, who is actually the electing and deciding God. If He is not that, and we cannot have faith in Him, it is only a short step to the denial of the existence of God. Or, to put it better, if we do not have faith in God, if we do not know Him as actually the electing and deciding God, His existence is, in fact, already denied.

In face of this very real danger of misunderstanding it is not necessary, nor would it be wise, to erase or abandon altogether the concept *decretum*[EN302]. The concept describes some-thing which cannot be denied but must seriously be recognised and taken into account. It tells us, in fact, of God's constancy, the faithfulness, the reliability, the absoluteness, the definitiveness of the free love of God in which He elected and predestinated at the begin-ning of all things with Himself. In this election and predestination God at all events remains unchanged and unchangeably the same. And we cannot think of His will and predestinating without forming for ourselves the concept of an authoritative and all-powerful decree which is once and for all, far above time and all that is in time; the concept of an ordinance. That notion of an eternal letter, posited once and for all and simply awaiting fulfilment in crea-turely life, is one which we cannot dismiss hurriedly and lightly. There can be no doubt that God *has* taken upon Himself a committal, an obligation, and that in perfect freedom (in the freedom of His love) He has decided to abide by it. If we would think in non-legal terms in

[183]

EN301 'decree'
EN302 'decree'

relation to this matter, we must see to it that in our fear of the concept *decretum*[EN303] we do not fall into the error of the *decretum absolutum*[EN304] which the older Protestant theology obviously thought that it could and should balance against a too pronounced legalism in the understanding of *decretum*[EN305]. We must still allow that in predestination we have to confess the divine law, and not an arbitrary divine power over-ruling the life of the creature. It is for this reason that we have always spoken of God's eternal will as His decree, and must continue to do so.

We must remember however—and in so doing we part company with the older teaching—that God's decree is a living decree, a decree that is infinitely more living than any decree of man. It is the letter of God in the beginning in virtue of the fact that this letter is determined and posited with all the constancy, the faithfulness and the dependability of God Himself, enjoying an authority and power greater than that of the letter of any possible human law. But it is also spirit and life in a way impossible even for the very best of the written laws of man as best expounded or applied. The fact that from all eternity God has predestinated, elected and decided has, of course, all the weightiness of the eternal *perfectum*[EN306]. It is something isolated and complete. It is the foreordination which precedes all creaturely life. It stands as hard as steel or granite before and above all things and all events. But in so doing, it has and is the life of God. It has really been predetermined from all eternity. It has the character not only of an unparalleled "perfect" but also of an unparalleled "present" and "future." And it remains because it is eternally before time. It is not left behind by time, but as that which is above time (for there is only one eternity with God) it accompanies time, and as that which is beyond time it outlasts it. It not only was but is and will be. It happened: never by any subversion can we weaken the fact that it happened, and happened once and for all. But it not only happened; it does happen and will happen. For it is the principle and essence of all happening everywhere. How, then, can it be anything else but a happening? How can it ever not happen? How can it have a part in one perfection of happening and not another? As God's foreordination, how can it happen only once and not continue to happen, giving place instead to that other happening, its execution and fulfilment, and itself becoming dead and obsolete, a happening which belongs only to the past? What meaning can there be in the word "then" when we are speaking of God's eternity? It is true, of course, that in that eternity there can be an "earlier" as there can be a "now" and a "later," for eternity is certainly not the negation but the boundary of time as such. But for this very reason "then" cannot mean only "earlier." When we speak of God's eternity we must recognise and accept what is "earlier" as something also present and future. God's predestination is a completed work of God, but for this very reason it is not an exhausted work, a work which is behind us. On the contrary, it is a work which still takes place in all its fulness to-day. Before time and above time and at every moment of time God is the predestinating God, positing this beginning of all things with Himself, willing and ordaining, electing and deciding, pledging and committing (us and first of all Himself), establishing the letter of the law which rules over all creaturely life. It is not the case, then, that God did will but that now He no longer wills, or wills only the effects of His willing. To speak in causal terms, God does will the effects, but in so doing He does not cease to will the cause. And He does not cease to be the living God in the cause. God is never an echo. He is and continues to be and always will be an independent note or sound. The predestination of God is unchanged and unchangeably God's activity.

[EN303] 'decree'
[EN304] absolute decree
[EN305] 'decree'
[EN306] perfect

2. The Eternal Will of God in the Election of Jesus Christ

The point that we have to make against the older doctrine is this, that while in other respects it laid too great stress upon God's freedom, in this context it came very near to thinking of this freedom in such a way that in predestination God became His own prisoner.

As against this tendency we must remember that *praedestinatio*[EN307], like *creatio*[EN308] and *reconciliatio*[EN309], like *vocatio, iustificatio, sanctificatio*[EN310] and *glorificatio*[EN311], describes a divine activity, and that there is no reason whatever why we should suddenly substitute for this concept a concept of isolated and static being. What we have to see and understand here is that it is unchanged and unchangeably God's activity, and that as such it is in the beginning with God. When we speak of the divine predestination we speak of an eternal happening. And we do not say this merely on the basis of abstract recollection. We say it because an analysis of the reality designated by the concept predestination has shown us that it can, in fact, refer only to a happening. We say it because when we speak of the electing of God and election of man to which the concept refers, when we speak of the intimate connexion between theonomy and autonomy, between divine sovereignty and human faith, we are not dealing with a systematic relationship but with one which can be the object and content only of a law which is itself spirit and life, concrete history. The reality of predestination is not merely history's *schema* and programme, but history itself as once and for all determined in God's own will and decree. Only as concrete decree, only as an act of divine life in the Spirit, is it the law which precedes all creaturely life. In virtue of its character and content this decree can never be rigid and fixed. It can never belong only to the past. Because it is God's decree it must, of course, be constant, authoritative and powerful. But because it has pleased God to let it be a concrete decree, it never ceases to be event.

Thus the eternal history, encounter and decision between God and man, the content of the Gospel in which we have to acknowledge the concrete content of predestination, cannot be thought of as breaking off or concluding with an effect which we then have to describe as the presupposition of all other temporal histories, encounters and decisions within the sphere of creaturely reality. How can that history, encounter and decision be eternal if it ceases as such with the beginning of time, if it can to some extent be replaced or supplanted by temporal events? Since it is itself history, encounter and decision, since it is an act of divine life in the spirit, since it is the unbroken and lasting predetermining and decreeing of Him who as Lord of all things has both the authority and the power for such activity, it is the presupposition of all the movement of creaturely life. This presupposition is not merely static but moving. It has authority, and it also authorises. It is powerful, and it exercises

---

[EN307] predestination
[EN308] creation
[EN309] reconciliation
[EN310] calling, justification, sanctification
[EN311] glorification

power. It happened, and it also happens. Who then, and what then, is unchanged and unchangeable? God Himself in His triune being as free love. And not only God, but God's decree, God's electing of man according to His own good-pleasure, an electing which resulted in the election of man, and man's electing of God and finding of his good pleasure in God. All these are as unchanged and unchangeable as God Himself and God's eternal will. All these are the eternal predestination of temporal events. But what is truly unchangeable cannot simply be immovable. What is truly unchanged cannot be unmoved. It is that which moves everything and as such it is moved within itself. What is unchanged and unchangeable is that the beginning of all things with God is itself history, encounter and decision. This is predestination. In saying this we do not launch predestination upon the general stream of world-events in time. Nor do we launch it upon the particular stream of the saving events in which world-events as a whole find their meaning and end. This history, encounter and decision between God and man was in the beginning with God, and is identical neither with the one nor the other. It is, rather, the secret which is hidden in world-history as such and revealed in the history of salvation as such. The secret of all life is the existence of the living God as the One who has created life and who sustains and governs it. The secret of everything that takes place in this world is the decision of God which eternally precedes it. All other events culminate in the history of salvation and take place necessarily for the sake of it. In this history God's decision which precedes everything, and therefore the divine electing of man and man's election by God, is made visible and becomes operative in time in the form of the Word of God proclaimed and received, in the form of the people Israel and the Church, in the form of the calling, justification, sanctification and glorification of man, in the form of man's faith and hope and love. For this reason we must see in all these things quite literally the divine predestination, the eternal decision of God's free love. These things are not in any sense a law unto themselves. There is no separation of the temporal from the eternal. Man's work and experience, what he wins and possesses, cannot be asserted over against the divine disposing. There can be no praise of man, no boasting or arbitrary pretension on man's part, but only discipleship, thankfulness and adoration. But for the same reason there is also in this relationship a royal self-awareness on the part of the Elect. Because the eternal predestination is made manifest to us in that history of salvation, we accept it as the secret of everything else that takes place in the world. We have, if not to understand, at any rate to consider and weigh up all other events, both in general and in detail, as we are instructed by what we know of that history. In principle, then, predestination is not concealed from us. It would be so if it consisted in that letter set up in an inaccessibly distant past eternity. But it is an act of divine life in the spirit, an act which affects us, an act which occurs in the very midst of time no less than in that far distant pre-temporal eternity. It is the present secret, and in the history of salvation the revealed secret, of the whole history, encounter and decision between God [186] and man. It takes place in time. It is revealed, and yet it still remains a secret, and is recognisable and recognised as such. It takes place in the proclamation of God's Word. It takes place in the foundation and existence and guidance of Israel and the Church. It takes place in the calling, justification, sanctification and glorification of man. It takes place in our awakening to faith and hope and love. What else are these things but the movement of the eternally electing God, the God who exercises His free love in the beginning? But predestination also takes place even where we do not recognise it directly, even where we do not understand it, even where, knowing of it (and having directly recognised and understood it in the history of salvation), we can only confess it as a hidden reality in world-events as a whole. In principle, it is never concealed. But the perception of it depends upon our direct or indirect interest in its occurrence, i.e., whether we are amongst those to whom it applies. There is no knowledge of predestination except in the movement from the electing God to elected man, and back again from elected man to the electing God. There cannot be, for predestination is this movement. This movement is, in fact, God's eternal decree. God willed this movement, willed it from all eternity, and continues to will it. In face of this movement, in face of predestination, we cannot be spectators. If we stood without and not within, we should not be able to see anything at all in this matter. Each glimpse of predestination that we get, even the very slightest, we can understand only as a challenge and invitation to understand and to conduct ourselves more radically and more seriously as those who are already caught up in this movement. In proportion as we do this, we are then challenged and invited to see and to understand predestination with greater clarity and fulness, both directly and also indirectly.

The fundamental significance of the character of predestination as act ought to be clear without further discussion. If it is unchanged and unchangeably the history, encounter and decision between God and man, there is in time an electing by God and an election of man, as there is also a rejecting by God and a rejection of man, but not in the sense that God Himself is bound and imprisoned by it, not as though God's decree, the first step which He took, committed Him to take a corresponding second step, and the second a third. If it is true that the predestinating God not only is free but remains free, that He does not cease to make use of His freedom but continues to decide, then in the course of God's eternal deciding we have constantly to reckon with new decisions in time. As the Bible itself presents the matter, there is no election which cannot be followed by rejection, no rejection which cannot be followed by election. God continues always the Lord of all His works and ways. He is consistent with Himself. He is also consistent with the prearranged order of election and rejection. But He is always the living God. And since His life is the [187] dynamic of that order, developments and alterations in it are always possible and do in fact take place. Neither in the history of Israel and the Church nor in the life of the individual can we dismiss these as mere appearance, a temporary obscuring of the inevitable outcome of things. On the contrary, it is in the developments and alterations as such, in their freshness, in their otherness, even in their conflicting nature as they succeed one another, that we must seek the inevitability of the divine predestination, the rule of the living God who is free to love where He was wroth and to be wroth where He loved, to bring death to the living and life to the dead, to repent Himself and to repent of His repenting. This is how predestination is described in the locus *classicus*, Rom. 9–11—a description which we cannot possibly reconcile with the understanding of predestination as a rigid and static law, but only with the understanding of it as a definition of God's eternal action in time.

But this activist understanding of predestination depends wholly and utterly upon the identifying of it with the election of Jesus Christ. Unless we start there, it is merely a case of one assertion against the other: the assertion of the divinity of static being as the beginning of all things against that of an activated history; a static and in the last analysis perhaps a quietistic view of life against a dynamic and activist. And the question arises: Which of these is right? How can we decide which of them is truly of God? Ultimately there is only one reason that we can give for deciding in favour of an activist understanding, and that is that the predestination which we know in the person and work of Jesus Christ is undoubtedly event, the history, encounter and decision between God and man. God's electing and man's election; God's self-humiliation and man's exaltation by God; the self-giving as it is effected in the Son of God and the Son of Man Jesus Christ, and as it is made manifest in Him as the eternal divine decree; the history of salvation in which we can see and understand predestination itself: all these are an act, or they are not what they are. They are an act, a definite act, concrete, completed. And this act does not contradict the being of God because in virtue of its definiteness it is letter as well as spirit, enjoying the authority and force of a law. At this point we must be very careful not to press the dynamic case against the static, or the activist case against the quietist. In different ways as much can be said against the former view as against the latter. In so far as we see the mystery of the divine decision in the concrete person of Jesus Christ we are against the activist view. And in so far as we think of Jesus Christ as the decision of the eternally living God we are opposed to the static. In the present context we are necessarily opposed to the latter. We could think of a *decretum absolutum*[EN312] as a lifeless and timeless rule for temporal life. But we can think of Jesus Christ only as the living and eternal Lord of temporal life. The Father loves the Son and the Son is obedient to the Father. In this love and obedience God gives Himself to man. He takes upon Himself man's lowliness in order that man may be exalted. When this is done, man attains to freedom, electing the God who has already elected him. But all this is history. It cannot be interpreted as a static cause producing certain effects. As

[188]

[EN312] absolute decree

the content of eternity before time was, it cannot remain beyond time. *Per se* it is in time as well as before time. And in time it can only be history. Who and what Jesus Christ is, is something which can only be told, not a system which can be considered and described. If, then, we accept the presupposition that predestination is identical with the election of Jesus Christ, the assertion of its actuality cannot be disputed. And this being the case, we cannot give to the assertion the same meaning as it has in that conflict between two opposing outlooks. It attacks the one outlook without commending the other. It is opposed to both. If it is to be theologically correct, it can be understood only in the light of this presupposed identity.

At the *Congrès international de théologie calviniste* held at Geneva in 1936, Peter Barth advoc-ated the activist understanding in his paper "The Biblical Basis of Calvin's Doctrine of Pre-destination" ("Die biblische Grundlage der Praedestinationslehre bei Calvin"). He did so with the express intention of correcting Calvin's interpretation. He claimed that God's free-dom in His judgment and mercy ought to be thought of as "God Himself in the activity of His kingly work: God, whose hands are not bound, creating light and darkness, opening and closing, binding and loosing, according to His own righteous good-pleasure .... Does not Holy Scripture everywhere bring us before the face of the God who is free at every moment to make His decision, who marches on from one decision to another, the unchangeable Lord of life and death, in whose power it is both to elect and to reject, both to raise up and to cast down? ... The concept of God's repenting cannot be thought away from the biblical presentation of God's thinking and action. According to the testimony of Scripture, God always reserves to Himself the freedom to put forth His own superior power in unforeseen and astonishing developments. 'The Lord killeth, and maketh alive: he bringeth down to the grave, and bringeth up' (1 Sam. 2⁶). At the same time Scripture shows us God the Lord—who can do what He wills—in a mysteriously living relation to us men. It speaks of God's earnest and urgent asking after us, of His seeking and knocking, of His patient waiting for our return. But this means that man is indeed put in the place of decision. The seriousness of our position cannot be altered by any foreordination of the outcome. 'Work out your own salvation with fear and trembling' retains its full validity, just because the willing and working is God's doing. It is obviously fatal when the concept *causa* (cause) is introduced into descriptions of the relationship between the divine will and the human. In Holy Scripture the supremacy of God's grace meeting us is shown always as God's act towards us in the Spirit. We can never divest this act of its existential character, or reduce it to a relationship of causality." We should translate Ex. 3¹⁴: "I will be that I will be"; God unlimited and unsearch-able in the freedom of His judgment and the freedom of His grace (*Transactions*, published under the title *De l'élection éternelle de Dieu*, Geneva, 1936, 21 f.; cf. 70 f.).

In Geneva these ideas met partly with obvious evasion and partly with open opposition. It was evident from the first that the wholehearted Calvinists who formed the bulk of the Con-gress would not accept the proposed correction of Calvin. After a preliminary and rather futile protest, one of the first speakers declared that he was "displeased" at the closing sec-tion of the paper. *Mais voilà; in cauda venenum*[EN313] (G. Oorthuys, 58). In the course of the debate it always came back to the same fundamental issue. What is to be made of the concept of God's repenting, which a biblical theology such as the Calvinist claims to be cannot possi-bly evade? Amongst other things, other very competent representatives of the ruling trend at that Congress said the following. First, we must distinguish in Calvin the standpoint of the

[189]

[EN313] There it is: the sting in the tail

exegete from that of the dogmatician, for in the two capacities Calvin had to tackle two very different problems. As an exegete (as in the exposition of Ezek. 18²³: "Have I any pleasure at all that the wicked should die?") Calvin could oppose a mechanistic exposition of the divine will and frankly confess that God calls everyone without exception to repentance and that He allows definite threats of punishment to be followed by equally definite promises of grace. As a dogmatician, however, out of the same spirit of loyalty to Scripture and in the fight against error he could bring forward his asseveration of God's hidden decree to convert only the elect (R. Grob, 68). Or again, in His eternity God is just as immutable (*immuable*) as in time He is capable of repentance, change and alternation between wrath and forgiveness. How can we reconcile these two facts? We cannot reconcile them, but it is *l'originalité de l'orthodoxie d'articuler ces confessions de foi avec un et tamen*^EN314, and yet, *und doch, et pourtant* .... *Oui Dieu se repent et puis oui il ne se repent pas; oui son décret est éternel, oui Dieu change dans le temps. Et nous ne savons pas*^EN315 (A. Lecerf, 66 f.). Statements like this can be Described only as an evasion of the problem. In this matter it is of no value simply to separate the spheres of dogmatics and exegesis, or eternity and time, and then to assert comfortably that there is an insoluble tension between the contradictory statements relating to these spheres. If God's eternal decree is as such immutable, then it is not an idly academic question which can be dismissed with a wave of the hand but a serious question of faith why "a mechanistic exposition of the divine will" should not prevail first and last. To put it in another way, if the Scriptures make statements about the self-activated will of God which are valid only in the temporal sphere, in what sense are we to take these statements seriously when we set them against the eternal reality of God? Have they any genuine seriousness with God, or have they not? And how can they have if they have no seriousness in eternity? We may reverse the question: On what authority, and from what loyalty to Scripture, may the dogmatician (even in the act of necessary confession against error) arrive at the point where he can use a quite different doctrine of God's eternal predestination to bracket and relativise and call in question his own exegetical findings as they relate to the manner of God's dealings with man in time? Who has called us to seek God's eternal predestination anywhere but in God's temporal dealings as such, or to understand it except as it is revealed and active in these dealings? Certainly the Bible does not invite us to do this. To create such contradictions artificially, and then to dismiss them as purely intellectual, and finally to leave them unexplained with a *nous ne savons pas*^EN316—that is not theology. At any rate it is hard to see what theological justification there is for making of the matter a riddle of this kind and then demanding that we should let it remain unsolved.

Other speakers in the discussion objected against the author that his asserting of an activist predestination would mean a return to the doctrine of the divine *potentia absoluta*^EN317, of a *Deus legibus solutus*^EN318, as held and taught in the later Middle Ages (M. J. Homines, 63). *On assiste à une sorte de jeu: on est soulevé par la miséricorde, on est précipité en bas par le jugement et l'on finit par ne pas très bien savoir où l'on en est*^EN319 (J. Rilliet, 64). The author's only answer was to repeat his statement: We must be taught by Scripture that God has entered into a mysteriously living relation to us men. But in this ambiguous expression there lurks a dilemma which to some extent spoils the otherwise excellent paper of Peter Barth, or, at any

[190]

---

^EN314 the originality of orthodoxy to articulate these confessions of faith as one
^EN315 Yes, God changes his mind, and yes, God does not change his mind. Yes, God's decree is eternal; yes, God changes in time. And we do not know.
^EN316 we do not know
^EN317 absolute power
^EN318 God free of laws
^EN319 One is playing a kind of game: one goes up the ladder of mercy, and falls down the snake of judgment. In the end, one does not very well know where one is in it.

rate, his intrinsically correct concluding thesis. This mysteriously living relation, including all that it is and means on man's part—in the free act of human faith—is the fulfilment of divine predestination, and it has been grounded and determined and ordained by God Himself. But can we really accept this as an end of the matter? There can be no doubt that that is what the author intended to maintain, and he did maintain it in forcible terms. But the more forcibly we maintain it, the more effectively there may be used against this thesis of an activist predestination the consideration advanced by its opponents, that for the fixed enactment to which man was subject according to the older doctrine this view now substitutes a mere game which God plays with man, a game which is completely bewildering in its hiddenness and unexpectedness. And in this game of judgment and mercy, what chance is there, if any, of a final knowledge of how one stands with God? To assert a mysteriously living relationship does not give us any answer to the difficulty if we really hold to the divine sovereignty in this relationship. We can thus understand rather better the objection of J. Rilliet (p. 64). As Rilliet saw it, the beauty and power of the Calvinistic doctrine of predestination consist in the idea of a pledged and static freedom of God in which He dominates the individual from all eternity in order *toujours et malgré lui*[EN320] to save him in time. Rilliet felt that the doctrine would be stripped of these qualities if the thesis of an activist predestination were accepted. The author does not seem to have felt the force of the argument. In his paper, and more particularly in the conclusion, he could find only one way to meet it: that of transferring the mysteriousness and life of the relationship into the "existentiality" of the decision in or before which man is placed by God's decision. God does not treat us like puppets, but like living men, created as such by God Himself. He puts salvation and perdition before us "in the form of a question." The question of God is a matter of life and death. In our own life a decision must be made. The inner movement of divine predestination, the possibility and reality of God's repenting and the living character of the relationship, correspond to this decision. But this brings us to the other side of that dilemma which engulfs those who adopt the activist thesis. If predestination is not a divine game which God plays with man, if it is not the capricious vacillation of a *potentia absoluta*[EN321], the only other possibility is that it is an ordination of God which is wholly conditional upon God's insight into the decision for or against Him made in the life of man. In this case, however, it is not an amendment of Calvin but of the Lutheran doctrine of *fides praevisa*[EN322], or even of the (in its own way) very mysterious teaching of Thomas about the co-operation of God and man in the communicating and receiving of grace. Without doubt the predestinating God is the living God, but only in so far as He has to do with the living man which He has created. Predestination is still decision, but the specific nature of the actual decision made is determined by the fact that it is related to the existential decision of man. It is quite clear that P. Barth never intended to say that and could not have meant it. But it is also understandable that he could not convince the Congress of the correctness of his thesis by an attempt at explanation which tended in this direction. On the contrary, the attempt caused real anger (*Transactions*, 19, 28 f.), and for two hours they screamed and shouted that the immutable double decree is God's eternal will and that is an end of the matter.

The whole proceedings are extraordinarily instructive because they show that the thesis of an activist predestination is purely formal, and that as such it stands just as much in the air, and under the same twofold threat of determinism and synergism, as does the traditional counter-thesis. Peter Barth thought it sufficient to substitute for the rigid divine decree which is fixed and static from all eternity the idea of the Lord who not only is free but

---

[EN320] always, and despite him
[EN321] absolute power
[EN322] foreseen faith

[191]   remains free and whose decrees are living and progressive. What is substituted is correct, but the correction of Calvin demands something more. The statement: *Idem est Deum praedestinare et praedestinasse et praedestinaturum esse*[EN323] is a magnificent one, but it derives from Duns Scotus (quoted from Loof's *Dogmengeschichte.* 4th edn. 1906, 595). In opposition to the twofold subtlety of Scotus it must be shown that the Lord neither decrees arbitrarily nor allows Himself to be conditioned by His counterpart in that decree. And to do this it is not enough to refer generally to God and man and to the mysteriousness and life of the relationship between them. For if we confine ourselves to generalities, we cannot escape the clutches of that dilemma.

In the discussion at the Congress there was raised one voice (apart from the later contribution of P. Maury, who, unfortunately, did not take part in the discussion) in favour of an adoption of the thesis. The voice was that of Pastor R. Abramowski of Riga. But this delegate also wanted attention to be directed to the only possible and solid basis for such a thesis, a basis which seemed to have been overlooked not only by the genuine Calvinists but also by the speaker. He did not gain any support, but the point which he tried to make was this. Predestination as election and rejection is "a *modus*[EN324] corresponding to God's redemptive work," and it is as such that it must be understood and proclaimed. In the Old Testament it stands in a strict relationship to the people Israel, and in the New Testament it stands in an equally strict relationship to Jesus Christ. It is impossible, then, to separate the doctrine of predestination from Christology and soteriology. Faith in the God of judgment and redemption has no direct connexion with the divine majesty, and must not be confused with an enthusiasm for God and for the glory of God. Together with our sins it must be "broken" by the cross of Christ. Now it is true that objections may be raised against this formulation. Predestination is not one *modus*[EN325] but the *modus*[EN326] of the divine work of redemption. It is not the *modus*[EN327] merely of this work, but of all God's work *ad extra*[EN328]. It not only corresponds to this work, but precedes it. Yet the direction indicated here is the direction in which we have to look. If it is presupposed that predestination is identical with the election of Jesus Christ the activist thesis is put on a basis against which no objection can be brought and is made secure from misunderstanding both on the one side and the other. Once we see this point it is settled that predestination does not antedate time, and all that is in it, and especially man and men in time, in the form of a letter, which, limited in this way, can mean only a dead letter. Predestination precedes time as a living act in the Spirit, similar to the cloud which went before Israel in the wilderness. It is settled, then, that predestination did indeed happen in the bosom of God before all time, but that for this very reason it happens and happens again before every moment of time. For the election of Jesus Christ is unchanged and unchangeably history. As such it is God's eternal will before all time, and also the eternal will of the living God in time. The fact that Calvin and the classical exponents of the doctrine failed to progress beyond a static understanding of God's eternal will was not due to their lack of a sufficiently "living" notion of God's working—in the last analysis Calvin could never be accused of that. We cannot help them, then, simply by placing a stronger emphasis upon the biblical doctrine of God's repenting and providing a new and better translation of Ex. 3[14]. Their failure was due rather to their non-adherence to the rule that the will of God as such, and therefore predestination, must be sought and found only in the work of God, i.e., in the core and purpose of that work, the name and person of Jesus Christ. Only by an

---

[EN323] That God predestines, and has predestined, and will predestine are one and the same.
[EN324] means
[EN325] means
[EN326] means
[EN327] means
[EN328] outside of himself

adherence to this rule can we really know God's eternal will as the will of the living God. Only in this way can we expose the falsity of the view which would assert the fixity of that will and thus reduce it to a dead letter. The correction of the older doctrine in this matter must definitely consist in an attempt to adhere to a rule which the Reformers themselves did not keep—the rule that the eternal God is to be known only in Jesus Christ and not elsewhere. If [192] this is first done, the belief in an activist predestination is then self-evident.

And if this is first done, it is possible to avoid the dilemma which entangled the discussion at the 1936 Congress.

If predestination is identical with the election of Jesus Christ, there can be no question of any confusion between God's living predestinating, deciding and electing, and the vacillation of a *potentia absoluta*EN329 or a game capriciously played by the Deity with its creatures. That there is no such confusion was rightly maintained by P. Barth at Geneva, but he could only maintain it and not prove it (except by an imperceptible surrender of the sovereignty of the divine decision over against man). If God's eternal will is not found in the election of Jesus Christ, where is it to be found except in the unsearchable sovereign act of the *decretum absolutum?*EN330 But if we accept God's sovereignty in this act, and yet think of this act as living and progressive, not something which happened once and for all but something which continues to happen, then unless we identify it with the election of Jesus Christ it is hard to see how this relationship of God to His creature can possibly be thought of except as the relationship of a player to his plaything, a relationship which takes on this or that form according to the whim of the moment. In these circumstances we can understand the inclination of the opposing faction to dispute a predestination in terms of act. We can understand their longing for the idea of a decree fixed before all time. In a decree of this kind the absoluteness of the act of freedom in which it arose does at least find rest. Even if in detail its content is always unknown, we do at least know that we have something definite to hold to. For it is quite impossible to see how a distinction can be made between predestination in terms of act and the *potentia absoluta*EN331 of the later Middle Ages. Only when we recognise that predestination is identical with the election of Jesus Christ does there arise at once a picture of God's will as it determined and ordered and to that extent limited itself even in its sovereignty. The history of this process is not any kind of history, but it has a definite content and it moves towards an appointed end. Its place cannot be taken by any other history moving perhaps towards some quite different end. In this history God's will is unequivocal. In Himself, God is free and He remains free. But in His freedom He decides in man's favour for the establishment and preservation of the covenant between Himself and man. He denies and hates the sin of fallen man with whom the covenant is to be made and maintained. But He wills an unequivocal affirmation and love of man himself, and it is in this affirmation and love that the covenant is willed and concluded. He decrees the rejection of the evil-doer, but in predestinating Himself to union with the Son of Man in His Son He decrees that this rejection should be lifted from man and laid upon Himself. In spite of man's unworthiness in himself, He wills and affirms and loves man, yet in so doing He does not will the continuance of man in his unworthiness. He wills rather that man should be exalted, and that (by the power of His grace) he should have a share in His own worthiness. He does not will the death of the sinner, but rather that he should be converted and live. The realisation of this foreordination of man is, of course, willed in such a way as to make man himself fulfil all the history which is the content of the divine will for him. From his supposed innocence he must be plunged into the depths of sin and misery, and from these depths he must be lifted up

---

EN329 absolute power
EN330 absolute decree
EN331 absolute power

again to the heights of real innocence, righteousness and blessedness. But God treads the way with him. God knows the goal and will not swerve from it. For the man who will accompany God on this road there can be no uncertainty with regard to the outcome. It is God who elects man. Man's electing of God can come only second. But man's electing does follow necessarily on the divine electing. In this history, then, there is nothing wholly dark or obscure. Even the mystery that it takes place at all, that God's will is in fact an affirmation and love of man, even this incomprehensible act of the divine freedom, is not as such dark but luminous; it is not obscure but clarity itself. This history is the sum and substance of all order, and for this reason it cannot be confused with the play of any actuality in itself and as such. It is not actuality in itself and as such, but one specific act. But if we say that this history does not end, if we say that God's eternal will is not left behind by time but precedes every moment of time, if we say that the God whose will is this history is not the prisoner either of Himself or of the historical process once and for all ordained by Him, it is utter folly to understand it to mean that man cannot know how he stands with God or what he may expect from Him, as though in and with the historical process God were merely playing a game with man. We arrive at its deep meaning from the fact that while the Bible does compare God's over-ruling will in creation with the will of a potter towards his work, while it does compare it, then, with the supreme will of a workman who plans, it does not compare it with the capricious will of a child at play, although the latter comparison would—apparently, but only apparently—be better calculated to bring out the sovereignty of the divine good-pleasure. The sovereignty of God bears no relation whatever to the sovereignty of whim or chance or caprice. On the contrary, we learn from the revelation of this sovereignty that the power of whim and chance and caprice is not a sovereign power. It belongs to the sphere of evil, and evil, as that which is denied and repudiated by God, has only the power of impotence. The sovereignty of God and of God's good-pleasure consists in the fact that it is a sovereignty which orders history, the content of God's eternal will. We must think of that eternal and self-ordered will as the will of the living God, a progressive and constantly renewed act of the Spirit. But in so doing we must also think of it as law, as a letter which can neither be reinterpreted nor replaced. We cannot, then, think of ourselves as tossed hither and thither by an incalculable fluctuation of divine decisions. If we know this eternal and living will, we know a rule which is completely trustworthy, and no dark suspicions can assail us. In face of this will we can and should know how it stands with us. Beyond this will we cannot and need not go.

But if predestination is identified with the election of Jesus Christ, it follows, secondly, that there can be no question of a limiting and conditioning of the freedom of God in which this decision is made by the mystery of the existentiality of a complementary human decision. The relationship between God and man is constantly renewed and refashioned, but there can be no question of its having two sources—the one in God's decision and the other in the corresponding decision of man to which God's decision is itself related. We might connect such a view either with Lutheran or indeed Roman Catholic teaching. Certainly it was not what Peter Barth intended when at Geneva he tried to present his thesis of a predestination in action. It is worth noting, however, that as far as this side of his assertion was concerned the Calvinists assembled at Geneva appeared to be less perspicacious, for they seemed not to take any offence at his efforts from this standpoint. Yet it is not at all clear how this view can really be avoided if we assert the actuality of predestination merely as a general truth of Scripture and not in specific and concrete relation to the central point of biblical testimony. If we would think of the relationship between God and man as a living relationship, then in presenting it we are almost necessarily forced to the conclusion that in their dealings with each other the two partners stand on a footing which is equal basically, although not equal in practice. The life of this relationship cannot, therefore, be one-sided. Even if God has a powerful advantage over man, it is still necessarily two-sided, and its mystery must be thought of as the mystery of the human decision as well as the divine. Generally speaking, and even in the Bible, if we abstract from that central point, God and man appear as two partners with capabilities and competencies which are different but still autonomous. A subtle synergism—the kind which is never acknowledged, the reproach of which is always avoided, which is never quite clear even to those who hold it—will always result from the presentation of this relationship when it is regarded only as a generality, even as a biblical generality, as was the case at Geneva when Peter Barth aimed (and rightly aimed) to show that this relationship is not a deterministic but an intrinsically living relationship. From this view of the matter it is only a step to a compromise in which the living quality of this relationship derives not from God only but also from His human partner. But if we see the eternal will of the living God concretely in the election of Jesus Christ we avoid this side of the dilemma too. There is no synergism of any kind in the history of Jesus Christ's election, for in this history neither the sin of man nor the prayer of man can play the part of an autonomous mystery, as man's decision complementary to God's. There can be no co-operation or reciprocal action of any kind between any such mystery in man and the mystery of the predestinating God. Both sin and prayer are active in this history—but in what way? Sin is active only as the ordination from which this man is released by God's grace, and which He does not, in fact, fulfil or accomplish. The rejection of this man is not, then, God's answer to His sin, but His rigorous answer to sin itself, to the sin of all other men. The rigour of the answer is thus borne by God Himself in the union of His Son with this man. But, again, the fact that this man does not commit sin, and positively, the prayer by which He for His part elects God, and the obedience in which He takes it upon Himself to bear the sin of all other men—these are no more than the confirmation of His election. It is not that His election is, as it were, the divine answer to His sinlessness and prayer. He has not ordained Himself to this decision but He is foreordained to it. By this decision He simply declares that He is this man, the Son of God who has become Son of Man. On this side, too, there is no autonomous or second mystery, the mystery of man, but only the revelation of the one divine mystery which is the mystery of God's omnipotence because it is the mystery of grace, of God's triumphant affirmation and love of man, and because it includes within itself the fact that man is allowed to be at all, and that in his rejection of sin and election of obedience he may in some degree be the image of the predestinating God. The glory and the life of all this history are God's. Certainly it is a history between God and man. Certainly there takes place within it a twofold human decision. But this decision takes place in such a way as to form, not the second point in an ellipse, but the circumference around the one central point of which it is the repetition and confirmation. If we think of predestination as identical with this history, there is no danger of the activist understanding leading us astray in the direction of synergism. In this history there is, of course, co-operation between God and man, but not of a kind which does not owe its origin entirely to the working of God. This history is a triumph only for God's grace and therefore for God's sovereignty. If we would do proper justice to the interests of predestination from this standpoint, we cannot do better than hold to the fact that its content is God's eternal will in the concrete form of this particular history. We must accept, then, the thesis which Peter Barth propounded at Geneva in 1936: but not without providing its necessary and only possible basis, the christological; not without safeguarding it in this way from the dilemma which opened up at Geneva. This is the lesson to be learned from the proceedings of that Congress.

INDEX OF SCRIPTURE REFERENCES

INDEX OF SUBJECTS

love as 81
man as covenant-partner in 176
of mand 59, 96, 157, 161
men divided through 41–2
mystery of freedom in 30
mystery of God and 20–1, 24–5
obedience demanded by 32
orientation of doctrine of 1–34
origin of 52
passive 125
place in dogmatics of 81–98
pre-decision in 44–5
providence and 85
reconciliation and 86, 89, 90, 93–5
Reformation theology and 66, 70, 73,
  76, 79–80
righteousness of God and 22, 24–5,
  32–4
will of God and 44, 46, 48, 49, 75,
  118, 171
will of God and election of Jesus
  Christ 156–203
the Enlightenment 155
evil 137, 148, 151–2, 173, 175, 179, 187

faith
  foreseen 78–9
  in Jesus Christ 168
  knowledge of 78, 171
Fatalism 37
Five Remonstrant Articles 70
foreordination 44, 48, 130, 177, 180, 192
foreseen faith 78–9
Formula of Concord 19, 61, 73, 76
freedom
  of choice 26
  of God 21–2, 28, 29–30, 165, 185–6, 202
  of grace 18
  mystery of, in election of grace 30
  predestination and 185, 199, 202

general hermeneutical principle 160
God
  activity of 3, 193, 195–6
  benevolence of 76–7
  choosing man for predestination 179
  decree of 190
  doctrine of 1–4, 8–9, 24, 82–4, 85, 190
  election by 59, 96, 105–6, 157, 161
  eternity of 192
  evil over-ruled by 137, 151, 153

evil permitted by 148, 179–80
freedom of 21–2, 24, 28, 29–30, 165,
  185–6, 202
fulfillment of love elected by 29
good-pleasure of 109–10, 113, 146,
  150, 165–7, 172–3, 175, 185, 190
grace of 46
history with covenant of 6–7
Jesus Christ as electing 109
Jesus Christ with 185
knowledge in Jesus Christ of 168
knowledge of kingdom/rule of 161–2
living 190
living to glory of 173
love of 3–4, 7, 27, 29, 81, 181, 185
man following 28
man's relationship to 5–6
mercy of 36, 80
moving towards man as Jesus Christ 5
mystery of 20–1, 24, 156–7
mystery of freedom in election of
  grace by 30
omnipotence of 44–6, 50
partners in covenant with 173–4, 176
pre-determination of 31
private relationships with 42–4, 49
righteousness of 22, 24, 32–4, 132
risk in covenant by 173, 175
self-determination of 51, 52–5, 96–7,
  106, 153
self-giving of 130, 177–8, 187
self-humiliation of 196
self-revelation of 35, 49–50, 53–4, 59,
  66, 93, 163, 166–7
self-sufficiency of 7
self-testimony of 1–2
silence before 21–2
sovereignty of 21, 29, 50, 152, 189
Subject 3–4
  as subject of predestination 185–6
  subordination to 166
  true 5
  tying self to universe 165
  unchanging 191
  will of 44, 46, 48, 49, 75, 118, 123,
    129, 152
  will of, in election of Jesus Christ 156–
    203
  wisdom from 22
  world-governance of 47, 50–1
  world's relationship to 5–6

209

INDEX OF NAMES

Index of Names

Oorthuys, G.   197
Otten, H.   36, 41, 91, 135

Pelagius   127
Peter Lombard   14
Polanus, A.   19, 46, 82, 117, 118, 143

Quenstedt, J. A.   19, 73, 75, 76, 79, 90

Rilliet, J.   198, 199
Rütimeyer, M.   72

Schlatter, A.   103
Schrenk, G.   122, 125
Schweitzer, A.   122
Schweizer, A.   135
Scotus, John Duns   200

Tersteegen, G.   120

Thomas Aquinas   14, 15, 18, 20, 45, 48, 60, 66, 83, 112, 113, 114, 116, 118, 127, 128, 154, 159, 199
Til, S. van   82
Turrettini, F.   82, 138, 139, 140, 141, 143

Vermigli, Peter Martyr   89
Vorländer, K.   21

Walaeus, A.   90, 118, 119
Weber, M.   10, 37
Wendelin, M. F.   82
Werenfels, S.   17
Witsius, H.   89
Wollebius, J.   46, 82, 119, 143
Wyclif, J.   14

Zahn, T.   101, 103
Zwingli, H.   15, 46, 82, 85, 86, 136